CHARACTERIZATION
IN THE GOSPELS

CHARACTERIZATION IN THE GOSPELS

Reconceiving Narrative Criticism

edited by

DAVID RHOADS AND KARI SYREENI

T & T CLARK INTERNATIONAL
A Continuum imprint
LONDON • NEW YORK

Published by T&T Clark International
A Continuum imprint
The Tower Building, 11 York Road, London SE1 7NX
15 East 26th Street, Suite 1703, New York, NY 10010

www.tandtclark.com

Copyright © 1999 Sheffield Academic Press
First published as JSNTS 184 by Sheffield Academic Press
This edition published 2004

British Library Cataloguing-in-Publication Data
A catalogue record for this book is available from the British Library

ISBN 0567043304 (paperback)

Typeset by Sheffield Academic Press
Printed on acid-free paper in Great Britain by The Bath Press, Bath

CONTENTS

PREFACE

In March 1994, the University of Helsinki granted special funding to four top-level research units. One of these 'centres of excellence' was The Research Unit for Early Jewish and Christian Culture and Literature, headed by Professor Heikki Räisänen. Among the four main projects to be carried out by this Unit was a Scandinavian-American project 'The Gospels as Stories'. This project was headed by Kari Syreeni, then Acting Professor of New Testament studies at the University of Helsinki. Aimed at a critical rethinking of narrative analysis of the New Testament Gospels, the project worked in close cooperation with Professor David Rhoads of the Lutheran School of Theology at Chicago.

The present collection is the fruit of the project's four years of work. In eight articles, the seven scholars who participated in the project discuss characterization in the Gospels as a case of applying narrative analysis to biblical texts. The critical and interpretive paths they suggest are neither identical in substance nor uniformly pronounced in presentation. Each author has his or her distinctive voice. At the same time, the multivoiced analyses do make something like a choir. At the University of Helsinki, New Testament exegesis has long been known for its strictly historical, redaction-critical mode of research. While this scholarly tradition pervades most of the contributions, the writers have also put much effort into combining this tradition with more literary and hermeneutical considerations. That such a combination is not without problems is one issue on which historical and literary scholars might agree. On the other hand, integrative and boundary-crossing efforts may also be the very thing that the increasingly specialized and fragmented biblical scholarship needs.

It is our belief that narrative analysis of the New Testament Gospels has a future, even if it is in a slightly renovated form. In his concluding article, David Rhoads is able to envision several areas of growth and expansion. Some of these are exemplified in the present volume; much remains to be done.

The writers of this volume have received funding from a number of sources. Together with the Department of Biblical Studies, The Research Unit for Early Jewish and Christian Culture and Literature at the University of Helsinki has made several extensive research periods possible through positions and grants. Additional grants were received from the 350 Years Foundation of the University of Helsinki, the Finnish Cultural Foundation, the Emil Aaltonen Foundation, the Alfred Kordelin Foundation, Jenny and Antti Wihuri Fund, and the Research Centre of the Finnish Evangelic-Lutheran Church. Thanks to these grants, members of the project were also able to study and work in Chicago and London. We wish to express our sincerest thanks for all material and other help we have received during the project's four years of research.

Chicago, Uppsala, Helsinki, May 1998
David Rhoads and Kari Syreeni

ABBREVIATIONS

AASF	Annales Academiae Scientiarum Fennicae
AB	Anchor Bible
ABD	David Noel Freedman (ed.), *The Anchor Bible Dictionary* (New York: Doubleday, 1992)
AnBib	Analecta biblica
ANRW	Hildegard Temporini and Wolfgang Haase (eds.), *Aufstieg und Niedergang der römischen Welt: Geschichte und Kultur Roms im Spiegel der neueren Forschung* (Berlin: W. de Gruyter, 1972–)
BBB	Bonner biblische Beiträge
BETL	Bibliotheca ephemeridum theologicarum lovaniensium
BEvT	Beiträge zur evangelischen Theologie
Bib	*Biblica*
BibInt	*Biblical Interpretation: A Journal of Contemporary Approaches*
BNTC	Black's New Testament Commentaries
BTB	*Biblical Theology Bulletin*
BZ	*Biblische Zeitschrift*
BZNW	Beihefte zur *ZNW*
ConBNT	Coniectanea biblica, New Testament
CBQ	*Catholic Biblical Quarterly*
CChrSG	Corpus Christianorum Series Graeca
CChrSL	Corpus Christianorum Series Latina
CurTM	*Currents in Theology and Mission*
EKKNT	Evangelisch-Katholischer Kommentar zum Neuen Testament
FC	Fathers of the Church
FRLANT	Forschungen zur Religion und Literatur des Alten und Neuen Testaments
GCS	Griechische christliche Schriftsteller
HNT	Handbuch zum Neuen Testament
HTKNT	Herders theologischer Kommentar zum Neuen Testament
HTR	*Harvard Theological Review*
ICC	International Critical Commentary
IRT	Issues in Religion and Theology
Int	*Interpretation*
JAAR	*Journal of the American Academy of Religion*

JBL	*Journal of Biblical Literature*
JR	*Journal of Religion*
JSNT	*Journal for the Study of the New Testament*
JSNTSup	*Journal for the Study of the New Testament*, Supplement Series
JTS	*Journal of Theological Studies*
LCL	Loeb Classical Library
MeyerK	H.A.W. Meyer (ed.), *Kritisch-exegetischer Kommentar über das Neue Testament*
NCB	New Century Bible
Neot	*Neotestamentica*
NIGTC	The New International Greek Testament Commentary
NovTSup	*Novum Testamentum*, Supplements
NRT	*La nouvelle revue théologique*
NTAbh	Neutestamentliche Abhandlungen
NTD	Das Neue Testament Deutsch
NTS	*New Testament Studies*
NTTS	New Testament Tools and Studies
PFES	Publications of the Finnish Exegetical Society
SBB	Stuttgarter biblische Beiträge
SBLBAC	SBL The Bible in American Culture
SBLDS	SBL Dissertation Series
SBLEJL	SBL Early Judaism and its Literature
SBLMS	SBL Monograph Series
SBLSP	SBL Seminar Papers
SC	Sources chrétiennes
SNTSMS	Society for New Testament Studies Monograph Series
SNTU	Studien zum Neuen Testament und seiner Umwelt
TDNT	Gerhard Kittel and Gerhard Friedrich (eds.), *Theological Dictionary of the New Testament* (trans. Geoffrey W. Bromiley; 10 vols.; Grand Rapids: Eerdmans, 1964–)
ThHK	Theologischer Handkommentar zum Neuen Testament
TTod	*Theology Today*
TU	Texte und Untersuchungen
USQR	*Union Seminary Quarterly Review*
WBC	Word Biblical Commentary
WMANT	Wissenschaftliche Monographien zum Alten und Neuen Testament
WUNT	Wissenschaftliche Untersuchungen zum Neuen Testament
ZNW	*Zeitschrift für die neutestamentliche Wissenschaft*

LIST OF CONTRIBUTORS

David Rhoads, lecturer and continuing education leader, is Professor of New Testament at the Lutheran School of Theology, Chicago.

Kari Syreeni is Professor of New Testament Studies at the University of Uppsala, Sweden.

Raimo Hakola, Arto Järvinen, Outi Lehtipuu, Talvikki Mattila and Petri Merenlahti are at the Department of Biblical Studies, University of Helsinki, Finland.

RECONCEIVING NARRATIVE CRITICISM

Petri Merenlahti and Raimo Hakola

Character and characterization are subjects of *literary* inquiry. During the last two decades, such inquiry has gained a permanent position in New Testament studies. As a result, new methodological approaches to biblical texts have come forth.[1] More broadly, some scholars have spoken of a 'new literary criticism'—the word 'new' here implying a distinction between this approach and the traditional *Literarkritik* which has been mainly interested in uncovering different sources behind the present biblical text.[2] In a yet broader sense, some have suggested a change of paradigms, that is to say, a replacement of the historical-critical exegesis for a (or sometimes even *the*) literary approach.

One prominent part of the new 'literary' exegesis has been the use of narrative theory in the analysis of the Gospels. In the late 1970s and early 1980s, a number of New Testament scholars sought a holistic approach that would give value to the compositional unity of the Gospel narratives. Narratological models, which at the time represented the avant-garde in literary studies, provided these critics with serviceable methodological tools.[3] What resulted was *narrative criticism*, a

1. Like the more traditional methods in biblical studies, the new ones, too, have been labeled as different types of 'criticism'. The book *The Postmodern Bible* by The Bible and Culture Collective (New Haven: Yale University Press, 1995) is able to introduce as many as seven new 'criticisms': reader-response criticism, structuralist and narratological criticism, poststructuralist criticism, rhetorical criticism, psychoanalytic criticism, feminist and womanist criticism, and ideological criticism.

2. Thus, for example, in the title of the collection of articles edited by E.S. Malbon and E.V. McKnight, *The New Literary Criticism and the New Testament* (JSNTSup, 109; Sheffield: JSOT Press, 1994).

3. The term 'narratology' was first proposed by T. Todorov (see his *Grammaire du 'Décaméron'* [The Hague: Mouton, 1969]). Originally, the term referred to the structuralist study of narrative. Later on, it came to be used in a broader

peculiar combination of narrative theory and redaction-critical study of the Gospels.[4] As such, narrative criticism still remains a popular application of literary theory to New Testament studies, especially in the United States—even though new avant-garde approaches (that is, poststructuralist or postmodern approaches) have already emerged to challenge its position.[5] However, narrative criticism has also faced severe critiques. In our view, the key question in this critique has been whether narrative-critical readings do justice to *the nature of the Gospel narratives*.[6] For narrative criticism, the true nature of the Gospels is *literature*. Narrative critics investigate the poetic function of the Gospels, that is to say, how the Gospels work *as literature*. This investigation takes place

sense, with reference to formal theories of narrative (and narrativity) in general. Such theories flourished especially in the late 1970s and early 1980s, when several comprehensive narratological syntheses appeared: G. Genette, 'Discours du récit', in *idem*, *Figures III* (Paris: Editions du Seuil, 1972); ET *Narrative Discourse: An Essay in Method* (trans. J.E. Lewin; Ithaca, NY: Cornell University Press, 1980); S. Chatman, *Story and Discourse: Narrative Structure in Fiction and Film* (Ithaca, NY: Cornell University Press, 1978); F. Stanzel, *Theorie des Erzählens* (Göttingen: Vandenhoeck & Ruprecht, 1979); ET *A Theory of Narrative* (trans. C. Goedsche; Cambridge: Cambridge University Press, 1986); M. Bal, *De theorie van vertellen en verhalen* (Muiderberg: Coutinho, 2nd rev. edn, 1980); ET *Narratology: Introduction to the Theory of Narrative* (trans. C. van Boheemen; Toronto: University of Toronto Press, 1985); G. Prince, *Narratology: The Form and Function of Narrative* (Berlin: Mouton, 1982); S. Rimmon-Kenan, *Narrative Fiction: Contemporary Poetics* (London: Methuen, 1983); W. Martin, *Recent Theories of Narrative* (Ithaca, NY: Cornell University Press, 1986).

4.   S.D. Moore, *Literary Criticism and the Gospels: The Theoretical Challenge* (New Haven: Yale University Press, 1989), pp. 51-55; *idem*, *Poststructuralism and the New Testament: Derrida and Foucault at the Foot of the Cross* (Minneapolis: Fortress Press, 1994), pp. 67-68, 131.

5.   For a general introduction to narrative criticism as a method of New Testament study, see, e.g., D. Rhoads, 'Narrative Criticism and the Gospel of Mark', *JAAR* 50.3 (1982), pp. 411-34 (originally a SBL 1980 seminar paper); M.A. Powell, *What Is Narrative Criticism?* (Minneapolis: Fortress Press, 1990); E.S. Malbon, 'Narrative Criticism: How Does the Story Mean?', in J.C. Anderson and S.D. Moore (eds.), *Mark and Method: New Approaches in Biblical Studies* (Minneapolis: Fortress Press, 1992), pp. 23-49. On poststructuralist critique of narrative criticism, see Moore, *Literary Criticism and the Gospels*, pp. 1-68; Moore, *Poststructuralism and the New Testament*, pp. 65-81.

6.   Thus also W.T. Shiner, *Follow Me! Disciples in Markan Rhetoric* (SBLDS, 145; Atlanta: Scholars Press, 1995), p. 3.

from a holistic point of view, which means that narrative critics focus on the narrative of each Gospel as a whole and try to come up with an integrated interpretation of all the elements of the narrative. This assumption of unity is, or at least narrative critics take it to be, a general feature of the interpretation of literary texts.

Indeed, in a literary context, our expectations of unity and coherence of a text appear to be stricter than usual. As readers of literature, we expect that even apparently incoherent features of the text are somehow, on a deeper level, interconnected. These expectations also involve an evaluative point of view: unity and coherence are among the criteria we expect a text to meet if we are to accept it as well formed. Accordingly, whenever narrative critics make a positive connection between parts and the whole of a Gospel narrative, they take unity and coherence to support the acclaim of the evangelist's artistic success: there is a place for everything in the Gospels, and everything is in its proper place. At this point, the critics' points of emphasis go hand in hand with the critics' aesthetic standards; narrative critics regard unity and coherence as characteristic of good literature.

Traditionally, however, scholarly considerations on the nature of the Gospel narratives have been quite different. They have emphasized the *episodic design* and *ideological purpose* of these narratives and concluded that these features make it difficult to regard the Gospels as genuine works of literature. Thus, as early as the middle of the second century, Papias, the bishop of the ancient Hierapolis, made the remark that even though Mark the evangelist failed to write down the Lord's sayings and doings *in order*, he was quite justified in doing as he did, because he did it on the purpose of giving an accurate account of the apostle Peter's preaching.[7] In other words, Mark's ideological objective resulted in solutions that deviate from what purely literary interests would have called for. Centuries later, modern critical scholarship followed in Papias's footsteps. At the turn of the century, scholars like Franz Overbeck, William Wrede and Clyde Weber Votaw considered the Gospels 'nonliterary' popular writings, or 'Volksliteratur', with a distinctive 'dogmatic' or ideological purpose. Later on, the form critics concluded that as folkloristic *Kleinliteratur* with a special 'cultic character', the Gospels were something quite unique in the entire history of literature. After form criticism came the redaction critics who regarded

---

7. Eusebius, *Hist.* 3.35.15.

the Gospels as distinctive 'theological achievements' of the evangelists. When seen against this background, narrative criticism's idea of the inmost nature of the Gospels as poetic, that is, literature for literature's sake, is indeed something new.

While a return in interest from ideological or theological to literary aspects was certainly due, not all teachings of the past should be forgotten. Episodic design and ideological purpose remain a most integral part of the nature of the Gospel narratives. In this essay, we seek to show that these two features present a serious challenge to the type of narrative analysis practiced by narrative critics.

First, we will take a look at how narrative criticism began. Initially, narrative criticism emerged in the midst of a redaction-critical discussion, where it contributed to back up one scholarly view against another on the origin and composition of the Gospels, most notably the Gospel of Mark. As we will see, this had implications as to what kind of application of narratology the narrative criticism of the Gospels turned out to be. Narrative criticism's situation of origin also provides us with at least a partial explanation as to why the issues of the literary unity and autonomy of the Gospels became so important for narrative criticism from the very beginning.

Second, we will consider more closely the issue of the literary unity of the Gospels. In addition to the question whether the Gospels indeed are as unified narratives as narrative critics take them to be, we will ask what narrative critics actually mean when they say that a literary work is 'remarkably unified'. We would also like to point out that, as a standard of aesthetic evaluation, the notion of unity is historically and culturally specific and varies from one place and time to another. The question is whether this notion, as understood and applied as standard by narrative critics, does justice to the historically and culturally specific nature of the Gospel narratives.

Third, we will focus on the nature of the Gospels as non-fictional narrative communication of a distinct ideological nature. Quite evidently, the Gospels display interests and present truth claims that exceed those characteristic of literary fiction. Although it is possible to read the Gospels exactly the same way as we read fictional narratives, this is hardly a reading that comes naturally. Rather, such reading would be a misjudgment of the type of narrative communication that the Gospels represent. Thus, when traditional scholarship has insisted on viewing the Gospels not only as literary artefacts but also as ideological discourse that originated in a particular real-life context, it has done this with good reason. Notably, a literary point of view of the texts of the Gospels needs not be rejected. Discussing the formal features of the Gospels as narratives certainly remains a meaningful and productive task. What is needed is a positively comprehensive approach that pays due attention to literary, ideological and historical dimensions of the text.[8]

The Origins of Narrative Criticism

Narrative criticism has its roots in earlier methodological approaches to the New Testament. Much of the work that led to the development of narrative criticism was undertaken in the Society of Biblical Literature Markan Seminar, chaired first by Norman Perrin, and then by Werner Kelber, between 1971 and 1980.[9] At the final year of this seminar, David Rhoads delivered a programatic paper called 'Narrative Criticism and the Gospel of Mark'.[10] In this paper he coined the term 'narrative criticism' to describe particular investigative areas of contemporary literary criticism as applied to the study of the Gospels. More precisely, the new approach involved 'investigating the formal features of narrative in the texts of the gospels, features which include aspects of the story-world of the narrative and the rhetorical techniques employed to tell the story'.[11] Referring to four categories of literary criticism as introduced by M.H. Abrams, Rhoads explained that such a study of narrative included '*objective criticism*' which 'describes the literary product as a self-sufficient world-in-itself' and '*pragmatic (or rhetorical) criticism*' which views the literary work as something 'constructed in order to achieve certain effects on the audience'. Significantly, all forms of *expressive* (or author-centered) as well as *mimetic* criticism (which

8. In our view, the most comprehensive and systematic theoretical framework for the analysis of these three aspects of biblical texts has been proposed in a number of writings by Kari Syreeni. See, e.g., his 'Separation and Identity: Aspects of the Symbolic World of Matt 6.1-18', *NTS* (1994), pp. 522-41.

9. Thomas Boomershine, Joanna Dewey, Robert Fowler, Norman Petersen, Robert Tannehill and Mary Ann Tolbert were among seminar members who were 'particularly influential in the development of the new discipline' (Powell, *What Is Narrative Criticism?*, p. 110 n. 24).

10. The paper was published two years later in *JAAR* 50.3 (1982), pp. 411-34.

11. Rhoads, 'Narrative Criticism', pp. 411-12.

takes literature primarily as *representation of reality*) were excluded.[12] According to Rhoads, the new 'literary' approach involved for him, as a New Testament scholar, two shifts of perspective. The first shift moved *toward a more holistic point of view*, that is, *an emphasis on the unity of the narrative*. Whereas traditional source-, form- and redaction-critical methods had cut the Gospels into small pieces of tradition and redaction, narrative criticism focused on the Gospels as *complete literary wholes*. The second shift involved moving away from the historical or theological questions concerning the Gospel's author or audience and toward *an exclusively text-oriented approach* that '*looks at the closed universe of the story-world*'.[13]

As to the first shift, there was, at the time, a particular call for a holistic approach in certain areas of Gospel studies. In the study of Mark's Gospel, the so-called creativity debate focused on the role of Mark the evangelist in the making of his Gospel—whether the earliest Gospel was to be considered the work of a genuine artist or instead a clumsily edited collection of diverse traditional material. This debate was hotly contested and, eventually, resulted in a split within Markan studies.[14] It was very much in the context of this debate that Rhoads and others first made the claim that 'a literary study of [Mark's] formal features suggests that the author succeeded in creating a unified narrative'.[15]

As to the second shift, the idea of the exclusive autonomy of the literary work had some decades earlier been one of the central tenets of a literary-theoretical movement called *New Criticism* (as had been the tendency to give special value to the literary work's unity and integrity, for that matter).[16] Although invoking that principle gave narrative

---

12. Rhoads, 'Narrative Criticism', p. 426; M.H. Abrams, *A Glossary of Literary Terms* (New York: Holt, Rinehart & Winston, 1971), p. 37. Cf. Powell, *What Is Narrative Criticism?*, pp. 11-12.

13. Rhoads, 'Narrative Criticism', p. 413.

14. On the debate, see H. Räisänen, *'The Messianic Secret' in Mark* (Edinburgh: T. & T. Clark, 1990), pp. 1-37.

15. D. Rhoads and D. Michie, *Mark as Story: An Introduction to the Narrative of a Gospel* (Philadelphia: Fortress Press, 1982), p. 3.

16. S.D. Moore was among the first to mark the family resemblance. See Moore, *Literary Criticism and the Gospels*, pp. 9-12; *idem*, *Poststructuralism and the New Testament*, p. 68; The Bible and Culture Collective, *The Postmodern Bible*, pp. 85-87. Soon enough, narrative criticism's debt to New Criticism became acknowledged by narrative critics themselves. See, e.g., Malbon, 'Narrative Criticism', pp. 24-26.

criticism a somewhat old-fashioned outlook (at least in the eyes of those well versed in contemporary literary theory), the strong influence of the new-critical thought on narrative criticism was only a small surprise after all. First, some earlier experiments using a 'literary approach' to the New Testament had been drawing extensively (and, in contrast to the early narrative criticism, explicitly) on New Criticism; in a sense, narrative criticism went along a beaten path.[17] Second, the essentials of the new-critical program had already found their way to such standard textbooks as René Wellek's and Austin Warren's *Theory of Literature*.[18] As such, New Criticism continued its influence in the American academic scene long after the methodological school itself had become *passé*. Class after class of students of literature would learn that 'the meaning of a work of art is not exhausted by, or even equivalent to, its intention. As a system of values, it leads an independent life.'[19]

When the New Critics first emphasized the autonomy of the literary work, their original objective was *evaluative*. According to them, the critics were not to let an author's intention play any part in judging the literary work's success. Instead, evaluation was to be based on a thorough 'objective' analysis of the work itself ('close reading'). Such analysis would give the work its due share of appreciation as literary art. This view received its classic treatment in a programatic essay by W.K. Wimsatt, Jr, and Monroe C. Beardsley, 'The Intentional Fallacy'.[20]

Wimsatt and Beardsley compared judging a poem to judging a pudding or a machine: 'One demands that it work'[21]—or, as the poet Archibald MacLeish put it, 'A poem should not mean but be'.[22] What was

---

17. Such experiments include the work of the Parables Seminar of the Society of Biblical Literature, involving scholars such as William Beardslee, John Dominic Crossan, Robert Funk, James Robinson, Robert Tannehill, Dan Via and (last but not least) Amos Wilder.

18. New York: Harcourt, Brace & World, 1949.

19. Wellek and Warren, *Theory of Literature* (repr.; Harmondsworth: Penguin Books, 1982), p. 42.

20. The essay appeared originally in *Sewanee Review* 54 (summer 1946), pp. 468-88. Our notes, however, refer to the collection by W.K. Wimsatt, Jr, *The Verbal Icon: Studies in the Meaning of Poetry* (Lexington: University of Kentucky Press, 1954), pp. 3-18.

21. 'The Intentional Fallacy', p. 4.

22. 'Ars Poetica', in *Collected Poems 1917–1954* (Boston: Houghton Mifflin, 1962), pp. 50-51.

essential to verbal messages of other than poetic nature was that they be understood correctly (that is, the way their maker intended them to be); what was essential to a poem or a machine or a pudding, was that it run smoothly: 'Poetry succeeds because all or most of what is said or implied is relevant; what is irrelevant has been excluded, like lumps from pudding and "bugs" from machinery.'[23]

After New Criticism, the point of emphasis changed. Instead of serving as a basis for *evaluative criticism*, the autonomy of the literary work became regarded as a standard of literary *interpretation*.[24] Now, it was not so much the merit of a work as the meaning of a work that was to be dealt with as independent of the author's intention. It was very much in this form that the idea of the literary work's autonomy was, in due time, assumed by the narrative critics of the New Testament as well. Significantly, however, the original, evaluative element remained visible. To quote Elizabeth Struthers Malbon:

> Narrative Criticism seeks to avoid the 'intentional fallacy' of redaction criticism. The narrative critic does not pursue the quest for the real author's intention. Instead, the narrative critic seeks to analyze and appreciate ... the text itself... They (we) focus on the text, partly in reaction to redaction critics' focus on the author, but mostly because we find the text so intriguing.[25]

It was the artistic merit of the biblical text that would make the study of its poetic aspect worthwhile. A 'close reading' of the Gospels was relevant, because the Gospels were good literature. Correspondingly, the disagreement between narrative critics and historical critics has been, essentially, a disagreement on the success of the Gospels as literary art. Critical voices have asked whether narrative criticism is not guilty of 'an uncritical admiration of the literary accomplishments of

---

23. Wimsatt and Beardsley, 'The Intentional Fallacy', p. 4.

24. See, e.g., Annabel Patterson, 'Intention', in F. Lentricchia and T. McLaughlin (eds.), *Critical Terms for Literary Study* (Chicago: University of Chicago Press, 2nd edn, 1995), pp. 135-46 (139-42).

25. Malbon, 'Narrative Criticism', p. 35. Another prime example of interweaving aesthetic and evaluative statements is given by Mark W.G. Stibbe, *John as Storyteller: Narrative Criticism and the Fourth Gospel* (SNTSMS, 73; Cambridge: Cambridge University Press, 1992), pp. 198-99. Stibbe says that he has, in his work, stated 'the obvious: that John's story is the work of a masterful storyteller'. Furthermore, according to Stibbe, the evangelist has succeeded in creating what is, 'by any standards, a quite brilliant literary achievement'.

the evangelists'.[26] Those on one side say those on the other do not have any eye for poetic beauty, while these, for their part, say love for the holy text has made the other party blind to the text's vices.

To make its case, narrative criticism assumed the task of exposing how a Gospel works as narrative. It sought to present the text's formal narrative structure, that is, the narrative mechanics according to which a Gospel was assumed to function as a structure of communication between the author and the reader. At first, some individual facets of these mechanics were investigated in topical studies.[27] The real breakthrough in the new approach, however, came with the appearance of two monograph studies: David Rhoads's and Donald Michie's *Mark as Story: An Introduction to the Narrative of a Gospel* and R. Alan Culpepper's *Anatomy of the Fourth Gospel: A Study in Literary Design*.[28] Both works aimed at presenting a comprehensive *descriptive poetics* of a Gospel. Both were also heavily influenced by one particular narratological synthesis of the time, namely Seymour Chatman's *Story and Discourse: Narrative Structure in Fiction and Film*.[29]

Concise, fluently written and easy to read, *Mark as Story* in particular became a highly influential book. Its bottom line, to be assumed by a great majority of narrative-critical syntheses to come, was that such literary analysis as represented by narrative criticism would reveal the

26. H. Räisänen, 'The New Testament in Theology', in P. Byrne and L. Houlden (eds.), *Companion Encyclopaedia of Theology* (London: Routledge, 1995), pp. 122-41 (128).

27. These include, e.g., T. Boomershine, 'Mark the Storyteller: A Rhetorical-Critical Investigation of Mark's Passion and Resurrection Narrative' (PhD dissertation, Union Theological Seminary, New York, 1974); R. Tannehill, 'The Disciples in Mark: The Function of a Narrative Role', *JR* 57 (1977), pp. 386-405; N. Petersen, '"Point of View" in Mark's Narrative', *Semeia* 12 (1978), pp. 97-211.

28. Philadelphia: Fortress Press, 1983.

29. Chatman's work has ever since remained the most important single source of inspiration for narrative criticism. The following lines with which Jack Dean Kingsbury presented his *Matthew as Story* (Philadelphia: Fortress Press, 1986) gave in a nutshell what much of the future of narrative criticism was to be like: 'One literary theorist, Seymour Chatman, has provided a useful outline for discussing the constituent parts of narrative, and David Rhoads has shown us with what profit this outline can be employed in investigating a gospel such as that of Mark. The present investigation of Matthew's Gospel will also draw from Chatman's outline, and supplement it as well with the work of others' (*Matthew as Story*, p. 1; see Moore, *Literary Criticism and the Gospels*, p. 51).

evangelist to be a masterful storyteller in full command of his material. As Rhoads and Michie put it,

> the writer [of Mark] has told the story in such a way as to have certain effects on the reader ... The author has used sophisticated literary techniques, developed the characters and the conflicts and built suspense with deliberateness, telling the story in such way as to generate certain emotions and insights in the reader.[30]

Over this very point, however, things started to become complicated. Redaction criticism had posed the same questions about the *author* of *Mark* (or Matthew, Luke or John): How did he work? So, also, Rhoads and Michie were talking about the author at this point. Doing that, however, took them far beyond the limits of any exclusively text-centered method. No text-centered method would take any interest whatsoever in either the origin or the reception of the text under consideration. Narratology confines itself to describing what the *narrator* (the one who tells the story, *as inscribed in the text*) does. The concepts of *implied author* and *implied reader* refer to the author and the audience *presupposed within the text itself*. If the critic yet wants to know what *the real author(s)* has (have) done (*with deliberateness*) with his or her material, it is (back) to the historical, 'extrinsic' methods he or she must turn.[31] Indeed, there is more at stake here than mere terminological purism. To avoid circular arguments, it is quite essential that the question 'what does the narrator do in the text?' will not be confused with the question 'what has the author/composer done?'

Certainly, narrative criticism never was a pure, straightforward application of narratology to the texts of the Gospels. While narrative critics drew upon narratological (and, later, reader-oriented) models to view

---

30. Rhoads and Michie, *Mark as Story*, p. 1. Culpepper's assessment of John's success is a more cautious one: 'The Gospel of John is therefore more unified and coherent than has often been thought because its unity is not found primarily in plot development, which as we have seen is rather episodic, or in the progression of action from scene to scene. It consists instead in the effect it achieves through thematic development, the spectrum of characters, and the implicit commentary conveyed through irony and symbolism. In other words, the unity of the "spiritual Gospel" is more evident in the subtle elements of its narrative structure than in the obvious ones. The eagle soars when it reaches for the sublime and the subtle, but it is clumsy when it has to walk through some of the ordinary elements of a narrative' (*Anatomy*, p. 234).

31. Cf. Moore, *Literary Criticism and the Gospels*, p. 12.

the texts of the Gospels as narrative communication, they nevertheless kept asking the same historical questions that redaction critics had asked before them.

Not that Rhoads's and Michie's conclusion would not have made sense. In its simple persuasiveness it resembled quite a lot the classical deist argument of a person who finds a clock and assumes that someone must once have made it. In this case, as applied to Mark, it went as follows: if a narrative-critical analysis is able to demonstrate consistent literary or artistic patterns going through the whole of the Gospel, there must once have been someone capable of putting them there. It takes a qualified artist to create a work with integrity.

Unity in the Gospel Narratives

Since *Mark as Story* and *The Anatomy of the Fourth Gospel*, numerous narrative-critical studies on the four Gospels and the Acts of the Apostles have appeared. Without exception, they all strongly emphasize the narrative unity of these works. Again and again the reader learns that the Gospels are

> of remarkably whole cloth: the narrator maintains a unifying point of view; the standards of judgment are uniform; the plot is coherent; the characters are introduced and developed with consistency; stylistic patterns persist through the story; and there is a satisfying overall rhetorical effect.[32]

By any standards, a strong emphasis on the inherent unity of the Gospel narratives must be considered the most salient single feature of narrative criticism.

At this very central point, however, serious confusion begins to appear. The seeds of this confusion lie in the fact that many narrative critics use the same term 'narrative unity' with reference to two entirely different matters. First, they maintain that a narrative analysis of the Gospels *shows* the Gospels to be 'of remarkably whole cloth'. This *argument of unity* implies that unity is a *discovery*, or result of analysis. Second, narrative criticism makes an *assumption of unity*, that is to say, it opts for *a holistic approach* that a priori sees every narrative as an autonomous, inherently unified world. In light of this,

---

32. D. Rhoads, 'Jesus and the Syrophoenician Woman in Mark: A Narrative-Critical Study', *JAAR* 62.2 (1994), pp. 343-75 (343); cf. Rhoads and Michie, *Mark as Story*, p. 3.

Narrative unity is not something that must be proved from an analysis of
the material. Rather, it is something that can be assumed. It is the form of
narrative itself that grants coherence to the material, no matter how disparate that material might be ... The presence of inconsistencies in no
way undermines the unity of a narrative but simply becomes one of the
facets to be interpreted. They may, for instance, signal gaps and ambi-
guities that must be either explained or held in tension. This is true
regardless of whether they are there by design or negligence ... the real
question is whether the poetic function of the Gospels in the form that
we now have them is a worthwhile subject for investigation.[33]

The key issue is, of course, that the two ways of understanding narrative unity must not be confused. Otherwise, we end up moving in
circles. After all, a claim such as 'analyses of the formal features of the
Gospel of Mark have shown this narrative to be of remarkably whole
cloth' does imply that under some circumstances matters could be
otherwise—that the unity shown *is* something more than just the unity
assumed.

Discoveries may not be assumed a priori. If narrative critics wish to
argue for a *particular* unity and coherence of the Gospels as narratives,
they will have to *prove* their case to their fellow scholars, whether in
the biblical or in the literary field.[34] In both cases, resistance should be
expected. On the one hand, the more traditionally oriented biblical critics are likely to continue their complaints that narrative critics ignore or
too easily dismiss inconsistencies in the Gospels due to the differences
between traditions and redactions in the Gospel material. On the other
hand, the perils of seeing too much unity and coherence in narratives
are widely recognized in contemporary literary scholarship as well. Let
us consider this issue first from a historical-critical, then from a literary-
theoretical point of view.

In simple terms, historical-critical scholars of the Bible fear that narrative-critical analyses smooth over inconsistencies and breaks in the

---

33. Powell, *What Is Narrative Criticism?*, pp. 92, 93.

34. Thus also M.C. de Boer, 'Narrative Criticism, Historical Criticism, and the
Gospel of John', *JSNT* 47 (1992), pp. 35-48, esp. p. 44: 'The data may well lead to
the conclusion, a narrative-critical one, that the text is unified, coherent whole, but
then again they may lead to the opposite conclusion, or at least a different one.
Coherence or unity, no more than incoherence or fragmentation, cannot be a methodological presupposition that stands beyond critical testing in the public arena and
empirical validation from the text itself, *whatever* method is used' (italics original).

text in favor of harmonizing interpretations. Such practice would be made possible by the narrative-critical 'assumption of unity' which, from the point of the more traditional biblical criticism, is equal to a practice of 'verdict first, trial second'. If *any feature* of *any text* can be interpreted in terms of the unity of the whole, there should, indeed, be no point in concluding that *some particular text* is 'remarkably unified'. So it seems, however, that quite a number of narrative critics would like to have it both ways. Consider Jeffrey Lloyd Staley's analysis of *the implied reader* of the Fourth Gospel.[35] As Staley takes it, a holistic, text-centered approach allows the critic to assume that every detail of the text plays a significant part in the narrator's rhetorical strategy. John's narrative strategy is, according to Staley, based on what Staley calls 'the victimization of the reader'.[36] Once critics have recognized this strategy, it will help them to analyze contradictory passages in the Gospel in terms of their effect upon the reader rather than in terms of their compositional history.[37] The critic may regard all the 'narrative-busting elements as heavily ironized rhetorical ploys' that 'force the implied reader into the role of an outsider, an error-prone reader who can never feel as though his grasp of Jesus or the life of faith is absolute'.[38]

35. J.L. Staley, *The Print's First Kiss: A Rhetorical Investigation of the Implied Reader in the Fourth Gospel* (SBLDS, 82; Atlanta: Scholars Press, 1988). Cf. also Staley's 'Subversive Narrator/Victimized Reader: A Reader Response Assessment of a Text-Critical Problem, John 18.12-24', *JSNT* 51 (1993), pp. 79-98. Staley himself places these studies in the theoretical context of *reader-response criticism* (*The Print's First Kiss*, p. 6). Nevertheless, his methodological starting point is a narratological one, namely Seymour Chatman's model of narrative communication (*The Print's First Kiss*, pp. 21-22). Because Staley's main focus is on how the narrator, as inscribed *in the text*, controls the reading process, Staley's method does not differ much from narrative criticism.

36. Staley borrows the term 'reader victimization' from J. McKee, *Literary Irony and the Literary Audience: Studies in the Victimization of the Reader in Augustan Fiction* (Amsterdam: Ropodi, 1974). See *The Print's First Kiss*, p. 95 n. 1; 'Subversive Narrator/Victimized Reader', p. 83 n. 21. Staley admits that the term is usually used in connection with modern novels. Nevertheless, as Staley notes, the term is not anachronistic in the Hellenistic era. A narrator who makes use of the strategy of reader victimization resembles the Socratic εἴρων who also 'feigns ignorance and occasionally suppresses his own knowledge in order to educate his audience' ('Subversive Narrator/Victimized Reader', p. 84).

37. Staley, *The Print's First Kiss*, p. 96.

38. Staley, 'Subversive Narrator/Victimized Reader', pp. 82-83. According to Staley, the reading conventions of the ancient Mediterranean world suggest that the

Most passages in John that, in Staley's view, 'victimize' the reader, are passages that traditional scholarship has sought to explain by referring to the multilayered editing of the Gospel. At the beginning of John 4, for example, there is a narrative comment that most critics would take as a later editorial gloss. In the course of the narrative, the narrator notes twice that Jesus baptized (3.22; 4.1). The comment in 4.1 is followed by an awkward correction which says that it was not Jesus himself but his disciples who baptized (4.2). It is customary to regard this correction as a secondary attempt to establish a clear difference between Jesus and John the Baptist. As such, the verse 'serves almost indisputable evidence of the presence of several hands in the composition of John'.[39] Staley, however, is not satisfied with this solution. He claims that the comment has *a rhetorical function*. It forces the implied reader to 'reevaluate his relationship to the narrator and the story'; the implied reader 'finds that he had only been set up to be hoodwinked by the juxtaposition of 3.22 and 4.2'. The rhetorical purpose of the narrator is 'to force the implied reader to realize that in spite of his high degree of knowledge, he still does not know everything. The gospel, as well as being an aesthetic whole, is a "learning program".'[40] Other passages that, according to Staley, make the Fourth Gospel a 'learning program' contain similar dissonance that traditional scholarship would explain by referring to different redactional layers.[41] In Staley's eyes, all these

first readers of the Gospels were male. Correspondingly, the implied reader of John is a 'he'.

39. Raymond E. Brown, *The Gospel According to John (I–XII)* (AB, 29; New York: Doubleday, 1966), p. 164.

40. Staley, *The Print's First Kiss*, p. 98.

41. In addition to Jn 4.1-2, Staley pays attention to the following passages in which the narrator 'victimizes the reader': 7.1-10, where Jesus says he is not going to the festival (v. 8), whereas the narrator tells that Jesus did go to the festival (v. 10); 10.40–11.18, where the narrator's information concerning the location of Bethany is confusing as compared to earlier information according to which Bethany was beyond Jordan (1.28); 13.1-30, where the unexpected appearance of an unnamed character called 'the beloved disciple' takes the reader by surprise; 20.35–21.25, where the reader is 'victimized' by the unexpected prolonging of the story in the beginning of ch. 21, and by the enigmatic closure of the narrative (21.24-25). These passages mark a process of growth which the implied reader goes through: at first, the implied reader is an outsider in company with the antagonistic Pharisees (ch. 4); then, the narrator moves the implied reader into the company of Jesus' unbelieving brothers (ch. 7); next, the implied reader is a few steps behind the disciples who misunderstand Jesus (ch. 11); then, the implied reader is at the

passages have a premeditated purpose.

The question is whether Staley's reading of John is a reading that comes naturally. After all, before Staley, not one real reader of the Gospel has ever grasped the 'rhetorical ploys' that supposedly hide in the seemingly contradictory passages of the Gospel. Instead, these passages have provoked one real reader after another to produce either overtly harmonizing interpretations or critical hypotheses about the composition history of the Gospel. Thus, in Staley's view, the whole history of John's interpretation is full of readers who have become victims of the Johannine narrator's rhetoric.[42] Is there not, however, something utterly disturbing in the idea that the Johannine narrator's rhetoric, supposedly comparable even to the irony of the Socratic dialogue, is only revealed to one modern and sensitive critic, whereas the text's entire earlier reception history consists of misunderstandings, misreadings and misinterpretations? Why is there so little evidence that any real readers ever experienced the text in the way Staley describes?[43]

Historical scholarship, on the other hand, might claim double evidence for its case. First, historical critics can refer to the comparative study of early Jewish and early Christian literature to explain why there is genuine dissonance in the text. In light of comparative study, we know that these writings often went through an editing process; one evangelist used another's text as a source; comments, corrections and

same level with the surprised disciples (ch. 13); finally, the implied reader shares Peter's position (ch. 21). (See *The Print's First Kiss*, p. 116.) Later, Staley has included Jn 18.12-24 among those Johannine passages that 'victimize the reader' (see 'Subversive Narrator/Victimized Reader').

42. For example, in Jn 18.19-24, there is a text-critical problem that Staley regards as an example of 'reader victimization': having first told that Jesus was questioned by the high priest (18.19-23), the text states that Jesus was sent to Caiaphas the high priest (v. 24). Several different manuscripts have tried to solve this problem by reordering the text. According to Staley, it is these attempts as well as 'numerous commentators' notes that paradoxically testify to the narrative's rhetorical power at the very moment those same real readers are falling victim to it' ('Subversive Narrator/Victimized Reader', pp. 96-97).

43. Cf. Moore on reader-response critical studies in the Gospels: 'Hearing how the implied reader of the Gospels forms expectations here only to revise them there... I am compelled to ask: Why do I experience none of these things when I read the text? Why is there so little evidence that the Church, historically, experienced them? And does the reader-critic who pulls the readers' strings actually experience them either?' (*Literary Criticism and the Gospels*, p. 106).

additions found their way into the text. Second, historical scholarship may look at how some early historical readers responded to the text *as narrative*; this helps to clarify what type of readings the text seems to invite as well as to assess how successful some rhetorical strategy, supposedly contained in the text, might have been. In light of this, a reading such as Staley's is not convincing. Apparently, no historical conventions of reading would support it. Genuine dissonance and discontinuity remain in the text, as well as in the eye of the reader.

The historical critics of the Bible are not the only ones to resist harmonizing readings. Narratology, let it be noted, had no specific interest in showing or assuming that narratives, some of them or all of them, are inherently unified. It was meant to be a descriptive theory, not a method of criticism. The models it proposed were designed to give a comprehensive formal description of any given narrative, no matter how unified or disjointed that narrative might be. In the closing lines of his *Narrative Discourse: An Essay in Method*, a distinguished classic of narrative theory, Gérard Genette explicitly refuses to end his description of the narrative structures present in Marcel Proust's *A la recherche du temps perdu* with a final synthesis that would show the inherent unity and coherence of Proustian narrative. This is because such unity and coherence is not to be found, and it would be 'unfortunate ... to seek "unity" at any price, and in that way to *force* the work's coherence—which is, of course, one of criticism's strongest temptations, one of its most ordinary (not to say most common) ones, and also most easy to satisfy, since all it requires is a little interpretative rhetoric'.[44]

Reading for unity is, of course, criticism's second nature. In another highly influential work of literary theory, *The Genesis of Secrecy: On the Interpretation of Narrative*,[45] Frank Kermode uses the very New Testament interpretation as a case in point to show how successive interpreters always seek and find more and more unity and coherence in the text. Aptly, Kermode calls all critics of all canons 'pleromatists', 'fulfillment men', 'programmed to prefer fulfillment to disappointment, the closed to the open'.[46] For a professional critic, this fulfillment is never hard to find; 'techniques of literary criticism provide us with a

---

44. Genette, *Narrative Discourse*, p. 266. On narrative criticism's independence of narratology, see Moore, *Literary Criticism and the Gospels*, pp. 51-55.

45. Cambridge, MA: Harvard University Press, 1979.

46. Kermode, *The Genesis of Secrecy*, pp. 64, 72.

range of devices for eliciting unified interpretations from apparent inconsequentiality; we are familiar with concepts of ambiguity, irony, symbolism, and other kinds of literary indirectness that help us bring *prima facie* ill-formed texts under proper control'.[47] What we just saw in Staley's reading of the Gospel of John was a perfect example of this.

While a narratologist like Genette may, for the sake of keeping descriptive poetics accurate, warn against forcing the literary work's coherence, poststructuralist critics of narratology go further and deny narratological models their internal coherence. Instead of universal structures, these critics maintain, theoretical models represent contingent constructions that are, as such, deconstructable. Where applied as critical method, literary deconstruction specializes in readings that demonstrate how texts successfully resist critics' attempts to perceive them as coherent, integral wholes. In Gospel studies, Stephen D. Moore has done pioneering work in this field.[48] In his treatment of water symbolism in the Gospel of John, Moore seeks to show that John's narrative does not allow such a fixed, stable way to interpret the concept 'water' as would be necessary for a fully coherent reading of the Gospel as a whole. At Jacob's well, the reader needs to take the words 'water' and 'thirst' in a spiritual sense in order to grasp the Johannine irony. However, when Jesus later asks for and receives a drink on the cross, and when fresh water flows from his side, it is quite essential that both 'thirst' and 'water' are material; this is a necessary precondition for the symbolic level of the narrative to work at all. So the narrative suddenly changes its basic rules of making sense—with the result that its internal logic collapses.[49] While Moore's analysis might be considered a rather

---

47. M. Heath, *Unity in Greek Poetics* (Oxford: Clarendon Press, 1989), pp. 1-2.

48. See Stephen D. Moore, *Mark and Luke in Poststructuralist Perspectives: Jesus Begins to Write* (New Haven: Yale University Press, 1992); Moore, *Poststructuralism and the New Testament*. Other applications of deconstruction to biblical studies include, e.g., D. Jobling, 'Writing the Wrongs of the World: The Deconstruction of the Biblical Text in the Context of Liberation Theologies', *Semeia* 51 (1990), pp. 81-118; D. Jobling, 'Deconstruction and the Political Analysis of Biblical Texts: A Jamesonian Reading of Psalm 72', *Semeia* 59 (1992), pp. 95-127; F.W. Burnett, 'The Undecidability of the Proper Name "Jesus" in Matthew', *Semeia* 54 (1991), pp. 123-44; D. Seeley, *Deconstructing the New Testament* (Biblical Interpretation Series, 5; Leiden: E.J. Brill, 1994); W.W. Bubar, 'Killing Two Birds with One Stone: The Utter De(con)struction of Matthew and his Church', *BibInt* 3 (1995), pp. 144-57.

49. See, e.g., Moore, *Poststructuralism and the New Testament*, Chapter 2,

tendentious counter-reading of narrative-critical approaches to John and other Gospels, he nevertheless takes home the point that, in the end, no descriptive model is truly descriptive. Models do not replicate any objective structures present in the text as such. Rather, they each produce another text, another narrative whose structures mirror the interests of those who developed the model and those who apply it.

Indeed, it seems that, as critics, most of us would expect the Gospels to be 'remarkably unified', if we were to appreciate them as good literature. Apparently, both historical critics and narrative critics share this expectation. Both historical critics and narrative critics assume that inconsequentiality in the Gospels, should there be any, must be seen as a deficiency—a case of bad design or a sign of the text's corruption. While historical critics take notice of points of incoherence and use these points to argue that the Gospels fail to satisfy as literary works, narrative critics assume that inconsequentiality is merely apparent and go on to propose integrated interpretations that establish overarching themes or structures that hold the seemingly incoherent elements together. In both cases, personal aesthetics is at stake; both the historical critics and the narrative critics would like the narrative to meet their own standards of good literature.

Certainly, an aesthetic tradition that gives value to the integrity of the literary work goes a long way back to antiquity. In his *Poetics*, Aristotle says that the parts of a tragedy 'must be so arranged that if one of them be transposed or removed, the unity of the whole is dislocated and destroyed. For if the presence or absence of a thing makes no visible difference, then it is not an integral part of the whole' (*Poet.* 1451a [LCL]). Likewise, according to Horace's classic formulation the literary work should be *simplex et unum* (*Ars Poet.* 23). It is also quite plausible to assume that, at least to an extent, the evangelists hoped their works to turn out a success by the standards applied to such works by their contemporaries. After all, each evangelist bothered to compose a linear, sequentially ordered narrative. Luke, for one, sets out 'to write *an orderly account*' (καθεξῆς γράψαι) of what was 'handed on to us' (Lk. 1.2, 3) and lets his audience know that other people, too, have undertaken a similar task (Lk. 1.1). At the same time, however, it is equally certain that the evangelists did not aim at such unity and

'Deconstructive Criticism: Derrida at the Samaritan Well and, Later, at the Foot of the Cross', pp. 43-64. The same textual example appears in many of Moore's writings.

coherence of composition as strict critical standards would expect. Otherwise, they would simply have done their work differently. They would not have been happy with introducing redactional additions, corrections, and some reorganizing to the material which they used as their source—in the manner we (who believe in the so-called two-source hypothesis) may witness Matthew and Luke to have treated their sources (that is, Mark and the sayings source Q). Instead, they would have thrown away or completely rewritten all such elements that failed to serve the whole, thus removing each and every irrelevant lump from their textual pudding.

A partial answer to the question why the evangelists did their work in the way they did will, of course, be that aesthetics and poetics were not their main concern. The interests of early Christian ideology and proclamation were far more compelling concerns. Even if it meant putting the unity of design at risk, the evangelists preferred not to do too drastic alterations to the traditions they had received. On the other hand, they felt quite free to break the linear flow of narrative in order to introduce commentary, to make sure that the readers would not get any wrong ideas of how the text should be understood. While the evangelists considered the essential contents of the traditional, authoritative *kerygma* untouchable, the same did not go with the design of their own narrative as a whole.

Yet one may also ask how much unity and coherence the literary standards of the ancient Greek poetics would actually have required. Indeed, there seems to be—to quote Malcolm Heath—a 'relative lack of interest in the concept of unity in ancient criticism; where it does play an important role—notably in Aristotle's *Poetics* ... the criteria of unity applied [are] tolerant of [diverging,] centrifugal practices'.[50] Besides, the notion of unity is subject to historical and cultural change: it seems that when the ancient Greek critics spoke of unity, they did not think so much of thematic integrity and interrelatedness.[51] Rather, they understood the unity of the work to mean that everything in the work's design on the formal level served the ends of the genre to which the work belonged.[52] Notably, Plato thinks that the philosopher is free to

---

50. Heath, *Unity in Greek Poetics*, p. 9. At this point, Heath is referring to an earlier discussion in his *The Poetics of Greek Tragedy* (London: Gerald Duckworth, 1987).

51. Heath, *Unity in Greek Poetics*, p. 3.

52. Heath, *Unity in Greek Poetics*, p. 150.

ignore the requirements of formal composition as long as the philosopher's arguments succeed in attaining truth.[53] Significantly, this is exactly the same point as Papias makes in order to defend the evangelist Mark: according to Papias, the Gospel's lack of order is not important, because the evangelist nevertheless succeeds in telling the truth about the apostle Peter's preaching.[54]

On a very basic level, the Gospels might probably be considered unified enough to meet the goal-oriented and genre-specific standards of their time. The primary goal of the Gospels was not beauty but truth; they were written 'so that you may come to believe' (Jn 20.31) or 'so that you may know the truth as it was handed on to us' (cf. Lk. 1.2). In the end, this self-appointed *telos*—especially the need to be faithful to traditions used as sources—necessarily meant accepting a considerable amount of diversity in literary presentation. This was sometimes considered a problem (as Luke's opening and Papias's comment on Mark seem to betray), but still a relatively minor one. Ultimately, the treasure inside was considered far more precious than the clay jars that contained it (cf. 2 Cor. 4.7).[55]

From the point of view of criticism, it is not necessary to see all the diversity and dissonance found in the Gospel narratives unambiguously as a vice. In some respects, aspects of diversity and dissonance can be positive qualifications as well.[56] In a classic work, *Problems of Dostoevsky's Poetics*,[57] Mikhail Bakhtin greeted the Russian literary genius Fyodor Dostoevsky as the inventor of an entirely new form of literary expression, namely *the polyphonic novel*. According to Bakhtin, polyphonic narration is characterized by the principle of *dialogism*, that is, interaction of several voices, consciousnesses and world-views, none of which is allowed to rule over others.

53. See *Theaetetus* 172de; Heath, *Unity in Greek Poetics*, pp. 22, 26.

54. Eusebius, *Hist.* 3.35.15; cf. p. 15 above.

55. This is not to say that the treasure inside is a single and unified one. For conflicting ideological elements in Paul's thinking, see H. Räisänen, *Paul and the Law* (WUNT, 22; Tübingen: J.C.B. Mohr [Paul Siebeck], 2nd rev. edn, 1987), esp. pp. 199-202; in Matthew, see K. Syreeni, 'Between Heaven and Earth: On the Structure of Matthew's Symbolic Universe', *JSNT* 40 (1990), pp. 3-13.

56. Indeed, in postmodernist thought, characterized by a 'suspicion of totalities', fragmentariness (as opposed to unity) is a core value. See F. Kermode, *History and Value* (Oxford: Clarendon Press, 1988), pp. 128-46.

57. Ed. and trans. by C. Emerson; Manchester: Manchester University Press, 1984.

As ideological literature whose omniscient narrators constantly seek to control their characters and readers, the Gospels would hardly qualify as genuine dialogic narratives in a full Bakhtinian sense of the word. They rather present a paradigm case of what Bakhtin called *monologic* or *authoritative* discourse. Yet at the same time—and this strange marriage is, we think, the ultimate key to the peculiar nature of these narratives—the Gospels still display many aspects of polyphony. They still echo the voices of different oral traditions; show traces of multiple authors and multiple contexts; display features of several different oral and literary genres; contain diverging ideological elements. Should this multivoiced, dialogic side of the Gospels not be considered worth some attention—and appreciation—as well? [58]

As to the application of models and theories, the principle of dialogism has other implications. A truly *dialogic criticism* will not dogmatically force the literary work to fit models imposed on it; nor will it be content with 'letting the work speak for itself', 'objectively'. For dialogic criticism, the work is not a static object of description or admiration but a dynamic conversation partner. This hermeneutic dialogue also involves an ideological level: the critic understands that both the critic and the text have their interests; that they each from one's own point of view have to be faithful to what they regard as true and valuable. [59] In the case of such openly ideological narratives as the Gospels, these ideological and, ultimately, ethical considerations, are particularly acute. It is to this side of the Gospel narratives that we will turn next.

Gospels in Context

The Gospels are not art made for art's sake. They were written to promote interests that transcend the limits of their exclusive storyworlds. As ideological narratives, their task was to induce the readers to believe in the values shared by the Christian community from which they emerged. The Fourth Gospel makes this quite explicit, as it reads: 'these

58. These aspects have recently been emphasized by W.L. Reed, *Dialogues of the Word: The Bible as Literature According to Bakhtin* (New York: Oxford University Press, 1993), and M. Jones, 'A Bachtinian Approach to the Gospels: The Problem of Authority', *Scando-Slavica, Tomus 42* (1996), pp. 58-76.

59. Here we take our lead from T. Todorov, *Literature and its Theorists: A Personal View of Twentieth-Century Criticism* (trans. C. Porter; London: Routledge & Kegan Paul, 1988), pp. 155-68.

things are written that you may believe that Jesus is the Christ, the Son of God, and that by believing you may have life in his name' (Jn 20.31). On the whole, the Gospels present their readers a most comprehensive existential and ideological challenge. It is quite natural that the readers' response is not restricted merely to the aesthetic aspect of these narratives.

The Gospels also repeatedly make truth claims that refer to the historical reality outside their exclusive storyworlds. Both Luke and John claim their narratives to be based on what eyewitnesses have experienced and testified (Lk. 1.1-4; Jn 19.35; 21.24). Whether these claims are true or not, they exemplify what the evangelists aim at: they seek to assure their readers that their narratives mediate the truth about what happened in the past of the storytime. Most readers have taken these claims more than seriously. The fierce attacks against the results of the historical-critical scholarship show how natural it is for any uncritical reader to take the referential aspect of the Gospel narratives for real. Even in antiquity, Christian apologists (and, apparently, their opponents as well) made the connection between the general trustworthiness of the Gospels and the validity of the truth claims they present. To increase the reliability of the Gospels, they established links between the would-be authors and the events presented in the narratives, even though not all the narratives themselves suggested such a relationship. Thus, in the second century CE, Mark's Gospel was believed to be based on Peter's reminiscences. All this was quite understandable, because both pious and hostile readers would more or less automatically take seriously the Gospels' claims (mostly implicit, yet, as shown by the previous quotations from Luke and John, occasionally explicit) to have presented an authentic record of the life and works of Jesus.

In light of the Gospels themselves and the way most readers read them, critical attempts to analyze the Gospels as narrative communication should not restrict readers' interest to the exclusive storyworlds of the Gospels. If critics claim to consider a Gospel a process of communication, should they not try to pay attention to all aspects—literary, ideological and historical—of this process? Most certainly, any critical treatment of the Gospels as literature must deal with the fact that these narratives contain truth claims that exceed those made in pure fiction.

Traditionally, the Gospels have not been read as fictional narratives, nor does it come naturally to think of them as such. It must be asked what consequences this has for narrative analysis. To answer this question we must first consider what the difference is between a fictional and a non-fictional narrative.

The difference between fictional and non-fictional narratives has to do with rules and conventions that guide the communication between the author and the reader.[60] The key question concerns the attitude that the author, on the one hand, and the reader, on the other, take toward the narrative. In the case of a non-fictional narrative, the authors commit themselves strictly to the story by guaranteeing its veracity. The authors assume that the reader takes the story seriously and believes it. In fictional narratives, however, narrative communication is not based on commitment and belief but on make-believe.[61] This difference becomes more evident as we consider what happens when we read fictional texts.

When writers of fictional narrative present their readers a storyworld and invite them to step in, both parties know that they are not dealing with 'reality' in the everyday sense of the word. It is as if all fictional works had a preface that reads 'I hereby present that ...' or 'I would like you to consider that ...'[62] The moment the readers accept the invitation, they enter into an unpronounced contract with the author. As a result, they grant the author privileges that would be out of place in

60. Cf. R.L. Brown, Jr, and M. Steinman, Jr, 'Native Readers of Fiction: A Speech-Act and Genre-Rule Approach to Defining Literature', in Paul Hernadi (ed.), *What Is Literature* (Bloomington: Indiana University Press, 1978), pp. 141-60 (149-50): 'A discourse *is* fictional because its speaker or writer intends it to be so. But it is *taken as* fictional only because the hearer or reader decides to take it so ... the decision to read a discourse as fictional or nonfictional is a decision to use one set of constitutive rules rather than another, and we really can't read it—interpret it—at all until we have made this decision'; M. Sternberg, *The Poetics of Biblical Narrative: Ideological Literature and the Drama of Reading* (Bloomington: Indiana University Press, 1985), p. 26: 'Both historiography and fiction are genres of writing, not bundles of fact or nonfact in verbal shape. In either case, then, it all boils down to the rules of the writing game, namely, to the premises, conventions, and the undertakings that attach to the discourse as an affair between writer and audience. What kind of contract binds them together? What does the writer stand committed to? What is the audience to assume?'

61. Cf. G. Currie, *The Nature of Fiction* (Cambridge: Cambridge University Press, 1990), p. 21.

62. Thus N. Wolterstorff, *Works and Worlds of Art* (Oxford: Clarendon Press, 1980), p. 233; A. Haapala, 'Fiktiivisyys kirjallisuudessa' [Fictionality in Literature], in A. Haapala *et al.* (eds.), *Kirjallisuuden filosofiaa* (Helsinki: Vapk, 1990), pp. 63-85 (81).

everyday communication. An adult author may freely use the voice of a child narrator to tell a story. Another author may recount matters that exist entirely in the future. It belongs to the common rules of fictional communication that readers do not question the rationale behind the author's actions. A reader who does so is simply misunderstanding the rules according to which one is supposed to read a fictional narrative.

As Kendall L. Walton suggests, we should regard fictional works of art as *games of make-believe* very much like those that children play.[63] To read fiction is to approach a work with expectations unlike those with which one faces a non-fictional—spoken or written—discourse. While the writer is free to establish and present an independent fictional world, readers know they are not supposed to believe that this world is true in any ontological sense. Wherever readers face demands of this kind, they find themselves out of the realm of fiction at a new playing field where a different set of rules is in force. While communication in fictional narratives can be described as a game of make-believe, in non-fictional narratives we meet a game of commitment and belief.

Because the difference between fictional and non-fictional narratives has to do with rules of communication, this difference lies beneath the surface level of each narrative, which makes it difficult to define what exactly it is that makes the difference. Evidently, the difference does not result from the presence or absence of particular formal features: forms and conventions typical of fictional narratives may be present in non-fictional narratives as well, which is shown by many narrative-critical studies that have successfully applied theoretical studies in the formal features of fiction to the narratives of the Gospels.[64] It should be noted, however, that even if fictional and non-fictional narratives make use of similar formal features, they do this on the basis of entirely different presuppositions. The difference becomes evident when we

---

63. Kendall L. Walton, *Mimesis as Make-Believe: On Foundations of the Representational Arts* (Cambridge, MA: Harvard University Press, 1990), p. 11, and *passim*. See also Currie, *The Nature of Fiction*, pp. 18-21; Haapala, 'Fiktiivisyys kirjallisuudessa', p. 81; M. Calinescu, *Rereading* (New Haven: Yale University Press, 1993), p. 188.

64. Cf. D.E. Aune, *The New Testament in its Literary Environment* (Library of Early Christianity, 8; Philadelphia: Westminster Press, 1987), p. 111: 'the literary styles and structures associated with fiction ... cannot exclude the use of narrative art in ancient cultures to mediate a historical view of reality'.

consider how different the narrator's role and functions are in fictional and non-fictional narratives.

Narratological theories emphasize the need to separate the act of *writing* from the act of *narrating*, that is, to distinguish between the *author* and the *narrator*. In fictional narratives, the narrator is a rhetorical device invented by the author in order to tell the story in a certain way. What kind of narrator the author chooses to bring in is a matter of the author's will. Thus, in fictional narratives, the narrator must not be confused with the author. At the same time, however, many narratologists note that in non-fictional, 'factual' narratives, matters may be otherwise. According to Gérard Genette, to identify the narrator with the author is 'perhaps legitimate in the case of historical narrative or a real autobiography, but not when we are dealing with a narrative of fiction, where the role of narrator is itself fictive'.[65] Elsewhere, Genette clarifies his point by saying that 'the rigorous identification' of the author with the narrator defines what he calls factual narrative; in these narratives 'the author assumes full responsibility for the assertions of his narrative and, consequently, does not grant autonomy to any narrator'.[66] Similarly, Dorrit Cohn concludes that 'the reader of a non-fictional narrative understands it to have a stable uni-vocal origin, that its narrator is identical to a real person'.[67]

In non-fictional narratives, therefore, the narrator represents the author. Consequently, in non-fictional narratives, the narrator and the narrative point of view from which the events are presented are not entirely matters of free artistic choice. In the Gospels, for example, events are seen from a retrospective point of view. This point of view is not accidental but results from the simple fact that the Gospels were written in particular historical situations. The writers tell their readers about events that have taken place in the past—perhaps two or three generations ago—which explains the temporal point of view of the story. Things are far from this simple in the case of fictional stories that can be told from whatever point of view the writer finds best for his or her purposes. In other words, in non-fictional narratives, narrative structures are more transparent as to the aims and purposes of the author

---

65. Genette, *Narrative Discourse*, p. 213.

66. Gérard Genette, 'Fictional Narrative, Factual Narrative', *Poetics Today* 11 (1990), pp. 755-74 (764).

67. Dorrit Cohn, 'Signposts of Fictionality: A Narratological Perspective', *Poetics Today* 11 (1990), pp. 775-804 (792).

than in non-fictional narratives. Instead of a yawning gulf, there is continuity between elements of 'reality' and elements of the narrative world.

Significantly, the difference between non-fictional and fictional narratives is not equal to the difference between what really happened and what was invented by an author. On the one hand, fictional narratives may be based on historical events or persons (like Tolstoy's *War and Peace*). On the other hand, not everything in non-fictional narratives is necessarily based on facts in the strict sense of the word. Although the Gospels contain material that is historically not entirely reliable, this does not yet make them fictional narratives. What counts is not the value the narrative has as a historical source but the explicit or implicit truth claims that make clear the purpose of the work.[68] Fictional works may try to imitate 'real' life; however, their writers do not mean that the things they tell in the narrative have actually taken place.[69] Their characters may be more or less realistic—indeed, they may be quite like the people we meet in our everyday lives—yet there is a notable difference between characters in fiction and living persons. The writers of fiction do not expect their readers to think that the characters of the story once lived or perhaps still continue living in the same world as the reader. Non-fictional works, on the other hand, really do purport to describe the real world.[70] For them to succeed in their task of factual narrative communication, it is quite essential that the reader does not doubt the writer's basic truth claims. A biographical narrative has failed to meet its goal if the reader at some point ceases to believe that the main character ever existed.

However, the difference between fictional and non-fictional narratives is far from an absolute one. There are texts that do not seem to fit properly in either group. Many modern and postmodern writers quite intentionally blur the line between fiction and non-fiction by introducing documentary material into a secondary fictional framework. These experiments do not, however, undo the basic difference between

---

68. Sternberg, *The Poetics of Biblical Narrative*, p. 25.

69. Calinescu, *Rereading*, p. 185: 'We must consider "real" or "literal" what is seriously meant when something is done or said in a specific situation or framework. We must consider "playful" or "nonliteral" or "fictional" what mimics or imitates or simulates or bears resemblance to a potentially serious message, nonverbal or verbal, without actually meaning it.'

70. Walton, *Mimesis*, p. 70.

fictional and non-fictional narratives. On the contrary, the effect these works have on their readers is based on the very fact that readers tend to respond to different texts in different ways. To end up reading a work of fiction in a way one would normally read non-fiction makes a confusing reading experience.[71] It is, of course, quite possible to read a fictional text as one would read a non-fictional one, and vice versa. But although individual readers may read historical accounts, biographies or news reports as they would read fictional narratives, it is still quite clear that, conventionally, the way we read these narratives and respond to them is different from the way we read fictional narratives.[72] We are likely to be shocked on reading or hearing of a murder in a news report; however, in a detective story, the same account would merely make us curious to know who the murderer is.

When speaking of a distinction between two different types of narratives, we are, in fact, speaking of reading conventions that make people read certain texts in certain ways.[73] Reading conventions provide readers with expectations about how the narrative relates to reality. These expectations have an impact on how readers approach each type of narrative, as well as an impact on what kind of questions the readers have in mind when they read. In the case of fictional narratives, it is natural for the readers to ask questions that do not transcend the limits of the story. It is of little use speculating what kind of childhood the character Raskolnikov of Dostoevsky's *Crime and Punishment* had or what exactly happened to Defoe's Robinson Crusoe after he had returned to England. The readers are expected to be satisfied with the information that the writer chooses to reveal in the work itself. In the case of non-fictional narratives, however, the readers' questions are by no means restricted to the internal world of the narrative. In non-fictional narratives, the readers do not construct the meaning of the

71. Perhaps the most famous of all works that have blurred the distinction between fiction and non-fiction is Orson Welles's radio production *The War of the Worlds*. In this fictional program Welles described the Martian invasion of the earth in extremely authentic terms. Many of the listeners took the program for an actual news broadcast.

72. Cf. Walton, *Mimesis*, p. 71.

73. This is emphasized by Stanley Fish, 'How to Do Things with Austin and Searle: Speech-Act Theory and Literary Criticism', in *idem*, *Is There a Text in This Class? The Authority of Interpretive Communities* (Cambridge, MA: Harvard University Press, 1980), pp. 197-245 (243).

work solely on the basis of the work itself; instead, they take into
account all they know about the relationship of the work to the 'real'
world. In order to make sense, non-fictional works need to be seen in
context.

Because a non-fictional narrative claims to refer to events and circumstances of the 'real' world, it is natural that the readers try to fill
any gaps the narrative may have, making use of all available information about the events and circumstances in concern. What readers of a
non-fictional narrative think of a character depends not only on what
the narrator reveals but also on what else the readers may know about
the person who is portrayed as a character in the narrative. Furthermore,
in the minds of the readers, certain historical persons may stand for
certain symbolic values, even if those values are not attached to these
persons as they are portrayed as characters in the narrative. All of this
makes narrative communication in non-fictional narratives a more or
less complicated event that is contingent upon a variety of things. Such
complexity is something any form of critical analysis should take seriously.

The portrayal of the Jewish leaders in the synoptic Gospels, and in
the Gospel of Matthew in particular, provides us with an excellent
example of how literary, ideological and historical aspects intermingle
in the narrative of the Gospels. Mark Allan Powell has described the
various, mostly negative, character traits that are attached to the Jewish
religious leaders in these narratives: the leaders are characterized as
fearful of the people, manipulative, hypocritical, deceitful and self-righteous. At several points in Matthew's narrative, the Jewish leaders are
identified simply as 'evil'. Now, according to Powell, the literary effect
of Matthew's portrayal 'is to impress upon the reader that God, in
Christ, has overcome evil, even though it succeeded at doing its worst.
If Matthew softened his characterization of the leaders, made them less
evil than they appear, the force with which this point is made would be
weakened.'[74]

In Powell's view, the characterization of the Jews is but a rhetorical
device that Matthew uses in order to bring home an important theological lesson. Consequently, Matthew's narrative does not intend to
describe Jewish groups in the real world. As Powell puts it, 'the religious leaders in Matthew's narrative do not "stand for" any real people

---

74. Powell, *What Is Narrative Criticism?*, pp. 66-67.

in the world *outside the story*, but are constructs of the implied author designed to fulfil a particular role *in the story*. The fact that Matthew's Gospel has aroused hostility towards Jewish religious leaders, and towards the Jews in general, is based on a misreading; such a reading 'represents a gross example of the referential fallacy and completely misses the point of the story'.[75] According to Powell, 'narrative critics are able to demonstrate that the intended literary effect of Matthew is not to foster anti-Semitism'.[76]

No one is likely to object to the way Powell describes Matthew's portrayal of the Jewish leaders. Problems begin only when Powell starts to make claims that go beyond the mere rephrasing of Matthew's text. Powell's suggestion that the function of Matthew's portrayal of the Jewish leaders is exclusively rhetorical calls forth serious questions: Is this a natural way to read such narratives as the Gospels? Are readers supposed to think that the Jewish religious leaders, as well as other characters in the Gospels, including Jesus, do not 'stand for' any real people? Have all those who have connected Matthew's portrait of the leaders to some Jewish groups outside the story (that is to say, virtually all readers before the invention of narrative criticism) indeed been misreading the narrative?

The answer to all these questions is obvious enough: Powell is grossly misreading Matthew by reading the Gospel as he would read a fictional narrative. The natural way to read a Gospel would be to make

---

75. Powell, *What Is Narrative Criticism?*, p. 66. Exactly the opposite, however, is proposed by Adele Reinhartz, 'The New Testament and Anti-Judaism: A Literary-Critical Approach', *Journal of Ecumenical Studies* 25 (1988), pp. 524-37. According to Reinhartz, a literary-critical reading of the Gospels clearly shows that the 'ideal readers' of the Gospels, that is, readers who assent to these narratives without critical reservation, are supposed to accept the villainous role of the Jews and the negative attitudes toward them (p. 532). The Gospels are, therefore, well capable of encouraging anti-Jewish attitudes, if actual readers read the story as the narrative expects them to read.

76. Powell, *What Is Narrative Criticism?*, p. 88. It is significant that Powell here speaks of the *literary* effect of Matthew, while he is, in fact, referring to the evangelist's *ideological* point of view. This is because Powell's idea of textual analysis can only reckon with two levels of meaning, namely literary and real-world. What should properly be the level of ideology is replaced with a blind spot. As a consequence, the ideology reflected in the text is seen as a mere literary device. See K. Syreeni, 'Metaphorical Appropriation: (Post-)Modern Biblical Hermeneutics and the Theory of Metaphor', *Literature and Theology* 9 (1995), pp. 321-38.

connections between character groups of the story and the 'real' groups
which those characters intend to portray. Just as the reader is not supposed to regard Matthew's Jesus as a character who only lives in the
pages of the narrative, the Jewish religious leaders are not a group
whose function in the story is only a poetic and not a referential one.
This means that questions concerning the function of Matthew's portrayal of the Jewish leaders cannot be sufficiently answered unless we
turn to what we know about the circumstances in which the narrative
was written. A purely 'intrinsic' approach to the Gospel leaves us only
halfway to a truly comprehensive understanding of Matthew's characterization of the Jewish leaders.

As long as we expect our analyses of the Gospels as narratives to be
something more than plain descriptions of the text's formal features, we
simply cannot neglect historical questions that concern the origins of
the Gospels. In the case of Matthew's portrayal of the Jewish leaders,
historical scholarship tends to explain the negative depiction of the
leaders by referring to a polemic between Jewish and Christian groups
in the first century. Now, this information is relevant not only from the
point of view of historical-critical scholarship; it is also highly important for a narrative analysis of Matthew's Gospel. If we hope to get a
truly comprehensive picture of Matthew's portrayal of the Jewish leaders, we must consider everything that may have contributed to the way
the leaders are presented. This means including historical and sociological questions that relate to the text's origin and reception.

As to actual, common readers of the Gospels (the original audience
of these works included), their response is hardly restricted to the formal, or poetic, features of the text but includes various religious and
ideological aspects as well.[77] In the case of Matthew, the narrative
requires that the readers accept, among other things, a polemical
portrayal of the Jewish leaders. In all probability, Matthew's original

---

77. Cf. S.R. Suleiman, 'Ideological Dissent from Works of Fiction: Toward a
Rhetoric of the *roman à thèse*', *Neophilologus* 60 (1976), pp. 162-77 (163): 'In the
"realistic" work, which has dominated the practice of the novel in the West until a
recent date, the kind of assent required from the reader has been not only formal,
but also, to varying degrees, social, political, ethical, philosophical—to use a catch-
all term, ideological. Since the novel has traditionally dealt with the actions or state
of being of a set of lifelike characters, an integral part of the reader's response to
novels has been an emotional reaction based on the explicit or implied judgments of
the text regarding these characters or their actions.'

audience was not supposed to doubt the accuracy of such a portrayal. Modern critical readers, however, cannot take this portrayal at face value. As recent developments in biblical studies have emphasized, the portrayal of the Jews and Judaism in the Gospels is a tremendous caricature and, as such, not based on what Judaism was like in the first century. To attain results that can stand critical scrutiny, narrative analysis of the Gospels, too, needs to include an ideological-critical point of view that allows interpreters to keep a critical distance from the ideology of the text and that will enable them to read against the grain whenever necessary.[78]

An 'intrinsic', text-centered approach does not seem to match properly the nature of the Gospels as non-fictional narratives. Furthermore, even in the study of fiction, exclusively text-centered approaches have long ago fallen into disrepute. This is because literary critics have come to realize that there never was, nor can there ever be such a thing as 'objective criticism'. On the contrary, all criticism and interpretation— formal, 'intrinsic' analysis included—have ideological implications. It is to these implications that we now turn; they make up our last argument for the need for narrative criticism to reconsider some of its starting points.

As paradoxical as it is, even New Criticism's decision to focus exclusively on the inherent, formal features of literary works had inevitable political implications. The New Critics became associated with political conservatives who likewise thought that art should concentrate on 'purely artistic' issues instead of giving attention to such 'political' matters as poverty or social unrest or, much worse, getting involved in (implicit or explicit) protests against the status quo. From the time of the Great Depression and the New Deal, the US government's official cultural policy was to support the politically indifferent

---

78. Thus also Reinhartz, 'The New Testament and Anti-Judaism', pp. 534-35. According to Reinhartz, actual present-day readers, who know more about historical Judaism and the history of the early church than the Gospels reveal, have the responsibility to deny any anti-Judaistic claims, implicit or explicit, in the text. Significantly, this ethically responsible reading is made possible by virtue of extrinsic, historical information: because the actual readers can understand that the portraits of the Jews in the Gospels are not historically accurate but reflect the troubled relationship between the early Christian communities and local synagogues, they are able to distance themselves from the anti-Jewish ideal readers of the Gospels.

current of modernism (the mirror image of the ideals of New Criticism) at the expense of the socially more critical current of realism. Correspondingly, New Criticism assumed the status of a norm for literary criticism in America. In the Soviet Union, of course, things went somewhat the opposite way. Socialist art was intentionally political and realistic, which is to say that realism came to be the only 'artistic method' that was accepted. From a Marxist point of view, all true art needed to be aware of its connections to prevailing social and historical circumstances. The circle became complete, as the East European dissident artists, revolting against the official Marxist views, took the nonchalant playfulness of 'reactionary' and 'degenerated' modernism as a symbol of freedom, creativity and resistance.

Thus, both in the West and in the East 'purely artistic' matters were far from being purely artistic. Art that claimed to be indifferent really supported the status quo. Likewise, a scholarly orientation that would detach the Scriptures from their historical contexts of origin and analyze them from a purely poetic point of view would for ideological reasons be warmly welcomed by some people, namely 'those who have been uncomfortable with the challenges posed by historical criticism'.[79] Indeed, some scholars have cherished the 'apparent compatibility between the goals of narrative criticism and the interests of believing communities' as well as the fact that 'by focusing on the finished form of the text narrative criticism seeks to interpret Scripture at its canonical level'. From their point of view, 'such scepticism [as demanded by historical investigation] is a far cry from the certainty of faith with which the gospel narratives appear to have been written and with which they obviously expect to be read'; luckily enough, 'by interpreting texts from the point of view of their own implied readers, narrative criticism offers exegesis that is inevitably from a faith perspective'.[80]

---

79. Powell, *What Is Narrative Criticism?*, p. 88. Cf. also M.W.G. Stibbe, 'Introduction', in *idem* (ed.), *The Gospel of John as Literature: An Anthology of Twentieth-Century Pespectives* (New Testament Tools and Studies, 17; Leiden: E.J. Brill, 1993), pp. 1-13. According to Stibbe, it remains to be seen to what extent 'new' literary criticism rescues the Gospels—in this case the Fourth Gospel—'from a form of scholarship which has alienated the Gospel(s) from both the church and society' (p. 13).

80. Powell, *What Is Narrative Criticism?*, pp. 88-89. Here Powell is strongly criticized by Moore, *Poststructuralism and the New Testament*, pp. 115-16.

It is rather obvious that new-critical ideas about the unity and autonomy of literary works would attract conservative Christians. Notably, the literary critic Vincent B. Leitch speaks of a congruence between fundamentalist Protestant exegesis and the new-critical 'close reading'. In Leitch's view, New Criticism built upon the tradition of the fundamentalist hermeneutic that, 'unlike the "higher criticism" of modern biblical scholarship with its attention to historical matters and textual flaws, conferred divine status on the work and then proceeded worshipfully to unravel the text'.[81] If the New Critics put the principles of fundamentalist hermeneutic in a new cloth, it is only natural that yet another recycling of these ideas would attract conservative Christians today.

Nor is it much of a surprise that some historical critics should become worried. From their point of view, a mere analysis of the formal features of texts as such falls fatally short of what is required for understanding those texts as writings that have been shaped by the ideas, attitudes and conditions of a particular historical moment. As such, a purely narrative analysis renders exegesis unable to perform its most essential task as a critical discipline, namely, that of being the 'historical conscience' of any theological use of the Bible, 'pointing out cases of overly strained application or downright misuse of the documents'.[82]

However, one may ask whether it really is the 'faith perspective' that makes narrative criticism so attractive to those not pleased with historical exegesis. In reality, the faith of the implied readers of the early Christian Gospels hardly comes close to the private, individualistic and doctrinal faith of the twentieth-century Christians. Facing this (de facto historical) difference might easily be just as painful as accepting the skepticism required by a historical approach. Perhaps a more likely reason for the conservative side to prefer a narrative-critical approach to a historical-critical or social-scientific approach might be narrative criticism's strong aesthetic emphasis, the promise to center on the poetic aspect of the Gospels and leave aside all conclusions that might concern the history, doctrine or policies of the church. As in the case of New Criticism, the very promise to ignore every ideological aspect might make the approach useful ideologically.

81. Vincent B. Leitch, *American Literary Criticism from the Thirties to the Eighties* (New York: Columbia University Press, 1988), p. 33.
82. H. Räisänen, *Beyond New Testament Theology: A Story and a Programme* (London: SCM Press; Philadelphia: Trinity Press International, 1990), p. 137.

As unfortunate as it is to anyone hoping for 'politically indifferent exegesis', however, most narrative critics would hardly keep away from matters beyond the 'purely artistic'. On the contrary, many of them have, especially in the recent years, become exceedingly involved in such matters as feminism, as well as the cause of the politically, racially and economically oppressed, along with different types of theology of liberation. The way David Rhoads concludes his recent analysis on Mark's *standards of judgment*—that is, those values and beliefs that implicitly govern the narrative world—is a fine case in point:

> Down through history, the standards of the Gospel of Mark have been reflected in ordinary folk who have lived courageous lives of service for others. Markan Christians are represented by the orders of the church that called people to give up their livelihood and security to preach the gospel or care for the poor and the ill. Countless missionaries who have left home and country to bring the gospel to remote parts of the world belong in the Markan trajectory. In modern times, their numbers will include those who risked their lives to rescue Jews in Nazi Germany. And we might point to all who joined Martin Luther King in the struggle for civil rights. Most recently, we can point to the sanctuary movement in this country, the base communities in Latin America, and the struggle of blacks in South Africa. In all nations, where people take courageous risks to bring life to others in the face of persecution, we find Markan Christians.[83]

Now that is hardly an exclusively poetic perspective on Mark's narrative.

In fact, narrative criticism has hardly ever restricted its interests to a mere structural analysis of the Gospels as narratives, or the simple descriptive question 'how do the Gospels mean?' From the very beginning, it has gone on to enter the arena of *interpretation* and make ideological judgments on the values and beliefs that those narratives promote. This is only natural, as it represents nothing less than 'interpreting texts from the point of view of their own implied readers'. These implied readers would certainly reckon that what they are reading is not only a work of *poiesis* but sacred history and prophetic proclamation. As such, it is bound to involve both material and spiritual realities beyond the narrative's exclusive storyworld. To read a Gospel is to gaze on history and to prepare for action in the present.

---

83. D. Rhoads, 'Losing Life for Others in the Face of Death: Mark's Standards of Judgment', *Int* 47.4 (1993), pp. 358-69 (367).

Conclusions

The literary unity of the Gospels should not be exaggerated. If judged by modern(ist) standards, there are 'bugs' in the narrative machinery of the Gospels, or lumps in the biblical pudding, to apply the witty new-critical imagery of Wimsatt and Beardsley. This is something that the evangelists themselves, however, would hardly have considered a vice—and the same goes in all probability for the original audience of the evangelists. After all, the evangelists were not so much interested in the purity of composition of their works, at least not according to the modern standards of unity. Rather, they sought to present an authoritative interpretation of what they had received from tradition as well as from other writings. While doing this, they maintained a dialogic relationship with the many voices they met in earlier traditions. This makes the Gospels multivoiced narratives in which a spectrum of historical voices can still be heard to proclaim the early Christian *kerygma*.

While we emphasize that the Gospels are non-fictional narratives by nature, we do not take this to mean that narrative criticism should stop making any questions that concern the 'literary' aspects of the Gospels and replace all such questions for 'historical' and 'sociological' ones.[84] What we do suggest, however, is that narrative analysis of the Gospels should be methodologically as inclusive and comprehensive as possible. This will help us to see narrative as a truly dialogic form of communication that takes shape in a process of interaction with the historical situation and ideology of the author and the readers. Once we

---

84. Narrative criticism's relationship to historical criticism is often presented in somewhat confusing terms. According to Powell (*What Is Narrative Criticism?*, p. 9), the two approaches do not overlap, apart from their common interest in the text. In another connection, however, Powell says there exists a symbiotic relationship between narrative and historical approaches; the methods cannot be used simultaneously, but they can be used side by side in a supplementary fashion (p. 98). In our opinion, an even closer relationship between the two approaches would be mutually beneficial. Learning how the Gospels work as narratives might indeed prevent historical critics from jumping to conclusions, as it comes to reconstructing the historical situation 'behind' the text. On the other hand, what historical criticism has to say about the origin of the Gospels might lead narrative critics towards a better understanding of what is, in fact, going on in the narrative. A narrative analysis should be *an integral part of* historical investigation, and vice versa.

have given proper attention to the dialogic relationship of the text with its ideological and historical environment of origin and reception, this will make it easier for us to recognize the rich polyphony of the diverse elements within the text as well.[85]

There is, finally, no need for a narrative approach to be an exclusively text-centered one, nor does 'intrinsic' criticism represent a more 'literary' point of view than 'extrinsic' criticism. In the case of the Gospels, forms of narrative analysis that are more open to questions concerning the ideological and historical background of the texts must be considered preferable, because they pay due attention to the nature of the Gospels as non-fictional narratives. These forms of analysis will welcome any relevant sociological or historical information that helps to understand the complexity of narrative communication in the Gospels. Consequently, they seek not rivalry but rather cooperation with the historical-critical method—which is only wise, because, however intriguing the exclusive storyworlds of the Gospels may be, 'nagging questions about the truth and value of realities envisaged in the Bible, refined as they are by sensitive readings, rightly continue to haunt the reader'.[86]

85. In this respect, the approach we are proposing parallels not only Bakhtin's early translinguistics but also some recent sociolinguistic and socio-rhetorical approaches to early Christian literature; see, e.g., V.K. Robbins, *Exploring the Texture of Texts: A Guide to Socio-Rhetorical Interpretation* (Valley Forge, PA: Trinity Press International, 1996); *idem*, *The Tapestry of Early Christian Discourse: Rhetoric, Society and Ideology* (London: Routledge, 1996).

86. M. Davies, 'Literary Criticism', in R.J. Coggins and J.L. Houlden (eds.), *A Dictionary of Biblical Interpretation* (London: SCM Press, 1990), pp. 402-405 (405).

CHARACTERS IN THE MAKING:
INDIVIDUALITY AND IDEOLOGY IN THE GOSPELS

Petri Merenlahti

This essay will focus on what might well be considered the most typical question of all concerning biblical characterization, namely, *representation of individuality*. In this respect, the mystery of biblical characters is the mystery of the mustard seed: how does so much come out of so little? How do figures who are sketched with only a few harsh strokes manage to give an impression of individuality and personhood?

My thesis is that characterization in the Gospels is disposed to changes that are due to ideological conditions. An attentive reader of the Gospels can detect two opposing lines of development. While some characters become increasingly subtle during the subsequent retelling of the story, others are stripped of their individuality and subjective performance and are turned into simple agents. Paradoxical as it may seem, the reason behind these changes appears to be the same in both cases: the narrative is striving to become more consistently monologic, which would enhance the ideological naturalization of all its elements.[1] For some characters, this means that their inner emotions, reactions and intentions need to be clarified, so that no misinterpretation on the reader's part will disturb the narrative's ideological impact. As a consequence, these characters become 'fuller'. As to some other characters, it is safer to deny them voice and vision altogether. Not surprisingly, the characters most liable to lose their share of narrative subjectivity are

---

1.   The concept of monologic narrative originates from Mikhail Bakhtin. In a monologic (as opposed to dialogic) narrative, the narrator's unifying voice and vision constitute the ultimate authority that rules over other voices, judgments and points of view. See M. Bakhtin, *The Dialogic Imagination* (ed. M. Holmquist; trans. C. Emerson and M. Holmquist; Austin: University of Texas Press, 1981); M. Bakhtin, *Problems of Dostoevsky's Poetics* (ed. and trans. C. Emerson; Minneapolis: University of Minnesota Press, 1984).

those characters whose actions, words or points of view somehow contest a dominant ideology.

Thus, in the Gospels, characters are only in the process of becoming what they are. Rather than static elements of design picked by a master author to fill a distinct literary or rhetorical purpose, they are constantly being reshaped by distinct ideological dynamics. This ideologically attuned nature of character presents a challenge for any theory or model of characterization for the Gospel narratives.[2] Rigid mechanistic models will need to be replaced with more flexible ones that treat the Gospels as part of a living, evolving tradition. Because there is 'a relation between ideological dominance and specific forms of representation', analysis of ideology should be an integral part of the analysis of the formal features of narrative.[3] This analysis need not necessarily be neutral. Perhaps the critic might consider the text not so much an object of formal description as a challenge to one's own personal convictions.[4]

---

2. Certainly, 'character' remains a complicated theoretical issue in its own right; some consider it 'both the most central and the most problematic concept of narrative theory', even to the extent that 'in the course of the long history of Western criticism and poetics, characters have never been described in a satisfactory way theoretically' (M. Bal, *Lethal Love: Feminist Literary Readings of Biblical Love Stories* [Bloomington: Indiana University Press, 1987], pp. 3, 105). The classification of characters by their 'fullness' is an essential part of this problem; see, e.g., S. Rimmon-Kenan, *Narrative Fiction: Contemporary Poetics* (London: Methuen, 1983), pp. 40-42; M. Bal, *Narratology: Introduction to the Theory of Narrative* (trans. C. van Boheemen; Toronto: University of Toronto Press, 1985), p. 81. For a brief review of these theoretical issues as related to biblical characters, see Outi Lehtipuu's chapter in this volume.

3. Bal, *Lethal Love*, p. 3. In her numerous works of the 1980s, Bal aimed at putting narrative theory in the service of ideology-critique, specifically feminism. Significantly, many of these works involved analyses of biblical texts. In addition to *Lethal Love*—and its earlier French version *Femmes imaginaires: L'Ancien Testament au risque d'une narratologie critique* (Utrecht: HES; Montreal: HMH; Paris: Nizet, 1986)—see her *Death and Dissymmetry: The Politics of Coherence in the Book of Judges* (Chicago: University of Chicago Press, 1988); and *Murder and Difference: Gender, Genre, and Scholarship on Sisera's Death* (Bloomington: Indiana University Press, 1988).

4. See T. Todorov, *Literature and its Theorists: A Personal View of Twentieth-Century Criticism* (trans. C. Porter; London: Routledge & Kegan Paul, 1988), pp. 155-68.

On the Impersonal Nature of Biblical Characterization

Obviously, many characters in the Gospels are individuals in the sense that they have, for example, a proper name and a particular setting. Yet their individuality is more or less impersonal: as agents, they remain subordinate to action; as types, they remain subordinate to the more general human (or sometimes superhuman) qualities they exemplify. While, of course, it makes a marked difference whether Jesus heals an anonymous blind person or a close friend named Lazarus, the more distinctive individuality of the latter does not yet make that character much of a personality. Even Jesus himself, the protagonist of the story, is typically characterized as the 'Son of God', a figure of a particular type, rather than a troubled, thoughtful young Nazarean, as modern literature would have him, for whom fate is not predestined but the result of personal choices.

Indeed, matters could hardly be otherwise. After all, psychological interest in the individual as personality is a relatively new phenomenon in Western art (just as the individualist idea of identity as selfhood has only emerged with modernity). In antiquity, characters had not so much 'personality' in the modern sense, as *ethos*—a static, unchanging set of virtues and vices.[5]

Even today, economical characterization and the use of simple, recognizable standard types (such as the *femme fatale*, the hypochondriac or the sage's stupid disciple) remain a practical necessity for all those forms of storytelling that are designed to make a simple point: the exemplary, educative or ideological story with a moral—as well as the *joke* whose every single feature is directed towards the punchline. In stories of this kind, character-types are most practical, because they give in a condensed form everything the audience needs to know about the figures presented. Any more detailed characterization would be superfluous and disturbing. Consider the example given by the American playwright David Mamet:

> 'Two guys go into a farm house. An old woman is stirring a pot of soup.'
> What does the woman look like? What state is the farm house in? Why is
> she stirring soup? It is absolutely not important. The dirty-joke teller is
> tending toward a punch line and we know that he or she is only going to

5. See, e.g., M.A. Tolbert, 'How the Gospel of Mark Builds Character', *Int* 47.4 (1993), pp. 347-57 (348-49).

tell us the elements which direct our attention toward that punch line, so
we listen attentively and gratefully.[6]

Quite similarly—and now I am quoting Erich Auerbach's famous
assessment of Mark's narrative,

> the author of the Gospel according to Saint Mark has no viewpoint
> which would permit him to present a factual, objective portrait of, let us
> say, the character of Peter. He is at the core of what goes on; he observes
> and relates only what matters in relation to Christ's presence and mis-
> sion; and in the present case [of Peter's denial] it does not even occur to
> him to tell us how the incident ended, that is, how Peter got away...[7]

The personal elements are there only insofar as they are necessary to
achieve the objective toward which the narrative is tending. In the
framework of an individual miracle story, this objective is the occurrence of the miraculous; in a controversy story, it is the final word
uttered by the protagonist silencing all objections; in a Gospel, it is
'Christ's presence and mission'.

The Role of the Reader in the Making of Biblical Characters

Thus, at least at first glance, ancient literary conventions and the evangelists' ideological objective appear to exclude any particular interest in
the individual and the personal. In biblical scholarship, the form critics
were quite emphatic about this, and their view remains dominant even
today.[8]

On the other hand, a number of literary critics have claimed that
while the Bible's sparseness in giving any formal portrayal of characters may be something rather unique even in ancient literature (compare
biblical figures with Homeric figures, or those of the Icelandic saga),
that very sparseness may result in a more dynamic and personal view of
character. This is due to the fact that reticence in characterization
invites the reader to play an active part in the making of characters.

---

6. D. Mamet, 'Radio Drama'. The article first appeared in *Horizon* and was
later published as a part of the collection 'Writing in Restaurants' in *A Whore's
Profession: Notes and Essays* (London: Faber & Faber, 1994), pp. 116-21 (118).

7. E. Auerbach, *Mimesis: The Representation of Reality in Western Literature*
(trans. Willard R. Trask; Princeton, NJ: Princeton University Press, 1953), p. 47.

8. See F.W. Burnett, 'Characterization and Reader Construction of Characters
in the Gospels', *Semeia* 63 (1993), pp. 3-28 (9).

Being given only sparse and ambiguous information, the reader simply has to infer, make guesses and interpretations, and correct those guesses and interpretations whenever his or her expectations are not fulfilled in the course of the narrative. The reading process becomes a drama with lines of development, which in itself conveys a particular (and, it would seem, rather modern) view of the human character as dynamic, full of surprises and capable of chance.

Again, it all returns to ideas first presented by Erich Auerbach. It was originally his grand idea that the retention and suggestiveness of the biblical narrative makes it 'fraught with background': 'Since so much in the story is dark and incomplete, and since the reader knows that God is a hidden God, his effort to interpret it constantly finds something new to feed upon.'[9] The silence of the text encourages the reader to fill the gaps. Both Robert Alter and Meir Sternberg have developed this idea in relation to characterization in the Hebrew Bible. Interestingly enough, both connect the (quite original, so it seems) strategies used in the rendering of biblical characters with biblical monotheism and the biblical view of humanity.

Sternberg's starting point is his general idea of the biblical narrative as an interplay between 'the truth' and 'the whole truth'. 'The truth' consists of the essentials that the narrative on every occasion makes perfectly clear to every reader: the storyline, the world order, the value system. 'The whole truth', in turn, is something the readers have to infer for themselves, filling in what the narrative purposefully leaves untold. The art of biblical narrative aims at getting the readers involved in a systematic process of gap-filling.[10]

---

9. Auerbach, *Mimesis*, p. 15.

10. Sternberg first presented this thesis in a programatic essay he wrote together with Menachem Perry. The essay was originally published in Hebrew in *Ha-Sifrut* 1.2 (1968), pp. 263-92, and later in English in *Poetics Today* 7.2 (1986), pp. 275-322, as 'The King through Ironic Eyes: Biblical Narrative and the Literary Reading Process'. It also forms the basis of Chapter 6 ('Gaps, Ambiguity, and the Reading Process') of *The Poetics of Biblical Narrative: Ideological Literature and the Drama of Reading* (Bloomington: Indiana University Press), a comprehensive 1985 synthesis by Sternberg. It is useful to note that Sternberg makes a distinction between 'what was omitted for the sake of interest and what was omitted for the lack of interest' (Sternberg, *The Poetics of Biblical Narrative*, p. 236). Omissions of the former type he calls 'gaps', the latter ones 'blanks'. It is only in intentional and purposeful systems of gaps in the biblical narrative that he is interested.

As to biblical characters, there are, according to Sternberg, marked differences between God and humans. In God's case, the narrator's reticence is related to the biblical view of God's qualitative distance from both humans and pagan gods. Only little is told, because there is not much to tell: most dimensions conventionally associated with character (such as physical appearance, social status, personal history, local habitation) simply do not apply to God. Furthermore, information is strategically withheld about God *and* human beings so as *to make reading a character a process of discovery.* Before the readers' eyes, the characters take shape gradually, often in unexpected ways, so that there is usually a notable distance between the first impression and the last. All along, the readers play an active part in the process. Because only a partial picture of the character is given, the readers must round it out by their own efforts. Yet again the qualitative distance between God and humans makes a difference. Whereas God is constant and stable, humans vary and change. While God *is*, humans are only *in the process of becoming* what they are. So while the readers can safely rely on whatever discoveries they make about God in the course of the narrative, they may never be quite sure about the biblical men and women.[11]

In a quite similar manner, Robert Alter likes to emphasize the biblical characters' *capacity for change*, which reflects 'a sense of the unknowable and the unforeseeable in human nature'.[12] Ultimately, this brings the biblical characters closer to character in modern literature than are the heroes of the Greek epics:

> Cognate with the biblical understanding of individual character as something which develops in and is transformed by time—pre-eminently in the stories of Jacob and David—is a sense of character as a center of surprise. This unpredictable and changing nature of character is one reason why biblical personages cannot have fixed Homeric epithets (Jacob is not 'wily Jacob,' Moses is not 'sagacious Moses') but only relational epithets determined by the strategic requirements of the immediate context: Michal, as the circumstances vary, is either 'daughter of Saul' or 'wife of David.' ... the underlying biblical conception of character as often unpredictable, in some ways impenetrable, constantly emerging

---

11. See the two chapters of Sternberg's *Poetics of Biblical Narrative* that center on character: Chapter 9, 'Proleptic Portraits', pp. 321-41, and Chapter 10, 'Going from Surface to Depth', pp. 342-64.

12. Robert Alter, *The Art of Biblical Narrative* (New York: Basic Books, 1981), p. 127.

from and slipping back into a penumbra of ambiguity, in fact has greater affinity with dominant modern notions than do the habits of conceiving character typical of the Greek epics.[13]

In New Testament scholarship, ideas similar to Alter's and Sternberg's have been presented, in a recent article, by Fred Burnett. Like Alter and Sternberg, Burnett, too, focuses on the reader's role in giving depth to the rather sketchy characters of the Gospels. He concludes that even though 'there is little doubt that in classical writers characters were presented as types',[14]

> it does seem plausible that [ancient] reading conventions that demanded that the reader infer character indirectly from words, deeds, and relationships could allow even for the typical character to fluctuate between type and individuality. If so, then it would seem wise to understand characterization, for any biblical text at least, on a continuum. This would imply for narratives like the Gospels that the focus should be on the degree of characterization rather than on characterization as primarily typical.[15]

The degree of characterization—that is, the extent to which characters stand out as mere functional agents as opposed to individual personalities—indeed varies at different points of each Gospel narrative. Jesus' disciples in Mark are a typical example. At one end of the continuum, they are, quite evidently, 'agents about whom nothing is known except what is necessary for the plot'.[16] This is true of the two anonymous disciples whom Jesus sends to fetch a colt for Jesus for his triumphal entry into Jerusalem (Mk 11.1-7) and the two he sends to make preparations for the Passover meal (14.12-16). In each case, the two disciples are needed for the miraculous to occur and for no other reason. At the other end of the continuum, there are figures like the one particular disciple whose portrait probably comes closest of all in the Gospels to deserve the attribute 'human', namely Peter.

---

13. Alter, *The Art of Biblical Narrative*, pp. 126, 129.
14. Burnett, 'Characterization', p. 6.
15. Burnett, 'Characterization', p. 15; cf. pp. 1, 19. Burnett refers at this point to A. Berlin, *Poetics and Interpretation of Biblical Narrative* (Sheffield: Almond Press, 1983), p. 32, who similarly suggests that one should think of degrees of characterization as points on a continuum of agent to type to character.
16. Cf. Berlin, *Poetics*, p. 32.

'*Peter the Image of Man*'

Through what specific means is this human portrait achieved? What exactly is it about Peter in Mark that invites the reader to view him as an individual personality? Let us begin with the following *distance factors* in Peter's characterization, as listed by Thomas Boomershine in a groundbreaking study in Mark's narrative: Peter is the first disciple to be named, to be called and to accept the call; he is mentioned separately in expressions like 'Simon and his companions' (Σίμων καὶ οἱ μετ' αὐτοῦ, 1.36), or 'his disciples and Peter' (16.7); in the official calling of the twelve (3.13-19), he is at the head of the list and is the only one given an individual surname; together with James and John, who are given a joint surname (and sometimes together with his brother Andrew), Peter forms part of 'the inner circle' of the twelve that is at times allowed to experience more than the other disciples (cf. 5.37; 8.2; 13.3; 14.33); he is the only disciple whose individual inner thoughts and emotions are described; together with John he is the only disciple whose words are ever reported (Peter five times: 8.29; 8.32; 9.5; 10.28; 11.21; John once: 9.38).[17]

Significally, one of Peter's narrative functions is that of expressing 'a human response that is totally believable'.[18] Peter represents a typical everyman who reacts in a way the reader might think anyone would. When Jesus tells his disciples about his suffering, Peter refuses to accept it (8.32); on the mountain of Jesus' transfiguration he does not know what to say, so he desperately seeks to make the blissful moment last (9.5); upon hearing that one has to leave everything for the kingdom, he quickly remarks that 'Well, that is exactly what we have done, haven't we?' (10.28); when he sees that the fig tree Jesus cursed has withered, he is openly astounded (11.21); when Jesus suggests that all his disciples will desert and deny him, Peter is determined to correct him: 'all except me' (14.29); finally, having denied Jesus after all, Peter bursts into tears (14.72).

Especially in the story of denial, Peter's character is treated in an intimate way, so that 'this scene encourages the reader to take an interest in

17. T. Boomershine, 'Mark, the Storyteller: A Rhetorical-Critical Investigation of Mark's Passion and Resurrection Narrative' (PhD dissertation, Union Theological Seminary, New York, 1974), pp. 136-39.

18. Boomershine, 'Mark, the Storyteller', p. 137.

the character or "personality" of Peter himself'.[19] Here as elsewhere in Mark's narrative, Peter is driven by what constitutes his primary dramatic need: the need to be a good disciple. More than anything else, it is actions generated by this very need that lay the basis for the readers' construction of Peter's character.

At first, it really seems as if things will turn out the way Peter said they would: in 14.50, we are told that 'all of them deserted him and fled'; in 14.54, we learn that Peter indeed was an exception and followed after Jesus' arrest into the courtyard of the high priest. The narrator may be playing a game with the readers' expectations at this point, delaying a little the information concerning Peter's part. Remembering the dialogue between Peter and Jesus in 14.29-31, the readers are likely to ask, 'How about Peter?' when they learn that all the disciples fled. Instead of immediately telling about Peter, however, the narrator reveals that *somebody else* tried to follow Jesus: a young man wearing nothing but a linen cloth (14.51-52). Only after the arresting party's mission is complete and Jesus is taken to the high priest (14.53) does the narrator point out that Peter indeed has followed along, at a distance, and is now at the courtyard. As Peter takes his place among the guards, warming himself in the firelight,[20] the narrator leaves him for a moment and goes on to report the nightly trial of Jesus.

With v. 14.66, the scene returns to *Peter's* trial. Peter is 'below' (κάτω) in the courtyard, while Jesus is 'above' in the high priest's house. A servant girl enters, and the readers are granted a view on Peter *from inside the narrative*: 'When *she saw* Peter warming himself, she stared at him and said...' (14.67). The distance has grown shorter. Suspense starts to grow gradually, beginning from the word that the girl 'stared [ἐμβλέψασα] at Peter'. Following 'The Rule of Three' that is

19. Burnett, 'Characterization', p. 22; see Boomershine, 'Mark, the Storyteller', p. 190; R.C. Tannehill, 'The Disciples in Mark: The Function of a Narrative Role', *JR* 57 (1977), pp. 386-405 (403); D. Rhoads and D. Michie, *Mark as Story: An Introduction to the Narrative of a Gospel* (Philadelphia: Fortress Press, 1982), p. 129.

20. According to Boomershine, it is significant that the word used of fire here is not τὸ πῦρ but τὸ φῶς. This makes the scene metaphorical: by following Jesus, Peter has ventured to *come into light*, running the risk of being identified and being caught. That such a risk exists becomes clear not only from the servant girl's questions to Peter a few lines later but also from the report that the young man who tried to follow Jesus actually got caught; his person, too, was unveiled, so that he had to flee naked, in a shameful way.

typical for folktale narration as well as for Mark, suspicion and denial take place three times. First the servant girl says to Peter: 'You also were with Jesus, the man from Nazareth.' Peter denies this and escapes to the forecourt. There the girl sees him again and reports her notion to others: the threat increases.[21] 'The bystanders' (οἱ παρεστῶτες) take up the servant girl's notion and start questioning Peter: the suspicion is spreading among those around Peter. A steadily escalating suspense is felt by the audience in relation to Peter: on the one hand, we hold our breath to see whether he will be caught for following Jesus; on the other hand, we are waiting to see if he will keep the promise he made to Jesus (14.31), or if it is rather Jesus' prophecy (14.30) that will come true.

At first, Peter does not deny Jesus directly; what he denies is 'knowing or understanding what the servant girl is talking about' (οὔτε οἶδα οὔτε ἐπίσταμαι σὺ τί λέγεις, 14.68.) When asked for a second time—this time Peter's words are reported indirectly—he denies 'being one of them' (καὶ ἡ παιδίσκη ἰδοῦσα αὐτὸν ἤρξατο πάλιν λέγειν τοῖς παρεστῶσιν ὅτι οὗτος ἐξ αὐτῶν ἐστιν. ὁ δὲ πάλιν ἠρνεῖτο, 14.69-70). Being asked the same thing three times is, finally, too much: Peter explicitly denies knowing Jesus.[22] The suspense is finally resolved, and the second cockcrow follows (14.72). Immediately after that—for the first time in the scene, so that the effect comes as if by a rapid zoom— we are granted Peter's own point of view by means of a remembrance: 'Then *Peter remembered that Jesus had said to him*, "Before the cock crows twice, you will deny me three times".' The prophetic words uttered by Jesus in v. 14.30 are repeated almost verbatim as they echo in Peter's head. Only after we have first been invited to see things from Peter's position do we get the report of his reaction, from zero distance: καὶ ἐπιβαλὼν ἔκλαιεν, 'And he broke down and wept'. This is where the scene ends, where we leave Peter—forever, for not once shall we meet him again in the Gospel—weeping in the courtyard of the high priest. Who would not feel sympathy for the poor man? Who is the reader who would not receive with great relief and welcome the extra mention by the young man at the grave, 'the disciples *and Peter*' (16.7), letting us know that for Peter, too, it will be all right? As Auerbach puts it:

---

21. Boomershine, 'Mark, the Storyteller', p. 186.
22. Cf. Boomershine, 'Mark, the Storyteller', p. 187; Tannehill, 'The Disciples in Mark', p. 151.

Without any effort on [the author's] part, as it were, and purely through
the inner movement of what he relates, the story becomes visually concrete. And the story speaks to everybody; everybody is urged to take
sides for or against it ... The incident [of Peter's denial], entirely realistic
both in regard to locale and dramatis personae ... is replete with problem
and tragedy. Peter is no mere accessory figure serving as illustratio... He
is the image of man in the highest and deepest and most tragic sense.[23]

How an Agent Becomes a Person

'*Without any effort on [the author's] part, as it were ...*' Auerbach's
words underline the random nature of Peter's personhood, pointing out
that the first disciple's personal tragedy sprouts up as an incidental by-
product of the more prominent, cosmic tragedy of Jesus' passion. Once
the seed of character is sown, it starts to grow, the sower does not know
how. This process is further described by Frank Kermode in an important literary study in the tradition history of the passion narrative as 'a
fabula, progressively interpreted'.[24]

Kermode points out how the narrative grows and becomes more
detailed due to interpretive retelling of the story: new details require
additional interpretation, which, in turn, calls for more narrative, and so
on: Achilles keeps chasing the turtle. During this process, characters
who on the atomistic level could be conceived as mere agents, plot functions, or actantial roles (such as 'betrayer' and 'deserter', or 'helper'
and 'opponent') gradually turn into more and more complex figures
with genuine personality traits. As a case in point, Kermode examines
the development of the figure of Judas.[25]

In the beginning, 'betrayal' is a motif included in the passion tradition. In 1 Cor. 11.23 Paul recounts: 'the Lord Jesus *on the night when
he was betrayed* took a loaf of bread ...' However, once Jesus' passion

23. Auerbach, *Mimesis*, pp. 47-48, 41.
24. Frank Kermode, *The Genesis of Secrecy: On the Interpretation of Narrative*
(Cambridge, MA: Harvard University Press, 1979), p. 81.
25. See Chapter 4, 'Necessities of Upspringing', of Kermode's *The Genesis of
Secrecy* (pp. 75-99). For a similar type of study in the character of Lazarus, see
R. Hakola's chapter in this volume. When mentioning plot functions of the *fabula*
and their actantial roles, Kermode is referring to V. Propp's classic *Morphology of
the Folktale* (trans. L. Scott; Bloomington: Indiana University Press, 1958) and the
equally well-known actantial model presented by A.J. Greimas in his *Sémantique
structurale: Recherche de méthode* (Paris: Larousse, 1966).

is presented in the Gospels as story, the character of the betrayer becomes necessary for performing the act of betrayal. So betrayal becomes 'Judas, one of the twelve', who is also introduced at the scene of the Passover meal.[26] But why should Judas want to betray Jesus? The answer is, for money, and so an episode in which Judas visits the chief priests is added to the story. Because the hero of the story—Jesus—is omniscient, it is necessary that he knows he is to be betrayed, and by whom. This, too, calls for a new narrative, namely a prophecy of Jesus to his disciples during the meal: 'one of you will betray me, one who is... dipping bread into the bowl with me' (Mk 14.17, 20). Like many features of the Passion narrative, this line is constructed on an Old Testament passage. In this particular case, the passage comes from the book of Psalms: 'Even my bosom friend in whom I trusted, who ate of my bread, has lifted the heel against me' (Ps. 41.9). Finally, on the Mount of Olives, Judas leads the arresting party to Jesus. The act of betrayal crystallizes in the famous 'inversion of the holy kiss that would have followed the sacred meal'.[27]

At this point, we have come to know Judas as he is presented in the Gospel of Mark. This is not very much yet—but certainly 'enough to ensure that there will be more'.[28] Matthew takes over, supplementing Mark's short report of Judas's visit to the chief priests (Mk 14.10-11) with an account of a dialogue: 'How much?'—'Thirty pieces of silver' (Mt. 26.14-16). Why thirty? Because in Zech. 11.12-13 the Lord refers to thirty shekels of silver as 'this lordly price at which I was valued by them'. 'Throw it into the treasury', says the Lord to Zechariah; later on, Judas goes and does likewise. What happens to the money then? 'They [the chief priests] used them to buy the potter's field as a place to bury foreigners' (Mt. 27.7). Why? Because 'then was fulfilled what had been spoken through the prophet Jeremiah' (Mt. 27.9).

---

26. Following J. Jeremias, *The Eucharistic Words of Jesus* (trans. Norman Perrin; London: SCM Press, 1966), p. 96, Kermode, *The Genesis of Secrecy*, p. 84, presumes that at an earlier stage, in a short traditional passion account, Judas had no part in the scene of the Last Supper. This is supported by the fact that in the scene of the arrest, Mark, Matthew and Luke all mention Judas in such a way as to make him seem like someone the reader has not heard of before. Mark and Matthew report that 'Judas, one of the twelve ['Ιούδας εἷς τῶν δώδεκα], arrived [Mk 14.43, Mt. 26.47]'; Luke speaks of 'the one called Judas, one of the twelve [ὁ λεγόμενος 'Ιούδας εἷς τῶν δώδεκα, Lk. 22.47]'.

27. Kermode, *The Genesis of Secrecy*, p. 86.

28. Kermode, *The Genesis of Secrecy*, p. 86.

While Mark's Judas remains a simple agent, Matthew starts to give him what might well be considered personal features. Whereas Mark simply makes all the disciples respond 'Surely, not I?' to Jesus' prophecy of his betrayal, Matthew gives an extra focus to the question by having Judas alone ask it. Moreover, it is Judas alone who gets an answer: 'You have said so.' After the necessary act of betrayal is performed in Gethsemane, Mark does not again mention Judas. Matthew, in turn, follows the poor man to the end. After everything is over, Matthew's Judas shows more than emotion: he repents (Mt. 27.3). Moreover, throwing down the money in the temple looks very much like a genuine act of despair.

As to what, ultimately, happens to Judas, different versions of the story give different answers, each of which presents the character of Judas in a slightly different light. In Matthew, Judas commits suicide. Because Matthew has earlier told us that Judas repented, Judas's decision looks like an effort to make amends for what he has done. This would allow us to think there was still a drop of dignity and nobility to his character. In Luke's version (preserved in Acts 1), Judas makes use of the money he gained. Evidently, Luke's Judas is all too obdurate ever to repent. God's curse falls upon him, however, as he 'falling headlong... burst(s) open and all his bowels gush... out' (v. 18). Still another tradition, preserved by Papias, says that 'Judas swelled up to such a size that a place where a wagon could pass was too narrow for him', which 'makes his death resemble those traditionally reserved for tyrants and very wicked men'.[29]

Both Luke and John report the exact moment when Judas the man, a greedy thief who stole from the common purse of the disciples (Jn 12.6), turns into Judas the betrayer occupied by Satan (Lk. 22.3; Jn 13.27)—an intriguing case of a character becoming possessed by his narrative role, as Kermode points out.[30] The famous Johannine supper scene makes a lot out of this diabolical metamorphosis. The magic moment when Jesus dips a piece of bread in the dish and gives it to Judas contains no less than three different exposures to Judas's horrific change of form: the prophecy of Ps. 41.10, 'who ate of my bread, has lifted the heel against me', is shown to come true; the identity of the betrayer is revealed to 'the beloved disciple'; and Satan is reported to enter into Judas (13.26-27). Judas's fate, decided in advance by God

29. Kermode, *The Genesis of Secrecy*, p. 87.
30. Kermode, *The Genesis of Secrecy*, p. 85.

(17.12) and put into effect by the devil (13.2), is (quite literally) in Jesus' hands. Eventually, it is Jesus who orders Judas to do what he is going to do. Judas obeys more or less automatically: 'So, after receiving the piece of bread, he immediately went out' (13.30). The overall effect produced by the scene is quite gloomy—and even more so, because Judas's departure is followed by the extremely dramatic words ἦν δὲ νύξ, 'and it was night'.

Later, outside the four canonical Gospels, Judas's character came to have an entire life of its own. In medieval legends, his bad habits were thought to be due to his harsh domestic conditions, and so on. To quote Kermode, the whole matter is

> really quite simple. Of an agent there is nothing to be said except that he performs a function: Betrayal, Judgment. When the agent becomes a kind of person, all is changed. It takes very little to make a character: a few indications of idiosyncrasy, of deviation from type, are enough, for our practised eyes will make up the larger patterns of which such indications can be read as parts.[31]

A Subject in Bud

In all their reticence and minimalism, biblical narratives make a most representative case of how little it takes for 'a kind of person' to emerge. Occasionally, these small seeds of individuality may grow as unchallenged as in Judas's case. At other times, however, they seem to have fallen on rocky ground and become scorched by the sun. Here the reception history of some minor characters of Mark provides us with a good example.

In a typical Markan healing story, the role functions given to characters follow a regular pattern. Recently, David Rhoads has examined 11 healing stories as representative of a 'healing type scene "A Suppliant with Faith"' in Mark.[32] The term 'type scene' originates from Robert Alter. A type scene is a scene with certain characters and interactions

31. Kermode, *The Genesis of Secrecy*, p. 98.
32. The 11 stories are: Simon's mother-in-law (1.29-31); the leper (1.40); the paralytic (2.1-12); the man with the withered hand (3.1-6); Jairus's daughter (5.21; 35–43); the woman with the hemorrhage (5.25-34); the Syro-Phoenician woman (7.24-30); a deaf-and-mute man (7.31-37); the blind man at Bethsaida (8.21-26); the father who brings a boy with an unclean spirit (9.14-29); Bartimaeus (10.46-52) (David Rhoads, 'The Syrophoenician Woman in Mark: A Narrative-Critical Study', *JAAR* 62 [1992], pp. 342-75 [349]).

that is repeated throughout the narrative. It sets up a convention, thus providing familiar patterns of expectation for the reader. Yet within the framework of 'the basic pattern that remains the same', the details, forms and features of the type scene vary and introduce new elements to the story.[33]

Evidently, there is a pattern that repeats itself in the episodes: Rhoads is able to list up to 12 different elements that comprise the type scene of the 'Suppliant with Faith'. In the particular case of the Syro-Phoenician woman, he is also able to recognize several points of contact with Mark's overall rhetorical/stylistic techniques, plotting, characterization, settings, standards of judgment, and so on. Furthermore, on the level of Mark's theology, the topical role of *faith* ties all the different episodes together.[34]

Importantly, however, some figures who perform a similar role in their respective 'healing type scenes' receive a greater amount of *narrative subjectivity* than others. That is, the narrative allows them more power to speak, act and perceive.[35] To illustrate this, I will consider two particular 'suppliants with faith', namely the paralytic whom Jesus heals in Mk 2.1-12 and the woman with the hemorrhage in Mk 5.25-34.

As to the story of healing the paralytic, it is Jesus' authority to forgive sins that is the point at issue. What Jesus is able to do to demonstrate that authority is decisive. An additional function of the story— taken that the story is seen both in its immediate context and as an integral part of the Gospel as a whole—is to contribute to the developing dramatic conflict between Jesus and his opponents.[36] These two func-

33. Cf. Alter, *The Art of Biblical Narrative*, pp. 47-61.

34. So, e.g., C.D. Marshall, *Faith as a Theme in Mark's Narrative* (SNTSMS, 64; Cambridge: Cambridge University Press, 1989). For structural and functional similarities between the stories—'the basic pattern that remains the same'—see also R.W. Funk, 'The Form of the New Testament Healing Miracle Story', *Semeia* 12 (1978), pp. 57-96.

35. Here I owe my choice of focus to Mieke Bal who has, since the late 1980s, put extensive effort to developing tools for the analysis of narrative subjectivity (for a synthesis, see, e.g., Chapter 6, 'Narrative Subjectivity', in D. Jobling [ed.], *On Story-Telling: Essays in Narratology* [Sonoma, CA: Polebridge Press, 1991], a collection of Bal's writings). In a wider perspective, Bal's work is part of her attempt to capitalize the ideological-critical potential of narratology.

36. Since W. Wrede's work on the pericope, 'Heilung Gelähmten (Mc 2,1ff)', *ZNW* 5 (1904), pp. 354-58, Mk 2.1-12 has conventionally been taken as an 'apophthegmatic narrative', consisting of a controversy apophthegm secondarily

tions interpenetrate the narration and dictate how much stage time each character gets.

As might be expected, it is Jesus who dominates the scene. The narrative includes patterns of three: three reports of a perception of Jesus; three references to his words 'your sins are forgiven'; three references to his words 'stand up and take your mat and walk'; and three references to the διαλογίζεσθαι, 'questioning', of the scribes against Jesus.[37] As to the person healed, the paralytic is brought to the stage very much like a material object: 'a paralytic carried by four was brought to Jesus'. There is, to be sure, a short private encounter between the healer and the paralyzed man. It is notable that Jesus calls the paralytic τέκνον, 'son' or 'child', but, because no more information of the latter is given, the address tells us more about Jesus than about the one to whom he is speaking. Significantly, *not once do we hear the voice of the man Jesus cures or see the events through his eyes.*

In the story of Jesus and the hemorrhaging woman, the situation is quite different. In this case, the audience is granted information about the healed person and also given an opportunity to see things from her point of view. The woman's past is given a vivid description; she is 'a woman who had been suffering from hemorrhages for twelve years; she had endured much under many physicians, and had spent all that she had; and she was no better, but rather grew worse' (Mk 5.25-26). In the Greek text, the series of five participles is quite a list of attributes to the single word γυνή, 'woman'. Her fearfulness and great trust in Jesus are further shown to us by means of an inside view in v. 28: 'for she said,

---

embedded into a miracle story (cf. R. Bultmann, *The History of the Synoptic Tradition* [trans. J. Marsh; New York: Harper & Row, 1963], pp. 14-16, 212-13). As such, the narrative opens a section of five controversy stories in Mk 2.1-3.6. In her 1980 dissertation *Markan Public Debate: Literary Technique, Concentric Structure, and Theology in Mark 2.1–3.6* (SBLDS, 48; Chico, CA: Scholars Press; see esp. pp. 109-43), J. Dewey has quite convincingly demonstrated that the section has a chiastic, concentric structure. It both begins and concludes with a healing story. The two healing stories are of a very similar type, constructed in a parallel manner as shown by form, content and linguistic details. Furthermore, 'along with the chiastic structure ... there exists also a linear development of [intensifying] hostility in Jesus' opponents' (Dewey, 'The Literary Structure of the Controversy Stories in Mark 2.1–3.6', *JBL* 92 [1973], pp. 394-401 [398]; cf. Dewey, *Markan Public Debate*, pp. 109, 116, 118).

37. Cf. Dewey, *Markan Public Debate*, p. 72; Marshall, *Faith as a Theme*, p. 81.

"If I but touch his clothes, I will be made well"'. As she makes her move, two additional inside views report *a sudden sensual realization.* Both accounts begin with the words 'and immediately' (καὶ εὐθύς), which indicates the simultaneous occurrence of the two inner sensations with which the hasty, rushing movement of the story is abruptly brought to a complete halt: 'Immediately her hemorrhage stopped; and she felt in her body [ἔγνω τῷ σώματι] that she was healed of her illness' (v. 29); 'Immediately aware [ἐπιγνοὺς ἐν ἑαυτῷ] that power had gone forth from him, Jesus turned about in the crowd and said, "Who touched my clothes?"' (v. 30). That indeed is the question: there are as many as five references to the woman's touch within just six verses (or six times in seven, if 'the whole truth', πᾶσαν τὴν ἀλήθειαν, in v. 33 is counted): 'she...touched his cloak' (v. 27); 'If I but touch his clothes' (v. 28); 'Who touched my clothes?' (v. 30); 'Who touched me?' (v. 31); 'who had done it' (v. 32). The references come from four different speakers: the narrator (v. 27), the woman (v. 28), Jesus (v. 30) and the disciples (v. 31).

In the very center is the secret interchange of power between the woman and Jesus. It is reported twice: once from the point of view of the woman, and once from the point of view of Jesus. This moment is surrounded by a five-piece montage of the outer action that caused the inner event to take place: the woman touching the cloak of Jesus. Narrative investment in one single motif is extensive. The disciples' comment in v. 31 takes care that no one in the audience misses the profoundly supernatural *intimacy* in the scene: pressed from everywhere by the crowd, Jesus still has felt the woman's touch—just as the woman in an immediate bodily sensation could feel the effect which that touch made.[38]

---

38. Kermode (*The Genesis of Secrecy*, p. 133) notes that what is said in v. 30 to have gone out of Jesus at the moment the woman touched him is called δύναμις, 'power', a word with sexual senses in the Greek language. The same can actually be said of the verb γινώσκω, 'to know', in v. 29 (cf., e.g., Mt. 1.25; Lk. 1.34, as well as Gen. 4.1, 17, 25; 19.8 in the LXX) and the verb ἅπτω, 'to touch' (cf., e.g., 1 Cor. 7.1). S.L. Graham, 'Silent Voices: Women in the Gospel of Mark', *Semeia* 54 (1991), pp. 145-58 (149), considers the event a parasexual act. While it would, of course, be too daring to claim that any sexual connotations in the narrative were intentional, the mere fact that they come so naturally to many interpreters nevertheless characterizes *the atmosphere of intimacy* so dominant in the episode.

In v. 33, the woman's inside thoughts and feelings are again in focus: she comes 'in fear and trembling';[39] she knows what has happened to her. She comes to Jesus—still on her own initiative[40]—and Jesus kindly calls her θυγάτηρ, 'my daughter', thus 'using the language of family to welcome her back into the community'.[41]

Evidently, while both the paralytic and the hemorrhaging woman play a parallel role of a 'suppliant with faith' in a Markan type scene, the way they are presented as narrative subjects differs significantly. While the paralytic is closest to a mere agent performing a necessary plot function, the woman is pictured as a character with personal feelings, sensations, relations and intentions.

Now, however minimal this increase of subjectivity may seem, it has been enough for Matthew and Luke to take material action in their use of Mark's text. It is to the evident ideological implications of this editorial work that I will turn next.

The Lost Self

Significantly, both Matthew (9.18-26) and Luke (8.40-56) omit what in Mark's earlier account were the most crucial moments of the hemorrhaging woman's story. Missing in both the Matthean and the Lukan version are the zoom-in brought about by an inside view to the woman's mind just before she touches Jesus and the double inner sensation Jesus and the woman secretly share at the moment of the touch. The story has changed to an extent that the representation of events and characters becomes more clearly focused to the point of, in Auerbach's

---

39. The numerous suggested explanations of the woman's fear (as listed by G. Theissen, *The Miracle Stories of the Early Christian Tradition* [trans. F. McDonagh; Philadelphia: Fortress Press, 1983], p. 134) include: breaking the purity regulations (W. Grundmann, *Das Evangelium nach Markus* [ThHK, 2; Berlin: Evangelische Verlaganstalt, 3rd edn, 1963], p. 115); shame at her disease (E. Klostermann, *Das Markusevangelium* [HNT, 3; Tübingen: J.C.B. Mohr, 4th edn, 1950], p. 51); the feeling of having stolen power without authority (H. Holzmann, *Die Synoptiker* [HNT, 1; Tübingen: J.C.B. Mohr, 5th edn, 1901], p. 135); realizing that her action could be mistakenly understood as either a love charm or an attempt to get rid of her disease by passing it on. Notably, all these readings add to the woman as narrative subject by further describing why and how she reacts.

40. Cf. Luke's version, in which the woman seems to have no other choice: 'When the woman saw that she could not remain hidden she came ...' (Lk. 8.47).

41. Graham, 'Silent Voices', p. 150.

words, 'Christ's presence and mission'. Moreover, the later versions evidently move toward greater narrative monologism, that is, one authoritative voice and one authoritative angle of vision (shared by the narrator and Jesus), with no deviations. Should other points of view, such as the woman's perspective, seem to challenge this authority, they are excluded.[42]

The trouble is, of course, that *any* rendering of personal experience tends to be challenging, at least in the long run. Indeed it has been suggested that forms which focus on personal experience will, as a rule, go hand in hand with a special *'culture of contestation'*, or *'contestatory symbolic forms'*, in folklore and premodern literature.[43] These are forms and signs that resist and challenge the ideological naturalization and mystification of the status quo in social relations. Whenever the individual and his or her experience is given a voice of its own, it tends to challenge any outwardly defined identity that is based upon affinity with the dominant, unified ideology (that is, the 'culture of affirmation'). This holds true especially for the experience of crisis (that is, a challenge to the dominant means of coping with whatever life brings on), especially crises experienced by those belonging to the subordinate class in the society. In its minimalist form, this challenge consists of the mere representation of individual experience as separate, independent, unintegrated, that is, as the voice of the *Other*.[44]

42. Cf. Bal, who notes that 'reception of such texts [whose subjectivity is problematic] shows a tendency towards naturalization, that is, a tendency to solve the problems and interpret the text in a unifying, reassuringly "natural" way'. The motive behind this is that the text's ideological impact should not become blurred (Bal, *Lethal Love*, p. 21).

43. See L. Lombardi-Satriani, 'Folklore as a Culture of Contestation', *Journal of the Folklore Institute* 11.1/2 (1975), pp. 99-121; and J.B. Thompson, *Ideology and Modern Culture: Critical Social Theory in the Era of Mass Communication* (Cambridge: Polity Press, 1990).

44. Interestingly enough, modern fiction has also shown exactly the opposite trend. Many modern writers have, in various ways, tried to dissolve the concept of individual character that they regard as a manifestation of bourgeois ideology. Likewise, for ideological reasons, many contemporary literary critics have been suspicious about a theory of character. As they see it, any such theory would require a stable, unified concept of self; such a concept is, however, a mere fiction that serves the interests of the ideological status quo. (See Rimmon-Kenan, *Narrative Fiction*, pp. 29-31; Bal, *Lethal Love*, p. 106.)

A Marxist scholar would typically examine 'contestatory symbolic forms' in light of the Marxist theory of class relations. Luigi Lombardi-Satriani writes:

> This contestation is on the part of the dominated against the dominators, on the part of the weak against the strong ... One of the most obvious examples is the relationship between the sexes where women assume the obligatory role of inferior creatures with respect to males who are the creators and depositors of values ...[45]

The story of the hemorrhaging woman focuses, of course, on an individual woman in crisis. Furthermore, it represents a contesting anomaly in terms of how the Gospels usually present Jesus. The norm is that Jesus is virtually omniscient. He can read people's thoughts at will. In the case of this particular woman, however, he is suddenly unable to do that. He is 'aware that power has gone forth from him', but he cannot tell who the beneficiary is. In the Markan and Lukan versions, the anomaly is allowed to prevail. The disciples' (in Luke, Peter's) comment (Mk 5.31; cf. Lk. 8.45) serves to soften the scandal: Jesus' abilities are still clearly of a supernatural kind. For Matthew, however, the deviation from the norm is too much: in his version the woman is caught in the act, so that Jesus' inner vision is never put to a test.

In Mk 7.24-30 (par. Mt. 15.21-28), Jesus meets yet another woman, and in this case, too, the inner logic of the story makes him act 'un-Jesuslike' in terms of a more general norm. During the short encounter, the woman—a Gentile, Syro-Phoenician by birth—persuades Jesus to heal her daughter, something that Jesus initially did not regard as proper. Jesus thus shows an ability to back up and reconsider his views when faced with someone who can match wits with him in making parables. The story is 'a classic example from the ancient Near East of the clever request of an inferior to a superior in which there is an exchange of proverbial sayings'.[46] The Jesus it portrays, as opposed to the normative Jesus of the Gospel *kerygma*, not only teaches with authority but also learns from other people.[47]

---

45. Lombardi-Satriani, 'Folklore as a Culture of Contestation', p. 103.

46. Rhoads, 'The Syrophoenician Woman', p. 358, referring to C. Fontaine, 'The Use of the Traditional Saying in the Old Testament' (PhD dissertation, Duke University, Durham, NC, 1979).

47. As Graham ('Silent Voices', p. 151) points out, nor is it too often that a woman's speech is recorded in the Gospel. Another such occasion is found in the story of John the Baptist's death—an exceptional story also for being the only one

Again, the later the version, the smaller the scandal. In Mark's version, Jesus gives due credit to the woman, saying, 'For saying that [διὰ τοῦτον τὸν λόγον], you may go—the demon has left your daughter' (Mk 7.29). Matthew, however, does his best to safeguard Jesus' authority: it is not for the woman's ability to outwit Jesus; nevertheless, *because of her faith* he grants her healing: 'Then Jesus answered her, "Woman, great is your faith! Let it be done for you as you wish"' (Mt. 15.28).

In neither of these two stories in Matthew does Matthew's Jesus ever lose control. Before Matthew, however, exactly the opposite was the case. The two women had the initiative, and Jesus had to adapt.

For Matthew in particular, 'silencing the other' seems to have developed into a policy with a fixed purpose. One representative feature of Matthew's way of compressing Markan miracle stories is the very *reduction in dialogues*. Apparently, in Matthew's view 'a Jesus who engages in conversation does not fit the picture of the miracle worker who acts with divine authority'.[48]

As noted by Norman Petersen, many redaction-critical studies seem to indicate that the 'literary peculiarities of Matthew's Gospel'—the way Matthew differs from its literary predecessor Mark—'make it look—and function—like a *manual of discipline* analogous to the *Qumran Community Rule* (1QS), and the Christian *Didache*'.[49] Such works intend to provide a community with a solid, unchanging (*incontestable*), enduringly homogeneous social structure of knowledge, belief and living. This is what Matthew is up to. It would, however, be rather unfair to condemn him as a petty propagandist for doing just that. After all, he is only exemplifying a more general line of development that took place when the Christian community became more stable and better adapted to the status quo.

As time goes by, radical colors fade (or initially monochrome radicalism begins to show more colors, depending on the way you look at it).

in the Gospel which does not center on Jesus.

48. Theissen, *The Miracle Stories*, p. 178.

49. N.L. Petersen, 'Can One Speak of a Gospel Genre?', *Neot* 28.3 (1994), pp. 137-58 (140), with reference to G. Bornkamm, 'End-expectation and Church in Matthew', in G. Bornkamm, G. Barth and H.J. Held, *Tradition and Interpretation in Matthew* (Philadelphia: Westminister Press, 1963); J.M. Robinson, 'The Problem of History in Mark, Reconsidered', *USQR* 20 (1965), pp. 131-47; and K. Stendahl, *The School of St. Matthew* (Philadelphia: Fortress Press, 2nd edn, 1968).

At first, a re-evaluation of socioeconomic relations appears to have been a part of the *metanoia*, the rethinking of the values and ways of life, that the early Christian communities proclaimed. According to Luke's testimony,

> all who believed were together and had all things in common; they would sell their possessions and goods and distribute the proceeds to all, as any had need... Now the whole group of those who believed were of one heart and soul, and no one claimed private ownership of any possessions, but everything they owned was held in common ... There was not a needy person among them, for as many as owned land or houses sold them and brought the proceeds of what was sold. They laid it at the apostles' feet, and it was distributed to each as any had need (Acts 2.44-45; 4.32, 34-35).

Luke's vision of the early Christian community is in perfect harmony with the command Jesus gives to the rich man in Mk 10.21 (par. Mt. 19.16-30; Lk. 18.18-30): 'go, sell what you own, and give the money to the poor'. According to Paul, no line of division drawn between different groups of people by social or religious institutions is valid in the Christian body. In Christ all men and women are equal: 'There is no longer Jew or Greek, there is no longer slave or free, there is no longer male and female; for all of you are one in Christ Jesus' (Gal. 3.28). Moreover, the coming eschatological rule of God would turn the present order upside down:

> Blessed are you who are poor, for yours is the kingdom of God. Blessed are you who are hungry now, for you will be filled. Blessed are you who weep now, for you will laugh ... But woe to you who are rich, for you have received your consolation. Woe to you who are full now, for you will be hungry. Woe to you who are laughing now, for you will mourn and weep (Lk. 6.20-21, 24-25).

That is, of course, about as 'contestatory' as it can get.

While proclaiming a new kind of order, the early Christian movement quite probably did (as would any social movement challenging aspects of the present order and proposing new ones) create what might be called 'emancipatory space'—room for those under domination to have a voice of their own. Correspondingly, in the early Christian folkloristic traditions (as represented, for example, by some of the miracle stories preserved in the Gospels) aspects of a personal, uninstitutionalized encountering of people with Jesus remain in focus. This kind of focus (besides being more or less 'contestatory' in itself) turns out to be, time after time, an occasion for unreservedly 'contestatory' actions and morals. Yet any revolution—a point of history at which social values and ways of living are truly open to question—lasts only for a limited time. Gradually, a new Christian order developed with a new kind of hegemony. Individual experience tends to suggest questions—to be 'contestatory' by nature—and where answers are to be proclaimed, open questions are not pertinent. In the subsequent retelling of the story, the hemorrhaging woman loses even that short moment of intimacy she initially shared with her healer, and the Syro-Phoenician woman's contest with Jesus (and triumph over him) is eventually turned into a humble affirmation of the rule of faith.[50]

Conclusions

In the Gospels, characters are most often not yet quite complete. In the event of being read, some of them will increase, while others must decrease. Which way it will go, depends on how each character relates to the ideology of each Gospel and to the ideology of its readers. In this respect, biblical characters resemble living organisms that mutate in order to adapt to their environments. This makes all static, comprehensive and harmonious interpretations of these characters problematic. As is the case with real-life personalities, partial truths are the only ones available.

Nevertheless, new, 'conclusive' interpretations of biblical characters are likely to be proposed in the future, too. Even if the evangelists did not succeed in making their narratives completely monologic, there will be sympathetic critics to help them in this task. Confident that 'the presence of inconsistencies in no way undermines the unity of a narrative but simply becomes one of the facets to be interpreted',[51] good-hearted critics will search until they find a literary interpretation that successfully integrates any inconsistent features into a complete whole. The trouble is that this can hardly be deemed as *critical* praxis. Even if one did not mind accepting the ideology of the evangelists, accurate

50. This line of development extends beyond the limits of the canon; as a rule, problematic biblical stories involving women subjects 'become less problematic, smoother, but also less interesting' in their later cultural uses (Bal, *Lethal Love*, p. 5).

51. Powell, *What Is Narrative Criticism?*, p. 92.

critical description alone would require that the ideological dissonance in the text be noticed.

As in narratives, so in criticism, the tendency towards unity and monologism is strong, because it is, ultimately, ideological. In biblical studies, this is natural, because 'the text that is considered is identical with that which believing communities identify as authoritative for their faith and practice'.[52] Furthermore, there may also be a deeper existential need in all of us to keep the world as one, conceivable and naturalized; perhaps Mieke Bal is right when she wonders whether 'the convention of unity, so powerful in our history of criticism, is seductive because of its potential to keep the disturbing uncertainty of the subject buried'.[53]

52. Powell, *What Is Narrative Criticism?*, p. 88.
53. Bal, *Lethal Love*, p. 21.

CHARACTERIZATION AND PERSUASION:
THE RICH MAN AND THE POOR MAN IN LUKE 16.19-31

Outi Lehtipuu

The Rich Man and Lazarus is one of the lively, long example stories[1] in the Gospel of Luke—one of the stories for which Luke has been described as 'a master of short story'[2] and 'the great storyteller of the New Testament'.[3] Indeed, the material unique to Luke is largely comprised of stories, mostly parables. Many of the Lukan parables belong to the best-known material in the New Testament, parables such as the Good Samaritan or the Prodigal Son. Since Luke places all his parables in the mouth of Jesus, it is the Lukan Jesus who is the 'master of short story'.[4]

---

1. The term 'example story' (*Beispielerzählung*) derives from Adolf Jülicher, the grand old man of parable scholarship. See his *Die Gleichnisreden Jesu*, I (Freiburg: Mohr, 1899), pp. 112-14.

2. J. Drury, 'Luke', in R. Alter and F. Kermode (eds.) *The Literary Guide to the Bible* (Cambridge, MA: Harvard University Press, 1987), pp. 418-39 (427).

3. M. Goulder, *Luke: A New Paradigm* (2 vols.; JSNTSup, 20; Sheffield: Sheffield Academic Press, 1989), I, p. 94.

4. Traditional students of the parables of Jesus, represented by scholars such as Joachim Jeremias, were convinced that they had found the authentic voice of the historical Jesus in the synoptic parables. In his classic *The Parables of Jesus* (trans. S.H. Hooke; New York: Charles Scribner's Sons, 2nd rev. edn, 1972), p. 11, Jeremias states: 'The student of the parables of Jesus, as they have been transmitted to us in the first three Gospels, may be confident that he stands upon a particularly firm historical foundation. The parables are a fragment of the original rock of tradition.' Since then, this view has been strongly criticized by those who consider the recovery of the *ipsissima verba Jesu* to be either impossible or irrelevant. To the latter group belong scholars who focus on the literary aspects of the Gospels and who are therefore not interested in Jesus as a historical figure but as a character in the Gospel story. See, e.g., J. Hintzen, *Verkündigung und Wahrnehmung: Über das Verhältnis von Evangelium und Leser am Beispiel Lk 16,19-31 im Rahmen des lukanischen Doppelwerkes* (BBB, 81; Frankfurt am Main: Anton Hain, 1991), p. 16.

A prominent feature in many Lukan parables is their lifelike, colorful characters. It is typical that 'the drama in Luke's parables arises ... from the mystery of human interaction'.[5] In his parables and example stories, Luke has created a number of memorable figures, like the rich fool or the unjust steward or the persistent widow and the unjust judge. Many of these figures are so vivid that the reader almost forgets that they are characters in story within a story and not real people whom Jesus meets in Luke's storyworld.

The characters in the Rich Man and Lazarus are no exception to this aspect of Lukan stories. Luke presents them in a way that makes the reader enter into the story and get emotionally involved. But why does Luke make such an effort to depict his characters? In the following, I will argue that Luke does not use characterization at random. On the contrary, he uses characterization to persuade his readers to share his own ideological program.

Problems with Analyzing Biblical Characters

The interpretation of biblical narratives faces several obstacles. A major problem is the temporal distance between the modern readers and the origins of the biblical texts. Both the text itself and its extratextual context are alien to us. This creates at least two kinds of difficulties. First, the stories contain terms that are altogether strange to us. For example, what does the expression 'Abraham's bosom' (NRSV: 'side') mean? Or what kind of a place is Hades? Second, there are familiar terms that do not necessarily bear the same meaning as today. For example, do the conceptions 'rich' and 'poor' refer to the same kinds of socioeconomic realities as today?[6] A great chasm has been fixed between our world and the world of the story by time and cultural changes, and we must be cautious not to give anachronistic meanings to familiar sounding conceptions found in ancient texts.

---

5.   J.R. Donahue, *The Gospels in Parable* (Philadelphia: Fortress Press, 1988), p. 126. In this aspect, Luke's parables differ from both those of Mark and those of Matthew. Mark's parables are almost exclusively nature parables in which the interest lies in natural phenomena and not human action. Like Luke, Matthew also sets his parables in the human world but his characters are close to black-and-white caricatures. See M. Goulder, 'Characteristics of the Parables in the Several Gospels', *JTS* 19 (1968), pp. 51-69.

6.   See discussion below on pp. 86-87.

A similar cautiousness must be employed when reconstructing images of biblical characters. We do not know very well how ancients viewed people or how characters in literature reflected that view.[7] It is generally presumed that the ancients did not view people individually and psychologically the way the moderns view people today in the Western world. Ancients were highly group-oriented, identifying themselves in terms of the social group to which they belonged.[8] Accordingly, characterization in ancient literature was based mainly on stereotypes with little or no psychological development.[9]

Another difficulty with analyzing biblical characters is that most of them appear only for a short time in the Gospel stories.[10] Most characters are presented only in their relationship with Jesus, and there is little interest in other aspects of their personality. After fulfilling their interactions with Jesus, they disappear from the scene, which makes it difficult, if not impossible for the reader to form a coherent impression of them. As no psychological development is involved, most biblical characters serve more as plot functions than as credible people. This view of characters as subordinate to plot—represented for example by V. Propp—is referred to as the 'functional' view of character. In this view, *who* does something is not as essential for the story as *what* is done. Propp drew his conclusions by analyzing folk tales, which certainly do not concentrate on character development. Because other kinds of narratives are more character-centered, not all literary theorists agree with Propp's functional view of character. At the other end of the spectrum, a 'realistic' view sees literary characters as one might see real people, who have a past and a future beyond the text.[11]

7. B. Hochman, *Character in Literature* (Ithaca, NY: Cornell University Press, 1985), p. 55.
8. This view is argued by B. Malina, who applies models of cultural anthropology to biblical texts. See, e.g., his 'Dealing with Biblical (Mediterranean) Characters: A Guide for U.S. Consumers', *BTB* 19 (1989), pp. 127-39; and *idem*, *The New Testament World: Insights from Cultural Anthropology* (Louisville, KY: Westminster/John Knox Press, rev. edn, 1993), esp. pp. 63-89.
9. See D. Rhoads and D. Michie, *Mark as Story: An Introduction to the Narrative of a Gospel* (Philadelphia: Fortress Press, 1982), p. 109.
10. This has been pointed out by R.A. Culpepper, *Anatomy of the Fourth Gospel: A Study in Literary Design* (Philadelphia: Fortress Press, 1983), p. 102.
11. For an overall discussion of various views about characterization, see, e.g., S. Rimmon-Kenan, *Narrative Fiction: Contemporary Poetics* (London: Methuen, 2nd edn, 1988), pp. 29-42.

Most recent theories of character fall in between these extremes. On the one hand, scholars argue that characters are not simply functionaries in a plot but have value in their own right.[12] On the other hand, characters must be distinguished from real people.[13] Even though characters resemble people and we have an ability to identify with them, there is a difference between knowing a person in daily life and knowing a person within a story. In real life it is more difficult to grasp a coherent picture of people, even though (or just because) our information about them is abundant, whereas in literature, even though the information is scarce, our image of characters can be more coherent. Characters in literature can be transparent: the narrator has the power to tell what a character is really like and she or he can let the reader have an inside view into the character's mind. In that sense, we can know more about literary characters than we know about real people.[14]

Another feature of character analysis emphasized in many recent narrative theories is the role of the reader in constructing characters. It is the reader who gives significance to the text; without readers, the characters are only words on a page. The characters are born into existence only during the reading process, in the consciousness of the reader.[15] Moreover, the reader easily sees the life of the character as a whole by imagining the events that must have happened before the character is introduced into the story and those that will happen after she or he disappears from it.

Where do biblical characters fall between these views? As noted above, most biblical characters seem to function more as a part of the plot; so it is difficult to apply to biblical figures the analyses done on

12. This view is held, e.g., by S. Chatman, *Story and Discourse: Narrative Structure in Fiction and Film* (Ithaca, NY: Cornell University Press, 1978), p. 112.

13. See Hochman, *Character*, pp. 59-60. According to him, after literary characters are written, they are finished. So, if people in literature resemble real people in any way, they resemble dead, not living people. See also M. Bal, *Narratology: Introduction to the Theory of Narrative* (trans. C. van Boheemen; Toronto: University of Toronto Press, 2nd edn, 1988), p. 80.

14. Culpepper, *Anatomy*, p. 102; Hochman, *Character*, pp. 61-62.

15. See Hochman, *Character*, p. 32. This is emphasized also by M. Sternberg, *The Poetics of Biblical Narrative: Ideological Literature and the Drama of Reading* (Bloomington: Indiana University Press, 1985), pp. 321-28. Cf. also Rhoads and Michie, *Mark as Story*, p. 112; F. Burnett, 'Characterization and Reader Construction of Characters in the Gospels', *Semeia* 63 (1993), pp. 3-28 (3).

characters in modern novels. However, it is also difficult to follow Propp's functional view to its logical limit. Not all biblical characters are the same; some characters are very lifelike and memorable. The life-likeness of biblical characters does not necessarily have to do with how long they appear in the narrative; it also has to do with how they are characterized and what kind of an impact they have on the reader.[16] The reader constructs the image of characters from the different character indicators in the text, and in this respect characters are presented in different ways.

It is customary to distinguish different biblical characters as 'round', 'flat' and 'stock' according to the number of traits they have. David Rhoads and Donald Michie depict the different character types in Mark's Gospel in the following way:

> Jesus is clearly a round character because he has many traits and is mysterious and acts in new and surprising ways. The disciples are also round characters, but for different reasons. The disciples are in conflict within themselves, and they change and develop as they face conflict and crisis. The authorities are flat characters with fewer traits and traits that do not conflict. They do not change and are rather predictable in their behavior. Yet they do vary in the means they use to deal with Jesus. The minor characters come closest to stock characters, although they are surprisingly rich in characterization, usually with more than one trait.[17]

Characters in the Gospel of Luke are defined similarly by Mark Powell. An example of a stock character is the poor widow in Lk. 21.1-4, her only role being to illustrate what 'sacrificial' means. Most religious leaders are flat, having such traits as 'unloving', 'hypocritical' or 'self-righteous'. The best examples of round characters are Jesus' disciples, because they can be 'humble', 'self-denying' and 'loyal', but also 'arrogant', 'status-conscious' and 'cowardly'.[18]

This division of characters into round, flat and stock is a somewhat peculiar combination of concepts from two scholars, E.M. Forster and Northrop Frye. The classic distinction between flat and round characters

16. An example of this is the way readers have been inspired to create new life stories for the biblical characters beyond the Gospel narrative. See R. Hakola's chapter on the many lives of Lazarus in this volume.

17. Rhoads and Michie, *Mark as Story*, p. 113.

18. M.A. Powell, *What Is Narrative Criticism?* (Minneapolis: Fortress Press, 1990), p. 55.

was made by Forster.[19] In his view, flat characters were 'two-dimensional' types or caricatures, and in their purest form built around a single idea or quality. According to Forster, flat characters are best when they are comic, because a flat character who is serious or tragic easily becomes boring. By contrast, round characters are complex, developing, many-sided and capable of surprising the reader. If characters have more than one trait to them 'we get the beginning of the curve towards the round'.[20] Clearly, biblical scholars have not based their definitions on the views of Forster. In biblical narrative theory, what Forster calls 'flat' is called 'stock', and 'flat' is something in between 'stock' and 'round'.

The conception of a stock character was introduced by Northrop Frye,[21] who based his view on Aristotle's *Ethics*. The term refers to *conventional* character types, ones that recur repeatedly in a particular literary genre. Frye took his examples from ancient comedies where he distinguished four different kinds of stock characters (an impostor, a self-deprecating character, a buffoon, a rustic character easily deceived). Other examples of stock characters might include such figures as an absent-minded professor in modern comedies or a fast-shooting sheriff in westerns or a wicked stepmother in fairy tales. The main feature of stock characters is the conventional use of them, not their minimal characterization. As such, stock characters can be created as convincing individuals. Thus, the way the term 'stock' is used in biblical narrative criticism does not have much to do with Frye's definition. It is true that sometimes these different definitions coincide; surely many of the minor characters in the Gospels would be considered stock figures. However, the category 'stock' is quite different from categories 'flat' and 'round'.

In any case, the original distinction between round and flat characters has attracted much criticism in several recent literary theories. According to Rimmon-Kenan, the term 'flat' suggests something two-dimensional, devoid of depth and life. In her view, however, many 'flat' characters can be very lively; to say that a character is simple does not

---

19. E.M. Forster, *Aspects of the Novel* (San Diego: Harcourt Brace Jovanovich, 2nd edn, 1955), pp. 67-78.

20. Forster, *Aspects*, p. 67.

21. See his book *Anatomy of Criticism: Four Essays* (Princeton, NJ: Princeton University Press, 3rd edn, 1973), esp. pp. 39-43 and 171-77; see also M.H. Abrams, *A Glossary of Literary Terms* (New York: Holt, Rinehart & Winston, 4th edn, 1981), pp. 185-86, for a helpful summary.

necessarily mean that the character is non-developing.[22] According to Hochman, the distinction between round and flat depends on point of view, that is, whether the character is seen from inside or outside. Only protagonists are seen internally, while secondary figures are seen externally. All figures are potentially round, but since secondary figures are seen from outside they seem to be flat.[23] In Bal's view, the problem is that the distinction between round and flat characters is based on psychological criteria and can thus be applied only to psychological narratives. However, there are many other genres of narrative, such as fairy tales and pulp fiction, where characters are always flat.[24] In general, there are at least two overall categories of narrative: plot-centered (apsychological) and character-centered (psychological) narratives.[25] The Gospels no doubt belong to the former group, because the whole conception of psychological characters is quite recent. It rose in the eighteenth century with the appearance of the novel.[26]

If Gospels are apsychological narratives, it would not be very fitting to use the terms 'round' and 'flat' to describe different kinds of biblical characters. After all, is Jesus 'clearly a round character'? Is he as many-sided as described above? Does his character develop? Surely we can attach several attributes to him, but that does not necessarily make his character more complex. Being 'hostile' toward the religious authorities and 'loving' and 'compassionate' toward the populace are two different sides of one trait. Moreover, how much is Jesus able to surprise us, especially as the first thing told about him is that he is the son of God (as in Mk 1.1), or, as in the case of Luke, that he will be called the son of the Most High (Lk. 1.32) and is born miraculously according to the words of an angel and confirmed by prophecies (Lk. 1–2)? If his actions, miracles and teachings are astonishing, does that make Jesus act 'in new and surprising ways'? Would he not surprise the reader only if he did not perform these miracles, if he refused to do them?[27] Perhaps

22. Rimmon-Kenan, *Narrative Fiction*, p. 40.
23. Hochman, *Character*, p. 43.
24. Bal, *Narratology*, p. 81.
25. This division was made by M. Todorov (see Chatman, *Story and Discourse*, p. 113).
26. Hochman, *Character*, pp. 56-57.
27. Only the story of the Syro-Phoenician woman in Mark seems to be somewhat of an exception in this respect, as Jesus at first refuses to heal the daughter and only due to the cleverness of the woman changes his mind. Perhaps this 'un-Jesus-

Jesus' association with sinners is a surprising action by one who is son of God, but this trait is consistently developed, especially in Luke's Gospel, and does not, therefore, add complexity to Jesus' character. Also, the suffering of the son of God no doubt is a shock, but, again, Jesus' passion is well anticipated within the Gospel story. Besides, suffering can hardly be counted as action at all.

The same argument can be applied to the character of the disciples in Mark. It is true that they have conflicting traits, but that is because they have conflicting roles in the narrative: that is, they have to play both the role of uncomprehending followers of Jesus and the role of successful healers and preachers, good examples for Christian readers. Within these roles, however, they seem to be non-developing types. The basic pattern is the same in Luke's Gospel. In the course of the story, the disciples have their moments. They get the power to heal and to exorcise (9.1; 10.17-19). Peter recognizes Jesus as Messiah (9.20). They are blessed to see what they see (10.23). Yet, the narrator also has several negative comments about them: they have little faith (8.25; 12.28); they do not understand Jesus (9.44; 18.34); and they seek positions of status and power (9.46; 22.24). Even at the very end, they act as uncomprehending as ever: they fall asleep in Gethsemane (22.45-46); one of them betrays him (22.47-51); and another one denies him (22.54-62). How have the disciples 'changed and developed'? The change comes only after the resurrection, and even then it is the risen Lord who solves the problem of the wrong attitudes of the disciples. First, he teaches them step by step how the Scriptures had to be fulfilled in him (Lk. 24.44). After that, he has 40 days prior to the ascension to instruct the disciples about the kingdom of God (Acts 1.3). Luke's overall tone concerning the disciples is not really very harsh—after all, they are the heroes of the book of Acts. In the Gospel of Luke, however, his interest in the disciples is only as counterpoints to Jesus. No other incidents of their lives are told. In this sense, they resemble the minor characters.

In fact, some minor characters seem to be more complex and more developed than the disciples. There are minor characters who seem to change—such as the sinful woman (7.36-50), the prodigal son (15.11-32) and Zacchaeus (19.1-9). Often Luke uses a brief soliloquy to reveal the inner thoughts of a character in a parable (see 12.16-21; 15.11-32; 16.1-8). However, all these changes and inside views serve a similar

---

like' behavior was one of the reasons why Luke omitted the story from his narrative. See further P. Merenlahti's chapter in this volume.

function. They are devices to get to the point of the story. So, the sinful woman is an example of one whose many sins are forgiven and who loves much. Similarly, Zacchaeus is an example of true repentance and the right use of wealth as a sign of repentance. The prodigal son has to return so that the father can welcome him. Again, it is the function that is most important.

Not all biblical characters are equally presented and equally important. However, the greatest difference between them is on the *symbolic* level. That is, some characters have greater significance for the reader than others; some have become symbols themselves, such as Jesus or Mary or Peter.[28] The figure of Jesus is not characterized in a more complex or psychologically convincing way than the rest of the biblical characters; nevertheless the symbolic depth of Jesus' character is much greater than that of the minor characters.[29]

To sum up, different biblical characters cannot be distinguished from each other by any psychological measures. The difference between characters is due to the degree of focusing and characterization employed to depict them. Luke, especially, builds many of his characters carefully, making them into convincing examples of human life. The way characters are depicted reveals what kind of a role they play in the Gospel narrative. In the parable of the rich man and Lazarus, the characters can be seen as types, yet attention can be paid to their characterization. Why are they depicted the way they are? How does Luke build his characters? What is the function of the characters both within the storyworld of the Lukan Jesus and within the storyworld of Luke? Before turning to the parable of the rich man and Lazarus, it is useful to take a closer look at how Luke builds his characters in general.

Character Building in Lukan Parables

The most thorough survey of Lukan characters has been done by John Darr.[30] His interest lies in the way the characters are presented to guide

---

28. For more discussion on a character as a symbol, see K. Syreeni's chapter in this volume.

29. The minor characters also vary in depth: some are more memorable and more easily identifiable than others. A concrete example of this is the treatment of different characters in the synoptic tradition: some figures grow and others diminish in their significance; see P. Merenlahti's chapter in this volume.

30. Besides his monograph *On Character Building: The Reader and the*

the reader's perception of the Gospel narrative. In Darr's view, the way Luke presents characters in his story about Jesus serves to make the reader respond in a proper way to the things she or he is reading. Luke's intention is to make the reader not only a witness *of* the story of Jesus and the disciples but also a witness *to* others about what she or he is reading. Luke's narrator, as presented in his prologue (Lk. 1.1-4), is a paradigm of such a witness. First he has traced everything closely, then he has recounted that to others. In the same manner, many figures in Luke's story serve as positive or negative examples of the proper perception for witnessing. On the one hand, as a positive example, Simeon sees in the new born baby Jesus the salvation of Israel (Lk. 2.25-35). On the other hand, as a negative example, the Pharisees constantly fail to understand who Jesus is. The way people respond to the story—both within the story itself and among readers—makes them either insiders or outsiders; and, of course, the reader is guided by Luke to see themself as an insider to the Jesus-story.[31]

Characterization guides the reader to choose the right ways of reading and to reject the false ways. Building credible portraits of characters and showing how they respond to what they have seen and heard, instead of just telling the reader how one should act, is a more powerful means to get the reader attached to the story.[32] Darr, however, only focuses on the characters of Luke's story about Jesus, not on characters in the stories told by the Lukan Jesus.[33] Yet, there is no reason why the

---

Rhetoric of Characterization in Luke–Acts (Louisville, KY: Westminster/John Knox Press, 1992), see 'Narrator as Character: Mapping a Reader-Oriented Approach to Narration in Luke–Acts', *Semeia* 63 (1993), pp. 43-60, and ' "Watch How You Listen" (Luke 8.18): Jesus and the Rhetoric of Perception in Luke–Acts', in E.S. Malbon and E.V. McKnight (eds.), *The New Literary Criticism and the New Testament* (JSNTSup, 109; Sheffield: Sheffield Academic Press, 1994), pp. 87-107. Darr relies heavily on Wolfgang Iser's reader-oriented criticism as is shown by B.W.R. Pearson, 'New Testament Literary Criticism', in S.E. Porter (ed.), *Handbook to Exegesis of the New Testament* (Leiden: E.J. Brill, 1997), pp. 241-66 (251-53).

31. Darr, *Character Building*, pp. 53-55; 'Narrator as Character', pp. 56-57.

32. Darr, 'Rhetoric of Perception', pp. 87-88.

33. The only exception is his brief analysis of the characters in the parable of the prodigal son; Darr, *Character Building*, p. 110. The same holds true with J.D. Kingsbury. In his book *Conflict in Luke: Jesus, Authorities, Disciples* (Minneapolis: Fortress Press, 1991), p. 32, he states that 'some of the most memorable figures in Luke's gospel story exist not as characters in his story world, but as characters in Jesus' parables'. He gives the good Samaritan, the rich fool, the prodigal son, the

same should not be applied to the characters in Lukan parables.

Luke builds credibile characters by depicting them and their circumstances in a lively manner. The vividness of the figures in Lukan parables has been strongly emphasized by Michael Goulder.[34] According to him, the impression of reality is due to the fact that Luke creates three-dimensional characters who have good as well as bad qualities. In the Prodigal Son, for example, the father is 'weak, warm-hearted, generous, exaggerated, tactful, balanced and restrained', the prodigal son is 'impatient, decisive, adventurous, improvident, unprincipled, independent, realistic and humble', and the elder son is 'cautious, resentful, hard-working, obedient, mean-spirited and slanderous'.[35] In the same manner, the rich man in the Rich Man and Lazarus 'is not a caricature blackguard, but a human being; neglectful and contemptuous of the beggar at his gate, but thoughtful for his brothers, even in torment'.[36] It seems, however, that Goulder is exaggerating his point. It is true that Lukan characters impress the reader by being somewhat realistic; yet it is worth asking whether Luke is really trying to create psychologically credible characters. Goulder finds two sides in the rich man, but what about the poor man Lazarus? Why is he not taken as an example? Obviously for the very reason that there is just one side to him: his destitute poverty. The figures in the Lukan parables seem to be representatives of their groups more than they are individual characters. This is further evident when the structure of the parables is examined closely.

Gerhard Sellin has argued that several Lukan parables have a common structure that is built around the characters.[37] These parables, such as the Two Debtors (Lk. 7.41-43),[38] the Good Samaritan (Lk. 10.30-35), the Prodigal Son, and the Rich Man and Lazarus, have three characters in a 'dramatic triangle'. Two of the characters are juxtaposed by

unjust steward and 'the poor man Lazarus' as examples, but he does not discuss them any further.

34. Goulder, *Luke*, I, esp. pp. 93-99.

35. Goulder, *Luke*, I, pp. 93-94

36. Goulder, *Luke*, I, p. 94.

37. See Sellin, 'Lukas als Gleichniserzähler: Die Erzählung vom barmherzigen Samariter (Lk. 10,25-37)', *ZNW* 65 (1974), pp. 166-89; *ZNW* 66 (1975), pp. 19-60.

38. The parable of the two debtors differs from the other above-mentioned parables as it is not a story, just 'a sketch of a story', see Sellin, 'Lukas als Gleichniserzähler', p. 180.

a common status but contrasted by their relationship to the third character who is a median figure in the story. In the parable of the two debtors, both of the men owe the creditor, but the one owes much, while the other owes little. Other parables are built in the same way: two travelers from Jerusalem to Jericho and the wounded victim,[39] two sons and their father, two dead figures in the afterlife and Abraham. The parable of the Pharisee and the tax-collector (Lk. 18.9-14) may also share the same structure. The missing third figure is substituted by Jesus' words in v. 18.14a.[40]

Another common feature for these parables is a change in values and attitudes.[41] At the beginning of the parable the one character is presented in a positive manner: the one who owes little, a priest/Levite, an obedient, hard-working son, a rich man, a Pharisee. At the end, however, the character who had the lesser status—the one owing much, the despised and ritually unclean Samaritan, the prodigal son, the poor man, the tax collector—attains the better outcome. Each parable includes a reversal, which also means a reversal in characterization. In each parable, the characters end up with characteristics and circumstances contrary to the stereotype they represent.[42] The Samaritan is characterized as loving, the priest/Levite as unloving; the prodigal son is accepted, the obedient son opposes his father; the rich man is in pain, the poor man in luxury; the tax-collector returns home justified instead of the Pharisee.

39. In the parable of the Good Samaritan, the antithetical characters are the Samaritan on the one hand, the priest and the Levite on the other, see Sellin, 'Lukas als Gleichniserzähler', p. 181 n. 73. The portrayal of the Samaritan as a third passerby is a literary convention typical of fairy tales, for example. The twofold division between well-doers and wrongdoers may include more than two characters, as is also the case in the parable of the talents (Lk. 19.11-27). Cf. D. Flusser, 'Aesop's Miser and the Parable of the Talents', in C. Thoma and M. Wyschogrod (eds.), *Parable and Story in Judaism and Christianity* (Mahwah, NJ: Paulist Press, 1989), pp. 9-25 (13).

40. Sellin, 'Lukas als Gleichniserzähler', p. 183.

41. Sellin, 'Lukas als Gleichniserzähler', p. 183.

42. This is noted by R. Tannehill in *The Narrative Unity of Luke–Acts: A Literary Interpretation*. I. *The Gospel According to Luke* (Philadelphia: Fortress Press, 1991), p. 119. He discusses only so-called quest stories, such as the Healing of the Centurion's Servant (Lk. 7.2-10), the Pharisee and the Sinful Woman (Lk. 7.36-50) and the Cleansing of the Ten Lepers (Lk. 17.12-19) but the same feature can be seen in many parables of Luke.

It seems that the point of these parables is the reversal itself, not the changes in the characters as persons. Rather, the characters are simply representatives of their group (the rich, the poor, the Samaritans, the Pharisees, etc.). Luke's lively description serves the typical; giving the stereotypes enough individual features makes them credible. Nevertheless, the characters remain close to caricatures. It is their function in the plot that is important, not the persons they are.

The credibility of Luke's characters and their paradigmatic function are emphasized also by Kari Syreeni.[43] According to him, Luke's characters are paradigmatic in the sense that they are not only typical representatives of a certain group, but also moral examples, suggesting a specific model of behavior in practical life worth imitating, or—in the case of a negative paradigm—worth avoiding. It is not at all insignificant how these paradigmatic figures are presented, because it is precisely the characterization that has an impact on the reader, guiding her or him to identify with one character and to reject another. By creating colorful, realistic figures, Luke leads the reader to be involved both morally and intellectually with the characters.[44] In this way, Luke manipulates the reader—she or he not only accepts the characters but also the narrator's ideology that is carefully disguised in the story. But the plan works only if the characters are convincing enough.[45]

According to ancient rhetoricians, there were three different aspects to argumentation. A successful speech had to appeal to reason, conscience and emotion.[46] As the parable of the Rich Man and Lazarus is a

43. 'The Gospel in Paradigms: A Study in the Hermeneutical Space of Luke–Acts', in P. Luomanen (ed.), *Luke–Acts: Scandinavian Perspectives* (PFES, 54; Helsinki: The Finnish Exegetical Society; Göttingen: Vandenhoeck & Ruprecht, 1991), pp. 36-57.

44. Syreeni, 'Gospel in Paradigms', pp. 44-45.

45. Credibility or *credibilitas* was one of the aims of the ancient rhetoricians; see E. Rau, *Reden in Vollmacht: Hintergrund, Form und Anliegen der Gleichnisse Jesu* (FRLANT, 149; Göttingen: Vandenhoeck & Ruprecht, 1990), pp. 87-89. The speaker used different means to achieve this goal, such as *evidentia*, or vivid description. Although rhetorical criticism is a different approach from narrative criticism, both share some aspects in common. This is shown by Dennis L. Stamps who treats both approaches under the same heading in his article 'Rhetorical and Narratological Criticism', in Porter (ed.), *Handbook to Exegesis*, pp. 219-39. According to him, both share a concern for the effects of textual strategies (p. 220).

46. See Aristotle, *Rhet.* 1.2.3-6 (1356a). The artistic proofs, which are dependent on the speaker's skill, are provided through three different modes: by *ethos*

story, not an argumentative speech, Luke tries to win over his audience by using other than logical or rational arguments. He appeals to his readers' emotions by a heart-stirring depiction of the two men, which leads the reader to sympathize with the poor man and reject the rich man. In addition, he creates a right kind of ethos or tone to his story. This has several aspects to it. First, there is the ethos of the narrator who has to be trustworthy and have authority for the audience. Second, there is the ethos of the parable itself that is based on 'Moses and the prophets', that is, on the tradition that everybody in the audience can agree upon. Third, there is the ethos of the characters.[47] It becomes evident that the ethos of the rich man is of a wrong kind, as his behavior is against the common set of values. The ethos of the poor man is not shown as clearly but he seems to be humble and content with very little, only longing to be satisfied with crumbs from the rich man's table. These aspects will be examined more closely as we now turn to analyze the parable in detail.

The Rich Man and the Poor Man in This Life

The parable tells a story of a rich man and a poor man, but what do these terms actually mean? According to Malina, in honor- or shame-based peasant societies, being poor does not primarily mean a person's economic rank. No matter if one's social rank is high or low, people are honorable as long as they live according to their ranks. Money does not determine one's social standing—birth does. Instead of an economic designation, being poor refers to an unfortunate turn of events that hinders persons from maintaining their inherited social status. This is evident in the several passages where Luke links the term 'poor' with circumstances such as imprisonment, blindness and oppression (Lk. 4.18); people who are poor are hungry, thirsty and mourning (Lk. 6.20-21), or crippled, lame and blind (Lk. 14.13, 21).[48]

Malina shows convincingly how one-sided it is to understand the term 'poor' as referring only to economic conditions. However, it is

(character), by *pathos* (emotion) and by *logos* (reason). See, e.g., A. Eriksson, *Traditions as Rhetorical Proof: Pauline Argumentation in 1 Corinthians* (ConBNT, 29; Stockholm: Almqvist & Wiksell, 1998), pp. 33-39.

47. Cf. Eriksson, *Traditions*, pp. 34-37, who speaks about ethos through character, ethos of the matter and ethos of the audience.

48. Malina, *New Testament World*, pp. 105-106.

hard to conclude that the term has no economic relevance and that it refers only to one's disability or changing circumstances to maintain her or his inherited status. The term 'poor' seems to have many relevant meanings in the Lukan world. For example, the poor are often explicitly mentioned as the opposite of the rich, as in the beatitudes and woes (6.20-26) or in Jesus' recommendation for the choice of guests (14.12-13). Moreover, in the beatitudes, for example, Luke seems to be familiar with a spiritual meaning of the word, common in the Hebrew Bible language. Especially in the Psalms, the word 'poor' refers to one who is in need and on whose side God has promised to be.[49] By contrast, the 'rich' are those who trust in themselves instead of God.[50] Thus, it is legitimate to interpret the term 'poor' as a *symbol*, as a word with a wide range of meanings, that can refer to different aspects in different contexts.[51]

If poverty is understood as a symbol, there is no need to make a sharp distinction between physical and spiritual poverty.[52] In both cases, poor is someone who is unable to take care of themself but is in need of help, either from other people or from God. A contrast to the poor are the rich, who have enough resources to survive without help from others.

The contrast between rich and poor is clearly shown in the parable of the Rich Man and Lazarus. The story opens up with a description of the rich man: 'There was a rich man who was dressed in purple and fine linen and who feasted sumptuously every day.' His wealth is defined by

---

49. D.P. Seccombe, *Possessions and the Poor in Luke–Acts* (SNTU, 6; Linz: DDr. A. Fuchs, 1982), pp. 27-38.

50. This interpretation of the rich is present throughout Luke's Gospel. See also the last chapters in *1 Enoch* (chs. 92–105).

51. However, scholars tend to emphasize only one aspect of the term 'poor'. For example, S.J. Glen (*The Parables of Conflict in Luke* [Philadelphia: Westminster Press, 1962], p. 65) suggests that since the conflict of the rich man and the poor man appears in a parable, it is 'essentially a moral and a spiritual problem and not exclusively economic and political'. He fails to see that the conflict of the rich and the poor appears also in several other Lukan passages, as shown above. Another extreme view is represented by W. Herzog (*Parables as Subversive Speech: Jesus as Pedagogue of the Oppressed* [Louisville, KY: Westminster/John Knox Press, 1994], pp. 14-16) who understands poverty only physically. He argues that the parables of Jesus were aimed at social reform and that Jesus' subversive teachings were the reason for his crucifixion.

52. R. Uro, *Jeesus-liikkeestä kristinuskoksi* (Helsinki: Yliopistopaino, 1995), pp. 46-62.

his external appearance and his daily lifestyle. The details of his daily life are not told but it is clear that he did not lack good food and drink, as indicated in the other passages where the verb εὐφραίνω is used. For example, the rich fool tells his soul (Lk. 12.19): 'relax, eat, drink, be merry' (ἀναπαύου, φάγε, πίε, εὐφραίνου). Similarly, in the Prodigal Son the father says, 'let us eat and celebrate' (καὶ φαγόντες εὐφρανθῶμεν in 15.23; the verb is repeated in vv. 24, 29 and 31). The sparse description is cleverly widened by the words καθ᾽ ἡμέραν (every day). They make the portrait of the rich man's life vague enough to allow the reader to imagine all that must have belonged to his daily lifestyle. They also tell what kind of a person the rich man really is.[53] This kind of iterative narration is typical for Luke. He uses the expression elsewhere to describe the right behavior of Jesus' disciples. Those who want to follow Jesus have to take their cross daily (ἀράτω τὸν σταυρὸν αὐτοῦ καθ᾽ ἡμέραν, Lk. 9.23). Also after the resurrection of Jesus, the disciples attended the temple and broke bread together day to day (καθ᾽ ἡμέραν) 'with glad and generous hearts' (Acts 2.46). The daily conduct of the disciples shows an example of the generous sharing of food, just the opposite of the conduct of the rich man.

As the scene shifts to the poor man, a totally different picture is drawn: 'And at his gate lay a poor man named Lazarus, covered with sores, who longed to satisfy his hunger with what fell from the rich man's table; even the dogs would come and lick his sores.' Again, a vivid description is used, this time to reveal a poor man in a pitiful condition. He is hungry and helpless. Some scholars stress his helplessness by interpreting the verb ἐβέβλητο in the passive voice ('he was laid'), thereby suggesting that the poor man is paralyzed.[54] The verb can also be translated in the middle voice ('he lay [himself]') which could also imply that he had nobody to help him. Had Luke wanted to stress Lazarus's being a paralytic he could have expressed that precisely, as he does elsewhere (Acts 3.2 and 14.8).[55]

Also other details in the description of the poor man's helplessness can be interpreted in different ways. Does the poor man have a skin condition or is he bleeding? It has been argued that in either case the

---

53. The sparse words καθ᾽ ἡμέραν tell what the rich man did repeatedly. Repeated action by a character is one of the features that helps the reader to construct the image of a character. See Bal, *Narratology*, p. 85.

54. E.g. Jeremias, *Parables*, p. 183.

55. This is argued by Hintzen, *Verkündigung*, p. 93.

poor man would have been impure and not able to beg publicly.[56]

However, already the mention of the dogs as Lazarus's companions depicts him as impure.[57] The function of the dogs can be understood in two different ways. Either they are adding to Lazarus's misery by not letting him alone, or they are the only creatures showing solidarity with him. Be that as it may, the touch by the dogs makes Lazarus impure, not able to be in contact with other people. Both the expression 'longed to satisfy' (ἐπιθυμῶν χορτασθῆναι) and the mention of impure animals remind the reader of the parable of the Prodigal Son. The prodigal son was also hungry and longed to be satisfied (ἐπιθύμει χορτασθῆναι) with the food of pigs—other impure animals. The link is even closer: the crumbs that fell from the rich man's table were considered food for the dogs, as shown by the Markan story of the Syro-Phoenician woman (Mk 7.24-30)—which Luke has omitted from his Gospel.[58]

The contrast of the two men is complete, as is shown by the parallel structure in which they are introduced. A certain man is rich, a certain man is poor; the rich man is inside his house, the poor man is outside at the rich man's gate; the rich man is satisfied by the sumptuous feasts, the poor man is hungry and unable to fill his wish to eat even the crumbs from the rich man's table; the rich man dresses in purple and fine linen, the poor man is covered by sores and licked by street dogs.[59] The characterization of the men in contrast to each other determines further what kind of an image the reader grasps of them.[60] In other words, the richness of the rich man underlines the poverty of the poor man, and vice versa. The contrast is further sharpened by the fact that they are physically so close to each other.

However, there is one feature in the description of the poor man that has no counterpart in that of the rich man: the name of the poor man. This is unique in the Gospels, for in no other parable is a person named.

---

56. For discussion, see, e.g., B.B. Scott, *Hear Then the Parable: A Commentary on the Parables of Jesus* (Minneapolis: Fortress Press, 1989), p. 150.

57. For more on purity/impurity, see Malina, *New Testament World*, pp. 149-83.

58. Cf. Goulder, *Luke*, II, p. 635.

59. This contrast is emphasized especially by R. Obermüller, 'La miseria de un rico: Un juicio neotestamentario—Lucas 16.19-31', in Lee Brummel (ed.), *Los pobres: Encuentro y compromiso* (Buenos Aires: La Aurora, 1978), pp. 45-66 (48-49); and F. Schnider and W. Stenger, 'Die offene Tür und die unüberschreitbare Kluft: Strukturanalytische Überlegungen zum Gleichnis vom reichen Mann und armen Lazarus (Lk. 16,19-31)', *NTS* 25 (1979), pp. 273-83 (277).

60. Cf. Bal, *Narratology*, p. 86.

Why the name Lazarus? And why does the rich man not have a name?[61] Many scholars interpret the name as depicting the situation of the poor man. 'Lazarus' derives from a Hebrew name with the meaning 'he whom God helps'. However, we have no proof that Luke knew Hebrew, and even if he did, his Greek speaking audience would certainly not have known Hebrew. So, if the etymology of the name was important, it would have been explained explicitly (as Luke does elsewhere, e.g. in Acts 4.36; 13.8). Nevertheless, other reasons can be given for naming the poor man. First, the name is needed in the story as a vital part of the dialogue. The rich man has to refer to Lazarus by some name. He cannot say 'the poor man', since Lazarus is no longer poor in Abraham's bosom. He has to use a name. Second, giving Lazarus a name helps to personalize him. It distinguishes him from all the other poor: he is not just any poor man, but this certain poor man.[62] It is easier for the reader to sympathize with him. Naming Lazarus reminds the reader of the fact that the rich man knows the poor man by name (see v. 24).[63] By contrast, the anonymity of the rich man makes him a more generalized character. He does not need a name.[64] He is called 'child' and 'you' by Abraham. That is sufficient.

The injustice of the life of the men goes on without a change every day as the rich man makes merry and Lazarus stays hungry. But change is to come. After the colorful description of the contrasting characters, the story continues with a remark about the death of each man: 'The poor man died and was carried away by the angels to be with Abraham. The rich man also died and was buried.' The life and the death of the men is told in a chiastic abb'a' pattern: first the rich man is described, then the poor man, then the death of the poor man, then that of the rich man. The pattern intensifies the story and anticipates the coming

61. In some manuscripts, the rich man does have a name. In the papyrus $\mathfrak{P}^{75}$ the name is Νευης, in sahidic translations ⲛⲓⲛⲉⲩⲏ, and in Priscillianus *Finees*. However, it is clear that neither these names nor any name belonged to the original parable.

62. A different conclusion is drawn by L.T. Johnson, *The Literary Function of Possessions in Luke–Acts* (SBLDS, 39; Missoula, MT: Scholars Press, 1977), p. 142. He states, 'They are simply τις πλούσιος and τις πτωχός, the name of the latter not having any particular significance for the story.'

63. This is noted by Seccombe, *Possessions*, pp. 174-75.

64. In English, the rich man is often called Dives (thus: the parable of Dives and Lazarus), which is simply Latin for 'rich'. This is unfortunate, since it prevents the reader from realizing the original anonymity of the rich man.

change.[65] The poor man is not buried; instead, he is carried off by the angels. The heavenly treatment initiates the full reversal that is recounted in the following verses. The rich man is said to receive the honor of burial, as would be typical for a wealthy man. The next verse, however, reveals the tremendous change. Without any previous warnings—wicked angels, for instance—the rich man is boldly stated to be in Hades, in torment.

The analysis of the characters so far shows that the general remarks about Lukan characters made above seem to be apt. It is clear that here we have an example of character types whose most important trait is wealth/poverty. Characters do not change or develop; they are the same until the day they die. Luke is using the description of the men in order to create credible types to emphasize their only important trait, their wealth or their poverty. The details as such are 'useless'; they are not necessary for the sake of the story itself. Rather, they have a different function. They are used in order to create an illusion of real life, a 'reality effect'.[66] The additional details make the image of the men more credible, which makes the reader get emotionally involved with the story. The image created by Luke is colorful but it is a still picture; the image does not move. Only the death of both men brings a change, and that change is a reversal.

The Reversal of Fortunes: The Rich Man and the Poor Man after Death

As the scene changes, also the point of view changes. The reversal of fortunes is now continued from the rich man's point of view: 'In Hades, where he was being tormented, he looked up and saw Abraham far away with Lazarus by his side.' The rich man finds himself in torment, and somewhere far away; yet he is close enough to be within speaking distance, and he sees Lazarus in the bosom of Abraham.[67] The word

65. This kind of a chiastic pattern is typical of Luke's reversal sayings, such as Lk. 1.52-53; 13.30; 14.11/18.14. See further below.

66. The term is adapted from R. Barthes, *The Rustle of Language* (trans. R. Howard; New York: Hill & Wang, 1986), p. 148; cf. Syreeni, 'Gospel in Paradigms', p. 45.

67. The idea of the good and the wicked seeing each other in the afterworld occurs also in Lk. 13.28-29. It was a well-known idea in Jewish apocalyptism. For example, *4 Ezra* 7.80-95 talks about seven rewards and seven punishments for the

κόλπος ('bosom'; NRSV: 'by one's side') has several meanings (cf. Jn 1.18; Acts 27.33), but it is here best interpreted as an honorary place for guests at a banquet (as in Jn 13.20). A messianic banquet was a widespread image in Jewish apocalyptic literature to describe the joys of heaven (e.g. *1 En.* 62.14). Luke is clearly familiar with the image, for he uses it frequently in his Gospel. For example, those who do not believe in Jesus are told that they will see 'Abraham and Isaac and Jacob and all the prophets in the kingdom of God, but you yourselves thrown out. Then people will come from east and west, from north and south, and will eat in the kingdom of God' (Lk. 13.28-29). A guest at a banquet declares: 'Blessed is anyone who will eat bread in the kingdom of God!' (Lk. 14.15). The disciples are promised that they will 'eat and drink at my table in my kingdom, and you will sit on thrones judging the twelve tribes of Israel' (Lk. 22.30). Other Lukan passages where Jesus refers to a meal image also have an eschatological tone to them (see Lk. 6.21, 25; 12.16-21, 45-46; 13.25-30; 14.12-14, 15-24; 17.27-28; 22.14-18).[68] Many of these scenes also include the idea of a reversal: those who are thought to be insiders, invited to a banquet, find themselves outside, and vice versa.[69] The image serves as a warning for those who enjoy luxury now and also as an assurance for those who have no access to earthly banquets.

The change of the scene from this world to the hereafter creates a problem: how to speak about the life after death in a convincing way? It is not easy to give a credible description of the hereafter. Besides some colorful details, such as the request by the rich man to have his hot tongue refreshed, Luke refrains from depicting the two dead men and their condition at length. Instead, he changes the structure of the narrative: a story told by a narrator turns into a dialogue. The focus shifts entirely to the rich man and Abraham, and Lazarus becomes a back-

souls after death as they wait for the judgment. One of the punishments for the ungodly is that 'they shall see the reward laid up for those who have trusted the covenants of the Most High'. Another punishment is that 'they shall see how the habitations of the others are guarded by angels in profound quiet'. Accordingly, one of the rewards for the just is that 'they shall see the perplexity in which the souls of the ungodly wander and the punishment that awaits them'. See *2 Bar.* 51.5-6 for a different kind of account.

68. The subject is treated persuasively, e.g. by D. Smith in his article 'Table Fellowship as a Literary Motif in the Gospel of Luke', *JBL* 106 (1987), pp. 613-38.

69. Other passages include Lk. 6.20-26; 13.25-30; 14.15-24. See further pp. 95-96 below.

ground figure. Only the rich man talks with Abraham while Lazarus does not utter a word. No more do we get *direct* comments by the narrator. The rest of the story, as well as the portrait of the characters, has to be reconstructed from the dialogue. 'He called out, "Father Abraham, have mercy on me, and send Lazarus to dip the tip of his finger in water and cool my tongue; for I am in agony in these flames."' The speech of the rich man reveals what kind of a person he is: in Hades he still views Lazarus as his inferior and thinks he can ask him to be sent according to his wishes.[70]

When Abraham denies his request to get comfort from Lazarus, he continues by asking Lazarus to be sent to his brothers: 'He said, "Then, father, I beg you to send him to my father's house—for I have five brothers—that he may warn them, so that they will not come into this place of torment."' Is this a sign of the many-sidedness of the rich man's character, a glance at his 'thoughtfulness for his brothers', as suggested by Goulder?[71] Rather than adding complexity to the rich man's character, the request seems to function as a device to move the story along. The people who resemble the rich man—who in the story-world of the parable are his brothers—will have to listen to Moses and the prophets, who call them to repentance. Otherwise, a similar fate awaits them.

The fate of the rich man is painful, and it is unchangeable, fixed by a chasm. The reversal has been complete, the situation of both men 'now' is the reverse of their situation 'then' (in their life).[72] Not only is the rich man now in pain, like Lazarus was in life, but also Lazarus is compensated for the bad things he experienced. The rich man has been humbled from his wealthy and honorary position into one of torment, while Lazarus has been exalted from being impure and despised by other people, into the friendship of Abraham. Now Lazarus is inside, taking part in the heavenly banquet, and the rich man is outside. The closeness of the two men on earth (πρὸς τὸν πυλῶνα) is contrasted with distance in the afterlife (ἀπὸ μακρόθεν). Now the men are separated not just by a gate, which could have been opened, but by an insurmountable chasm.[73] Now the rich man has to beg for a drop of water,

---

70. See D. Gowler, 'Characterization in Luke: A Socio-Narratological Approach', *BTB* 19 (1989), pp. 54-62.

71. See p. 83 above.

72. See Scott, *Parable*, p. 154.

73. The significance of the boundaries has been emphasized by Schnider and

and his request is refused, just as he had refused Lazarus even a crumb of food from his table. The rich man did not pity Lazarus, but now he is asking Abraham to pity him. What is the reason for the reversal? The poor man is not characterized as being particularly pious, nor the rich man especially ungodly. The only explanation for the reversal is given in v. 25: 'But Abraham said, "Child, remember that during your lifetime you received your good things and Lazarus in like manner evil things; but now he is comforted here, and you are in agony"'. The contrast of 'your life there' and 'his life here' is intensified by the same abb'a' structure that was used to describe their lives on earth (vv. 19-21). The moral evaluation of the characters must be concluded from the standards of judgment Luke has introduced previously in his story. 'Standards of judgment' refer to the values that are present in the narrative, either explicitly or implicitly, that give to the reader the basis to judge the goodness or badness of the characters and their actions.[74]

The Lukan standards of judgment about wealth and poverty are seen in the instructions given by John the Baptist and Jesus. As the kingdom is drawing near, people are required to behave accordingly. Since the kingdom means good news to the poor (Lk. 4.18), the rich must stop oppressing them (3.12-14). Since it means an end to hunger (6.20), people must share their food (3.11).[75] Those who have power and wealth are urged to share what they have with those who have not. The wealthy must guard themselves against greed (Lk. 12.15). The disciples are instructed to sell all they have and give to the poor (Lk. 12.33; cf. Lk. 18.22). Another prominent standard is the call to repentance (Lk. 3.8; 5.32).[76] Those who fail to repent will be destroyed (Lk. 13.3, 5) The right use of wealth, the repudiation of exploitation and wrongdoing are concrete signs of repentance (Lk. 3.13-14; 19.1-9). Those who have nothing will be included in the fellowship (Lk. 14.13; 15.25-32).[77] One should imitate God's mercy (Lk. 6.36). All of this means

Stenger, 'Offene Tür', p. 277; and Scott, *Parable*, p. 146.

74. See Rhoads and Michie, *Mark as Story*, p. 110.

75. These examples are given by Seccombe, *Possessions*, pp. 182-83.

76. The theme of repentance in Luke is treated by J. Kiilunen in his article 'Sanoma kääntymyksestä—Luukkaan toimintaohjelma kirkolle', in L. Aejmelaeus (ed.), *Aimo annos eksegetiikkaa* (Festschrift Aimo T. Nikolainen; Helsinki: Kirjapaja, 1992), pp. 103-24.

77. This is emphasized by R. Piper, 'Social Background and Thematic Structure

living according to the word of God, which one should hear and obey (Lk. 11.28). If the wealthy and powerful fail to act according to these standards, God will intervene. God is on the side of the poor and oppressed, and promises them an eschatological reward. The mighty and powerful will be put down and the lowly and humble exalted (Lk. 2.52-53).[78]

The theme of reversal is repeatedly present in Luke's Gospel.[79] Luke has received several reversal sayings from his tradition but has prominently widened the use of the reversal pattern. He is especially fond of double reversals where the situation changes both upside down and downside up (or inside out and outside in). The hungry will be satisfied, the sated will be sent away empty (Lk. 1.51-53; 6.21, 25). The poor will be invited and comforted, the rich will find themselves outside (6.20, 24; 14.16-24). Other 'vertical' reversals (in terms of upside down) include the instruction to choose last places in the banquet (14.8-10) and the parable of the Pharisee and the tax-collector (18.9-14), for 'all who exalt themselves will be humbled, and those who humble themselves will be exalted' (14.11/18.14). Other 'horizontal' reversals (in terms of inside out) include sayings like 'those who want to save their life will lose it, and those who lose their life for my sake will save it' (9.24), and 'some are last who will be first, and some are first who will be last' (13.30).

As noted above, the Rich Man and Lazarus combines both a 'vertical' and a 'horizontal' aspect of reversal: Lazarus, who was outside and down (in poverty, outside the gate) is exalted inside and up (to an honorary place at Abraham's bosom; NRSV: 'side'); accordingly, the rich man's position changes from inside and up (at a table inside a house) to outside and down (torments in Hades). Reversal is present also in other Lukan parables. In the Good Samaritan, the honorable priest and Levite are put to shame, the shameful Samaritan is honored. In the Prodigal Son, the obedient brother finds himself outside while his

---

in Luke 16', in F. Van Segbroeck *et al.* (eds.), *The Four Gospels* (Festschrift Frans Neirynck; BETL, 100.2; Leuven: Leuven University Press, 1992), pp. 1660-61.

78. See Tannehill, *Narrative Unity*, p. 109.

79. This has been most recently argued by J.O. York, *The Last Shall Be First: The Rhetoric of Reversal in Luke* (JSNTSup, 46; Sheffield: JSOT Press, 1991). Another recent treatment of the theme is presented by D. Rhoads, 'The Gospel of Luke: Society with Mercy', in *idem*, *The Challenge of Diversity: The Witness of Paul and the Gospels* (Minneapolis: Fortress Press, 1996), pp. 99-116.

prodigal brother is inside at a party. The pattern of reversal can be seen
also in the way Luke presents Jesus' life and actions. Jesus, who is born
in a lowly manger to humble people and who dies rejected, is raised up
from death, ascends to heaven and becomes lord of all.[80] God's chosen
one also has to humble himself before exaltation. Jesus' life will cause
the 'falling and the rising of many in Israel' (Lk. 2.34). His teaching
honors a sinful woman and puts a Pharisee to shame (7.36-50). His
healing of a crippled woman includes her in God's family, while the
religious leaders are judged to be hypocrites (13.10-17).

Thus, the reversal of the fates of the rich man and Lazarus is based on
the justice of God. In the mercy of God, it is unbearable that the one
lives in luxury while the other suffers. Fatal for the rich man was the
inequality in this life that he did not try to overcome in any way.[81] The
inequality is compensated in the life after death—whether we think of it
as being fair or not is a different matter.[82] The rich man's inability to
meet God's standards becomes more apparent as the dialogue in the
parable goes on. The discussion about the brothers makes clear that the
rich man had not repented, that he had not heard Moses and the prophets. The importance of the Scriptures is emphasized by the repetition

80. Rhoads, *The Challenge*, p. 104.
81. See Scott, *Parable*, pp. 150, 153. The gate could have functioned in two
ways: it could have let in as well as kept out. Yet the rich man failed to open it, and
it was not until being in torment in Hades that he sought to bridge the separating
boundary.
82. It seems not to have been a problem for Luke's audience since the reversal
of status of rich and poor was a widespread concept in Jewish apocalyptism (*1 En.*
92–105). See also the articles by G. Nickelsburg ('Riches, the Rich, and God's
Judgment in 1 Enoch 92–105 and the Gospel According to Luke', *NTS* 25 [1979],
pp. 324-44), and R. Bauckham ('The Rich Man and Lazarus: The Parable and the
Parallels', *NTS* 37 [1991], pp. 225-46). To modern readers, such an idea does not
seem to be justified. In his novel *The Last Temptation of Christ* (trans. P.A. Bien;
New York: Simon & Schuster, 5th edn, 1960), N. Kazantzakis makes Jesus tell
another ending to the story: 'When Lazarus heard Abraham's words he sighed and
addressed God in his mind: "God, how can anyone be happy in Paradise when he
knows that there is a man—a soul—roasting for all eternity? Refresh him, Lord,
that I may be refreshed. Deliver him, Lord, that I may be delivered. Otherwise I too
shall begin to feel the flames." God heard his thought and was glad. "Lazarus,
beloved", he said, "go down; take the thirster by the hand. My fountains are inex-
haustible. Bring him here so that he may drink and refresh himself, and you refresh
yourself with him." ... "For all eternity?" asked Lazarus. "Yes, for all eternity,"
God replied' (p. 202).

of the expression 'Moses and the prophets'.[83] The Jewish writings, the law and the prophets, clearly show the ideal behavior for the wealthy. Yet the rich man did not even share the scraps from his table. In his selfish care for himself only he was a rich fool, just like the man who built larger barns to store his grain (Lk. 12.16-20) who also had his good things (τὰ ἀγαθά μου/σου) in his life. Elsewhere, Luke gives examples of proper behavior for the wealthy. Had the rich man invited Lazarus to share his banquet, as instructed by Jesus (in Lk. 14.13), he would have received his reward in the resurrection of the just (Lk. 14.14). Another counterpart for the rich man is the unjust steward (Lk. 8.1-9). In his behavior, he resembles those who do not fail to make friends with unrighteous mammon and who, therefore, are received in eternal dwellings.[84]

The Role of Abraham

What is the role of Abraham in the afterlife? The simple answer is that the structure of the story demands a partner for the rich man in the dialogue. It obviously cannot be God, since God cannot be seen (cf. Exod. 33.20) nor does God speak in Luke's Gospel except for the two occasions when he names Jesus as his son (Lk. 3.22; 9.35). On all other occasions, God makes his will known through messengers, like angels (e.g. Lk. 1.11-20; 2.26-38; Acts 1.10-11) or Jesus (e.g. Lk. 10.22). In the afterlife, Abraham is a fitting spokesperson for God. In the Old Testament the expression used for dying was 'to go to one's ancestors' or 'to lie down with one's ancestors' (see Gen. 15.15; 47.30; Deut. 31.16; 1 Kgs 1.21; 2.10; 11.21; 1 Macc. 2.69). In later Jewish and early Christian literature there are several passages that talk about the three patriarchs Abraham, Isaac and Jacob in the afterlife (e.g. *4 Macc.* 7.19; 13.17). Luke himself pictures the three patriarchs in the kingdom of God (13.28-29).

83. Luke uses a similar expression in two key passages in his two-volume work. In Lk. 24.27 the risen Jesus explains 'beginning from Moses and all the prophets' how the Scriptures prophesied about him (cf. v. 44). In a parallel passage, at the end of Acts, Paul tries to convince the Jews in Rome about Jesus 'both from the law of Moses and from the prophets' (Acts 28.23).

84. The contrast of the two parables in Lk. 16 is suggested by A. Feuillet, 'La parabole du mauvais riche et du pauvre Lazare (Lc 16,19-31) antithèse de la parabole de l'intendant astucieux (Lc 16,1-9)', *NRT* 111 (1979), pp. 212-23.

Besides being the necessary interlocutor for the rich man, Abraham
has several other roles. The rich man's address to Abraham as his father
reminds the reader of the words of John the Baptist at the beginning of
Luke's Gospel: 'Bear fruits worthy of repentance. Do not begin to say
to yourselves, "We have Abraham as our ancestor"; for I tell you, God
is able from these stones to raise up children to Abraham' (Lk. 3.8).
The 'fruits worthy of repentance' is exactly what the rich man failed to
do, as shown by the end of the parable. And if the brothers of the rich
man do not repent, their destiny will also be the place of torment. Calling Abraham a father does not help. The true children of Abraham are
those who live accordingly.

Being a child of Abraham means belonging to God's family. Luke
uses the image of Abraham as father elsewhere, as in the story of Jesus'
healing a crippled woman on a Sabbath (Lk. 13.10-17). When the religious authorities oppose his healing, Jesus replies: 'And ought not this
woman, a daughter of Abraham whom Satan bound for eighteen long
years, be set free from this bondage on the sabbath day?' (Lk. 13.16).
The woman also belongs to the family of God and it is right to free her
from her bondage, just as the religious leaders would have saved
another member of the family, their son, had he fallen in a well on a
Sabbath (cf. Lk. 14.5; here, however, the image of untying the ox and
the donkey from bondage is used, as it is parallel to untying the woman
from her bondage). A similar expression occurs in the story of Zacchaeus (Lk. 19.1-9), a story that tells about a rich man who repented and
gave to the poor. When Zacchaeus declares he will give half of his possessions to the poor, and in addition pay back four times to those from
whom he has taken unjustly, Jesus replies: 'Today salvation has come
to this house, because he too is a son of Abraham.' Though lost, Zacchaeus is a member of the family who has found his way back home.
So instead of grumbling (19.7) the others should rejoice over the lost
brother who is found (cf. Lk. 15.7, 10, 32).

The reference to Abraham as father can also be seen from a different
angle. The rich man appeals to Abraham for a favor and so the word
'father' is used as an honorary title. The appeal echoes a patron–client
relationship common to peasant societies. An honorary title is used by
the inferior to evoke a positive response from the superior.[85] A similar
kind of appeal is made by the blind beggar near Jericho who addresses

---

85. See Malina, *New Testament World*, pp. 101-102.

Jesus with the title 'Son of David' (Lk. 18.38-39). But in the parable the appeal of the rich man does not help. Even though Abraham does not deny the relationship (he calls the rich man 'child'), Lazarus has taken the place of the rich man. Besides, Abraham is unable to help the rich man, had he wanted to. It is too late, for God has fixed a chasm between them. Abraham explains: 'Besides all this, between you and us a great chasm has been fixed, so that those who might want to pass from here to you cannot do so, and no one can cross from there to us' (v. 26). This may imply that Lazarus would have been willing to come to the rich man's aid, should he be able to. In so doing, Lazarus would be merciful like his Father is merciful (Lk. 6.36), showing a contrast to the rich man's conduct in life.

Another role for Abraham is to be companion and consoler to Lazarus. In his life, the rich man did not consider Lazarus as a child of Abraham, and the poor man had nobody to help him. Now Lazarus has the friendship of Abraham, and the rich man has to recognize the kinship between the two. If both men are Abraham's sons, Lazarus is the rich man's brother, belonging to the same family with the rich man.

Some scholars also see other nuances in the figure of Abraham. According to Scott,[86] Abraham was known for his hospitality. In Genesis (Gen. 18.1-15) Abraham receives three strangers, one of whom is the Lord. Later, in the rabbinic literature, this scene was interpreted as an ideal of hospitality; it shows Abraham's virtue exceeding that of Job's because Abraham fed strangers while Job fed only those accustomed to eating. Thus the figure of Abraham contrasts with the rich man's failure at showing hospitality. However, it is somewhat doubtful whether Luke and his audience were familiar with Abraham as a symbol of hospitality. Instead of hospitality, Herzog[87] emphasizes the background of Abraham's wealth, implied by several Hebrew Bible passages (Gen. 13.2; 14.13-24; 23.13-16; 25.7-11). Because Abraham is also rich, it would be natural to consider the rich man as his kin. The shock value of the parable increases as the figure of Abraham, who supposedly represents the existing social order, is presented as an advocate of the poor. But would wealth really be the trait of Abraham that comes first to the mind of the reader? Besides, Abraham does not deny his kinship to the rich man. He would be willing to receive also the rich man, had he lived according to God's will.

86. *Parable*, pp. 153-54.
87. *Subversive Speech*, p. 130.

There is another important role for Abraham: he is the authoritative voice in the story who mediates God's judgment. Abraham's authority is emphasized by the fact that he gets the last word in the story. In this regard, Abraham resembles another father in another Lukan story: the father of the prodigal son. Both of them have the last word, just as Jesus usually has the last word in his controversies with religious leaders (cf. Lk. 14.6; 20.1-8, 26, 40). Abraham serves as a commentator inside the story explaining to the rich man what has happened and why. His role is to explain God's point of view. He does this not only to the rich man in the storyworld but also beyond it to Jesus' audience in the Lukan storyworld. And not only is he speaking to Jesus' audience, but also to Luke's audience, the readers. Thus, a threefold audience is gathered around him. First of all, there is the rich man listening to Abraham. Second, there is Jesus' audience in Luke listening to Jesus telling the story of a rich man listening to Abraham. And third, there is the reader who is reading Luke's story telling about the audience listening to Jesus telling the story of the rich man listening to Abraham. Abraham mediates the voice of God for all these audiences.

The Story as a Call to Repentance

The end of the parable consists of an exhortation and a warning aimed at the rich man's brothers: 'Abraham replied, "They have Moses and the prophets; they should listen to them." He said, "No, father Abraham; but if someone goes to them from the dead, they will repent." He said to him, "If they do not listen to Moses and the prophets, neither will they be convinced even if someone rises from the dead."'

A hortatory ending is another typical feature of Luke's parables, which often have an 'imperative intention'[88] to guide the readers into action. In the parable of the rich man and Lazarus, the action is repentance leading to generosity for the poor. In the Good Samaritan, the reader is guided to go and do likewise and love their neighbor (Lk. 10.30-37). In the Prodigal Son, the reader is encouraged to accept a repentant brother (Lk. 15.11-32). The reader is guided to use wealth wisely like the unjust steward (Lk. 16.1-8), not as the rich fool (Lk. 12.16-21), and to be humble like the tax-collector and not arrogant like the Pharisee (Lk. 18.9-14).

---

88. Goulder, *Luke*, I, p. 101.

The right kind of action is associated with the verb 'listen'. The theme of listening is constantly present in Luke–Acts (see Lk. 6.27, 47; 8.8-15, 18, 21; 9.35; 10.16, 39; 11.28; Acts 3.22, 23; 4.19; 28.28). The one who hears what Jesus says and does accordingly is like a wise man (Lk. 6.47-48). Those who listen to Jesus and obey him are his real family (Lk. 8.21). On the other hand, the parable teaches that those who do not hear Moses and the prophets will not believe in resurrection either. The law and the kingdom of God are linked together in Jesus' teaching (Lk. 16.16), which shows the Lukan view of salvation history. The 'right' kind of Jews are those who have piously obeyed the law and who have believed in John the Baptist. They are also likely to become followers of Jesus. The Scriptures bear witness to Jesus so that no other sign is needed.[89]

But how does Abraham's warning function in the story? How do the different audiences react to his words? We are not told how the rich man reacted, but, clearly, for him it is too late to repent. However, the parable is left open-ended as far as the fate of the brothers is concerned. Did they begin to listen to Moses and the prophets and repent? By leaving the end open, Luke suggests that there is still hope for the brothers. They still have time to repent and revalue their lives. This can hardly mean that Luke actually expects the brothers to begin to listen to what Moses and the prophets say. After all, they are figures in a parable. The open end serves as a rhetorical device to guide the listeners to reconsider their lives.

What about the people listening to Jesus? Who are they? Most scholars point out that they are Pharisees, as may be indicated by v. 14. There Luke blames the Pharisees for being lovers of money. This accusation, which can hardly be associated with the real Pharisees of Jesus' time, links the Pharisees closely with the rich man of the parable. Therefore, in Luke's view, the warning of the parable is suitable for them. On the other hand, in v. 1 the disciples are said to be Jesus' audience for the parable of the unjust steward. These two parables are linked together, for Luke describes the Pharisees overhearing the first parable aimed at the disciples (16.1-8). As the Pharisees get angry, Jesus turns to them and tells them the second parable (16.19-31). But the disciples do not go away; so now it is their turn to overhear a story.

---

89. Luke uses the verb διαμαρτυρέω in Acts as a technical term to refer to the apostles' witness of Jesus; cf. Acts 2.40; 8.25; 10.42; 18.5; 20.21, 24; 25.11; 28.23.

It seems that the parable has a double audience,[90] just like some other Lukan teachings (6.20-49; 8.4-8; 15.1-2; 20.45). The primary audience is the Pharisees (the rich), but there is also a secondary audience, the disciples (the poor). The parable functions well for both audiences. The other side of the warning to the rich is assurance for the poor. The message depends on whom the listener identifies with in the storyworld.

The story is told mainly from the rich man's point of view, perhaps because the Pharisees are the primary audience. In this way the Pharisees are led to identify themselves with the rich man and experience what their life is going to be like if they do not repent, if they do not share their goods with others. The same technique is used in the Good Samaritan. As the story is told from the point of view of the wounded, the lawyer has to identify himself with him, and in the end, admit that it is the Samaritan who is his neighbor.[91]

If the Pharisees are guided to identify themselves with the rich man, is Jesus wanting to lead them to identify with an outsider for whom there is no hope? Not necessarily. As the brothers of the rich man are introduced and as the dialogue concentrates on them, they offer a new point of identification. They are still alive, and they still have time to change—as have the Pharisees. Even though the fate of the rich man is sealed, Abraham does not treat him in a hostile way. In fact, there are some reasons for seeing also the rich man as an insider; after all he is still a child of Abraham, a member of the family. In this respect, the rich man resembles the older brother in the Prodigal Son. The difference between them is that the older brother has the chance to decide whether to go into the house and become an insider or not, while the rich man in this parable does not. But his brothers still have the chance. Also, the 'brother' language, the use of another kinship term, gives the suggestion of an interfamily affair.

Luke's portrayal of the Pharisees and the rich is negative, but his tone is more tragic than hostile.[92] Also, the rich can be saved, as the story of Zacchaeus shows.[93] Luke does not view the leaders as evil characters with no hope. The outsiders are seen as potential insiders.[94] This is

---

90. This kind of a double audience for the parables in ch. 16 is argued by Piper, 'Social Background', pp. 1641-42.

91. Sellin, 'Lukas als Gleichniserzähler', p. 24.

92. Cf. Piper, 'Social Background', p. 1643.

93. Tannehill, *Narrative Unity*, p. 107.

94. This is different from the Gospel of John, for example. There characters are

clearly evident in other Lukan parables, too. Both of the two debtors (Lk. 7.41-43) were loved, even though the one did not need as much forgiveness. Also the older brother was invited to come in (Lk. 15.11-32), even though he did not need repentance (cf. Lk. 15.7). In regard to the good Samaritan, the call for the reader to be an insider functions on another level of the story, for the lawyer who is first viewed negatively (10.25) is promised eternal life, if he lives according to the law. The same promise holds true for the rich man's brothers, but here the parable introduces a new twist: they need to repent.[95] In other words, not only are the despised accepted (the poor man, the Samaritan, the prodigal, the sinful woman) but also the 'honorable' ones are accepted (the rich man, the lawyer, the obedient brother, Simon the Pharisee)—if they live according to Moses and the prophets, who, in turn, point to Jesus (cf. Lk. 24.27, 44; Acts 28.23).

But how likely is it that the Pharisees would heed the parable and repent? And what would happen if they did repent? Would they become believers in Jesus? At least for a Christian reader—for whom Luke most probably wrote his Gospel—Abraham's last words include an allusion to Jesus' resurrection. Of course, it is impossible to expect the Pharisees in Luke's Gospel to believe in Jesus' resurrection, which has not even happened yet in the storyworld. These outsiders never become insiders. In Luke's ideological view, also the Pharisees have missed their chance. As v. 14 links them closely to the parable, the story suggests that actually the Pharisees are like the rich man in the parable. This is, of course, not stated explicitly but it is hard to avoid the impression that also the Pharisees ignore their neighbor and do not listen to what the Scriptures say. What explicitly is an exhortation to repent and to take care of the poor, hides an implicit ideological message of what the Pharisees are like.[96] An insurmountable chasm separates them from the true makers of the law, the followers of Jesus.

By alluding to Jesus' resurrection, Luke shows that he has his reader in mind all along. At the end of the parable, the different narrative levels merge into each other. The voice of Abraham and that of Jesus fade to the background to give space for Luke's voice and for his

portrayed as either insiders or outsiders according to their understanding or misunderstanding Jesus. For the outsiders not much hope is given; cf. Culpepper, *Anatomy*, p. 164. The same holds true with Mark's Gospel.

95. Cf. Piper, 'Social Background', p. 1661.
96. Cf. Syreeni, 'Gospel in Paradigms', p. 47.

message to his audience. The call to repentance is too late for the rich man. It is also too late for the Pharisees. Thus, the only ones who still have a real chance to change their lives and repent are the readers. For a Christian reader, the parable functions in two ways. On the one hand, it serves as an exhortation among insiders: repent and accept your brother while you still have time. On the other hand, it strengthens her or his view of Jesus' opponents, those who stubbornly stay outsiders.

Conclusions

Luke combines many of his favorite themes in the parable of the Rich Man and Lazarus. By making use of a reversal pattern, he deals with wealth and poverty and emphasizes the validity of the law. Most of all, he stresses the importance of repentance. A sign of true repentance of the rich is the right use of their possessions, sharing with those who have not. The parable serves as a warning for the rich and as an assurance for the poor. God is on the side of the poor and will pay them if the rich fail to accept them. Luke's story guides the reader to revalue their life and to act accordingly.

The characterization of the rich man and the poor man Lazarus also serves this purpose. Both characters are stereotypes of their representative groups; one with wealth, the other without it. The detailed description of them, with purple and linen, bleeding sores and licking dogs, creates an illusion of reality around them. As the characters are presented vividly, the reader is guided to get emotionally involved in their story. Showing what happens to these lifelike characters is a powerful rhetorical device. Its purpose is to lead the reader to right kind of action and to share Luke's ideological view. In this way the point of the parable is very similar to the overall point of Luke–Acts.

Luke's rhetorical use of characterization is not limited to his parables. Many of his other stories function similarly. The sinful woman, who is brave enough to enter among those who despise her in order to anoint Jesus, is an ideal model of one who loves, and she deserves the reader's sympathy and forgiveness. Zacchaeus, even if short in stature, shows his greatness through his change of conduct. Such paradigmatic characters occur frequently in Acts, too. There are positive examples, such as Stephen (6.8-7, 50), and the Ethiopian eunuch (8.26-40), as well as negative examples, such as Ananaias and Sapphira (5.1-11). Each of them gives a good or bad model of behavior. And in each case, by presenting the characters in a credible and memorable way, the narrator leads the reader to make a personal commitment to live according to the model given. Luke guides the reader carefully according to his own ideological intentions. The parables of the Lukan Jesus are a vital part of the ideological program of the evangelist. The persuasion is delicate, but it is so intense that it penetrates different narrative levels. The Lukan Jesus speaks in the Lukan voice and becomes an advocate of Luke's ideology, a tool to persuade the reader. Thus, while at the same time the readers admire Luke's masterly characterization and his narrative rhetoric, they should not ignore the narrator's deeper intentions, the ideological message of the story.

PETER AS CHARACTER AND SYMBOL
IN THE GOSPEL OF MATTHEW

Kari Syreeni

While Jesus is the main character of the Gospel narratives at large, Peter undoubtedly occupies the second most important role. This is especially true for Matthew's Gospel. Yet there seems to be 'a somewhat disconcerting inconsistency' in the Matthaean characterization of Peter.[1] Certainly, at the very least, there is a wide range of readerly responses to Matthew's presentation of Peter. While one reader sees in Matthew's portrayal of Peter as an authoritative teacher 'little more than a historicized literary cliché',[2] another reader argues that, at places, Peter 'approaches characterhood and even "personality"'.[3]

Peter's literary portrait poses a typical narrative-critical challenge, to be assessed by means of a theory of characterization.[4] But surely the

---

1.   R.E. Brown, K.P. Donfried and J. Reumann (eds.), *Peter in the New Testament* (Minneapolis: Augsburg; New York: Paulist Press, 1973), p. 107.

2.   K. Syreeni, 'Between Heaven and Earth: On the Structure of Matthew's Symbolic Universe', *JSNT* 40 (1990), pp. 3-13 (5). The present article will slightly modify and substantially detail the position taken there. The quotation concerns Matthew's presentation of Peter's authority on halachic issues. In this respect, my position has remained unaltered, but admittedly there is much more to Matthew's portrait of Peter than that.

3.   F.W. Burnett, 'Characterization and Reader Construction of Characters in the Gospels', *Semeia* 63 (1993), pp. 1-28 (22-23).

4.   As will appear, my application of the theory of characterization is somewhat heterodox. The major expositions of and contributions to the more customary narrative-critical theory of characterization include R. Scholes and R. Kellogg, *The Nature of Narrative* (Oxford: Oxford University Press, 1966), esp. pp. 160-206; S. Chatman, *Story and Discourse: Narrative Structure in Fiction and Film* (Ithaca, NY: Cornell University Press, 1978), esp. pp. 107-38; Baruch Hochman, *Character in Literature* (Ithaca, NY: Cornell University Press, 1985), esp. the taxonomy of characters, pp. 86-140; S. Rimmon-Kenan, *Narrative Fiction: Contemporary Poetics* (London: Methuen, 1988), esp. pp. 59-70; M. Bal, *Narratology: Introduction to*

character of Peter keeps intriguing readers for deeper, ideological reasons and is open to other approaches than narrative-critical ones. One is struck by the variety of interpretations in this respect, too. At the one extreme, there is the tradition—and redaction-historical claim that Peter the first apostle is the chief authority behind the first Gospel, so that the Gospel of Matthew is really 'the Gospel of Peter'.[5] At the other extreme, a recent deconstructionist reading suggests that Jesus' pronouncement to Peter in Mt. 16.13-20, historically interpreted to provide legitimacy for the church, paradoxically if unconsciously undermines the foundation of the entire Gospel. If the deconstructive endeavour is successful, we should be able to see 'both an institutional church in ruin and a Gospel in the process of self-deconstruction'.[6]

Clearly, both extreme interpretations fall beyond a strictly narrative-critical scope. Even the most rigorous analysis of the ways Peter is characterized in Matthew's Gospel will not provide ready answers to questions concerning Matthew's use and evaluation of previous traditions. Nor can narrative criticism protect the text world Matthew created against such 'wonders of distortion' as may be performed by readers with an overdose of bad faith.[7] This is no surprise, of course. A

---

the Theory of Narrative (trans. C. van Boheemen; Toronto: University of Toronto Press, 1985), esp. pp. 25-37, 79-93; M. Sternberg, *The Poetics of Biblical Narrative: Ideological Literature and the Drama of Reading* (Bloomington: Indiana University Press, 1985), esp. pp. 321-64; E.S. Malbon, 'Narrative Criticism: How Does the Story Mean?', in J.C. Anderson and S.D. Moore (eds.), *Mark and Method: New Approaches in Biblical Studies* (Minneapolis: Fortress Press, 1992), pp. 23-49 (28-30). The otherwise useful book by R.W. Funk, *The Poetics of Biblical Narrative* (Sonoma, CA: Polebridge Press, 1988), is one-sidedly action-oriented and thus less pertinent to the theory of characterization.

5. W. Schenk, 'Das Matthäusevangelium als Petrusevangelium', *BZ* 27 (1983), pp. 58-80 (72). Schenk here quotes with approval C. Kähler, 'Zur Form- und Traditionsgeschichte von Matth. 16.17-19', *NTS* 23 (1976–77), pp. 36-58 (57).

6. W.W. Bubar, 'Killing Two Birds with One Stone: The Utter De(con)-struction of Matthew and his Church', *BibInt* (1995), pp. 144-57 (156-57).

7. Cf. Sternberg, *The Poetics of Biblical Narrative*, p. 50. Sternberg there discusses 'foolproof composition', which he thinks is typical of biblical (or Old Testament) texts at large. Matthew's Gospel as a whole exemplifies foolproof composition fairly well; its message is transparent enough and its theological bias is unmistakable. The portrayal of Peter is much more opaque and contradictory, however, and especially Mt. 16.13-20 suggests that Bubar's interpretation need not be a mere counter-reading; but certainly it is an overreading.

method necessarily has its limits; without limits there would be no identifiable methods.

However, the historical and theological implications of Matthew's
portrayal of Peter are too far-reaching to be left totally out of the scope
of narrative critical analyses. Therefore an attempt will be ventured
here to correlate the narrative-critical question of the characterization of
Peter with other exegetical methods.[8] The approach here will make use
of a three-world model of reality—a general hermeneutical framework
expounded elsewhere in more detail—although no knowledge of this
model is presupposed in what follows.[9] The main methodological
concern is to show that the narrative-critical approach itself calls for a
wider interpretative framework. However, the ultimate goal is not a
methodological one. Rather, the goal is simply to contribute to a better
understanding of how and why Peter is characterized in Matthew's text
the way he is.

Methodological Issues: Character, Symbol, Person

Mirror, Mirror: Mimetic Illusions

Narrative critics, and literary critics in general, are accustomed to
thinking in terms of the binary distinction between 'text' and 'reality'.

8. All customary exegetical tools, such as tradition and redaction criticism,
will be used here to the extent they serve to illuminate the main narrative-critical
issue. It is interesting that a recent redaction-critically oriented study by A.J. Nau,
*Peter in Matthew: Discipleship, Diplomacy, and Dispraise—with an Assessment of
Power and Privilege in the Petrine Office* (Good News Studies, 36; Collegeville,
MN: Liturgical Press, 1992), shares many of the conclusions reached in the present
article.

9. For an exposition of the three-world model, see my 'The Gospel in
Paradigms: A Study in the Hermeneutical Space of Luke–Acts', in P. Luomanen
(ed.), *Luke–Acts: Scandinavian Perspectives* (PFES, 54; Helsinki: Suomen Ekse-
geettinen Seura; Göttingen: Vandenhoeck & Ruprecht, 1991), pp. 36-57; 'Separation and Identity: Aspects of the Symbolic World of Matt 6. 1-18', *NTS* 40 (1994),
pp. 522-41; 'Metaphorical Appropriation: (Post-)Modern Biblical Hermeneutic and
the Theory of Metaphor', *Literature and Theology* 9.3 (1995), pp. 321-38. See also
P. Luomanen, 'Entering the Kingdom of Heaven: A Study on the Structure of
Matthew's View of Salvation' (Dissertation, University of Helsinki, 1996), esp.
pp. 32-38. Luomanen's work is the first full-length monograph on Matthew applying aspects of the three-world model as a general theoretical framework. It is typical
of the model that Luomanen in his detailed analysis combines narrative-critical and
social-scientific methods to approach Matthew's symbolic universe.

Typical of this innate dichotomy is the definition by Robert Scholes and Robert Kellogg in their *The Nature of Narrative*.[10]

> Meaning, in a work of narrative art, is a function of the relationship between two worlds: the fictional world created by the author and the 'real' world, the apprehendable universe. When we say we 'understand' a narrative we mean that we have found a satisfactory relationship or a set of relationships between these two worlds.

Were the 'fictional world' in this definition consequently understood as containing both the literary and the ideological creation, most of the shortcomings of the two-world model could be avoided or compensated for. There has been, however, a remarkable reluctance among literary critics to deal with the ideology of the text. Two major lines of thought have converged to produce this reluctance. A long aesthetic tradition suggests that ideological concerns only stain the artistic purity of literature. Along with this puristic conception of literature goes the mimetic tradition, which views narrative as imitation of real life. Both traditions, taken together, result in focusing on 'pure' text-world phenomena in their relationship to the 'real' world.

And why not indeed focus on these two worlds? The aesthetic-mimetic reduction has an undeniable prima facie appeal, and narrative texts with their 'characters' are the most powerful instance of this appeal. While in real life we meet persons, in the narrative world we encounter their literary representatives, the characters. It is only too natural to juxtapose the two and take a character for a person's mirror image: not quite the person, but similar enough to make a pair. It seems even more so with a factual character such as Peter, perhaps in part because of the presence of the proper name. A factual character, having a reference to a real historical figure and even bearing the same name, is truly a powerful image. It is suggestive not only of an irreducible identity of the character and the person, but also of a secret reference that ties together the real person and the one named after him in the narrative world.[11]

10. Scholes and Kellogg, *The Nature of Narrative*, p. 82.

11. For proper names and the mystery of identity, see, e.g., Sternberg, *The Poetics of Biblical Narrative*, pp. 330-31, and Burnett, 'Characterization', pp. 17-18. The term 'secret reference' comes from T. Moore and C. Carling, *The Limitations of Language* (London: Macmillan, 1988); see esp. Chapters 5 ('Secret Reference: A Grand Illusion?') and 6 ('Words and Things: A Second Secret Reference'), pp. 31-44.

But can we really assume such a secret identity between Peter the man and Peter the character? Surely narrative critics have warned against this mimetic illusion in many and various ways, reminding us that the inhabitants of the text world, 'imitation' though there may be, are 'fantasy, fabricated creatures; paper people, without flesh and blood'.[12] We are told that these creatures range from 'round' to 'flat' characters, to stock people, and to anonymous, even non-human actors who function as mere exponents of the plot.[13] We are even told that a character such as Peter in Matthew's text 'fluctuates' between a type and a fully developed character.[14] Such reminders should make it clear that there is a substantial gap between person and character, a gap huge enough methodologically to warrant an intervening instance.

Recognizing the gap in a narrative, we are perhaps tempted to fill it with additional personlike (or characterlike) entities, namely the implied author or the narrator. The temptation is understandable, for it is true that Peter the character was created by a living person, an author, and was not simply brought about by an inanimate duplicator. In other words, the category of *poiesis* is needed to complement the other basic Aristotelian concept of *mimesis*. Unfortunately, the Aristotelian concepts still make it possible to understand *poiesis* narrowly as a matter of technique, as if creative production were just a sculptor's skill in manufacturing a realistic text-world image.

With the introduction of the author into consideration, the whole issue of authorial intent would come up, to the aesthetic critic's dismay. It was a fine compromise when Wayne C. Booth coined the term 'the implied author'. According to Booth, the concept would enable the critic to discuss the moral values and ideological tenets of the text without directly referring to the real author.[15] But then another chain of

12. Bal, *Narratology*, p. 80. Bal, too, observes the mimetic bias that resists attempts at drawing a clear dividing line between human person and character: 'The resemblance between the two is too great for that: we even go so far as to identify with the character, to cry, to laugh, and to search for or with it.'

13. A fuller discussion of 'round', 'flat' and 'stock' figures is given in Lehtipuu's article earlier in this volume.

14. Burnett, 'Characterization', pp. 18-23.

15. W.C. Booth, *The Rhetoric of Fiction* (Chicago: University of Chicago Press, 2nd edn, 1983), pp. 67-77. The mimetic logic of the concept is still seen in his paraphrases of the implied author as the author's 'second self' or implied image. Other approximations of the concept discussed by Booth are 'style' and 'technique'

mirrors emerged from 'real author' via 'implied author' to 'narrator' and 'characters'. These mirror images are somewhat illusory, for apparently 'implied author' and 'narrator' are hard to distinguish in the Gospel narrative,[16] while 'narrator', especially from the reader's perspective, can even be seen as a special case of 'character'.[17] Then we are again left with the basic dichotomy between real world and text world. This time it is not treated simply as a mimetic illusion; there is an additional poietic element to it. But behind the poietic relationship between creator (author) and creation (character) there still lurks a mimetic anthropomorphic illusion, to the effect that creator and creation are of the same kind.

Put otherwise—in terms of intentionality and communication—the poietic-mimetic illusion suggests two analogical worlds: the actual world and the narrative world, both of which have people/characters communicating with each other. This two-world image suggests that the real world is people in action, and that the artistic creation imitates the real world by showing people in action. But such an action movie world is hardly the best point of departure for assessing the symbolic depth dimension of both the empirical and the artistic reality. There is an intervening instance between the actual world where the author is situated and the fictional world that the characters inhabit. In order to

(p. 74), which are farther away from the mimetic imagery. The ideological tone becomes evident when Booth discusses the implied author's 'values', 'various commitments' and 'combinations of norms' (p. 71). Thus, for instance, 'the implied Shakespeare is thoroughly engaged with life, and he does not conceal his judgment of the selfish, the foolish, and the cruel' (p. 76). For Booth, the implied author's (moral) values naturally lead to the issue of readerly responses; see his *The Company We Keep: An Ethics of Fiction* (Berkeley: University of California Press, 1988). In spite of his interest in the ethical dimension of literature, Booth remains within the confines of the aesthetic (or rather aesthetic-didactic) tradition; the ethical critic's task is 'to help us avoid ... miseducation' (*Ethics of Fiction*, p. 477). An ideological critic, however, will have to go beyond the issue of (good or bad) taste.

16. Cf. Funk, *The Poetics of Biblical Narrative*, p. 29. To Funk, the real author, the implied author, and the teller within the narrative itself are the three 'facets' or 'masks' of the narrator. For more discussion of author/implied author/narrator, see Rimmon-Kenan, *Narrative Fiction*, pp. 94-103, and Merenlahti's and Hakola's joint article in this volume.

17. Cf. J.A. Darr, 'Narrator as Character: Mapping a Reader-oriented Approach to Narration in Luke–Acts', *Semeia* 63 (1993), pp. 43-60.

do justice to this depth dimension of reality, we need to add a new level of analysis—a whole new *world* to be studied.[18]

Three Levels of Analysis

The above discussion has led us to assume (1) a poietic axis between author and reader and a mimetic axis between text and reality[19] and (2) three levels of analysis: the text world, the concrete world, and an intervening interpretive level—in more daring words, an ideological intervention.[20] Figure 1 (p. 114) illustrates this theoretical framework. In fact, a threefold distinction (mainly along the mimetic axis) was already articulated by Scholes and Kellogg when they spoke of the ways in which 'illustrative, representational, and esthetic elements' are combined in characterization. The main point in Scholes' and Kellogg's discussion is the difference between illustration and representation. Alternative descriptions for these principal terms are given generously, for instance: 'The illustrative is symbolic; the representational is mimetic.'[21]

According to Scholes and Kellogg, in representational/mimetic (or empirical, realistic) narrative, characters are an attempt to create 'a

18.   It provides no remedy for the mimetic two-world view to stress the mutual interdependence of the two worlds and to urge readers to imagination, artistic emotion, and participation in the possible world of fiction, as does D. Maitre, *Literature and Possible Worlds* (London: Middlesex Polytechnic Press, 1983). In Maitre's view, her account is sufficient to challenge the mimesis theory: 'Works of art, rather than imitating the world as it is, imitate the world as it might or could be—but this is to give a rather attenuated or even distorted use to the term "imitate"; for possible worlds do not so much represent what is, as present what could be for the first time. In fact the superimposition of the fictional world on the actual world creates new meaning for the actual world on the model of metaphor-making ...' (pp. 118-19). What remains hidden here—as a hermeneutical blind spot—is the symbolic creation or, in terms of the metaphor model, the creation of the tertium (comparationis). It may not be incidental, then, that biblical texts and characters are absent from Maitre's discussion; instead, the index has entries for fairy stories, fantasy, ghost stories, talking animals, Cinderella, Winnie the Pooh, etc.

19.   For the necessity of simultaneously viewing both directions, see T. Todorov, *Theories of the Symbol* (trans. Catherine Porter; Oxford: Basil Blackwell, 1982), pp. 285-92. Todorov describes the crucial move from classicism to romanticism as a shift in attention from imitation to production.

20.   Cf. S. van Tilborg, *The Sermon on the Mount as an Ideological Intervention: A Reconstruction of Meaning* (Assen: Van Gorcum, 1986).

21.   Scholes and Kellogg, *The Nature of Narrative*, p. 100.

replica of actuality'. A factual character in a diarist's or a historian's account is the most rudimentary example of representational character, but even a fictional character like Robinson Crusoe presents an individual 'whose most important attribute is that he may pass for real'. This specific representation may shade into a more generalized kind of mimesis dominated by the notion of the typical; Crusoe is also 'a type of the middle class man'. Beyond the notion of typicality the mimetic function gives way to illustration, which 'does not seek to reproduce actuality but to present selected aspects of the actual, essences referable for their meaning not to historical, psychological, or sociological truth but to ethical and metaphysical truth'.[22] In other words, illustrative characters give utterance to ethical values and ideological concepts.

Scholes and Kellogg keenly point to various combinations in which an author deliberately straddles 'this precipitous border between the illustrative and the representational' and 'works on both sides of the gap'.[23] But a careful reader will observe that they assume yet another gap between the illustrative and the aesthetic. Thus, for instance, an able allegorist in creating a 'mixture of representational, illustrative, and purely esthetic qualities' must have 'a deep commitment to ideas, balanced by an esthetic commitment to the art of narrative'.[24] Such statements are clearly suggestive of a methodology that reckons with three levels: representational, ideological, and aesthetic levels of analysis. With little imagination the levels can be seen as three worlds: the concrete world of everyday reality, the symbolic world of values and ideas, and the aesthetic world of narrative.

Meaning, we recall, according to Scholes and Kellogg is *a relation between worlds* (and we now have three of them). This seems sensible, but two things must be added. First, relations *within* one specific world also contribute to meaning. Thus, for instance, relations within the text world of Matthew's Gospel have an *intratextual* meaning in terms of characterization, temporal sequences and plot development.[25] Second,

22. Scholes and Kellogg, *The Nature of Narrative*, pp. 84-86, 88.
23. Scholes and Kellogg, *The Nature of Narrative*, p. 89.
24. Scholes and Kellogg, *The Nature of Narrative*, p. 108. Cf. also p. 109: 'The illustrative may be combined with the representational, as in Dante and Joyce, or with the esthetic, as in Spenser.'
25. Scholes and Kellogg prefer not to speak of 'meaning' in the sense of intratextuality (coherence) or intertextuality (relations between texts). The aesthetic tradition seems operative here, because, according to them, 'pure' literature should be

relations between specific worlds *on the same level of analysis* must be reckoned with. Thus, the text world of Matthew's Gospel has *intertextual* relations with its predecessor, Mark's Gospel. The same holds true for symbolic and real worlds respectively. The elements of Matthew's symbolic world must be assumed to have some inner coherence, and obviously there are connections between Matthew's ideology and other early Jewish and Christian thought-worlds. By the same token, the real world around Matthew has some coherence (a network of people, sites, etc.) and stands in relation to other historical settings, including the everyday life of his modern readers.

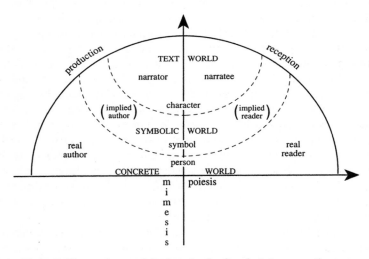

Figure 1. *The two axes and the three levels of analysis in a narrative text*

conceived in terms of being, not meaning (*The Nature of Narrative*, pp. 84-85). This tenet leads to rather surprising conclusions. Scholes and Kellogg name a romance adventure with its 'highly patterned and virtually meaningless configurations' as a near equivalent of 'pure' literature. It follows that the purest kind of literature is that which is meaningless, and that cheap novels are literature *par excellence*! At the same time, the reference to 'highly patterned … configurations' reveals that even the most 'meaningless' text has an *intertextual* meaning as a representative of a genre. The reader may know the hero of a romance adventure beforehand, as the hero of previous similar texts, by recognition of a general type (e.g. the lonely rider) and/or a uniting proper name (e.g. Zorro).

In sum, following the hints from Scholes and Kellogg, we arrive at a three-world scheme where the ideological level of reality is given its due.[26] The meaning and the means of characterization are thus related to:

(1) the narrative world (intra—and intertextuality);
(2) the symbolic world (authorial/traditional/readerly ideology);
(3) the real world (authorial/historical/contemporary concrete reality).

In this scheme, Peter is (1) a character in Matthew's Gospel, having an intratextual meaning within Matthew's story and an intertextual meaning as a Gospel character in relation to the Markan story; (2) a symbol for ethical values, doctrinal options, social and religious commitments, party strifes, or the like; (3) a historical person, whose contribution to the Matthaean character is indirect but vital; he is the *sine qua non* of all subsequent historical developments.

We have seen that a three-level mode of analysis can be deduced from Scholes' and Kellogg's understanding of narrative. Other narrative-critical theories, such as Seymour Chatman's elaborate structural model in his *Story and Discourse*, are more resistant to such reformulation. Chatman defines character as 'a paradigm of traits'.[27] According to him, the readerly construction of a character's traits 'does not seem to differ in kind from our ordinary evaluations of human beings that we meet in the real world'.[28] This remark is well in keeping with the dualistic conception. No doubt a reader's perception of character resembles, to a degree, the way one is likely to construct personality in real life. However, this analogy itself presupposes an intermediary instance where both text-world and real-life entities are *interpreted*. The interpretive level often remains transparent enough to pass unnoticed; we do not always recognize the ideological intervention. Yet, if a person in

26. In my terminology, 'ideology' is a neutral term referring to a relatively firm and stable set of interconnected features within a symbolic universe. It does not necessarily imply 'a false consciousness', even though some ideologies may be criticized for distorting or neglecting important aspects of concrete reality.

27. Chatman, *Story and Discourse*, p. 126. Cf. Rimmon-Kenan, *Narrative Fiction*, p. 59 ('a network of character-traits').

28. Chatman, *Story and Discourse*, p. 128. In fact, however, there are notable dissimilarities in the way one constructs a character and a real person. A reader familiar with the genre of a romance adventure may adequately construct the villain and other characters of the story from a few hints. If one assesses persons in real life with similar ease, one is simply prejudiced.

real life or a character in the text world is said to be 'Satan', as the
Matthaean Peter is (Mt. 16.23), we are likely to pay attention to the
ideology behind the utterance. In such cases, we recognize that there is
a third entity between character and person, namely an ideological
symbol.

Character and/as Symbol
If, then, Peter can be viewed as character and symbol in Matthew's
Gospel, how are the two aspects connected? Are we to imagine two
Peters, a text-world character and a symbolic-world figure, only united
by the proper name? Obviously not. Insofar as Peter the symbol is
manifested in and through Peter the character, there must be an intimate
relationship between the two.

The togetherness of text world and symbolic world is, to a certain
degree, comparable to the union of a person's everyday world and symbolic universe.[29] In both cases there is an experienced more-or-less-
unity in the form of one, interpreted world—a 'world-that-makes-
sense'. Yet, sometimes a person's real-world-that-makes-sense unexpectedly splits: a gap emerges between the real world and the way it is
supposed to make sense. Reality is at odds with ideology. Not much
differently, the narrated-interpreted textual reality usually holds together as a 'text-that-makes-sense' but may suddenly fall apart. The
text does not make sense as it goes, or it suggests too much hidden
sense to be a mere text world. The ideological intervention is too heavy:
the text loses its supposed integrity.

The fragile unity of the narrated-interpreted world is closest to the
breaking point in the Gospel of John, where scholars often speak of
'narrative symbolism' or 'symbolic narratives'.[30] The Johannine text

29. Note the terminology. 'Symbolic universe' as a term comes from Berger's
and Luckmann's sociology-of-knowledge approach, which is one of the corner-
stones of the three-world model. It refers to what is basically a social construct (a
person's or a group's world-view) objectified in the concrete life. 'Symbolic world',
on the other hand, comes from a literary approach and refers to an entity objectified
in a literary (or other artistic) product. This double terminology is instructive when,
for instance, a community's ideology has changed after the production of a document. Matthew's and his community's symbolic universe made its way into the
Gospel as its symbolic world; but the community's world-view may not have
remained quite the same in the decades to come.

30. See D.A. Lee, *The Symbolic Narratives of the Fourth Gospel: The Interplay
of Form and Meaning* (JSNTSup, 95; Sheffield: JSOT Press, 1994), esp. pp. 11-35.

affects readers in different ways. Some readers find in the close unity of narrative and symbolic meaning the miracle of incarnation: the Johannine narratives are not signs of something absent but symbols that bring to expression a present reality. Other readers prefer to deconstruct the alleged unity and find much confusion and elements of harsh dualism.[31] In Matthew, the stilling of the storm (Mt. 8.23-27) is a prime example of a narrative with palpable symbolism: the narrative world is suggestive of a symbolic vision of reality that interprets both the narrative situation and the situation of Matthew's contemporary readers.[32] Another celebrated example in Matthew is the motif of the mountain. Far from providing a mere existent or a setting-element in the text world, 'the mountain' in Matthew is a loaded ideological symbol.[33]

In non-theological language, the issue of narrative and ideological unity vs. duality parallels the distinction between 'sign' and 'symbol' or between 'metaphoric' and 'metonymic'. Is Peter the character only an arbitrary narrative 'sign' of a symbolic-world entity, or is he the visible (readable) part of a fuller entity, Peter the symbolic character? Or, to put it bluntly, are there two Peters in Matthew or are they one flesh? Let us assume, as an initial compromise, that Peter the narrative character and Peter the ideological symbol are something like twin brothers. But, as it happens with twins, the interconnection may in principle range from non-identical to identical and Siamese twins. How it is with the Matthaean Peter(s) remains to be examined.

Lee herself favours the term 'symbolic narratives' and defines these rather narrowly as six passages in John where 'a common narrative structure is discernible which revolves around a central symbol' (p. 12).

31. Contrast Lee's (*The Symbolic Narratives of the Fourth Gospel, passim*) incarnational enthusiasm (oneness of form and symbolic meaning) and search for an authentic reader response (faith) with S.D. Moore's deconstruction of Johannine water symbolism, e.g., in his *Literary Criticism and the Gospels: The Theoretical Challenge* (New Haven: Yale University Press, 1989), pp. 159-63.

32. Cf. my 'Metaphorical Appropriation', p. 328.

33. For 'the mountain' as a theological (ideological) symbol in Matthew, see T.L. Donaldson, *Jesus on the Mountain: A Study in Matthew's Theology* (JSNTSup, 8; Sheffield: JSOT Press, 1985). K.C. Hanson's 'Transformed on the Mountain: Ritual Analysis and the Gospel of Matthew', *Semeia* 67 (1994), pp. 147-70, approaches the mountain scenes from a wider cultural anthropological point of view, with emphasis on the ritual aspects of the mountain symbolism (see also P.F. Esler's response in the same volume 'Mountaineering in Matthew: A Response to K.C. Hanson', pp. 171-77).

Characterization, Symbolization and the Layered Structure of Reality
In principle, the historical Peter is one contributor to the Matthaean character that bears his name. His personal impact is mediated through the stories about him and the symbolic meaning he had in the minds of Matthew and his readers. This mediation is complicated by the layered structure of reality. Textual and symbolic reality is layered through countless turns of intertextuality and intersymbolism. The structure of layers tends to confuse the boundaries between the worlds.

When a character gives utterance to an ideological stance, it is not a priori evident whether the ideology is only a text-world feature (Matthew reproduces and develops the 'paper-ideology' of the Markan character in order to make a better story), a symbiosis of literary and symbolic contributions (Peter is made to represent Matthew's own ideology through the use and development of the Markan character), or a still more complex bundle of contributions (e.g. Peter represents Matthew's ideology indirectly by representing a false or defective ideological stance criticized and modified by Matthew in the story itself). Hence the means of indirection, notably the various shades of irony, must be carefully analysed. Not all ideological elements plainly indicate the authorial ideology. Some elements may be in literary use as text-world ingredients; other elements may convey the authorial stance by way of contradiction or modification; still other elements may reveal a genuine but optional use of a scheme;[34] and ultimately some elements reflect the author's firm ideology.

Besides the vertical layered structure between textual, symbolic and concrete reality, there is the horizontal layered structure between author, work and reader. While the vertical axis is the line of meaning, that is, the function of the relationship between the worlds, the horizontal axis is the highway of communication (creation, transmission and exchange of meaning). Analogy—underlying representation—is the basic feature of the vertical axis, while causality and intentionality are the basic horizontal forces. Yet the axes intersect in such a way that analogy and causality seldom appear in pure forms.

One specific case of such impurity is the fact that a character may assume a *shadow function* on the vertical axis by being suggestive of some aspects of the (implied) reader on the horizontal axis.[35] According

---

34. For 'scheme' as a conventional element of ideology, see my 'Separation and Identity', pp. 531-37.
35. Generally speaking, 'shadow' is the function of a character as a partial text-

to Ulrich Luz, the disciples in Matthew take on a shadow function in relation to the reader. In Luz's vocabulary, the disciples are 'transparent' characters who are so typified as to be models for Christians in Matthew's community.[36] Thereby Luz opposes Georg Strecker's thesis, according to which Jesus and the disciples in Matthew are 'historicized' characters set in an unrepeatable, holy past; that is, they only represent the historical Jesus and his original followers.[37] Obviously the two interpretations are not mutually exclusive. Luz, too, admits that the disciples in Matthew also stand for the historical apostles; and Strecker's interpretation allows for a mythic relationship between the narrative characters and the present readers (the 'holy past' is to be actualized and re-enacted in the community). The question remains, however, to what extent and in which ways the mimetic element is bound to historical representation and to the shadow function. The

world representative of the author or the reader. The character may function as the reader's shadow by presenting a recognizable similarity to their symbolic universe, but the similarity may also be less comprehensive and non-ideological. The 'shadow' function concerns only references to the author or the reader as is suggested by the linear metaphor (the shadow is cast 'forward' or 'backward'). Other analogical relations between characters and concrete persons may be described in terms of the characters' 'representative' functions. The peculiarity of the 'shadow' function lies with the fact that normally the author and the reader should not be found within the story proper. Shadow functions are a means of enhancing readerly involvement and directing the reader's responses.

36. U. Luz, 'The Disciples in the Gospel According to Matthew', in G. Stanton (ed.), *The Interpretation of Matthew* (Issues in Religion and Theology, 3; Philadelphia: Fortress Press: London: SPCK, 1983), pp. 98-127. As to Peter, Luz offers an overall interpretation in the second volume of his commentary to Matthew (*Das Evangelium nach Matthäus* [EKKNT, 1.2; 3 vols.; Zürich: Benziger Verlag; Neukirchen–Vluyn: Neukirchener Verlag, 1990], II, pp. 467-71). Luz finds in Matthew's Peter a mixture of individual and typical traits (p. 468: 'Die Verbindung des Einmaligen und des Typischen'); thus Peter is not wholly 'transparent' in Luz's view. (Cf. also Luz, *Matthew in History: Interpretation, Influence, and Effects* [Minneapolis: Fortress Press, 1994], pp. 57-74.) On the other hand, Luz has recently pushed the idea of 'transparency' in Matthew still further: the Gospel as a whole is transparent for the history of Matthew's community (*Die Jesusgeschichte des Matthäus* [Neukirchen–Vluyn: Neukirchener Verlag, 1993], pp. 75-79). One may ask how useful a concept 'transparency' is in this widest use.

37. G. Strecker, 'The Concept of History in Matthew', in Stanton (ed.), *The Interpretation of Matthew*, pp. 67-84.

layered nature of reality and of communication suggests that the answer may be complex indeed.

Sequential Analysis: Characterization and Symbolization of Peter in Matthew

In the following sequential analysis of the Petrine scenes in Matthew both text-world and symbolic-world observations will be made simultaneously. This is advisable because of the interwovenness, not the identity, of character and symbol. As segments of the narrative, the Petrine scenes offer cumulative insights into the character Peter. Little by little the reader will learn his individual traits and how the character contributes to the unfolding plot. The cumulative process is also vital to the interpreter's understanding of the symbolic values attached to Peter. In order for a character to be perceived by the reader as a symbol, a character such as Peter has to reappear on several occasions.[38] Gathering the hints, the interpreter gradually becomes aware of the presence of symbolism, learns to pose relevant questions, and eventually reproduces the set of ideological values and suggested pragmatic responses that make up the symbolic content of the character's presentation.[39]

---

38. In aesthetic and literary theories, it is often suggested that an object can only become a symbol through recurrence or prominence in a work of art. Recurrence is the main principle in R. Wellek and A. Warren, *Theory of Literature* (New York: Harcourt Brace & World, 3rd edn, 1956), esp. p. 189. Both recurrence and prominence count in M.C. Beardsley, *Aesthetics: Problems in the Philosophy of Criticism* (New York: Harcourt, 1958), esp. pp. 406-408. But outside artistic literature the more usual development is that a real-world object (e.g. the cross) or person (Jesus, Peter) takes on symbolic depth and only secondarily becomes a literary entity (a narrative existent). Hence the symbolism, or part of it, may be an inherited feature in the text world. In the Gospels, Jesus—as the Christ, Son of Man, Kyrios, etc.—is a character with symbolic depth already in his first appearance, no matter how flatly the narrator presents him. So, too, is Peter in the four Gospels, even if to a lesser degree.

39. My analysis presupposes the two-source theory, even though I avoid building too much on it. I also assume that the implied reader knew (something of) Mark's Gospel and the Sayings Gospel Q, but I will not speculate on the possibility of purposeful intertextuality (i.e. the possibility that Matthew's implied reader is supposed to pay attention to the dis/similarities between the present text and Mark/Q). Methodologically, narrative criticism includes the reader's perspective to a certain degree. A more reader-oriented approach has its distinctive problems. Cf. H. Frankemölle, 'Johannes der Täufer und Jesus im Matthäusevangelium: Jesus als

The First Disciples (4.18-22)
As in the Markan story, Peter enters Matthew's Gospel at the point
where Jesus begins his public ministry and calls his first disciples. This
position marks Peter in a double way. Unlike John the Baptist, Peter
appears as a character only through Jesus' action. He is a follower of
Jesus; his childhood or pre-Gospel life has no bearing on Matthew's
story. But from the very start of Jesus' public career[40] he occupies a
prominent role among the followers. The reader will observe that Peter
is mentioned first, before his brother and the second pair of brothers.

Yet Matthew does not underline Peter's special role more than the
Markan story does. Unlike Mark (1.16), he does mention the double
name of Simon Peter (Σίμωνα τὸν λεγόμενον Πέτρον, 4.18), but in this
context it hardly brings anything new to the portrait of Peter. In fact, at
16.18, it only adds to the confusion of the reader. The name 'Peter' is
first introduced as an ordinary name (τὸν λεγόμενον). Later on, it
appears to be an honorific name, given—or at least interpreted—by
Jesus himself.[41]

Nachfolger des Täufers', *NTS* 42 (1996), pp. 196-218 (202-204). For instance, the
principle of 'successive reading' (*sukzessives Lesen*, p. 203; cf. my 'virgin reader'
or 'first-time reader') is vulnerable in so far as it precludes many possible and plausible, even intended, readerly conventions (handbook use, pericope reading, etc.). A
formalist concept of reader is advocated by R.A. Edwards, *Matthew's Narrative
Portrait of Disciples: How the Text-Connoted Reader Is Informed* (Harrisburg, PA:
Trinity Press International, 1997). To judge from Edwards's analysis, the 'text-connoted reader' is ideologically blind.

40. It is less advisable to view the calling of the first disciples as the conclusion
of the Matthaean Vorgeschichte; thus H. Frankemölle, *Matthäus: Kommentar* (2
vols.; Düsseldorf: Patmos Verlag, 1994), I, p. 197. This interpretation would lend
more symbolic weight to Peter as a 'primordial' character who must be introduced
before the story can properly begin. However, in Matthew's outline, the transition
from pre-(hi)story to story proper is more plausibly to be drawn between 4.17 and
4.18. The temptation of Jesus—the final preparatory test—is completed at 4.11; the
fulfillment citation is given at 4.15-16; the decisive narrative marker ἀπὸ τότε is
launched, and the summary of Jesus' public proclamation is given at 4.17. Moreover, the calling of the first disciples and the healings at 4.23-25 belong closely
together, introducing as they do the double audience of Jesus' first speech (NB the
chiastic order: disciples 4.18-22/ crowds 4.23-25/ crowds 5.1a/ disciples 5.1b).

41. One may, of course, argue that the mention of the double name in 4.18
anticipates the name-giving episode. The *first-time* reader, however, will have a
hard time recognizing any salvation-historical depth in the name 'Peter' in this
context. Apart from the *general* symbolism of Peter's name ('Peter' means 'Rock'),

Another Matthaean nuance is the prominence of the theme of brotherhood. Before Peter is mentioned, the reader is told that Jesus saw two brothers (δύο ἀδελφούς). The same phrase is found at v. 21 (Jesus saw ἄλλους δύο ἀδελφούς). The use of the phrase twice tends to diminish the impact of the fact that Peter is mentioned first. That is, Jesus first sees two brothers, not Peter alone. Whether or not 'brother' here has symbolic depth as a term for community solidarity (Christian 'brotherhood') is impossible to determine. Such a symbolization is near at hand for a reader who thinks of the call story in relation to the community speech (Mt. 18), but nothing in the calling story as such makes this interpretation cogent. What seems more obvious here is Peter's representational (vis-à-vis the historical real world) function as one of the 'founding brothers'.

Peter and the rest of the 'brothers' also have a representational function within Matthew's text world. According to 5.1, 'the disciples' came to Jesus to hear his sermon. Actually the reader has only been informed of Peter, Andrew and the two sons of Zebedee; now, all of a sudden, 'the disciples' appear on the scene. Matthew hardly meant that only the four named disciples were around Jesus. More likely the two pairs of brothers are representative of a larger group of disciples. This *pars pro toto* representation looks natural enough in the reader's eye because Matthew has juxtaposed the brothers who at once 'followed' Jesus (4.20, 22) and the great crowds who 'followed' Jesus from all corners of Palestine (4.25).[42] The mention of a great mass of followers effectively creates the impression that other disciples were called, too. Hence the reader will probably not be puzzled by the appearance of a larger group of disciples. Yet it is symptomatic of Matthew's symbolic preferences that these four disciples were given such an inner-text-world representational role.

Matthew's addition τὸν λεγόμενον Πέτρον sounds as trivial as the parallel remark τὸν ἀδελφὸν αὐτοῦ after Andrew's name. Nau (*Peter in Matthew*, p. 70 n. 4) considers it to be 'a case of the 'Matthew 16.17-19 syndrome' in action' to take 'Peter' in 4.18 or 10.2 as a title, not just a proper name.

42. The importance of the theme of 'following' Jesus in the pericope is often noticed; see, e.g., E. Schweizer, *Das Evangelium nach Matthäus* (NTD, 2; Göttingen: Vandenhoeck & Ruprecht, 1981), p. 42.

Peter's Mother-in-Law (8.14-15)

Peter's first appearance in Matthew was voiceless but full of action. The second time he enters the stage he is both voiceless and somewhat invisible. Even his presence on the occasion of his mother-in-law's healing remains conjectural. Jesus entered Peter's house, but the reader is not told whether Peter went there with Jesus or was already there to receive Jesus or indeed whether he was even at home during the healing.

In Mark the narrative opens clumsily: Jesus 'entered the house of Simon and Andrew, with James and John' (Mk 1.29), which obviously means that Simon (Peter) and Andrew, too, were present. The plural form 'she served *them*', at the close of the narrative (Mk 1.31), also is easily interpreted to include Peter as well. In Matthew, Jesus enters 'the house of Peter'. Matthew's version of the narrative is quite elegant in omitting Andrew, James and John. Incidentally, Lk. 4.38 makes the same omission while retaining 'Simon' for Peter. But only Matthew tells that the healed mother-in-law 'served *him*' (i.e. Jesus).

The peculiarities of Matthew's version have a double impact. On one hand, Peter's explicit role is even more marginal than in Mark's narrative. On the other hand, the omission of other disciples makes Peter appear a more prominent character. The notion that Jesus entered Peter's house makes the reader aware of an intimate relationship between Jesus and Peter. The healing itself[43] is a minor incident in comparison with other Matthaean accounts of Jesus' powerful deeds (cf. 11.5: the blind receive their sight, the lame walk, lepers are cleansed, the deaf hear, the dead are raised up). Moreover, the reader will not meet the healed mother-in-law later on in the story. Obviously, then, the episode is not primarily about healing a sick person or about Peter's mother-in-law. Rather, the story illuminates how Jesus cared for *Peter's* household.[44] Matthew's persistent use of the name 'Peter' reminds the

---

43. Actually there is no explicit mention of healing in the pericope. The customary paraphrase 'the healing of Peter's mother-in-law' is therefore an arbitrary event labelling, as is rightly noticed by Funk, *The Poetics of Biblical Narrative*, p. 50.

44. There is no doubt, of course, that the narrator focuses on the healing, too. The episode is told together with other healing stories and leads to the summary in 8.16-17. Yet the episode as such is a rather modest illustration of how Jesus fulfilled Isaiah's prophecy (v. 17: note the heavy salvation-historical symbolism!). A sensitive story-teller might well have omitted the whole episode if no other narrative interests had been present.

reader that this indeed was the name by which Simon was called (ὁ λεγόμενος, 4.18).

The Twelve Apostles (10.1-4)

It is peculiar to Matthew that the calling or election of the twelve apostles is not narrated. The calling of two pairs of brothers was recorded at 4.18-22, from whence a larger group of disciples was tacitly assumed but never defined. At 9.37-38/10.1-5, a sudden turn is taken. There, without hardly any warning, 'the disciples' become 'his twelve disciples', 'the twelve apostles', 'these twelve'. Obviously the reader is supposed to know the existence of a group of twelve disciples (from Mark and/or Q?), but even so the narrator seems negligent. An effort is made to prepare the reader for a larger group of disciples who will take on leadership (cf. 9.36: μὴ ἔχοντα ποιμένα) and are given a special mission (9.37: ἐργάται). But precisely this effort creates a distinction between the disciples of 9.37 and those (the twelve, as it will appear) who will be sent out in 9.38.

An attentive reader, then, is faced with a problem. Inasmuch as the narrator had tried silently to identify the 'disciples' mentioned in chs. 4–9 as the twelve apostles introduced in 10.1-4, his narration in 9.36-38 seems strangely counteractive. Is there simultaneously an attempt to divide the representational functions of 'the disciples' and 'the twelve', with the former providing a mirror for the reader-community and the latter being more a representative of the historical apostles? Or is the representation a double one, with 'the disciples' and 'the twelve' standing, in part, for two factions within Matthew's community (the senders or the rank and file members vs. those who are sent or provided with special authority)? In the latter case, a link might be suggested between the two functions of 'the twelve' as representatives of the historical disciples and as shadows for the later community authorities (e.g. did the leadership legitimate its authority by referring to the twelve?).[45]

While such distinctions may occur to the reader, a clear-cut division of functions seems impossible. That the 'disciples' and the twelve

---

45. If one is allowed to speculate further still, has the markedly Jewish-Christian horizon of 10.5-6, 23 to do with the possible division of the functions of 'the disciples' and 'the twelve'? For instance, does the narrator suggest that the restricted mission of 'the twelve' to Jews remains a special task for the Jewish-Christian faction of the community?

'apostles' are much the same group is evident from the fact that the first four names in the list of the apostles are the two pairs of brothers whose calling was recorded earlier (4.18-22). As there, so also in the list of the twelve, Peter takes pride of place: πρῶτος Σίμων ὁ λεγόμενος Πέτρος (10.2). That Peter is 'first' (πρῶτος) can be understood as both a text-world and a symbolic-level device. Within the text world the reader is reminded of Peter's election as the first disciple; at the same time, Peter's firstness is a symbol of honour and authority.

As yet, of course, the virgin reader cannot fully substantiate the symbolic meaning Peter is given. The epithet ὁ λεγόμενος Πέτρος gives no further symbolic hint, for it was given already in 4.18. Possibly the repetition should (in the narrator's mind) alert the reader to the significance of the epithet, but that is by no means obvious. Granted the laxity of narration elsewhere in Matthew, the reader is not necessarily tempted to assume a refined repetitive technique here. The impact of the repeated epithet may then also be, simply, that the reader will remember that Peter was usually called Peter and not Simon.

A Man of Little Faith (14.28-31)

When Peter comes on the scene for the fourth time, a new pattern begins to emerge. As the notion of Peter's 'firstness' gradually unfolds, the reader will recognize that Peter's prominence is strikingly ambivalent. Here, he is one with courage (vv. 28–29) and also a man of little faith (vv. 30–31). The aspects change rather abruptly. At first, Peter's action in the Galilaean night seems successful. He is the only one to respond to Jesus. Still a bit uncertain of the ghostlike figure's identity, Peter is curious to find out if it really is his master (κύριε, εἰ σὺ εἶ) and is ready to approach him. The reader is just about to conclude that Peter managed to reach Jesus (ἦλθεν πρὸς τὸν Ἰησοῦν, v. 29), when the narrative suddenly takes a new turn. Peter saw the wind, became afraid and began to sink, and cried out: 'Lord, save me.' And so Jesus did save him, albeit also reproaching Peter for his little faith (ὀλιγόπιστε, εἰς τί ἐδίστασας; v. 31).

Precisely how the two sides of Peter's action and character are to be connected is difficult to conclude. Three sorts of readerly responses are possible. At worst, Peter is a man who confounds pretentious enthusiasm with faith. He fails and desperately needs Jesus' salvation. More favourably, Peter is a typical disciple both in his willingness to obey his master and in his insufficiency of faith. Still more favourably,

Peter is given pre-eminence among the disciples. While he may have had insufficient faith by that time, Peter already had the first glimmerings of faith. After all, he did walk on water.[46]

A decision between the various options will depend on how the relative weight of the diverging narrative hints is estimated. Should the reader focus on the incident between Peter and Jesus? This would still leave open several options. Is the main point Peter's eagerness and failure or is it Jesus' assistance to the distressed disciple? In the former case the narration is seen to accentuate either Peter's individual, personal traits or his symbolic value as a less than trustworthy community authority. In the latter case, with the stress being laid on Jesus as the helper to those in need, Peter would be a typical disciple, and the whole community would be able to identify with him. This sort of edifying interpretation might seem suggestive; but then the narrator would have told just another version of the stilling of the storm (8.23-27; there the disciples in unison stand for the distressed community).

Or is the decisive point to be read from the conclusion in v. 33, where the disciples worshipped (προσεκύνησαν) Jesus and confessed, 'Truly you are the Son of God'? If Peter as a typical disciple is included in the confessing group, his character is here ultimately coloured in a positive way. The faith and understanding the disciples show here (as they do in 13.51) are general rather than personal traits. As an embodiment of these virtues Peter would make a powerful symbol for real discipleship. Yet the conclusion of the narrative episode remains ambivalent, for actually the narrator says that when 'they' (Jesus and Peter) got into the boat, 'those in the boat' (the rest of the disciples) made the proper christological confession. It is true that Peter here is given pre-eminence among the disciples; but is he simultaneously separated from the confessing community?

Of course, the reader need not pay attention to the particular formulation; and possibly the author meant no such sharp difference between Peter and the rest of the disciples. But there are other more striking formulations. Peter's failure was that he doubted (εἰς τί ἐδίστασας, v. 31).[47] Did his doubts vanish immediately so that he could

46. The three options are presented in R.E. Brown, K.P. Donfried and J. Reumann (eds.), *Peter in the New Testament* (Minneapolis: Augsburg; New York: Paulist Press, 1973), pp. 81-83.

47. Cf. Nau, *Peter in Matthew*, pp. 102-103. The (relatively rare) verb διστάζω means 'to hesitate, waver' rather than 'to disbelieve'. It 'means that the person con-

join the worshipping disciples? The answer cannot be deemed self-evident, for at the close of the story the resurrected Jesus still meets both worship and doubt among his disciples (28.17: προσεκύνησαν/οἱ δὲ ἐδίστασαν). Nevertheless, Peter's little faith (ὀλιγόπιστε, v. 31) seems to be a typical rather than an individual feature among the text-world followers of Jesus (cf. 6.30 and especially 8.26). Even after the confession of faith in 14.31, the disciples as a group remain people of little faith (16.8, 17.20). In this light, Peter's little faith does not seem to be a distinctive trait in his character. Yet the somewhat unclear relation between Peter and the other disciples in this episode world may alert the reader to the possibility that Peter does not unequivocally symbolize the Christian community at large. An implicit division of roles becomes visible, even though the virgin reader cannot yet see the implications.

One more peculiarity is found in Peter's reply to Jesus, κύριε, εἰ σὺ εἶ, κέλευσον, etc. (v. 28), which curiously echoes the devil's words in the temptation narrative (εἰ υἱὸς εἶ τοῦ θεοῦ, εἶπε, etc. 4.3).[48] There are marked differences between the episodes, to be sure, for example, the quite different geographical settings (desert vs. sea). And Peter does not really tempt Jesus; so Jesus does nothing wrong in agreeing to Peter's request. Rather, it is Peter who, on his own initiative, is put to the test; and he fails, although not fatally this time. Such differences do not diminish the affinity between the episodes but rather lend the latter episode a touch of irony. The irony may be unintentional and seems mild in any case; but it prepares the reader for subsequent scenes in which Peter does take the tempter's role (16.22-23) and where he fails much more bitterly (26.75).

Still without Understanding (15.12-20)
In his next appearance, Peter is seemingly in a less arbitrary position.

cerned is divided in his conviction. The disbelieving man has made a stand against belief; the doubtful man cannot make up his mind whether to believe or not. The existence of faith is implied, but it is imperfect' (I.P. Ellis, '"But Some Doubted"', *NTS* 14 [1967–68], pp. 574-80 [576]). Thus the verb is well in coherence with the preceding vocative ὀλιγόπιστε. It has the same meaning in 28.17.

48. Peter's words also echo Jesus' preceding announcement ἐγώ εἰμι (v. 27). These words of Jesus sound much like a divine self-revelation (thus, e.g., R. Schnackenburg, *Matthäusevangelium* [Neue Echter Bibel; 2 vols.; Würzburg: Echter Verlag, 1985], I, p. 138). But does not Peter in his initial words reveal his little faith, as he questions Jesus' own announcement? In this light, Peter's action seems a failure from the start.

He is singled out, but not separated from the rest of the disciples; he addresses Jesus on behalf of all the disciples. A comparison with the Markan parallel, where the disciples address Jesus in unison (Mk 7.17), raises the question as to why Matthew's narrative has Peter alone as the addresser. It is often suggested that Peter's prominence here has to do with the issue of Jesus' teaching.[49] The teaching concerns purity rules, which are an important halachic matter. If Matthew's readers were aware of a tradition that granted Peter special authority in halachic matters (cf. 16.16-18), it comes as no surprise that Peter here appears as the prime recipient of Jesus' teaching.

However, should the activity of Peter the character in this episode reflect the authority and leadership Peter the man once had or was traditionally claimed to have had, then the knowing reader will also be alerted by Jesus' words against blind guides: 'If a blind guide leads a blind man, both will fall into a pit' (v. 14). That was said of the Pharisees, but it concerns the Christian group as well, for Peter's question immediately triggers Jesus' worried comment 'Are you also still without understanding?' (v. 16). Supposing that the prominence of Peter the character here reflects his symbolic value as a (past) community authority, an uncomfortable juxtaposition seems to emerge. If Peter the guide to the community is blind, the whole community will fall into a pit.

Naturally Matthew's readers need not infer from these hints that Peter and his followers should be equated with Pharisees. Peter is, after all, on Jesus' side, listening to his teaching against the Pharisees. Nor does Jesus blame Peter alone; it is the whole group of disciples ('you') that he addresses. Yet Jesus is possibly launching an indirect warning to Peter and his followers, for it may not be purely incidental that Matthew has Peter enter the stage immediately after Jesus' parabolic utterance in v. 14 (to the effect that Peter's plea, 'Explain the *parable* to us', seems to refer to, or include, the parable of blind leaders).

Taken as a whole, the episode 15.1-20 suggests that the disciples more or less have a *shadow* function as representatives of the addressees in Matthew's community. At the same time, the text-world

---

49. So especially G.D. Kilpatrick, *The Origins of the Gospel According to Matthew* (Oxford: Oxford University Press, 1950), pp. 38-40; R. Hummel, *Die Auseinandersetzung zwischen Kirche und Judentum im Matthäusevangelium* (BEvT, 33; Munich: Chr. Kaiser Verlag, 1963), pp. 59-63; J. Gnilka, *Das Matthäusevangelium* (2 vols.; Freiburg: Herder, 1988), II, p. 25.

disciples seem to symbolize a double set of values. Initially, in v. 2, the Pharisees and scribes observe a clear transgression of the tradition of the elders on the part of the disciples. Jesus readily admits that the observation is valid, and goes on to attack the 'precepts of men' (v. 9). Up to this point, the disciples seem to side wholly with Jesus: they have violated the tradition of the elders and Jesus defends their freedom. But then, as if frightened by Jesus' harsh words, the disciples turn to Jesus: 'Do you know that the Pharisees were offended (ἐσκανδαλίσθησαν) when they heard this saying?' (v. 12). Did they feel that Jesus went a bit too far?

But Jesus does nothing to soften his words. To the contrary, his reply is even more offensive than his original attack.[50] Precisely at the point of escalation of the scandal, Peter opens his mouth on behalf of the disciples, and Jesus rebukes them for not understanding his teaching. The impression is that Jesus now speaks for a freedom that Peter and the disciples were not (yet) fully capable of realizing. The disciples, who initially seem to have transgressed the tradition of the elders without much ado, suddenly get anxious about the teaching of Jesus. They recognize that the new teaching offends Pharisaic hearers; and now Peter gets involved.[51]

Thus the reader may recognize a very subtle division of roles among the disciples. Peter here seems to represent the disciples; but then the disciples no longer seem to reflect transparently the Matthaean community as a whole. Here, as already in the preceding episode, there are some indications that Peter represents values that are shared only by a faction among Matthew's audience.

Confession and Offence (16.13-23)
In the next Petrine episode—which is actually two separate but closely related episodes—the ambivalence is heightened to the extreme. How

---

50. Well noticed by Margaret Davies, *Matthew* (Readings: A New Biblical Commentary; Sheffield: JSOT Press, 1993), p. 113.

51. Schweizer (*Das Evangelium nach Matthäus*, p. 213) assesses Peter's role in this episode as follows: 'Peter receives prominence when a new understanding of the law in the community is under discussion... although he must in turn make inquiry of Jesus, and thus can only expound Jesus' will.' The first conclusion is valid, but the rest of the comment seems an understatement. Not only must Peter ask Jesus for an interpretation, he is also ignorant of the right interpretation of the law and misunderstands Jesus' will.

can Peter be the foundation of the church and Satan in one character? Why does the helper of the hero so suddenly become the chief antagonist, or how can the receiver of God's revelation (v. 17) lose his divine gift (v. 23) so completely? A side glance at Mark (8.27-33) suggests that the narrative dichotomy is not Matthew's invention. Nevertheless, Matthew has not removed the uneasy juxtaposition; his fuller narrative rather makes the dichotomy worse. At first, Peter is blessed by Jesus for his right confession (as in Mark), even renamed (?) and promised an outstanding future position (not in Mark). A few lines later, Peter has become Satan (as in Mark) and a stumbling block to Jesus (σκάνδαλον, not in Mark).

Some features of Matthew's fuller narrative might be designed to motivate both the helper and the antagonist aspect of Peter. Thus Peter's confession is somewhat enriched: 'You are the Christ, the Son of the living God.' Mark had Peter say only 'The Christ'.[52] By the same token, while Mark summarily paraphrases Peter's rebuke to Jesus (ἤρξατο ἐπιτιμᾶν αὐτόν), Matthew adds Peter's direct speech: 'God forbid, Lord! This shall never happen to you!' (v. 22). But such slight amplifications are mainly cosmetic, hardly equipping the reader with new insight into the diverging aspects of Peter's character or into their connection within the larger narrative plot. The reader will not learn why a complete change takes place.

Still worse, some Matthaean inventions tend to confuse the reader more than the Markan account does. In 16.16, the double name 'Simon Peter' is used (Mark and Luke have simply 'Peter'). This seems to indicate that the narrator is preparing the reader for the name-giving. But the device is unsuccessful in that the reader knows quite well that Simon was customarily called Peter. What is new—but ought to have been familiar to the reader—is the original full name Simon Bar-Jona, by which Jesus calls Peter in v. 17. Jesus then renames Simon Bar-Jona: 'You are Peter.' That does not make much sense to the reader, because Simon was 'renamed' from his first appearance (4.18). Of course, the fatal mistake was made already there. Little could be done in ch. 16 to amend it, and that was done in v. 16 by reminding the reader of Peter's

---

52. The additional epithet 'the Christ' hardly makes Peter's confession superior to Mark's formulation or to confession of the disciples in 14.33. It might be seen as an attempt to characterize Peter as Jewish (Christian) and thus to give him a partisan shadow function. However, this designation is not alien to the narrator himself (e.g. 1.17, 18 and 11.2).

original name. The reader, then, might pardon the narrator's lapse.

But was it just a lapse—what if the author's intent was to undermine beforehand the name-giving episode that his special tradition insisted upon?[53] Another of Matthew's peculiar choices makes this suspicious question more suggestive than it might first seem. As was observed, Matthew had the disciples (not Peter) make the proper christological confession earlier (14.33). True, the narrator's voice may have been indistinct, or the disciples may have in the meantime become less understanding (cf. 15.15 and 16.8-12). Yet the narrator hardly implies that Peter all of a sudden has become the most understanding among the disciples. So, when Peter answers Jesus' question on their behalf (cf. ὑμεῖς, v. 15), the reader cannot expect that the rest of the disciples should have given an inferior answer (and v. 20 confirms that they agreed with Peter's answer). Placed after the confession of the disciples in 14.33, the blessing, the praise and the outstanding promise Peter receives are something of a surprise, to say the least.[54]

Jesus' words in vv. 18-19 are peculiar to Matthew, and it is easy to see how awkward these are in the present context even on formal grounds (e.g. v. 20 now seems misplaced). Undeniably Matthew has inserted here a special tradition. But why offer it here, together with an entirely different view of Peter? If Matthew wished to undermine the special tradition about Peter, the grounding figure and key-holder, by introducing it in an improper context, his narrative is cleverly designed; if not, he is a poor storyteller.

The brilliance or awkwardness of the narrative design can be appreciated more fully in what follows. In v. 21, 'Jesus Christ'—a remarkable combination that corresponds to 'Simon Peter' in v. 16—begins to show his disciples that he must go to Jerusalem to meet his destiny. Peter's reaction is quite sympathetically rendered, with the vocative 'Lord' expressing his aspiration to loyalty and with the cry ἵλεώς σοι (may God spare you) sounding spontaneity and intimacy. Never should those awful things happen to Jesus! This is no malevolent

---

53. Again, Davies (*Matthew*, p. 119) perceptively observes that Simon Peter's nickname, which should have indicated his stone-like quality of firmness, 'perhaps functioned ironically'. What is particularly striking is that the placement of the name-giving/interpreting episode makes the irony even stronger.

54. Commenting on 14.33, Schweizer (*Das Evangelium nach Matthäus*, p. 209) makes the point more sharply: 'This confession [sc. of the disciples] in fact depreciates the confession of Peter in 16.16.'

person speaking; Peter is a worried and deeply involved friend. (That is, of course, were it not for the concluding words in Jesus' prediction that on the third day he will be *raised from the dead*; but obviously the reader should not dwell on that inconsistency.) But then Jesus' reply sounds all the more unfriendly—not hostile, but unfriendly, withdrawing, creating a distance. Denied his proper name as well as the honourable name he just received, Peter is now described by his negative function as 'Satan', the stumbling block.

Obviously, heavy and diverging symbolism must be at work beneath the explicit narrative, even though the dialogue cannot really help the reader understand what is going on. It is interesting how Peter's and Jesus' speeches differ in the way in which the narrative and symbolic levels are interrelated. Peter's speeches are more at home within the narrative and fit into the plot: he answers to Jesus' direct question and reacts to his passion prediction. Jesus, on the othe hand, transcends the narrative limits (by speaking of his future ἐκκλησία) and in effect destroys Peter's characterhood, indeed his personhood, in favour of symbolic representation. In Jesus' speeches, Peter is positively the 'rock' on which the church will be built; negatively, he is the 'stumbling block'. In neither case is he viewed as a character; rather, he is petrified, turned into a symbol.

The reader may try to view Peter as a character, but Jesus' repressive words cannot be ignored. In fact the reader is forced to take Jesus' symbolic stance in order to make sense of the dichotomous narrative.[55] Only so is it possible *simultaneously* to imagine Peter as the foundation of the church and the archetypal enemy of God's plans. Despite occasional efforts at creating a plausible character out of Peter, Matthew, in designing the double episode, reveals to his readers that there is more to Peter than a character; namely, he is a highly ambivalent ecclesiological symbol. This inherent depth-dimension, the 'more' of the character of Peter, may sometimes add to his characterization, as is evident at v. 22. There, the loaded symbolism and the coerced literary design has made Matthew look for alleviating narrative devices that round Peter towards full characterhood. Paradoxically, however, the symbolic depth at the same time flattens Peter in the narrative world into 'less' than a

---

55. The 'text-informed reader' only receives a kind of 'variation' in portrayal, and concludes that 'Peter and the disciples cannot, no matter how hard they work, arrive at the goal without the assistance of the Father' (Edwards, *Matthew's Narrative Portrait*, p. 77).

character. From now on, the reader will not be content to ask whether this or that trait suits the plot or builds the Petrine character. The reader will also ask for the symbolic meanings that attach to this character.

Witnessing the Transfiguration (17.1-8)

The necessity of treating Peter as a symbol apart from his character and his participation in the narrative plot is evident in the scenes that follow. The gloomy episode of 16.21-23 is soon forgotten. However, when Jesus addresses his disciples in 16.24, it is difficult to infer whether or not Peter should be included. Perhaps a slight distinction is still palpable, that the rest of the disciples should learn from Peter's unhappy reaction and not behave as he did. Rather, they should accept Jesus' tragic fate and take up their own cross in obedience to God's will. But the reader may also conclude that Jesus' words to Peter 'get behind me' (ὀπίσω μου, v. 23) are readily fulfilled and Peter is again among those who will 'come after' Jesus (ὀπίσω μου, v. 24) in humble self-denial.

In any case, 'after six days' (17.1), Jesus and the formerly satanic Peter are great friends again. Peter and the sons of Zebedee are led up a high mountain, and Jesus is transfigured before their eyes. In Matthew's version of the transfiguration narrative, Peter's role is slightly emphasized (ποιήσω, v. 4; Mark and Luke have ποιήσωμεν) and the narrator's comment on Peter's clumsy gesture in Mk 9.6 (οὐ γὰρ ᾔδει τί ἀποκριθῇ, etc.) is absent. The respectful vocative κύριε in Peter's mouth (v. 4; Mark has ῥαββί) together with the polite expression εἰ θέλεις (v. 4; not in Mark) make Peter appear in a rather positive light. On the whole, Matthew's narrative is different from Mark's in that he emphasizes the awe of the three disciples rather than their bewilderment.[56] After the disaster of 16.23, the reader might think that Peter recovered quite marvellously. But obviously the continuity of the plot and the psychology of Peter's character are not the narrator's concerns here.

Is there any recognizable pattern in Matthew's treatment with Peter thus far? Why does the narrator here tone down all disquieting traits while at other places he is more critical of Peter? It is too early for an overall judgment, but one notes that Peter's role as a prime witness to

---

56. F. Kermode, 'Matthew', in R. Alter and F. Kermode (eds.), *The Literary Guide to the Bible* (Cambridge, MA: Harvard University Press, 1987), pp. 387-401 (397).

Jesus' transfiguration, sonship and salvation-historical status is ¹not
questioned.[57]

The Policy of No Offence (17.24-27)

Quite a different tone is heard in the narrator's voice in the pericope on
the temple tax. The episode comes from Matthew's special tradition,
and again—as in 16.17-19—it is vital to notice how a piece of tradition
is placed and accentuated in Matthew's narrative.

It is commonly assumed that the temple-tax pericope is thematically
related to the community discourse (Mt. 18).[58] This seems correct; however, two complications must be noted first. A first observation that
makes the assumed thematic connection difficult to see is that the
temple-tax pericope suggests a contrast between the tax-collectors (and
the religious ideology they represent), on one hand, and Jesus, Peter and
the disciples, on the other hand. This contrast parallels the contrast in
the teaching of Jesus (v. 26) between outsiders and Matthew's own
people. What is at stake symbolically seems to be the relationship of the
Christian community to Judaism.[59] Since the community discourse

57. Nau's (*Peter in Matthew*, p. 80) efforts to show that Matthew's inserted
Petrine pericopes establish 'a kind of comparison, or contrast, situation between
Jesus and Peter or Jesus and the disciples' are often plausible but seem less convincing in the present pericope. It is to be expected, then, that the pattern Nau dis-
cerns in Matthew's presentation of Peter is one-sided. Matthew's aim is not simply
to disparage or to cast shame upon Peter.

58. So in different ways, e.g., Schweizer, *Das Evangelium nach Matthäus*,
p. 233; H.B. Green, *The Gospel According to Matthew* (New Clarendon Bible;
Oxford: Oxford University Press, 1975), p. 157; W.G. Thompson, *Matthew's
Advice to a Divided Community: Mt 17,22–18,35* (AnBib, 44; Rome: Pontifical
Biblical Institute, 1970), pp. 245-52; D. Patte, *The Gospel According to Matthew*
(Philadelphia: Fortress Press, 1987), p. 244. Those who deny any substantial thematic connection usually interpret the passage separately from the context or regard
the placement as determined by geographical considerations (i.e. Matthew inserted
the Petrine passage in a context where Capernaum was mentioned, because that
town was connected with the profession of tax collecting, Mt. 9.1, 8-13; thus
Brown, Donfried and Reumann [eds.], *Peter in the New Testament*, p. 101).

59. There is some discussion whether the pericope deals with the Jewish temple
tax (which ended with the destruction of the temple) or the Roman poll tax imposed
on Jews (*fiscus iudaicus*) after 70 CE. See Luz, *Das Evangelium nach Matthäus*, II,
pp. 527-28 for literature. Luz is obviously correct in excluding the latter interpretation, but we must question his conclusion that the pericope therefore had no contemporary bearing for the community but was preserved by the redactor only

deals with inner-community relations, a thematic and symbolic affinity does not immediately suggest itself—unless the community discourse, too, somehow deals with the community and Judaism. A second confusing observation pertains to the catchword connection between the two pericopes. The pericopes are joined by the catchword σκαν- δαλίζειν, which in 17.27 obviously means *causing offence* (to the tax-collectors or authorities) but in 18.6 is usually taken to mean *causing* (the little ones) *to sin*. If that is correct, the catchword connection would seem superficial and irrelevant. The question, however, is precisely whether the two occurrences of σκανδαλίζειν really differ in meaning.

A third observation is more promising. The theme of *self-denial* for the sake of others, which is developed in various ways in the community speech, is already launched here in the temple-tax pericope.[60] Jesus submits himself to an obligation from which, in principle, he is free. The demand of self-denial is paradoxical; one chooses to do what one actually would not have to do. The self-denial theme is carried on in ch. 19, where it is said that some disciples voluntarily refuse marriage for the sake of the kingdom of heaven (19.10-12). Finally, there is the observation that Peter's role is a positive link in both sections. In 17.24-27, he makes the crucial decision concerning the temple tax in the name of Jesus and, it seems, in the name of the community. His resolute 'yes' immediately proves to be problematic and provokes Jesus' critical comment. In 18.21-22—the only narrative intrusion in the community discourse—Peter returns to the scene to ask a question on behalf of the community, proposes an answer, and is mildly corrected by Jesus.

Obviously the issue of the temple tax is a symbolic one. The joyful proclamation, 'Then the sons are free' (v. 26), as well as the compromising practical principle, 'not to give offence to them', seem to imply a contemporary debate. The debate could hardly be about the Roman *fiscus iudaicus*, for in that case neither the freedom of the sons

because of piety towards his tradition. The temple remained a religious symbol, with the result that issues concerning the temple worship continued to be discussed. In the present narrative, the temple symbolism is metaphorically transferred to the synagogue. A transference from temple tax to synagogal and other religious duties is quite natural considering such concrete issues as voluntary contributions to the beth-din in Jabneh (Thompson, *Matthew's Advice*, p. 68) or attending synagogue services and giving alms (cf. Mt. 6.2-4).

60. Patte, *The Gospel According to Matthew*, pp. 244-46.

nor the principle of avoiding offence would make sense to the reader. The actual debate, rather, might concern the community's financial (and other) ties with the synagogue, which is the issue of 6.1-18 (cf. esp. vv. 2-6 on almsgiving). Should members of Matthew's community financially support the synagogue, or should they rather withdraw from it and collect money only for their own widows, orphans and poor ones?

If that was the burning issue, what would Matthew's implied reader make of the temple tax issue? The fronts now appear to be inside the community, with Peter and Jesus representing two slightly different attitudes towards the Jewish obligations. The tax-collectors unmistakably go to Peter, the great authority of the community. As usual (as the reader has learned by now), Peter is more than eager to accept the leader's role. His answer is firm and ready: Yes, of course we shall pay the tax. But the answer was premature, necessitating a comment from a still greater authority, Jesus himself. Jesus' private lesson (in a house) to Peter is slightly ironic. 'What do you think, Simon?' sounds just a bit too kind and humble—as if Peter and Jesus were equals. The use of Peter's original name Simon is also finely tuned, suggesting both intimacy and lack of final authority. The reader knows that the founding father should have been addressed as Peter, the rock (cf. 16.18: 'I tell you, *you are* Peter'). But the real authority lies with Jesus, as the rest of the episode makes clear. In what is nearly a piece of Socratic dialogue, the master reveals the disciple's error through a clever question. Peter cannot but give the right answer and thereby contradict his earlier statement. The sons are free; they do not need to pay.

Unexpectedly, Jesus goes on to qualify Peter's solution. Even though Peter's policy was spurious, there was another consideration that justified his solution in practical life, namely the principle of avoiding offence (ἵνα δὲ μὴ σκανδαλίσωμεν αὐτούς, v. 27). This principle reminds the reader of Peter's earlier conduct (σκάνδαλον εἶ ἐμοῦ, 16.23). This situation was the right occasion to avoid giving offence and to exercise self-denial. The sons are free, but they are also called to sacrifice themselves in humility—another lesson that Peter had a hard time understanding (cf. 16.22/24). The pericope ends with another spoonful of mild irony. Peter, formerly a fisherman, is sent to his pre-discipleship occupation for a while. That might seem humiliating, but, as earlier (14.31), Jesus actually *saves* Peter in the eyes of the disciples. Peter had acted too eagerly and without having the right insight. In the end, however, Jesus restored the situation: Peter's solution stands, if only in the way it was modified by Jesus.[61]

What the compromise meant in the community's everyday life is not quite obvious. Was the lesson that all community members were to support the synagogue, or was it a free decision for each individual member?[62] It is typical of Matthew that the reader will not know the precise practical implications. Indeed, an observation from the narrative plot suggests that the author/narrator was less than willing to offer clear-cut solutions. What the anecdote implies is as ingenious as it is impractical. The temple tax is paid and the Jewish authorities have their due. At the same time, Peter and Jesus need not give money from their purse; they pay with money miraculously found. To a pious reader that might suggest that God will provide all the money that a double loyalty (to the community and the synagogue) costs. Unfortunately, in real life, coins from a fish's mouth are in short supply.[63]

Peter as Spokesman for the 'Little Ones' (18.21-23)
In 17.24–18.35, the narrator has made it difficult for the reader to know who accompanies Jesus. In 17.24 (ἐλθόντων αὐτῶν) all the disciples are included; but, in the dialogue of vv. 25-27, Peter and Jesus are alone. Jesus then summons Peter to go and cast a line in the lake (v. 27), and 'at that time' (18.1) the disciples come to Jesus. Does the narrator mean to say that on that occasion Peter is away (catching the fish) and only arrives at 18.21? This reading may be far-fetched, but one can ask whether the shifts in Jesus' audience serve some thematic

---

61. R. Feldmeier ('The Portrayal of Peter in the Synoptic Gospels', in M. Hengel, *Studies in the Gospel of Mark* [London: SCM Press, 1985], pp. 59-63 [61]) aptly notes that in this anecdote 'there is probably already a reflection of the position of Peter after Easter; while he is instructed by Jesus, he does give authoritative answers to questions'. But, to be more precise, in the narrative, Peter first answers the question and only then is instructed (and corrected) by Jesus!

62. If the moral of 6.1-18 applies here, the latter option is preferable. Those who wish to be loyal to the synagogue may do so (as Peter taught); those who know that they are free (as Jesus taught) should consider how to practise the freedom without giving offence to anybody. Thus Davies seems to be on the right track. On the one hand, he says, ' "the sons are free" seems to give readers a freedom not to pay'. On the other hand, '[t]he rhetoric of the story leaves open the possibility that Jewish Christians might pay this tax ...' (*Matthew*, p. 126).

63. Coins from a fish's mouth are found more often in narrative worlds; see Luz, *Das Evangelium nach Matthäus*, II, p. 535 n. 49.

purpose. If so, then Peter's coming to the fore may mark a turn in the flow of thought in the community discourse. Elsewhere in Matthew's great discourses a narrative intrusion is coupled with a dramatic shift in the audience and in the contents of the speech (13.36; 24.1). Several outlines have been proposed for the community discourse, the most popular divisions being two parts (1-14: the worth of the little ones/ 15-35: brotherliness and forgiveness) or four parts (1-4: greatness in the kingdom of heaven/ 5-14: the care of the little ones/15-20: discipline of a brother/ 21-35: forgiveness of a brother).[64] The main question concerns the borderline between vv. 14 and 15. Is it a minor shift or a major thematic watershed? One terminological difference speaks for the latter option. In vv. 1-14, the theme word is 'the little ones' (vv. 6, 10, 14) while in vv. 15-35 the theme word is 'brother' (vv. 15, 21, 35).[65]

Do the theme words imply different groups? The answer, to some extent, depends on how the parable of the lost sheep (vv. 12-14) is to be understood. If the parable speaks of a sinner, as do vv. 15-17, then the thematic shift from v. 14 to v. 15 would be smooth, and no shift in audience need be assumed. In the Lukan parallel of the lost sheep there is no question that the lost sheep is a sinner: 'There will be greater joy in heaven over one sinner who repents than over ninety-nine righteous people who do not need to repent' (Lk. 15.7). In Matthew, however, the lost sheep is identified as 'one of these little ones' (cf. vv. 10 and 14). These 'little ones' must not be despised ones, since they have guardian angels in heaven (v. 10). Losing any of 'the little ones' would be against the will of the heavenly Father (v. 14). Taken at face value, these remarks grant 'the little ones' a special status that scarcely fits ordinary sinning members of the community.[66]

64. Cf. R.H. Gundry, *Matthew: A Commentary on his Literary and Theological Art* (Grand Rapids: Eerdmans, 1982), p. 358.

65. H. Frankemölle, *Jahwebund und Kirche Christi: Studien zur Form- und Traditionsgeschichte des 'Evangeliums' nach Matthäus* (NTAbh NF 10; Münster: Chr. Kaiser Verlag, 1974), p. 181.

66. For discussion and literature on 'the little ones', see, e.g., G. Stanton, *A Gospel for a New People: Studies in Matthew* (Edinburgh: T. & T. Clark, 1992), pp. 214-18. Stanton rightly concludes that 'the little ones' in 25.31-46 and elsewhere in Matthew denote disciples. He fails, however, to recognize (1) the oscillation in the shadow/representational functions of the disciples between an elite group (those who have 'left everything', who 'preach the kingdom' and are 'persecuted' and should be 'received' by people), and a broader group (including all other community members who receive the teaching, show hospitality to mis-

Nor does the fragmentary storyworld of the parable[67] imply that the lost sheep is a sinner.[68] The parable concentrates on the shepherd's efforts to find the sheep. Everything should be done to rescue a straying 'little one'—even at the risk of neglecting the other sheep. Thus the notion of evil-doing does not seem to be the main qualification of 'the little ones'. The idea is rather that these should be paid special attention. A similar idea is found in the preceding passage, vv. 6-9, where Jesus warns against 'scandalizing' any of 'these little ones'. Again, the emphasis is not on the conduct of 'the little ones', but on how others

sionary workers, etc.), and (2) Matthew's modest efforts towards democratizing the elite ideology to embrace the whole community. Often, when a distinction is made between 'the little ones' (or their equivalents in Matthew's community) and the rest of the community, it is thought that 'the little ones' are the despised and powerless ones; thus recently J. Roloff, 'Das Kirchenverständnis des Matthäus im Spiegel seiner Gleichnisse', *NTS* 38 (1992), pp. 337-56 (342) ('the little ones' = the settled people in distinction from wandering charismatics). But this interpretation over-looks the social dynamics of the paradoxical (self-stigmatizing) names of honour. A reading of Paul is instructive in this respect: note how keenly he argues for being 'the least' of all the apostles (1 Cor. 15.8-11; cf. also 1 Cor. 1.20-31 and 2 Cor. 11.30)!

67. The construction of the parable is apparent already within the discourse world of Mt. 18: Jesus puts the parable forward hypothetically (ἐὰν γένηται, vv. 12, 13), and the incident is told indirectly by way of actions that are assumed by the audience (οὐχὶ ἀφήσει, v. 12) or assured by the storyteller (ἀμὴν λέγω ὑμῖν ὅτι χαίρει, etc. v. 13). Thus, the literary character of Jesus' discourse is argumentative rather than narratival; it is not really a story about a shepherd who has a hundred sheep, then loses one and searches for it, and rejoices having found it. Hence, it is often not considered to be a parable (cf. Gnilka, *Das Matthäusevangelium*, II, p. 130 n. 3).

68. Cf. the parallel in the *Gospel of Thomas* (107): 'The kingdom is like a shep-herd who had a hundred sheep. One of them, the largest, went astray. He left the ninety-nine and looked for that one until he found it. When he had gone to such trouble, he said to the sheep, "I care for you more than the ninety-nine" ' (The Nag Hammadi Library; ed. J.M. Robinson; trans. T. Lambdin; Leiden: E.J. Brill, rev. edn, 1988). Here, as in Matthew, the straying sheep is of special value and is not qualified as a sinner. Note also that the shepherd does not stand for a community leader. The ending ('I care for you more ...') and the christologically oriented con-text (log. 108) suggest that the *Gospel of Thomas* identified the shepherd with Jesus, and the sheep with the solitary Gnostic who finds the kingdom. The other Gnostic parallel in the *Gospel of Truth* (31.35–32.9) is somewhat more remote, but there, too, there is no suggestion of moral defiency.

should behave with regard to them.[69] In fact, the whole opening part of the discourse asserts that the little ones are the greatest in the Kingdom. Every disciple should try to 'become' a little child by 'humbling one-self' (v. 4). Instead of complete transformation, ideological accommodation will do: if one cannot actually become a child (i.e. join 'the little ones'), then at least one should take account of their needs (v. 5),[70] avoid offending them (vv. 6-7), abstain from things that are dangerous in their eyes (vv. 8-9), and see that they not become lost (vv. 10-14).

This line of reading distinguishes vv. 1-14 from the latter half of the speech. It is not so much the little ones who sin, but those who do not receive them. The little ones may also sin, but theirs is the sin of being scandalized, and of leaving the flock. The second half of the community speech then focuses on the problem of sinners in the community from another perspective. The point of view is now that of the offended person: how should such a one deal with a sinning brother? Here the sinner is not about to leave the flock; on the contrary, he is there until, perhaps, he is deliberately put out: 'you must treat him as you would a pagan or a tax-gatherer' (v. 17).

The addressees of Jesus in vv. 1-14, the 'you' of the discourse, are obviously the disciples of the main narrative (v. 1). Since the 'you' are contrasted with the little ones (v. 10), it is difficult to identify them with the narrative disciples. A new narrative audience is not directly indicated; yet, notably, it is Peter who in v. 21 reacts to the new teaching that began in v. 15 (note the catchwords ἁμαρτανεῖν, ἀδελφός σου/ μου, εἰς σέ/ἐμέ). While Peter is absent or silent, the rest of the disciples are told not to scandalize the little ones. But when the little ones are addressed, Peter is right there to receive the teaching and to ask for an

69. It is frequently assumed that the parable of the straying sheep primarily addresses the leaders of the community, who should look after the weak ones of their herd (typically J. Jeremias, *Die Gleichnisse Jesu* [Göttingen: Vandenhoeck & Ruprecht, 6th edn, 1962], p. 36). Undoubtedly, the leading members might understand the parable in this sense, but the context in Matthew does not really suggest that; v. 14 has no obvious addressee but only restates the special value of the straying sheep.

70. Cf. Mt. 10.40-42, where giving a cup of water to one of 'these little ones' is juxtaposed to 'receiving' a prophet or a righteous man. Nothing indicates that 'the little ones' are contrasted with the prophets or righteous men here (so Luz, *Das Evangelium nach Matthäus*, II, p. 152); rather they, too, are itinerant Christians who must be 'received' in the community (by offering water after the journey).

explanation. The conclusion is near at hand that *Peter is the narrative advocate for the 'little ones'*. He is allegedly the one with authority to excommunicate—that is, not to forgive—sinning members. As such, Peter not only represents the 'little ones' but also seems uncomfortably similar to the unforgiving servant (vv. 21-35). Obviously, Peter himself thinks he is liberal enough; but again his judgment is premature. Jesus' answer, in multiplying the number of transgressions Peter suggested, ridicules the very attitude Peter exemplifies. The irony in Jesus' dealing with Peter in 17.24-27 thus continues in the community speech. Jesus takes a double role, in part siding with Peter and the little ones and in part siding with the disciples or the 'you' of the discourse in vv. 1-14. In 17.24-27 Jesus accepts Peter's practical decision, but compels him to rethink the matter from a new viewpoint. This new angle corresponds to that of the disciples with regard to 'the little ones' in 18.1-14. That is, Jesus instructs Peter to treat the tax-collectors similarly to the way the disciples are to treat the little ones. In both instances, the instruction involves compromising, self-denial and avoiding offensive behaviour. Tolerance is required on both sides.

None of this makes sense unless 'the little ones' represented by Peter have a counterpart in the author's and the implied reader's concrete world. The social and ideological characteristics of the people in question, however, are only dimly seen in their partial, oscillating narrative representations.[71] Matthew's ancient readers must have known 'the little ones' much more closely than do modern critical readers who are left with Matthew's veiled text-world hints. Yet these hints yield to a general picture of a conservative Jewish-Christian faction within Matthew's community, with some—perhaps only informal and disputed— disciplinary authority. Matthew also envisages the danger that these people might leave the community, obviously to (re)join 'the lost sheep of the house of Israel' (10.6; cf. 18.12-14 and 9.36)—that is, the synagogue.

71. It is possible, though, that the real-world people actually called themselves 'the little ones'. The designation is comparable to the 'babes' of Q (Luke) 10.21, with whom the implied reader of Q obviously knew to identify (even if the implied reader/member of the Q community hardly was called 'a babe' in everyday speech).

Reward and Warning to the Privileged Ones (19.23-30)
The partisan role Peter was allotted in the setting of the community
speech seems to vanish in the next Petrine episode. In 19.23-30, Peter is
clearly the spokesman for the group of twelve disciples, as the dialogue
shows: Jesus addresses the twelve (v. 23), they are astonished and pose
him a question (v. 25), Jesus replies (v. 26), this time Peter reacts on
behalf of the twelve ('we', v. 27), and finally Jesus replies to 'them'
(v. 28). However, the preceding episodes have made the reader suspicious enough to look behind the outward distribution of roles. Is there
some symbolism at work?

The thematic ties to the community discourse and to the narrative of
19.1-22 suggest that this might be the case. The theme of childlikeness,
introduced in 18.1-4, crops up again in 19.13-15. In the community
discourse the paraenesis about childlikeness is intertwined with the
special status of 'the little ones', which in the author's and implied
reader's concrete world was a designation for a powerful, conservative
Jewish-Christian faction within the community. Their privileged
position was taken for granted, and fellow Christians were recom-
mended to exercise considerable caution in dealing with 'the little ones'
for fear they would leave the community. At the same time, a veiled
warning was directed at 'the little ones' through the images of Peter and
the unforgiving servant.

In ch. 19, the childlikeness issue is connected with other themes that
are very instructive in pointing to the inherent symbolism. While
already in 18.7-9 an ascetic ideology is suggested, the inner connection
between childlikeness and ascetic self-denial is made explicit in 19.3-
12. The disciples rightly infer from Jesus' teaching that a perfect follower will not consider marriage. Jesus then explains that this perfection is meant only for a select group of people who are ready to make
themselves 'eunuchs for the sake of the kingdom of heaven' (v. 12).
This would be childlikeness at its most specific: being neither male nor
female, but innocent like angels in heaven (cf. 22.30).

Another concrete case of childlikeness, ascetic self-denial and perfection is expounded in the story of the rich young man (19.16-22).
Keeping the commandments is basic, even if one could well conceive
that it was 'the little ones' who boasted about doing and teaching the
whole law down to 'the least of the commandments' (and were therefore 'the greatest' in the kingdom, 5.19; cf. 18.1). Real perfection is to
give away one's possession and follow Jesus (v. 21). In practical life,

this ideal was met by wandering charismatics, prophets and apostles who counted on the hospitality of the communities that received them; for 'the labourer (of the kingdom) deserves his food' (10.10 = Q/Lk. 10.7; cf. 1 Cor. 9.14).

It appears that the ideology of perfection Jesus advocates here is very much like that of 'the little ones'. It is the ideology of Jewish-Christian missionary workers and charismatics, or better, it is the ideology of those who in the post-70 period cherished and imitated the missionary way of life in perfect obedience, humility and poverty. It is the ideology of those who thought they could make claims for the traditions of Jesus' original followers, including Peter. It is not incidental, then, that Peter responds to Jesus and says (v. 27), 'Lo, we have left everything and followed you, What then shall we have?' Peter represents all twelve apostles, to be sure; but this time (as occasionally before), the twelve seem to share the Petrine values. The representational role of the twelve, too, oscillates between the whole community and the elite group.

The oscillation here is produced mainly by Peter's question. Peter—who else—gives expression to the elite ideology: 'We have left everything...' Jesus, however, in his reply redefines the disciples' representational function by separating the historical/narrative twelve from latter-day Christians. The special role belongs only to 'the twelve' who will 'sit on twelve thrones, judging the twelve tribes of Israel' (v. 28). As for the other followers,[72] Jesus only assures them that 'every one who has left houses or brothers or sisters ... will receive a hundredfold, and inherit eternal life' (v. 29). In the contemporary world of Matthew and his readers, there seems to be no special reward for the elite.

This subtle turn might indicate the author's effort (through the narrator and Jesus) to play down the Petrine group's claims for special status. If so, then the previous narrative that seems to take the elite ideology for granted would be a little *unreliable*; the reader will be left in some doubt as to whether 'the little ones' as members of a

---

72. In the narrative world, the other followers are those outside the group of twelve. In Matthew's concrete world, the reference is not quite so obvious. In principle, the other followers might be those outside the elite group of 'the little ones'. However, since Matthew seems to question their privileged status, it is more likely that the twelve apostles are regarded here only as the historical elite. Also, the concrete numerical equivalence (twelve apostles, twelve thrones, twelve tribes) makes it difficult to attach a symbolic meaning to the twelve apostles.

contemporary group in Matthew's community really have special guardian angels in heaven (18.10), whether the revered doers and teachers of 'the least commandments' (5.19) really will have the best seats in the coming kingdom, whether they really have the authority to excommunicate other people. Insofar as Peter here stands for the elite ideology, he is also warned not to take his privileged status in the kingdom for granted. For it truly sounds a warning when the lesson ends with Jesus' words (v. 30) to Peter, the *first* disciple: 'But many that are first will be last, and the last first.'[73]

Unwatchfulness and Denial (26.30-75)

Incidental or not, the next and final Petrine scenes present a disciple who is the *first* one to declare, 'Though they all fall away because of you, I will never fall away' (26.33), and 'Even if I must die with you, I will not deny you' (v. 35), but who in the end denies his master three times.

The main lines of the denial story are found in Mark. Matthew's alterations are relatively slight and do not substantially change the general picture. Yet the minor deviations show that Matthew is fully engaged in what he narrates. Most of the peculiarities in Matthew's version are rather neutral to Peter; thus, for example, the cock only crowed once (vv. 34 and 74 differ from Mark; the Matthaean narrator's consistency is worth noting—he is quite vigilant in telling the passion narrative). Some details perhaps slightly alleviate Peter's burden (v. 40 differ from Mk 14.37: 'Simon, do you sleep?' is omitted and Jesus' address takes the plural form). But then again some of Matthew's details are more negative toward Peter. The pregnant formulation of v. 33 (differ from Mk 14.29) accentuates Peter's failure. Similarly, the mention of Peter's denial ἔμπροσθεν πάντων (v. 70; not in Mk 14.68) and his taking an oath (v. 72; not in Mk 14.70) bring the *maxima culpa* to the reader's attention. On the whole, Matthew's account of Peter's denial of Jesus is scarcely less harsh toward Peter than the Markan story.[74]

---

73. Cf. also Mt. 20.16. The placement of the parable of the labourers in the vineyard and the parallelism between 19.30 and 20.16 lend more weight to the warning spoken to Peter in 19.30.

74. Nau (*Peter in Matthew*, pp. 87-91) is impressed by Matthew's 'devastating' redaction of the denial episode. In Matthew's hands, it became 'a sad climax' of Peter's story.

Aesthetically, the Peter of the Matthaean denial story comes very close to full characterhood. Here he is momentarily 'rounded' for the reader.[75] And certainly there have been perceptive readers who know how to appreciate this extraordinary depth of characterization. In his classic, *Mimesis: The Representation of Reality in Western Literature* Erich Auerbach was so impressed by the synoptic narrative of Peter's denial and self-recognition that he placed it 'entirely outside the domain of classical antiquity'.[76] Be that as it may,[77] the question is whence the force of the narrative comes. Does the narrative really encourage the reader to take an interest in Peter's character or 'personality', or does it rather make the reader look for a *symbolic* meaning?

Especially one thematic hint suggests that, at least in Matthew's version, the reader is directed to a symbolic level. The narrator is keen to point out beforehand that the flow of events illustrates Peter's and the disciples' *falling away from faith in Christ* (πάντες ὑμεῖς σκανδαλισθήσεσθε ἐν ἐμοί, v. 31; the words ἐν ἐμοί are not found in Mk 14.27). This is what Peter specifically denies (v. 33; note again ἐν σοί). The emphasized ἐν ἐμοί/σοί gives the narrative a touch of intimacy, thus adding to its *text-world* appeal. At the same time, however, this emphasis recalls the earlier scenes with Peter and Jesus where the personal touch has *symbolic* significance. However intimate a friend Peter purports to be, the real 'I' of Jesus remains a mystery for him. As in 16.22, so in the denial narrative, Peter just cannot understand Jesus' real nature and mission. More importantly, the theme of 'being scandalized' in the denial narrative recalls how the narrator played that theme on previous occasions. By now the reader will understand that Jesus' harsh words σκάνδαλον εἶ ἐμοῦ (16.23) point to a central trait in

---

75. Burnett, 'Characterization', p. 21.

76. E. Auerbach, *Mimesis: The Representation of Reality in Western Literature* (Princeton, NJ: Princeton University Press, 1953), p. 45.

77. Auerbach was impressed by the prominence of Peter as a secondary character and by the unnecessary details about Peter in the passion story. However, if Peter is viewed as one of the main characters in Matthew, the denial story will appear less extraordinary. It is also typical of early Christian literature that seemingly minor characters sometimes attract narratorial interest for reasons other than aesthetic: either the character represents a known, historical person (Simon of Cyrene, Mk 15.21), or provides a symbol that fits the narrator's concerns (Lazarus in the Gospel of John). Obviously, in Matthew (and Mark), Peter is conspicuous for both reasons.

Peter's character, or rather, to a central symbolic meaning of Peter's portrayal.

The Silent Peter (28.16-20)

The last thing the reader is explicitly told of Peter in Matthew is that 'he went out and wept bitterly' (26.75). What then happened is left ambiguously open for the reader to fill in. How did Peter recover after the tragedy? Indeed, did he ever recover?

Some specifically Matthaean details indicate that the narrator by no means sought to diminish the reader's anxiety concerning Peter. Right after Peter's denial, Matthew narrates the death of Judas, the betrayer of Jesus (27.10). Judas confessed his sins before the chief priests and the elders, yet he had to die. Did Peter's recognition (26.75) lead to a more positive outcome? Nothing to that effect is suggested. There is no narrative of Peter's presence at the empty tomb (cf. John). Even Mark, while not having Peter see the empty tomb, lets the young man at the tomb mention Peter: 'Go and tell his disciples and Peter that he is going before you to Galilee; there you will see him ...' (Mk 16.7). This positive hint of Peter's recovery is curiously absent from Matthew (28.7). Does the narrator imply Peter's inclusion among Jesus' disciples? If so, then the narrative tension is relaxed with surprising ease. Why first worry the reader so thoroughly about Peter and then simply *imply* that all ended well for him?

Another Matthaean peculiarity meets the careful reader's eye in 28.9-10, in a seemingly superfluous incident when the risen Jesus meets the women who fled from the tomb. The short episode brings no new information. Jesus only reiterates the message of the angel (v. 7)—with one notable exception: Jesus now calls the disciples his 'brethren' (v. 10). Even though the narrator in 28.16 returns to the customary terminology, 'the disciples', the mention of 'brethren' may have some pregnant meaning. The theme of brotherhood was introduced in the opening Petrine episode (4.18-22), so a faint resonance might be felt here. But what kind of hint should that be: is it just a narrative decoration? Does it symbolically restore Peter's relationship to Jesus? Or does it rather imply that Peter and the rest of the disciples are now equals as the brethren of Jesus (i.e. as the 'founding brothers' of the Christian community of brothers and sisters)?

The scanty narrative in itself allows no firm conclusions. The fact remains in any case that Peter's role in the conclusion of Matthew's narrative is modest indeed. Paul knew a tradition according to which Peter was the first witness to the risen Lord: ὤφθη Κηφᾷ, εἶτα τοῖς δώδεκα (1 Cor. 15.5). Luke, too, was aware of a special appearance of Jesus to Peter (24.34). In John (21.1-14), there is an impressive appearance story in which Peter takes the leading role among a group of disciples. Matthew will not tell his reader anything of the sort. The minimalistic, pale description—hardly a real narrative—of Jesus' appearance, declaration of authority, and commissioning concerns 'the eleven disciples' (28.16), of which no one is specified. Since Judas is dead by now, the reader will conclude that Peter is among the eleven. But the narrative silence around Peter is remarkable in comparison with the expectations the reader has been led to have about Peter's central role. Was not Peter the first disciple, the spokesman for the twelve, the foundation of the community, and the holder of the keys of the kingdom? Why did he lose his voice at the final triumphal scene? Or, considering his grave failure and lack of faith on some occasions, why was he not given a new chance or a word of consolation (in the style of Lk. 22.31)?

Arguments *e silentio* are always risky, and it is possible that the reader may have appreciated the narrator's spartan style. Ideologically, the conclusion of the Gospel effectively highlights Jesus as the sole teacher of the community. Yet there is one visible sign that should alert the reader to the silence of and about Peter. The narrator says that 'when [the disciples] saw [Jesus], they worshipped him; but some doubted' (v. 17).[78] The notion recalls 14.31-32, where Peter 'doubted' while (the rest of) the disciples 'worshipped' Jesus. In light of all that the reader has learned about Peter, the question is inevitably raised whether Peter still had his doubts. No answer is given; but surely the reader is left with some doubts about Peter.[79]

78. The peculiar remark οἱ δὲ ἐδίστασαν has been discussed vividly, see, e.g., Luomanen, *Entering the Kingdom of Heaven*, p. 167 n. 30. The usual translation 'but some doubted' is grammatically quite possible and seems the correct one. P.W. van der Horst ('Once More: The Translation of οἱ δέ in Matthew 28.17', *JSNT* 27 [1986], pp. 27-30) notes that 'it is a well-known and frequently used syntactical device to indicate a division of a group of persons or things into two (or more) subgroups only in the second half of the sentence' (p. 28; several examples are given).

79. The 'text-connoted reader', in Edwards, *Matthew's Narrative Portrait*, is unaware of the problems concerning Peter. *All* disciples doubted (p. 132), but the reader also gets 'every indication that the disciples' limitations should not paralyze them' (p. 135).

Conclusion: Facets of Peter in Matthew

It remains to summarize and evaluate the main lines of the sequential analysis. The Petrine twins—the character and the symbol—are separated now, if only momentarily. How coherent a 'paradigm of traits' can be constructed out of Matthew's characterization of Peter? Can another set of interconnected features be formed to describe the ideological symbolism attached to Peter, and how tightly are the two paradigms interwoven?

Peter as Character

Matthew's Peter is a many-sided character. Often flatly presented, he is at times surprisingly vivid and full of mimetic appeal. To begin with, he is the first disciple to be called by Jesus. This notion is made very clear to the reader, albeit with a certain mannerism, as is evident particularly in the list of the twelve apostles. This suggests that the implied reader is supposed to know Peter's special status beforehand, that it was a known fact from the community's tradition. The narrator occasionally deepens this rather flat side of Peter's character by showing that Peter really was a close friend of Jesus. This is indirectly shown in the minor healing episode in Peter's house and in the episodes where Jesus is accompanied only by his closest disciples. The intimacy contributes to the reader's perception of Peter as a 'real' person, a perception that then might invite a modern reader to psychologize further about Peter's personhood and inner motives. Several incidents show how eager Peter was to follow Jesus, but also how thoughtless and weak in faith he was.

This touch of full characterhood may explain why the narrator's many negative hints either pass unnoticed or tend to be interpreted in a lenient, atoning light. Peter was weak, but is that not just typically human? 'The spirit is willing, but the flesh is weak' (26.41). So, when Peter saw what he had done and 'wept bitterly' (26.75), the reader is likely to recognize here a human tragedy. And, knowing that the Gospel narrative is not really a Greek tragedy, the reader is also likely to anticipate a final turn to the better for Peter (as Luke did, 22.31-32). That turn is only hinted at vaguely, however, with the result that the reader is left with considerable uncertainty about Peter.

While much of the characterization of Peter makes sense within Matthew's plot, there are several instances where the narrator is surprisingly unconcerned about narrative continuity. Thus, for instance,

Peter participates in the transfiguration scene as if the incident six days earlier had never taken place. Such narratorial slumbers make the reader look for other, deeper-lying traits in Peter that would help explain why he can be depicted in such seemingly unmotivated ways, at least from the narrative viewpoint.

Another set of surprising features in Peter's behaviour as character also point in this direction. On many occasions, Peter seems to take on a representational, in part even illustrative role. As a spokesman of the group of disciples he still remains within the confines of the narrative; this role only highlights his prominence as the first and closest disciple of Jesus. Yet a pattern emerges to the effect that Peter becomes the spokesman in issues that concern the interpretation of the law, discipline, and division of honour within the community, as well as the community's relationship to Jewish society. Here the narrative world begins to lose its integrity and to point to deeper levels of reality, as shown, for instance, by the mention of the 'community' (ἐκκλησία) of those who believe in Jesus.

Thus, while mostly walking comfortably as a character along the surface of the narrative world, Peter every now and then sinks into deeper waters, towards being an illustrative symbol and, at bottom, a partisan hero and villain in Matthew's contemporary church.

Peter as Symbol

As a symbol, Matthew's Peter embodies both positive and negative values. The positive symbolism is mostly attached to the narrative notion of Peter as Jesus' first and closest disciple. The transfiguration scene is an instructive point of departure in assessing these brighter sides of Peter's symbolic value. As eyewitness and hearer of the heavenly voice, as guarantor of salvation-historical continuity, and as the historical seal of the trustworthiness of the Christian proclamation, Matthew's Peter is an unwavering uniting, pan-Christian symbol, much as he is in 2 Peter (cf. 2 Pet. 1.16-21). Also, his christological confession remains valid for all time. This aspect of Peter the symbol coheres with the 'historicized' Peter the character whose status as the first disciple was fully appreciated by the narrator. Yet there is much more to Peter's positive symbol than his historicity. Not a mere historical person, Peter is a revelation-historical symbol with abiding theological value.[80]

---

80. One might indeed speak of Peter's 'salvation-historical primacy' in

More ambiguously, but with unmistakably positive connotations, the Matthean Peter illustrates the brighter as well as the darker sides of Christians of all times. The 'first' disciple is the archetypal Christian in his eagerness to follow Christ and in his weakness, his little faith, and his defective understanding of God's ways. These are the facets of Peter that Christian interpreters best recognize. Understandably so, for such paradigmatic traits can be deduced rather simply from the narrative. Here aesthetic and ideological aspects converge. The character and the paradigmatic symbol are truly Siamese twins. Paradigmatic features easily disturb an aesthetically oriented reader as being too poignantly illustrative. However, especially in the denial story, Matthew's touching narration precludes the reader from any possible criticism to that effect. There the symbolic level and the text world are happily conjoined: a devoted reader will learn from the moral paradigm, while an aesthetic critic will appreciate the vivid characterization.

But there is a deeper level where the symbolic message no longer finds an adequate counterpart in the narrative. There, the 'first' disciple's historical and theological primacy, which Matthew seemingly took for granted and aptly exploited for a general paradigm, ceases to pass unquestioned. Peter is only in part an all-Christian symbol. He also embodies the traditions and values of a Jewish-Christian group in Matthew's community. Where Peter's partisan role comes into play, the narrative logic often suffers or becomes more complex. The distribution of roles becomes opaque or ambivalent, and here the narrator uses indirection as the means of characterzation. Irony, sometimes mild but sometimes appearing more sinister, can be felt. The narrator suggests to the reader that not all of what was said of Peter concerning his leadership and authority should be taken at face value. Thus, 'the very

Matthew, as does J.D. Kingsbury, 'The Figure of Peter in Matthew's Gospel as a Theological Problem', *JBL* 98 (1979), pp. 67-83 (71, 75). What Kingsbury's sympathetic mainstream reading does not capture, however, is that Peter's 'salvation-historical primacy' already was a theological (and practical) problem for Matthew. Against Kingsbury's view, S. Byrskog (*Jesus the Only Teacher: Didactic Authority and Transmission in Ancient Israel, Ancient Judaism and the Matthean Community* [ConBNT, 24; Stockholm: Almqvist & Wiksell, 1994], pp. 252-53) rightly points out that 'the authorization of Peter in 16.18f. points to the future, not the past'. But then again, Matthew has seriously damaged this proclamation of Peter's future authority by historicizing/narrativizing it (cf. the scene immediately following), by democratizing it (cf. ch. 18), and, in the concluding scene of the Gospel, by silencing Peter and emphasizing Jesus as the only authority.

favourable view of Peter in Matthew'[81] is partly an illusion.

Through the partisan character of Peter, 'the little ones'—be they teaching authorities, ascetics, supporters of Petrine traditions, or those concerned for the purity of the community and its good esteem among the Jewish society—are seriously appealed to. Matthew may stand relatively close to their symbolic universe; at any rate he is fully aware that they are heirs to Jesus' historical disciples. By the time Matthew wrote the Gospel, the community seems to have included a considerable number of non-Jews and was increasingly aware of its worldwide mission. Matthew's community would lose its legitimacy if the Jewish-Christian group decided to leave it and (re)join 'the lost sheep of the house of Israel'. Yet Matthew does not side with this group whole-heartedly. True, the author admonishes the non-Jewish or liberal faction to show much patience and self-denial. The author even urges them to make the Jewish Christian group's symbolic world their own. But the Petrine front, too, is admonished to forgive a sinning brother. Peter's lack of understanding in halachic and disciplinary matters suggests that the author indirectly questions the Jewish-Christian understanding and application of the law. Matthew also warns that the 'first' may become the last and the 'last'—the Gentile newcomers—may become first.

The most ambivalent feature in the symbolic role of Peter is in his role as 'a stumbling-block' to Jesus. The themes of scandal, offence and going astray pervade the Matthaean portrayal of Peter and have spread beyond Peter himself to those who relate to him in the narrative world. Not only is Peter a scandal to Jesus and scandalized by Jesus, he also reacts when Jesus seems to offend the Jewish authorities. Astonishingly, even Jesus' behaviour and teaching are contradictory in this respect. In 15.12-14, he deliberately offends the Pharisees so that Peter and the disciples are terrified. In 17.24-27, Jesus' attitude is much more tolerant, and throughout the community discourse he keenly admonishes his followers to avoid all forms of offending behaviour.

This variety, it seems, has origins that are deeper than the narrative and thematic level of the text. Peter's ambivalence at the ideological level points to a fundamental problem in Matthew's symbolic universe,

---

81. Brown, Donfried and Reumann (eds.), *Peter in the New Testament*, p. 75. The phrase is taken over by A.F. Segal, 'Matthew's Jewish Voice', in D.L. Balch (ed.), *Social History of the Matthean Community: Cross-Disciplinary Approaches* (Minneapolis: Fortress Press, 1991), pp. 3-37 (8).

to his understanding of Jewish and Christian relations within and without the community. This is too vast an issue to be discussed here, but, concerning Peter and Jesus, one final conclusion can be reached.

In Matthew, Peter remains a dubious symbol—a figure of authority and legitimation, a pan-Christian paradigm of discipleship, yet also a partisan figure, a scandal to the expanding church of Christ. Therefore, no matter how high he was esteemed by the ecclesiastical tradition, Peter could not really hold the keys of the kingdom over other disciples. Consequently, there is a democratizing tendency in Matthew towards a community of brothers and sisters. The most that Peter reasonably could be was a 'founding brother' *par excellence*, with all his extra-ordinary vices and virtues. Matthew's ultimate answer to the Petrine dilemma, however, is the christocentric programme of 23.8 and 28.16-20. All teaching authority belongs to Jesus; all authority in heaven and on earth belongs to Jesus alone. While Peter is silent and invisible, Jesus has the last word; Matthew's church will be built on his abiding presence.[82]

---

82. A similar conclusion is reached by Nau (*Peter in Matthew*, p. 134): 'Judging from the effect of Matthew's redaction, then, the goal of the evangelist was to show that even Peter provided no real competition to Jesus, leaving Jesus ultimately to stand unrivaled with all authority, *exousia*, in heaven and on earth.'

NAMING THE NAMELESS: GENDER AND DISCIPLESHIP IN MATTHEW'S PASSION NARRATIVE

Talvikki Mattila

The power of naming is crucial. Through naming, God created the world. Through naming, our experience is expressed and shaped—human reality is created and transformed. Feminist theology claims that up till now the naming has been done by men and therefore it is partial. Men should name only their own reality. When males name women's reality, it renders women invisible, silent and subdued. This has challenged women into a process of creating new language so that women can speak out their own reality.[1]

New language leads to a new feminist reading of Scripture, which will be illustrated here through a study of the passion, death and resurrection of Jesus in the Gospel of Matthew (chs. 26–28). Seen in the context of Matthew's whole Gospel, these stories reflect something that

---

1. For the ideology and goals of feminist theology, see further, e.g., L. Isherwood and D. McEwan, *Introducing Feminist Theology* (Sheffield: Sheffield Academic Press, 1993); C.P. Christ and J. Plaskow (eds.), *Womanspirit Rising: A Feminist Reader in Religion* (San Francisco: Harper & Row, 1979); E. Schüssler Fiorenza, *In Memory of Her: A Feminist Theological Reconstruction of Christian Origins* (New York: Crossroad, 1983); *idem, Bread Not Stone: The Challenge of Feminist Biblical Interpretation* (Boston: Beacon Press, 1984); *idem* (ed.), *Searching the Scriptures*. I. *A Feminist Introduction*; II. *A Feminist Commentary* (London: SCM Press, 1994–95); R. Radford Ruether, *Sexism and God-Talk: Toward a Feminist Theology* (London: SCM Press, 1983); J. Capel Anderson, 'Feminist Criticism: The Dancing Daughter', in J. Capel Anderson and S.D. Moore (eds.), *Mark and Method: New Approaches in Biblical Studies* (Minneapolis: Fortress Press, 1992), pp. 103-33; J. Capel Anderson, 'Matthew: Gender and Reading', *Semeia* 28 (1983), pp. 3-27. Especially for Matthew see also E.M. Wainwright, *Toward a Feminist Critical Reading of the Gospel According to Matthew* (BZNW, 60; Berlin: W. de Gruyter, 1991), and A.-J. Levine, 'Matthew', in C.A. Newsom and S.H. Ringe (eds.), *The Women's Bible Commentary* (London: SPCK, 1992), pp. 252-62.

can be called 'the logic of Matthew's imagination'.[2] This imagination is very much dependent on the Old Testament. The old text is fulfilled in the new, for Matthew looks at the old text from a new angle.[3] He[4] expresses his code of understanding this way: 'Therefore every scribe who has been trained for the kingdom of Heaven is like the master of a household who brings out from his treasure what is new and what is old' (13.52).

Just as Matthew tried to transform and reinterpret old texts in the first century, feminist readings can do the same in the twentieth century in order to make these texts relevant to us today. Elaine Wainwright finds a parallel in this image of the scribe trained to implementations of the inclusive *basileia* vision, which she sees as a symbolical image of 'revisioning'. This kind of revisioning needs to take account of both 'the old text' and new critical reading.[5]

I will try here to approach the narrative world of Matthew from the angle of gender. The focus will be on women who appear as characters in the passion narrative. They will be considered in the wider perspective of discipleship. Analysis of character presentation helps to explore the gender codes surrounding the women characters. Also, comparisons and contrasts between characters on the basis of gender will be made in order to point out the gender biases in the text. All this can be considered as a new angle to the old text.

Before entering into a more detailed analysis of the texts concerning women, some general observations about discipleship are appropriate. Discipleship—even if the concept is neither explicitly expressed nor defined—is a very typical way in Matthew to depict the group relation-

2.   The expression is from F. Kermode ('Matthew', in R. Alter and F. Kermode [eds.], *The Literary Guide to the Bible* [London: Collins, 1987], pp. 387-401 [388]).

3.   Kermode sees in this process a typological relation between the old and the new. The old text is fulfilled in the new and the new is validated by the old, but the new also contains and transcends the old text. The demand of fulfillment is a constant excess in everything, and excessive deeds bring out the question of authority. According to Kermode, Matthew needed to explain the *exousia* of Jesus as a manifestation of something new that was an excess of something old, namely the law, the old source of authority. The themes of excess, transformation and authority are in various ways visible in Matthew's Gospel (Kermode, 'Matthew', pp. 388-94).

4.   The authorship of the Gospel will not be discussed in this context. I assume that the evangelist whom I here call Matthew, was a 'he'.

5.   E.M. Wainwright, 'The Gospel of Matthew', in Schüssler Fiorenza (ed.), *Searching the Scriptures*, II, pp. 635-77 (635-36).

ships in the community.[6] In the world in which the New Testament was written, 'disciple' was a technical term for the pupil of a philosopher or a teacher. The term and the social institution it implies were known both in early Judaism and in Hellenistic society at large. Comparable relationships are the teacher–student relationships of the Jewish scribes and and later rabbinic schools. The Jewish institution of discipleship shows many similarities with the form of discipleship in early Christianity.

There are, however, considerable differences, especially in regard to questions concerning the substance of teaching and the person of the teacher. The rabbinic scholar is bound to the Law, which is, in principle, supreme over the teachings of any individual rabbi, while Jesus' disciples are connected to the person of Jesus in a particular way. The rabbis are chosen by their students while Jesus takes for himself the initiative to call whom he chooses. In Greek culture, the teacher–student relationship took varying forms, but generally discipleship involved adherence to a great teacher and his particular way of life. The early Christian form of discipleship, with its emphasis on the person of Jesus, comes closer to the individualistic Hellenistic teacher–disciple relationship.[7] The person-oriented, christological nature of discipleship in early Christianity is seen in the fact that the discipleship language was extended beyond the original reference to disciples of the earthly

6. The verb μαθητεύω occurs in the New Testament 4 times, 3 of which are in Matthew. The noun μαθητής is used in Matthew 73 times (261 in the New Testament as a whole), which is far more than in Luke or Mark. The word is never used outside the Gospels and Acts. Within the Gospels it is never used of a woman. Of a woman it is used only once in Acts 9.36.

7. H. Weder, 'Disciple, Discipleship', *ABD*, II, pp. 207-10 (209). According to Anthony J. Saldarini, the master–disciple relationship does not come from Second Temple Judaism, which is the cultural context of Jesus' ministry; rather, Matthew is using early Jesus traditions and a Greek model rather than a Hebrew model, and at the same time resisting the early rabbinic movement of the late first century. During the Hellenistic period, the most common referent of a disciple was an adherent of a great teacher, one committed to a movement or a way of life (Saldarini, *Matthew's Christian-Jewish Community* [Chicago: University of Chicago Press, 1994], pp. 95-96). S. Byrskog argues for a continuity between the concerns of the Jewish culture and the transmission of the Matthean community as related phenomena (Byrskog, *Jesus the Only Teacher: Didactic Authority and Transmission in Ancient Israel, Ancient Judaism and the Matthean Community* [ConBNT, 24; Stockholm: Almqvist & Wiksell, 1994]).

Jesus. In the Gospel of Matthew, Jesus is presented as a teaching authority for both the historical disciples and the generations to come (23.8-12; 28.18-20). Jesus' mastership is not, however, commensurate with that of the rabbis or other teachers. In the narrative world that Matthew creates, Jesus' unique and incompatible authority is expressed, for example, by letting only outsiders address Jesus as teacher (e.g. 8.19; 9.11; 12.38; 17.24). His own disciples do not use this expression in the narrative.[8] Jesus' unique authority has implications for the understanding of discipleship. One becomes a disciple when called to follow by Jesus himself. The meaning of discipleship is not merely to learn from a teacher; it represents a life relationship, a commitment to Jesus. In this sense it is not restricted to the historical figures of the past, but includes as well the recipients of the Gospel in the Matthaean community.[9] An analogy might be seen in the prophet's vocation. As God himself called the prophets, so did Jesus call people to be his disciples.[10] Yet the question of discipleship is still more complex. The disciples in Matthew are followers of Jesus and, having received special teaching from him (13.10-12; 15.15; 16.5-20) become proclaimers of

8.   Saldarini, *Matthew's Christian-Jewish Community*, p. 96. Byrskog, on the other hand, argues that Jesus is primarily the teacher of his own chosen disciples. According to Byrskog, the disciples are not, however, merely ideal figures of the past. The readers in the Matthean community could identify with them. Byrskog claims that 'the author identified himself as one among Jesus' disciples and pupils' (*Jesus the Only Teacher*, pp. 234-36). It is obvious that the narrative has different layers of understanding. In the narrative world, Jesus is the leader of a limited group of followers. Because Jesus' authority in Matthew's community extends beyond and is legitimated by his death and resurrection, the circle of disciples is extending beyond the narrative to Matthew's social world. The point, however, is not the extension in time and space, but the substance of Jesus' teachership.

9.   J.D. Kingsbury argues that the Gospel does not make a difference between the time of the church and the time of Jesus. These are overlapping (*Matthew: Structure, Christology, Kingdom* [Philadelphia: Fortress Press; London: SPCK, 1975], pp. 31-37). Also, U. Luz emphasizes the transparency of the disciples: they are to be models for Christians in Matthew's community ('The Disciples in the Gospel According to Matthew', in G.N. Stanton [ed.], *The Interpretation of Matthew* [IRT, 3; Philadelphia: Fortress Press; London: SPCK, 1983], pp. 98-127). G. Strecker, however, sees the disciples as historical characters in an unrepeatable past, as he emphasizes the 'historicizing' perspective in the Gospel narrative ('The Concept of History in Matthew', in Stanton [ed.], *Interpretation of Matthew*, pp. 67-84).

10.   Weder, 'Disciple, Discipleship', p. 209.

this teaching to new disciples (28.18-20). The disciples are often specified as 'the twelve', but sometimes a larger undefined group of followers is indicated. Discipleship is also a designation for insiders (cf. 11.25-27; 13.11). These observations evoke the following questions: Is everyone who follows Jesus a disciple or is it a title restricted to a limited group? What is the symbolic content of the term? How are disciples defined in terms of characterization? If discipleship is a construct for insiders, how does this relate to gender—what is the status of women among the followers in Matthew?

I have chosen to track the theme of gender in relation to discipleship in the passion narrative (chs. 26–28) as a whole. The table that is included overleaf shows the appearances of two different character groups in the narrative: disciples and women. The disciples refer here to different groupings. They are sometimes 'the twelve', and sometimes a smaller group or even a larger group of followers. The specific expression 'the twelve' is used three times in chs. 26–28. Two of these are connected to Judas, who is said to be 'one of the twelve'.[11] The one who betrays is one of the chosen twelve. The third occurrence is connected to the Passover meal, where the twelve are the only ones present with Jesus (26.17-30). A closer circle is mentioned also in 28.16, where 'the eleven' are gathered in Galilee for instructions after the resurrection. All these references clearly concern groups of males.

The italicized and underlined passages show how the female presence frames the passion narrative. Just as the whole Gospel in a sense is framed by women—the women in the genealogy and the witnesses of the death and the resurrection of Jesus—also the passion narrative begins and ends with episodes including women. The italicized, but not underlined, passages mark the other appearances of women. A clear and immediate observation from this table is the alternating presence of women and disciples during these events. At the beginning of the narrative, the disciples are present all the time with Jesus. Jesus tells them that he is going to be crucified; they witness the anointing by an unknown woman, the meaning of which they hear Jesus himself explain. The twelve have the Passover meal with Jesus, and some of them are present at Gethsemane. But when Jesus is arrested, they flee; and the next time they are present in the story is in Galilee after the resurrection. What is in between here? Besides the unknown woman in the

11. Mt. 26.14; 26.47.

anointing story, there are women who are introduced to the narrative only *after* the male disciples—the twelve—have fled. These are women looking at the cross and witnessing his death, sitting near the tomb, and finally witnessing the resurrection. These women are commissioned to proclaim the good news to the disciples who have fled. But when the eleven are getting instructions from the risen Jesus for a worldwide mission, women are no longer present.

	disciples	women	
Instruction to disciples 26.1-2	X		
Leaders plot against Jesus 26.3-5			
Woman anoints Jesus 26.6-13	X	X	
Betrayal of Judas 26.14-16	X		–One of the twelve
Passover 26.17-30	X		–The twelve
Peter's betrayal foretold 26.31-35	X		
Prayer in Gethsemane 26.36-46	X		–Three of the twelve
Betrayal and arrest 26.47-56	X		–Disciples flee
Jesus before Jewish Council 26.57-68	X		–Peter
Peter's Denial 26.69-75	X	X	*–Two women*
Jesus before Pilate 27.1-2			
Death of Judas 27.3-10	X		–One of the twelve
Trial before Pilate 27.11-26		X	*–Pilate's wife*
Soldier's response 27.27-31			
Crucifixion 27.32-44			
Death of Jesus 27.45-53			

Responses to his death 27.54-66		X	–Centurion
			–Joseph of Arimathea
			–Mary of Magdala
			–Mary, the mother
			    of James and Joseph
			–the mother of Zebedee's
			    sons

Women witness the empty tomb *28.1-8*		X	–Mary of Magdala –The other Mary
Commissioned to proclaim *28.9-10*		X	–Mary of Magdala –The other Mary
Leaders plot 28.11-15			
Instructions to the disciples 28.16-20	X		–The eleven

The twelve (the eleven) are clearly the chosen, symbolic group of insiders. They are with Jesus during the Passover meal. They are the ones Jesus sends to proclaim the good news all over the world. They are definitely a male group. But then why, all of a sudden, are women brought into the story? What is the function of women in this narrative? Let us consider two different answers to this puzzle. According to Carla Ricci, the redactor was unable to cite the witness of the male disciples because they had fled, and the narrator was thus forced to refer to the women who stayed. The story describes the end of Jesus' earthly existence. The women have been with him from the beginning, but only now, when the women are the only ones present, must their presence be acknowledged. If Matthew had been able to refer to the presence of the apostles at the foot of Jesus' cross, women would not have been mentioned, and the great silence—as Carla Ricci calls it—would have been total.[12]

Elizabeth Struthers Malbon's interpretation approaches the problem from another angle. Malbon sees the verses about women at the cross as a repeating analepsis, a retrospective section that fills in an earlier missing element. This means that the reference to the women disciples/ followers was deliberately delayed until the moment when the true meaning of discipleship could be understood by the reader. This would mean that the experience of the crucifixion and the resurrection is central to followership/discipleship.[13]

Which of these opposite interpretations seems more true to Matthew's purpose? The real point, I will argue, is missing in both interpretations. Women's presence or activities do not guarantee their discipleship. Women may have followed Jesus. Still, the fact remains that they are not called disciples and the references to them are reduced almost to a minimum. Ricci's position is therefore well grounded, but is it the whole truth? A closer look at Matthew's narrative is needed to fill out the picture. As a test case, I will analyse the women as characters in the

12. C. Ricci, *Mary Magdalene and Many Others: Women who Followed Jesus* (Minneapolis: Fortress Press, 1994), p. 26. Ricci notes also the presence of women at the Passover meal: apostles were there, and they could be quoted. There was no need to mention women. Consequently, Ricci calls the approach in her book 'the exegesis of the silence'.

13. E. Struthers Malbon, 'Fallible Followers', *Semeia* 28 (1983), pp. 29-48 (41-42). Malbon's article is about the structure of the Markan passion narrative, not about the Matthaean narrative.

passion narrative. It is not sufficient, however, to observe the female characters. It is necessary to compare the characterization of women with the main characteristics of discipleship in general. This comparison can give clues to a revisioning of discipleship.

Women in Matthew's Passion Narrative

The narrative structure of Matthew 26–28 can be divided into three main sections: 26.1-56; 26.57–27.53; and 27.54–28.20. The first section illustrates preparation for Jesus' death, the second one his death, and the third one the events after his death.[14] In the structure of Matthew's passion narrative, women appear at the crucial turning points of the story. In the beginning, there is a woman pointing toward Jesus' destiny, and, in the moment of his death and resurrection, women act as witnesses and intermediaries. Also, other brief appearances of women—the female servants and Pilate's wife—serve as contrasts in the process of the narrative communication.

A Woman Anoints Jesus (26.6-13)[15]

Matthew has abbreviated Mark's story (cf. Mk 14.3-9) and introduced some changes, but the basic content remains the same. According to Mark, those who disapproved were vaguely 'some'; Matthew has 'disciples'.[16] The statement in Mark, 'She has done what she could', is left out.

---

14. J.P. Heil names these sections: (1) Jesus prepares for and accepts his death; (2) the innocent Jesus dies as true King and Son of God; (3) the authority of the risen Jesus prevails through witnesses of his death, burial and resurrection (*The Death and Resurrection of Jesus: A Narrative-Critical Reading of Matthew 26–28* [Minneapolis: Fortress Press, 1991], pp. 1-19).

15. The story about anointing appears in every Gospel, but in somewhat different forms. In Matthew and Mark the episode is placed in Bethany in the house of Simon the leper, and the name of the woman is not told. In Luke (7.36-50), a woman whose identity is not told, but who is defined as 'a sinner', anoints Jesus' feet, not his head as in Mark or Matthew, and the place is the house of Simon the Pharisee. Finally, in John (12.1-8), there is an anointing episode in Bethany, and the woman who anoints (his feet this time) is Mary, the sister of Martha and Lazarus.

16. The Matthaean redaction here may portray disciples as representative Christians. The issue would then be the traditional discussion between almsgiving (helping the poor) and good works (*Almosen und Liebeswerk*). The original context of the anointing pericope is thus seen in the situation of Matthew's church, and the

There are two pericopes of ill-will in the beginning of the passion narrative. The Jewish leaders plot against Jesus, and one of the twelve betrays him. The anointing story is placed between them. The contrast is clear. After the hostile gathering of the Jewish priests and elders, Jesus is described here in the middle of table fellowship with his own followers. The place is the house of Simon 'the leper', which means that Jesus is once more associating with social outcasts and eating with them. This is something to which the Pharisees had already objected (cf. 9.10-13). There appears here an unknown woman[17] who by her action shows her love and devotion to Jesus. The focal point of the anointing is in the future. According to Jesus' own explanation, anointing is a preparation for burial, it is 'good work'. The priests and elders plan to kill Jesus, and here is a woman who holds fast to a deeper instinct concerning the meaning of the moment. This does not mean that she really knows the implications of her anointing, only that she may feel them on a deeper level of her being.

The story implies still another meaning. The word 'Messiah' means 'the anointed'. In ancient Israel, each new king was anointed. Samuel anointed first Saul and later David by pouring oil over their heads. This is exactly what the unknown woman does in this story. But she is no famous prophet, just a woman without identity, status or background— a person who as a representative of her gender is an outsider. She has no voice of her own, even if disciples speak to her and her actions are the cause of the dialogue between disciples and Jesus. As a character, she lacks all personal features. She carries out a prophetic action at a crucial moment of Jesus' life.

The situation in this story is somewhat problematic. All events occur during a meal. The indignation of the disciples could have occurred merely because of the presence of the woman. A female with access to a male dinner was anomalous. In antiquity, meals were ceremonies where the roles and statuses were predictable and legitimated. The social relationships during a meal were an image of social relationships in the society in general. Eating together implied sharing a common set

---

problem is solved here in favor of good works. Cf. D. Senior, *The Passion Narrative According to Matthew: A Redactional Study* (Leuven: Leuven University Press, 1975), pp. 32-33.

17. Heil extends the antithesis to include also the high priest who is named Caiaphas. The priest has a name, the woman does not (Heil, *The Death and Resurrection of Jesus*, p. 26).

of ideas and values. In a luxury meal, servants could anoint guests with perfumed oil.[18] However, the presence of the woman seems not to be the problem in the story. The problem is not even her deed, but the waste. The oil must have cost a lot. It is said explicitly that the ointment was expensive and could have been sold 'for a large sum'. Mark has been more specific. His valuation of the ointment is 'more than three hundred denarii'. According to Matthew (20.1-16), one silver denarius was the wage paid to a man who has worked all day in the fields. For this woman it could have meant one year's earnings.[19] This serving is for Jesus only, and it is a luxury, not for daily needs. This is what annoys the disciples. They think the money should have been given to the poor. They have still not understood what Jesus told them about his death (26.2).

The woman is an image of prophetic commitment to Jesus. Even if the chosen representatives of the insiders, the male disciples, are present, the acknowledgment is in the hands of a woman. In the Matthaean narrative, the woman symbolizes understanding. In her deed, the meaning of Jesus' kingship becomes visible. The symbolic meaning of gender is clearly perceptible. The woman's personal identity is not essential. On the contrary, because she has no identity it is her action that is in the spotlight. Her action underlines her gender, because what she does breaks the rules and conventions of her time. Her gender is a symbol. It is a contrast to the disciples, the chosen insiders who fail to understand. Jesus has told the disciples about his crucifixion. After that, Matthew introduces a female prophet who anoints Jesus. This anointing implies kingship that has nothing to do with earthly ruling, but will be realized in a shameful death in this narrative. Preparation for a burial and messianic kingship are two sides of the same coin.

A little earlier (16.16), Peter has boldly confessed, 'You are the Messiah, the Son of the living God', but he has not really understood the meaning of his words. In 26.2, Jesus has told the disciples about his coming crucifixion, which they fail to accept. The woman in the narrative, on the contrary, is characterized as somebody who, on the deeper

---

18. B. Malina and R. Rohrbaugh, *Social Science Commentary on the Synoptic Gospels* (Minneapolis: Fortress Press, 1992), pp. 135-37.

19. L. Schottroff has very thoroughly shown the economic situation of women in New Testament times. Women earned less than men, and one denarius was enough for two days' provisions and other needs (*Lydia's Impatient Sisters: A Feminist Social History of Early Christianity* [London: SCM Press, 1995], pp. 92-95).

level of her being, identifies herself with Jesus' suffering and death. Her prophetic commitment to Jesus has been described as 'a sterling model of true discipleship' in sharp contrast to the male disciples.[20] In the narrative, Jesus authoritatively acknowledges and legitimates her action in spite of the indignation. Jesus' authority gives the woman her full humanity and acknowledges her as a true disciple. What happens here is the emerging of a new liberating consciousness that forms the new content of discipleship.

The relationship between this episode and the Passover meal, where there are only the male disciples present, is somewhat interesting. A woman prepared Jesus for burial in a meal setting, and then Jesus prepares his disciples for his departure.[21] Because the Passover meal is a significant rite that is central to the Christian community, it may have been important for the narrator to explain who was present. The rite involved eating: it was a meal. A meal meant table fellowship, social cohesion and shared values. Jesus ate the Passover meal with his disciples, which is a symbol of a new family. But the family consists only of male disciples. The androcentric values of the time are clearly present in this episode. Ricci comments that women were not mentioned because there were males present at the historical last supper and women could thus be forgotten.[22] However, the point in the story lies not in a historical report about what really happened, but in the symbolic content of the story. Symbolically, women are excluded.[23]

As in Mark, the last verse in the anointing story binds this event to the worldwide proclamation of the gospel. The prophetic act of love will be told as a part of the gospel 'in memory of her', even if her name is not recorded and her presence in the house of a leper is not explained. This story has provided the title for Elisabeth Schüssler Fiorenza's feminist reconstruction of Christian origins, *In Memory of Her*. In the

---

20. Cf. Heil, *The Death and Resurrection of Jesus*, p. 27; Schüssler Fiorenza, *In Memory of Her*, pp. xiii-xiv.

21. Levine, 'Matthew', p. 261.

22. Ricci, *Mary Magdalene and Many Others*, p. 26.

23. L. Schottroff sees in this episode about Passover the symbolic dispossession of women's work. Women made the bread, but both in Jewish and in Roman mealtime rituals, the paterfamilias performed the ritual and symbolic acts which included breaking the bread. In the Passover meal, Jesus takes the role of the paterfamilias who takes the bread, blesses, breaks and gives it. The work of women is rendered invisible (*Lydia's Impatient Sisters*, p. 85).

first pages of her volume, Schüssler Fiorenza confronts the problem of naming. This woman is virtually forgotten, because her name is lost to us. The stories about Peter and Judas are still continuously repeated, but the name of this faithful disciple is forgotten, because she was a woman.[24] A name is something that gives a person identity, but I would still claim that part of the significance of this story is due to the fact that the woman is not identified. The story will be told in memory of a female disciple and a female prophet.

The Two Female Servants and Pilate's Wife (26.69-75; 27.11-26)
Matthew has abbreviated the Markan story about Peter's denial and also made some changes. In Matthew, there are two different young women asking the questions (in Mark it was the same one). In the Matthaean version, when Peter denies Jesus the second time, he takes an oath that underlines the denial. Matthew plays with contrasts here. Whereas Jesus fearlessly confesses his messiahship in front of the high priest, Peter denies Jesus in front of two female servants.Whereas the high priest questions Jesus under oath if he was 'the Christ, the Son of God', Peter takes an oath denying that he even knows Jesus.

The two women in the story are not developed characters, but their questions are an essential part of the plot. Furthermore, in the structure of the story these women may be seen as counterparts to Peter. In front of female servants who are in the margins of the society because of both their gender and their status, a disciple denies his master, whom he has boldly acknowledged as Messiah earlier.[25] According to 26.35, Peter insisted that he was ready to die with Jesus. Here he is in the position to meet the challenge, but he fails to prove his discipleship. His identity as a disciple is exposed by the female servants.[26] Throughout the Gospel, Peter is described as a spokesman of the disciples; he is the first among the twelve. But even he fails to be faithful.

When Jesus is in front of Pilate, there is the voice of a woman in the story. Matthew is the only Gospel telling about Pilate's wife. She does

24. Schüssler Fiorenza, *In Memory of Her*, p. xiii.
25. Wainwright wants to see more here. According to her, the affirmation of the women symbolically places them on the side of Jesus so that they symbolize the truth, while Peter symbolizes falsehood as one who is unfaithful to Jesus at this crucial moment (*Toward a Feminist Critical Reading*, p. 137). I think falsehood is too strong an image here; rather, Peter symbolizes fallibility.
26. J. Kopas, 'Jesus and Women in Matthew', *TTod* 47 (1990), pp. 13-21 (20).

not appear in the story; there is only her message. She has had a dream, and she sends a message to her husband: 'Have nothing to do with that innocent man, for today I have suffered a great deal because of a dream about him.' The expression 'because of a dream' recalls the infancy narrative in chs. 1–2, where Joseph gets divine messages through dreams. Her words are a contrast to the climate of ill-will and accusation in the narrative. It is a voice outside the world of power. An outsider, a woman and a Gentile, with no personal connection to Jesus, offers the only voice of protest.[27] It is a prophetic voice—divine communication on Jesus' behalf, as significant as the dreams in the infancy narrative.

The two female servants and Pilate's wife—unlike the unknown woman who anoints Jesus—have a voice in the story. They have an essential part in the plot, in the process of communicating the truth, even if they are unable to change the course of events. In the Matthaean narrative, it is possible to acknowledge the symbolic meaning of their presence. The female servants confront Peter with his association with Jesus—something that implies Peter's confrontation with his discipleship. He is not only unprepared to die with Jesus as he had promised, but he is also unable to understand what it means to be a disciple. The women speak the truth that Peter could not. So does Pilate's wife, even if she is unable to save Jesus.

Women at the Cross and at the Tomb (27.54-66; 28.1-8)
At the beginning of the passion narrative, there was a woman sending Jesus to his kingship, which meant death. When Jesus dies there are again women present. 'Many women were also there, looking on from a distance; they had followed Jesus from Galilee and had provided for him. Among them were Mary Magdalene, and Mary the mother of James and Joseph, and the mother of the sons of Zebedee' (27.55-56). These women are 'looking on from a distance'. Later, Mary of Magdala and the other Mary are said to be 'sitting opposite the tomb' (v. 61).

The passion narrative is framed with stories about women. Even if Matthew seems to be very patriarchal and androcentric in many respects, he has no difficulty placing women in roles of foretelling and witnessing. Matthew mentions 'many women' already in the beginning of the episode (v. 54), where Mark has only names. Mark introduces

27. Here again Wainwright places a woman—Pilate's wife—on the side of Jesus and truth against falsehood (*Toward a Feminist Critical Reading*, p. 137).

'many other women' only later. It may not seem very significant, but nuances can be revealing. In Matthew, the picture is that of many women following Jesus *from Galilee* (not in Galilee as in Mark); they joined him on his way to Jerusalem. Matthew seems to say that these women were with Jesus and served Jesus *after leaving for Jerusalem*, instead of the Markan version that depicts women who had followed and served Jesus *already in Galilee before the journey*. This difference needs to be kept in mind when we consider the relationship of the terms 'following' and 'serving' to discipleship.

These verses come after the account of Jesus' death. The following verses describe several responses to Jesus' death. First, the centurion and his men acknowledge Jesus as the Son of God. Like Pilate's wife, they also are rather unexpected witnesses as Gentiles and outsiders. The centurion and his men are mentioned before the women are mentioned. After the women are mentioned there is a wealthy man from Arimathaea, who 'was also a disciple to Jesus' and wants to bury him.[28] I want to point out here the possible clue in the words καὶ αὐτός. If Joseph *too* was a disciple,[29] the verse refers back to the women in previous verses whom Matthew then counted as disciples. As such, it is still not sufficient evidence and the καὶ can be interpreted with a less significant meaning: here is one more disciple who verifies his discipleship in this way; he performs the service of a disciple, buries his master, and then departs. After this, the male disciples are out of the scene.

Women are described in these verses in a passive way; they are not giving any signs of response. Their silence contrasts with the dramatic confession of the centurion produced by Jesus' death. Women are presented as helpless witnesses watching in silence. What is important from the narrative's point of view is that they are *there*, present. The

---

28. That Joseph is said to be both rich and a disciple can be seen as incongruous according to Jesus' earlier sayings about the rich and entering the kingdom of God (19.23-24). Still, as 'a rich disciple' Joseph can request and receive the body from Pilate (Heil, *The Death and Resurrection of Jesus*, p. 93).

29. The identity of Joseph varies in the Gospels. In Mark it is said that he was a member of the council and 'was also himself waiting expectantly for the kingdom of God', as also in Luke. Matthew does not say that he was a member of the council, but that he was a disciple. In John he is also a disciple, but in secrecy, and he is not mentioned as a member of the council. As for Matthew, it might be significant to notice the different wording. Matthew does not use here the noun 'disciple', but a corresponding verb that he 'was also a disciple' to Jesus. The same verb is used in 28.19 in the sense 'to make disciples' of all nations.

centurion confesses, Joseph from Arimathaea acts as a disciple, women are just 'looking on from a distance' and 'sitting opposite the tomb'. What does this passivity tell us?

Before trying to suggest any answers, it would be important to look at the scene in 28.1-8, where women are again mentioned. Now they act as witnesses at the empty tomb. Here again there are some differences compared to Mark. In Matthew, there is no mention about the women going to anoint Jesus' body. Women are reduced from three in Mark to two in Matthew. The women are 'Mary Magdalene and the other Mary', who are the first ones to know about the resurrection and whom the angel commissions to proclaim the news. The mother of the sons of Zebedee, who was mentioned in the scene at the cross, has disappeared. The audience is limited to the disciples, to 'brothers'. The women are to go to the disciples and tell them that they are to go to Galilee. According to Wainwright, 'contrary to the patriarchal structuring of society whereby men carry out the significant tasks, the divine message and mission is here given to women rather than men'.[30] In my opinion, the text here proves exactly the opposite. It has already been noted that women are probably mentioned here because it was not possible to refer to any man. But the whole situation is patriarchalized. Women are given the smallest possible role, and they have no voice and carry out no actions. As witnesses they are needed to fill up the gap when men are not available, and they are forgotten as soon as possible. Their role is reduced to the minimum.

From the group of 'many women', Matthew names three. This is the only place in the Gospel—besides Mary and the foremothers in the infancy narrative and Herodias—where women have names. Matthew tells about Peter's mother-in-law, about the ruler's daughter and the hemorrhaging woman, about the Canaanite woman and her daughter, but none of them is named. But these women at the cross and at the tomb not only have names, two of them are also very carefully identified through their sons, who are known as disciples. Is there intentional irony in this? The men flee, but their mothers remain faithful. These women are not meant to be seen only as substitutes[31] for their sons or male disciples in general but as faithful witnesses in their own right. The mother of Zebedee's sons has a double connection to men, to

---

30. Wainwright, *Toward a Feminist Critical Reading*, p. 144.
31. This is how Heil sees them (*The Death and Resurrection of Jesus*, pp. 91-95).

the father and to the sons, but her own name is not given.[32] It is interesting that this mother of Zebedee's sons appears also a little earlier in Matthew's narrative (20.20-21). Then she is said to have asked Jesus for a favour for her sons. According to Mark (10.35-36), the men ask for themselves. In Matthew's narrative, it is possible to imagine that families were the ones following Jesus. If there were sons and mothers, it is likely that there were daughters too. In the feeding miracles in Matthew (14.21; 15.38), it is said that many men shared in these meals, 'to say nothing of women and children'. In the crowd following Jesus, there were men, women and children. The inner circle of disciples might have consisted of families, in which there were twelve men who afterwards were chosen as the symbolical group for the new Israel. So even if the women were not mentioned by name and not counted, Matthew does not hide them altogether. They become visible in terms of the dynamics of the patriarchal world in the narrative.

The author needed the women at the cross and at the tomb as witnesses. There had to be some known and defined persons to serve that role. This is the reason for mentioning names and sons of the women. But if that much was granted for women, it was because there was no one else. As soon as possible, the significant tasks were returned to men. The worldwide mission is reserved for males only in the story. Once again, female gender forms a limitation in a patriarchal society.

Another group of characters present in the passion narrative are the Jewish leaders. They are a male group, but they also symbolize authority and power, which in this narrative means power to judge, to execute. The narrative begins with their plotting against Jesus. They are the ones who accuse Jesus and the ones who take the blame and get the blame in the story. They are present mocking at the cross; they set guards in front of the tomb and plot after the resurrection. The three character groups—disciples, women and Jewish leaders—embody a symbolic function in the narrative: disciples are weak, fallible; women are faithful followers;

---

32. The names differ from Mark. In Mark there is at the cross Salome instead of the mother of Zebedee's sons as in Matthew. Is Salome the name of this mother? In Matthew, women at the tomb were Mary Magdalene and 'the other Mary', which in Mark is Mary, Joseph's mother. It is also puzzling to have the verb in v. 61 in singular. Is it possibly referring to Mary of Magdala alone?—in Mt. 28.1 the women are Mary of Magdala and the other Mary, while in Mark there were three women: Mary Magdalene, Mary mother of James, and Salome.

and the Jewish leaders are the guilty ones. The contrast is between the disciples and the women. The disciples are those who fail, and the women are those who remain faithful. Against this it is possible to argue that women can also be considered as 'fallible'. In 27.55 it is said that 'they were looking on from a distance' (ἀπὸ μακρόθεν) just as Peter followed Jesus 'at a distance' (ἀπὸ μακρόθεν) when he was arrested (26.58). For Malbon this means that women were also fallible; stronger followers would have drawn nearer. Remaining 'at a distance' is a sign of fallibility.[33]

Still, the fallibility of the women is on a different level than that of Peter. Maybe it was easier for women to be present at the crucifixion than for male supporters; it was less conspicuous and less dangerous. Their gender might also have prevented them from going nearer. The disciples, on the other hand, are given a prominent status among the followers; they receive special revelation and teaching from Jesus, and they still fail. The fallibility of women is really vulnerability in the patriarchal structures, where they were not counted. Jane Kopas presents an opposite view: in her opinion the women were faithful to a heroic degree.[34] This faithfulness is shown in terms of their gender in a patriarchal society. But, fallible or not, the women and the disciples are on the same side. Failure does not exclude discipleship. It must also be taken into consideration that there are negative female characters in Matthew: vengeful Herodias and her daughter and the mother of Zebedee's sons who wanted her own sons to have more dignified positions in the coming kingdom. It cannot be said that the Matthaean disciples are all 'bad guys' and that all women are models of faith. The real 'bad guys' are the Jewish leaders.[35] It is much more crucial to see the controversy between the Jewish leaders and the women. The leaders have power, women have none. The leaders stand against Jesus because they

33. Malbon, 'Fallible Followers', p. 43. In this article, Malbon wants to point out that even if the disciples were fallible, they did not thereby become non-followers. Malbon's article is about disciples in Mark, where, on the whole, the theme differs from the theme of disciples in Matthew.

34. Kopas, 'Jesus and Women in Matthew', p. 21.

35. These groups of characters are treated here on a literary level. The historicity of these accounts is not the point here. The question about historicity and the tendency to describe the Jewish leaders as the guilty ones rather than the Roman leaders is dealt with profoundly, e.g., in J.D. Crossan, *Who Killed Jesus?* (San Francisco: Harper & Row, 1995).

fail to understand, while women remain faithful because they do understand.

Commissioned to Proclaim (28.8-10, 16-20)

The women are sent twice to the disciples, first by the angel at the tomb and then by Jesus whom they meet on their way. As in Mark, the women are said to be filled with fear, but Matthew also describes them as running away from the tomb 'in great joy'. Their meeting with Jesus is told very concretely. They grasped his feet and worshipped him. The passive, silent women at the cross and at the tomb are transformed into confessing messengers. Jesus sends women 'to his brothers' which can be seen as underlining the role of women as mediators in the reconciliation of the disciples with Jesus.[36] This can lead to an image of women as substitute disciples who are not needed any more after they have fulfilled their role. Yet they are not substitutes; rather, they form a reliable and indispensable bond with the reality of Jesus' death and resurrection, as witnesses and disciples in their own right.

Women and Discipleship

The prophetic anointing by a woman, the presence of women at the cross and at the tomb, and the lack of understanding and absence of those who are called disciples—all these narrative traits lead to the question of women's discipleship. I will next consider some of the general elements that belong to discipleship in Matthew in order to see if they are in some sense compatible or comparable with what has been said above about the women. If there is compatibility to be found, I think there is also ground for a revisioning of discipleship.

Considering discipleship as such, it is first necessary to find out what the main elements of discipleship in Matthew are. The word μαθητής[37] is first mentioned in the beginning of the Sermon of the Mount (5.1). The disciples come to Jesus, and he begins to teach them. This group of followers seems to be well known to the author and his audience, because it is not explained in any way. Some clue as to who belonged to this group is found in ch. 4, where Jesus calls four men to follow

---

36. Cf. Heil, *The Death and Resurrection of Jesus*, pp. 99-102.

37. On μαθητής as a key term to discipleship, see M.J. Wilkins, *The Concept of Discipleship in Matthew's Gospel as Reflected in the Use of the Term 'μαθητής'* (Leiden: E.J. Brill, 1988).

him. These men immediately leave the work they were occupied with and their father in order to follow Jesus. What is noteworthy here is that the narrator does not formally designate these four men (Peter, Andrew, James and John) as disciples. The key word here is ἀκολουθεῖν (to follow), which in the literal sense means 'following', 'going behind', but even in ancient Greek includes also following in an intellectual or religious sense.

The same pattern repeats itself: 'following' is clearly something essential to those who belong to the disciples. The occurrences of the verb ἀκολουθεῖν,[38] however, point to a more inclusive definition about discipleship and raise some questions. It seems important that when Jesus calls, he calls people to follow him, but the word 'disciple' is not always mentioned. What seems decisive is that Jesus calls, not the decision of the recipient. Jesus takes the initiative, as in the calling of these two pair of brothers (4.18-22) or in the call of Matthew (9.9). On the other hand, it seems that people who themselves turn to Jesus, are unable to follow, like the scribe who comes up to Jesus and says: 'Teacher, I will follow you wherever you go.' The narrative does not say that he ever did (8.19). Or the rich young man who approaches Jesus and to whom Jesus said: 'If you wish to be perfect, go, sell your possessions ... then come, follow me.' The narrative says that the man went away (19.16-22).

'Following' is clearly essential in the language of discipleship, and it includes more than just being in the company of Jesus. The calling is a definite, immediate and total break with the past. The disciples were not offered any positions of honor or power, which is pointed out very clearly:

[A]nd whoever does not take up the cross and follow me is not worthy of me (10.38).

If any want to become my followers, let them deny themselves and take up their cross and follow me (16.24).

38. The verb occurs in Matthew 25 times, in Mark 18 times, in Luke 17 times and in John 18 times. Outside the Gospels the occurrences are limited: 4 times in Acts, once in 1 Corinthians and 6 times in the book of Revelation. This can mean that the verb ἀκολουθεῖν is an indication of following the earthly Jesus. At least it demonstrates a close association with Jesus himself (cf. Weder, 'Disciple, Discipleship', p. 207).

The fact that the verb ἀκολουθεῖν characterizes the central quality of the existence of a disciple, is really not a matter of disagreement.[39] But is it a parallel expression to μαθητής? Do the 'followers' represent those who stand in a special and intimate relationship with the earthly Jesus? Or is it the case that disciples and 'followers' represent two different levels of supporters? There is also the crowd who is said to 'follow' Jesus (4.25; 8.1; 12.15; 19.2; 20.29; 21.9). At the beginning of the Sermon on the Mount the audience seems to be a distinct group of disciples, and the reader of Matthew's Gospel is puzzled by the identity of this group. There were the four fishermen who were called in ch. 4 to follow, but in v. 4.25 the narrative says that 'great crowds followed him (Jesus)'. The response of the crowd is described with the same word ἀκολουθεῖν. There seems to be no reason to distinguish the crowd and the disciples in 5.1. For Matthew, discipleship is open for all.[40] In 7.28, at the end of the sermon, the distinction has vanished, and it is 'the crowds' who are impressed by Jesus' teaching. So the depiction of who is a follower fluctuates. There is a crowd that follows; there is the group of twelve whom Jesus calls to follow him; but there are also others who are called to follow (8.18-22; 19.16-26; 20.29-34). And to blur things even more, there is Joseph from Arimathaea who is also a disciple but who is not among the twelve.

What can be concluded here is that the term μαθητής clearly has a restricted usage and does not extend to all who follow Jesus in the Gospel.[41] In this context, I find very helpful the illustration that Michel

39. See especially J.D. Kingsbury's article 'The Verb *akolouthein* ("to follow") as an Index of Matthew's View of his Community', *JBL* 97.1 (1978), pp. 56-73. Among others also Weder, 'Disciple, Discipleship', p. 207; K. Corley, *Private Women, Public Meals: Social Conflict in the Synoptic Tradition* (Peabody, MA: Hendrickson, 1993), p. 173; R.F. Thiemann, 'The Unnamed Woman at Bethany', *TTod* 44 (1973), pp. 179-88 (182).

40. U. Luz says in his commentary: 'following on the part of the disciples does not distinguish them from the people who are sympathetic to Jesus, but the people, by following, belong together with the disciples' (*Matthew 1–7: A Commentary* [Minneapolis: Augsburg, 1989], p. 201). Kingsbury, on the contrary, is of the opinion that the 'following' of the crowds is only descriptive and lacks any connotations of discipleship ('The Verb *akolouthein*', p. 61).

41. Thiemann sees the term 'disciple' as being systematically ambiguous. The true followers, the authentic disciples, are those who recognize that Jesus' mission leads to crucifixion, and they embark on a journey that may lead to the loss of their own lives for his sake. According to Thiemann, the only authentic disciples in the

MATTILA *Naming the Nameless* 173

Clevenot has produced in his materialist reading of Mark. His idea is that Jesus' person creates a sort of 'magnetic field'. Around his person are formed several concentric circles, and the text situates people to these circles. Closest are Peter, James and John; then the twelve; then the disciples; then the crowd. The distance to the centre (Jesus) differs, but all these different groupings belong to Jesus' magnetic field.[42]

The term 'disciples' itself remains ambiguous. It refers in Matthew to different groupings. They are 'the twelve', some smaller groups, or possibly a larger group of followers. This is a question of dispute. Some scholars think that in Matthew's understanding the term 'disciples' refers only to the twelve or their equivalent.[43] Others see in 'disciples' a more inclusive, larger group.[44] The discussion is based on different ways of understanding the question. It is possible to take 'disciples' as a broader concept of following or just a way of defining a certain restricted group among the followers. The question is not without importance, because it clearly involves the problem of women's status among disciples in Matthew.

Discipleship is an image of determined commitment. But commitment to what? In 28.19, Jesus gives instructions for the worldwide missionary work to the eleven disciples. He sends them to make all nations his 'disciples' (μαθητεύσατε πάντα τὰ ἔθνη). The verb μαθητεύω indicates a wider perspective for discipleship. The verb occurs in the New Testament only four times, three of which are in Matthew. The two other occurrences are in v. 13.52, where it is used of a teacher of the law who becomes a disciple in the kingdom of heaven and in 27.56 of Joseph of Arimathaea. All three of these are clearly connected to discipleship other than that of the immediate group of people following Jesus. From this perspective, everybody in the community of believers

passion narrative are Joseph of Arimathaea and the women ('The Unnamed Woman at Bethany', p. 182).

42. M. Clevenot, *Materialist Approaches to the Bible* (Maryknoll, NY: Orbis Books, 1985), pp. 86-89. What is interesting is that the crowd is also present in the other magnetic field—the counterforce around the temple—as the last circle.

43. Anderson, 'Matthew: Gender and Reading', p. 20; S. Love, 'The Place of Women in Public Settings in Matthew's Gospel: A Sociological Inquiry', *BTB* 2 (1994), pp. 52-65 (57); M. Sheridan, 'Disciples and Discipleship in Matthew and Luke', *BTB* 3 (1973), pp. 235-55 (237-38).

44. Corley, *Private Women, Public Meals*, p. 174; U. Luz, 'Die Jünger im Matthäusevangelium', *ZNW* 62 (1971), pp. 141-71 (142-43); Thiemann, 'The Unnamed Woman at Bethany', p. 185.

is a disciple. 'Following' is a word describing movement. Jesus calls followers and these followers are instructed to invite new members to the community. This kind of understanding would leave space for all kinds of people to be considered as disciples, both male and female, both Jew and Gentile.

Still, there is in the Gospel the small group of the twelve to whom the explicit word 'disciple' most often refers. The twelve are chosen by Jesus from the 'crowd' and they are 'the sent ones' (ἀποστολοί).[45] The explicit phrase 'the twelve' occurs most frequently in ch. 10 where these men are mentioned by name and where Jesus gives them instructions and sends them on. Their task is to proclaim the kingdom of heaven, to heal the sick, to raise the dead, to cleanse the lepers and to exorcise demons. In this way they are supposed to be following Jesus by doing the same miracles he did; but more than simply following is at stake here.

From the reader's point of view the situation is puzzling. The names of the twelve appear rather late in the narrative and already before ch. 10 the 'disciples' are mentioned several times. Does the narrator mean that before the mission of the twelve in ch. 10, the disciples were a larger group of followers? From this group Jesus then chose the twelve, and the 'disciples' as a group after ch. 10 are always the twelve? The twelve are mentioned explicitly only in 19.28, when there is a question of reward: the disciples are going to sit on twelve thrones and govern the twelve tribes of Israel. In 20.17, Jesus takes the twelve aside and speaks about his death. In the passion narrative there are three references, two to describe Judas as one of the twelve and the third to underline the participants during the Passover meal. The twelve are clearly associated with the Jewish-Christians among the readers. The twelve are sent to the lost sheep of Israel (10.6),[46] not to the Gentiles. Thus they fill here a very specific symbolic function, but they do not exhaust the whole content of the concept of discipleship.

There are two different ideas of discipleship interwoven with each other. On the one side, there are the twelve who symbolize the male Jewish fellowship, which apparently had its function in the Jewish-Christian community of Matthew. The twelve symbolize the claim of

45. The word ἀπόστολος (apostle) is used only once in Matthew, in 10.2 in reference to the listed names of the twelve.

46. In neither Luke nor Mark is there a parallel to these words. Cf. Mk 6.7-13 and Lk. 9.1-6.

Jesus on all of Israel. Everyone of the twelve was a disciple, but every disciple did not belong to the twelve.[47] On the other side, the other 'group' is too vague to define, but certainly they had some common denominators with the twelve. The followers in the Gospel are a group physically moving from one place to another with the earthly Jesus, but they are also a group of insiders within the community of believers, who are entrusted with the secrets of the kingdom (13.10-11; 13.36).

Thrones and governments—elements of power and hierarchy—have already been mentioned. Quite opposite to these is the approach to discipleship in 23.8-12. There, the hierarchical model is put upside down: 'The greatest among you will be your servant.' The key word is διάκονος. The same idea occurs in 20.26: 'Whoever wishes to be great among you must be your servant.' This implies that the idea of serving is somehow closely connected to discipleship. The verb διακονεῖν occurs five times in Matthew. The first occurrence is in the account of the temptation in the wilderness where, as in Mark, 'the angels came and waited on (διηκόνουν) him' (4.11). The fact that it was angels doing the service certainly makes it look like something more than 'ordinary service'. The second occurrence is in the story of the healing of Peter's mother-in-law (8.14-15); the woman 'began to serve (διηκόνει) him' after being cured by Jesus. This differs from Mark, where she is said to serve *them* (Jesus and the disciples). Matthew's singular pronoun underlines the quality and object of this serving. The third reference is found after the request by the mother of Zebedee's sons for positions of honour for her sons. Jesus tells the twelve that 'whoever wishes to be great among you must be your servant, and whoever wishes to be first among you must be your slave; just as the Son of Man came not *to be*

---

47. Like the majority of scholars, Weder considers that 'the twelve' was an entity instituted by Jesus. According to him, the description that Judas was 'one of the twelve' speaks against a post-Easter origin of the establishment of the twelve, and also it is much easier to understand the later meaning of the group if it was instituted by Jesus (Weder, 'Disciple, Discipleship', p. 208). Also, Sheridan considers it difficult to see how the concept of the twelve could be so deeply embedded in the tradition if it did not have a historical foundation, at least in the latter part of Jesus' ministry (Sheridan, 'Disciples and Discipleship in Matthew and Luke', p. 239). On the other side is Crossan, who thinks that even if Judas was a historical follower of Jesus, he could not have been one of the twelve, because the symbolic grouping of the twelve new Christian patriarchs to replace the twelve ancient Jewish patriarchs did not take place until after Jesus' death (Crossan, *Who Killed Jesus?*, p. 75).

served [διακονηθῆναι] but to *serve* [διακονῆσαι] and to give his life a ransom for many' (20.26-28). Matthew takes this over from Mark. The fourth reference is in the context of the parable of the last judgement (25.44): 'Lord, when was it that we saw you hungry or thirsty or a stranger or naked or sick or in prison, and did not take care of you?' (οὐ διακονήσαμέν σοι). This has no parallels in the other Gospels. Finally, there are the women at the cross who had followed Jesus from Galilee and 'had provided [διακόουσαι] for him' (27.56). All these five occurrences indicate something more than just ordinary serving. The verb διακονεῖν is seen as depicting the ministry of Jesus and also characterizing the life of the followers of Jesus.[48] The women who are serving (Peter's mother-in-law and the women at the cross) are actually described as doing what all disciples were supposed to be doing.

Here is the very heart of what discipleship is about. The word disciple is insufficient by itself and therefore another kind of language is needed. The male and female discipleship/followership is described differently: Men follow and are said to be disciples, women follow and are said to serve.[49] The members of the new movement should be referred to by another word. 'Disciple' is a concept from patriarchal society and it is reserved for men only. But through the portrait of male discipleship, revisioning of followership is possible. There are other than male followers also, the existence of which is challenging us to discover new expressions and ways to define what it means to belong to the group of insiders. There are healing stories in chs. 8 and 9 where Jesus' calling is narrated in a different way, and the responses are from those of the marginal and vulnerable people in the society: women, Gentiles, lepers. They are people of faith, as also are the unknown woman who anoints Jesus and the Canaanite woman in ch. 15. If 'following' and 'serving' are attributes of followership, so also are 'faith' and 'understanding'. The separation of male and female followership is due to the difference in language used even if the words refer to the same thing. The attributes 'following' and 'serving' are explicitly the words used in 27.55 and connected to the women who were witnesses at the cross. They had

48. Wainwright, *Toward a Feminist Critical Reading*, pp. 86-87; M.A. Tolbert, 'Mark', in Newsom and Ringe (eds.), *The Women's Bible Commentary*, pp. 263-74 (267); J. Dines, 'Not to Be Served, but to Serve: Women as Disciples in Mark's Gospel', *The Month* (November 1993), pp. 438-42 (440-41).
49. Dines, 'Not to Be Served but to Serve', p. 442.

left everything, followed Jesus, and served him. These women fulfil the demands of discipleship, but nevertheless they are not called disciples.

Stuart Love argues that the term 'disciples' refers only to the twelve, but he adds that this does not suggest that other members of the Matthaean community were not disciples. The point is 'to underscore the authority and responsibility of the teaching ministry which belongs only to those known in the Gospel as the disciples'. He wants to point out that though women are not counted among the twelve and that there is no evidence that they were teachers in the Matthaean church, it does not mean that they were not considered full members of the kingdom or 'models' for the male disciples.[50] These comments show quite clearly the ambiguity of the question. Women were not counted among the disciples, but they could still be 'models'. It remains a fact that their gender prevents their identification as disciples.[51] Those designated as Jesus' disciples are male, but the concept of discipleship is vague. It also leaves out others in addition to women. If, rather than 'discipleship', the ideas of 'following', 'serving', 'faith' or 'understanding' are taken as a description of those who belong to the insiders, there becomes evident a more inclusive gathering of the new movement. Such a movement was not exclusively male and Jewish as the twelve were but could also include women and Gentiles, and all other 'nobodies' as well.

The question of 'fallibility' of characters in the passion narrative was discussed earlier. The disciples and the women are not to be put in contrast with one another. The disciples are not to be seen as bad examples for discipleship while women are positive examples of faithful followers. The male disciples are still disciples, even if they fail, and women are not in the story to oppose them. Men and women symbolize different reactions and attitudes. Another readily made contrast is between the women of great faith (the Canaanite woman, the woman who suffered from hemorrhage, Peter's mother-in-law, the unknown woman who anoints Jesus) and the disciples 'of little faith' (6.30; 8.26; 16.8; 17.19-20).[52] Their leader Peter is a man 'of little faith' (14.31). In 16.22-23, Peter is rebuked by Jesus and his denial in the passion narrative is quite obvious.

---

50. Love, 'The Place of Women in Public Settings in Matthew's Gospel', p. 57.
51. Cf. Anderson, 'Matthew: Gender and Reading', p. 20.
52. Corley, *Private Women, Public Meals*, p. 175.

Conclusion

At the beginning of this article, I referred to two different approaches by Carla Ricci and Elizabeth Struthers Malbon. Ricci's exegesis of silence wanted to prove that women were there, even if they were invisible in the text. In Malbon's view, the real essence of discipleship in the form of women was reserved to a later stage, because of the connection to the death and resurrection of Jesus. Without countering the positive significance of women being present in the central experiences of Jesus' death and resurrection, I would argue that when discussing discipleship, both of these interpretations are substantially insufficient. On the one hand, the crucial point is that women nevertheless are not called disciples, even if they can be assumed to be silently present and even referred to on the decisive points of the narrative. On the other hand, the fact that women in Matthew's narrative were not really noticed until in the death scene, is not quite accurate. Women are mentioned a few times also before in the Gospel—in the miracle stories especially where there are glimpses of other kinds of responses and followership of Jesus. Therefore, I have here tried to shape a third alternative for approaching the question about discipleship.

In my view, women in the passion narrative are representatives of prophetic commitment and communication. They are not to be called models, because being 'a model' can mean that one is not really inside. One can be praised but not counted. Women are experiencing the status of being outside. They are insiders who are 'outsiders'.[53] The 'little ones' who are not to be despised, appear in the context of ch. 18, where in fact the model for disciples is a child, an ideal member of the new movement. Ideal membership involves humility and the total lack of power. Jesus is clearly identified with the weak and the defenseless. As part of patriarchal society, women and children are 'outsiders'. As outsiders they live in an unidentified, vulnerable position. Nevertheless, Matthew has ways of claiming them as insiders. The fact that the women at the cross were 'watching from a distance' does not prove fallibility; rather, it indicates the status of women in a patriarchal society. They are simply not allowed to be in the centre. They are unique witnesses to the death and to the resurrection, but are still kept aside. For Matthew—the ancient storyteller from a patriarchal society—there was

53. See also Kopas, 'Jesus and Women in Matthew', pp. 13-14.

no getting beyond that position, even though some elements of his Christian identity seem to question the inherited values. Nevertheless, through a consideration of male discipleship, it is possible *for us* to start to revision the inclusive followership. In doing so, we can appreciate the positive hints Matthew has given and strive for a further goal. The patriarchal structures once deprived women of the name, but they could not deprive them of the substance.

THE SON OF MAN AND HIS FOLLOWERS:
A Q PORTRAIT OF JESUS

Arto Järvinen

The narrative approach has already been around in the study of the Gospels for nearly two decades. Still, the early Christian document that most scholars think was a source for Matthew and Luke and that conventionally has been termed 'Q' seems to have caught little if any attention as a narrative text. Reasons for this may be manifold. First, the Q 'text' is only a reconstruction and always debatable in details; how can we be sure about the wording, order or extent of it?[1] Second, many critics have tended to view the document as a 'speech collection' rather than an organized, plotted text with narrative patterns.[2] Third, according

---

1. Apart from the Greek/English reconstructions of the International Q Project (cf. n. 4 below) the reader may consult the reconstructions and translations of B.L. Mack, *The Lost Gospel: The Book of Q and Christian Origins* (San Francisco: HarperSanFrancisco, 1993), pp. 71-102, and M. Borg, T. Moore, M. Powelson and R. Riegert (eds.), *The Lost Gospel Q: The Original Sayings of Jesus* (Berkeley: Ulysses Press, 1996), pp. 33-121. Both books share, to be sure, an interest in making Q known to the wider audience and as such do not qualify as critical presentations of the Q text.

2. M. Dibelius is well known for his scepticism concerning the degree of knowledge that one can wish to obtain about the character of Q. In his classical study *Die Formgeschichte des Evangeliums* (Tübingen: J.C.B. Mohr [Paul Siebeck], 2nd rev. edn, 1933), p. 236, he states: 'Was wir bei dem heutigen Stande der Forschung von der Quelle Q wissen, berechtigt uns eher von einer *Schicht* als von einer *Schrift* zu reden ...', and classifies the Q material as 'Worte Jesu' (p. 237) and 'diese stückweis erschlossenen Texte' (p. 235). Later on, some scholars even intensified the sceptical outlook toward a documentary Q text (e.g. W.F. Albright and C.S. Mann in their Matthew commentary: 'As a single, ordered source, oral or written, "Q" will not stand' [*Matthew: Introduction, Translation, and Notes* (AB, 26; Garden City, NY: Doubleday, 1984), p. 53]; cf. also D. Hill, *The Gospel of Matthew* [NCB; London: Oliphants, 1972], p. 25) but mostly the view has moved toward a growing optimism. J.S. Kloppenborg's words are representative of

to the dominant conception of Q, the document's narrative framing—
the little that we 'have' of it—is a late secondary development. Bearing
this in mind, it is not really difficult to see why the study of Q has
remained primarily within the realm of traditional exegesis,
notwithstanding a growing interest in sociological reflections and
rhetorical inquiries. On the other hand, far-reaching compositional theories and various reconstructions of the social history of the Q community have been proposed during the last 30 years of scholarship.

The goal of the present article is to broaden the methodological scope
of Q research in the direction of narrative criticism by approaching Q
with Jesus' self-characterization 'Son of man' as a vantage point. As
the reader will see, I am not suggesting that the 'new' literary approach
should be an exclusive methodology, but should rather supplement
more traditional composition-critical methods. Questions related to
(1) the literary nature of the Q document as well as those related to
(2) the social phenomena in the document's historical setting will be
asked. This means that sociological applications will occasionally be
included along the literary analysis. I will pay special concern to (3) the
symbolic world of the text, which is the merging point of the aforemen-
tioned two realms: the textual/narrative world and the real world.[3] I
accept the current standard practice of referring to Q-passages in the
order in which they are presented in Luke's Gospel; for example, Q 3.7
equals Lk. 3.7. Apart from few exceptions, Luke (rather than Matthew)

present-day Q studies: 'Q is very far from being a "random collection of sayings"
and is erroneously regarded as a pure sedimentation of oral tradition. It is, on the
contrary, a carefully constructed composition which employs literary techniques
characteristic of other ancient sayings collections' (*The Formation of Q: Trajectories in Ancient Wisdom Collections* [Studies in Antiquity and Christianity; Philadelphia: Fortress Press, 1987], pp. 323-24). Regarding Q's genre, V. Taylor fore-
shadowed many later studies, and also the present majority view, according to
which Q grew from 'a sayings-source pure and simple' toward a clustered document of both sayings and 'Pronouncement-Stories' (i.e. chreias); cf. V. Taylor, *The
Formation of the Gospel Tradition: Eight Lectures* (London: Macmillan, 2nd edn,
1945), pp. 182-84.

3. The 'symbolic world' of the text is contained in a given literary entity and is
a reflection of (but should not be mistaken for) the *'symbolic universe'* of its
author(s). On the concept 'symbolic universe', see P. Berger and T. Luckmann, *The
Social Construction of Reality: A Treatise in the Sociology of Knowledge* (London:
Allen Lane/Penguin Books, 1971), pp. 110-46. See also Kari Syreeni's article in
this volume.

is generally considered to be more faithful to the original Q-order of pericopes.[4]

I shall argue that the 'Son of man' functions as an important symbol that helped the Q community to interpret the rejection and failure of its mission to Israel. Jesus' role as the scorned Son of man and his glorious parousia—two quite contradictory phenomena—provided the Q community with applicable analogues to their own situation. The experienced hardships were evaluated from the perspective of the anticipated reward at the parousia soon to take place. The experience of rejection and the hope of compensation are discernible in the Q 'Son of man' language. If read in this manner, the passages that portray Jesus as the Son of man provide a narrative thread for the overall rhetoric of the document Q and contribute significantly to its thematic coherence.

The Study of Q and Literary Approaches

Modern Q-scholarship is methodologically characterized by an approach that is usually called *stratigraphical analysis*. This enterprise views the Q-text first as a complete literary product, penetrating then into clusters of projected older traditions.[5] The high esteem for the final

4. See Kloppenborg, *Formation of Q*, pp. 69-80. Where English translations of Q texts appear, they are in the form determined by the International Q Project (IQP) of the Society of Biblical Literature. The critical Greek reconstructions and their English translations as well as the explanations of the employed sigla can be found in *JBL* 109.3–114.3 (1990–95). The IQP's suggestions for verse order are accepted here, unless otherwise stated. Concerning the contents and extent of Q, I include the following Matthew and Luke parallels into a kind of 'minimal Q': 3.7-9, 16-17; 4.1-13; 6.20-23, 27-33, 35-49; 7.1-2, 6-10, 18-19, 21-28, 31-35; 9.57-60; 10.2-16, 21-24; 11.2-4, 9-20, 23-26, 29-35, 39-44, 46-52; 12.2-12, 22-31, 33-34, 39-46, 49, 51-56, 58-59; 13.18-21, 24, 26-30, 34-35; 14.16-24, 26-27, 34-35; 15.4-7; 16.13, 16-18; 17.1-4, 6, 23-24, 26-27, 30, 33-35, 37; 19.12-13, 15-26; 22.28-30. This list is a simplified version of J.S. Kloppenborg, 'The Sayings Gospel Q: Literary and Stratigraphic Problems', in R. Uro (ed.), *Symbols and Strata: Essays on the Sayings Gospel Q* (PFES, 65; Helsinki: Finnish Exegetical Society; Göttingen: Vandenhoeck & Ruprecht, 1996), pp. 1-66 (4 n. 12).

5. See L.E. Vaage, 'The Son of Man Sayings in Q: Stratigraphical Location and Significance', *Semeia* 55 (1992), pp. 103-29 (105, 121); Kloppenborg, 'Sayings Gospel Q', pp. 50-57. Quite similarly, see A.D. Jacobson, *The First Gospel: An Introduction to Q* (Foundations and Facets; Sonoma, CA: Polebridge Press, 1992), pp. 43-46. Jacobson uses 'composition criticism/analysis' (p. 43) to evaluate the literary integrity of Q blocks, then he evaluates the emerging tendencies from the viewpoint of identifying different strata.

product is partially responsible for the growing number of studies that are labeled under rubrics like 'rhetorical' and 'literary'.[6] These approaches have proven very important, especially as a means to demonstrate the relatively significant thematic and compositional coherence of Q.

There are *similarities* worth noting between the stratigraphical analysis and narrative criticism. On some points the common ground is real, while on other points it may be ostensible. Both approaches have their point of departure in the emphasis on the literary whole, but the interests of stratigraphical analysis lie ultimately in the fields of form and redaction criticism. If something is considered 'redactional', according to J.S. Kloppenborg, it is not primarily because of the subject-matter ('content'), but is a result of form-critical and literary observations.[7]

Yet a noticeable tension in the interaction of the two different foci (composition criticism and redaction criticism, most notably) is evident in many modern Q-studies. In applying different methods of divergent origins, scholars are often forced to make a choice between them. Present day studies on Q have much too easily adopted a preference for form-critical distinctions, even when rhetorical/literary analysis accentuates the *integrity* of a given literary unit.[8] In effect, literary

---

6.   No explicitly narrative-critical Q-studies have thus far been published. However, J.S. Kloppenborg's article 'City and Wasteland: Narrative World and the Beginning of the Sayings Gospel (Q)', *Semeia* 52 (1991), pp. 145-60, comes very close to being a narrative-critical treatment.

7.   Kloppenborg ('Sayings Gospel Q', p. 51) claims that the opponents of his Q-redaction hypothesis have failed to understand the 'point' ('it needs to be reiterated') regarding the discrimination of literary layers of Q: '[S]trata delineation of Q based on content-considerations has expressly been rejected by the present author and others'.

8.   For similar criticism, see P. Hoffmann, 'The Redaction of Q and the Son of Man: A Preliminary Sketch', in R.A. Piper (ed.), *The Gospel behind the Gospels: Current Studies on Q* (NovTSup, 75; Leiden: E.J. Brill, 1995), pp. 159-98 (187-88). Particularly telling is how W. Cotter treats the Q episodes on John the Baptist (3.7-9, 16-17 and 7.18-23, 24-28, 31-35): on the one hand, she argues that both blocks of text are skillful compositions (which, of course, is foremost an aesthetical evaluation), and on the other hand, she distinguishes independent prior traditions; cf. W. Cotter, ' "Yes, I Tell You, and More Than a Prophet": The Function of John in Q', in J.S. Kloppenborg (ed.), *Conflict and Invention: Literary, Rhetorical, and Social Studies on the Sayings Gospel Q* (Valley Forge, PA: Trinity Press International, 1995), pp. 135-50. Without entering into details, it is easy to agree with W. Arnal ('Redactional Fabrication and Group Legitimation: The Baptist's Preaching in Q

observations are subordinated to a traditional exegetical paradigm—in spite of the explicit claim that stratigraphical analysis is primarily based on 'literary-critical observations' (which is quite an ambiguous expression!).[9]

Herein lies the main *dissonance* between narrative criticism and the stratigraphic approach. Whereas structural anomalies and shifting foci are (traditionally) considered to be indicators of redactional activity in the latter approach, a narrative critic looks for rhetorical reasons for the contrasts in question. Shifts and tensions can often be viewed as quite deliberate ways to get the attention of the reader and thus need not be taken as evidence of a clumsy redactor. A scholar utilizing stratigraphical analysis may find recurring motifs with similar forms and tones as an indicator of the document's literary layering,[10] while a narrative critic might assume that the pattern is supposed to serve as a particular signal to manipulate the reader's interpretation in a desired direction. This point will be illustrated in the analysis to follow.

However, I wish to point out first that the Gospel texts themselves are made up of many individual and originally independent traditions, and a significant number of these, most likely, were already joined together in the oral phase in order to form pairs or small clusters of sayings (etc.).[11] It would be unwise to think that such a procedure of material aggregation has not resulted in tensions and often artificial compositions. While there undoubtedly was a certain redactional logic operative at the very first stages of this process, it is not at all clear that the subsequent (whether oral or literary) redactors were still fully aware of it. Nevertheless, in many cases the pre-existing composition was most

---

3.7-9, 16-17', in Kloppenborg [ed.], *Conflict and Invention*, pp. 165-80 [170]), who considers it likely that these units were created by one and the same hand.

9. Kloppenborg, 'Sayings Gospel Q', p. 51.

10. Cf. Kloppenborg's criteria for assigning substantial portions of Q to secondary redaction(s) in *Formation of Q*, pp. 167-70.

11. Reference can be made to the famous model of H. Schürmann, in which various stages of material growth can be detected in the Gospels; his article on the Son of man sayings in Q is illustrative ('Beobachtungen zum Menschensohn-Titel in der Redequelle: Sein Vorkommen in Abschluß- und Einleitungswendungen', in R. Pesch, R. Schnackenburg and O. Kaiser [eds.], *Jesus und der Menschensohn: Für Anton Vögtle* [Freiburg: Herder & Herder, 1975], pp. 124-47 [128-30, 140-44]). See also Kloppenborg's description of Schürmann's model (which Kloppenborg terms 'aggregation model'), 'Sayings Gospel', pp. 25-26; similarly Vaage, 'Son of Man', pp. 105-106.

likely preserved. We have evidence of this in Q when we encounter sayings that have been attached to each other with almost nothing connecting them except a thematic or a catchword linking.[12] It would be exaggerating, however, to state that there are many compositions of this kind in Q. All in all, my aim is to argue for a quite unified rhetoric in Q. Acknowledgment of the complexity of its tradition-history should not hinder one from asking: what is the unifying principle that the final author of Q has followed and that has enabled her or him to consider the text coherent enough to have relevance for its readers?[13]

Redactional Layering—Or Narrative Unity?

Nowadays many Q-scholars acknowledge Kloppenborg's redactional layering as their basic hypothesis, and it follows that most scholars share his methodological presuppositions. According to his redactional theory, judgmental motifs are deemed secondary, whereas wisdom teaching is the original core.[14] Also, the narrative framework is considered a secondary trait in the composition.[15] Accordingly, the Jesus of Q^1 is a teacher of wisdom,[16] quite foreign to the menacing celestial figure in Q^2, the 'Son of man'. The descriptions of Jesus in Q are held to be so divergent that the predominant explanation has been to suggest

12. Cf. such units as Q 6.43-45; 11.33-35 and 16.13, 17-18.

13. Cf. the emphatical statements of M.A. Powell, *What Is Narrative Criticism? A New Approach to the Bible* (London: SPCK, 1993), pp. 6-10. The essentiality of a 'unifying principle' is also underlined by N. Friedman, *Form and Meaning in Fiction* (Athens, GA: University of Georgia Press, 1975), pp. 51-52. C. Tuckett stresses the need to view Q as a unified whole (regardless of any stratification theory) in his Son of man analysis ('The Son of Man in Q', in M.C. De Boer [ed.], *From Jesus to John: Essays on Jesus and New Testament Christology in Honour of Marinus de Jonge* [JSNTSup, 84; Sheffield: JSOT Press, 1993], pp. 196-215 [202-203]).

14. The material distinction between the layers Q^1, Q^2 and Q^3 (symbols that denote literary layers; Q^1 is the earliest of these) is conveniently and compactly illustrated by W. Cotter, 'Prestige, Protection and Promise: A Proposal for the Apologetics of Q^2', in Piper (ed.), *Gospel behind the Gospels*, pp. 117-38 (117 n. 1).

15. See Kloppenborg's summary of the composition history of Q in *Formation of Q*, pp. 317-28. B.L. Mack presents more radical redactional conclusions in 'The Kingdom That Didn't Come: A Social History of the Q Tradents', in David J. Lull (ed.), *SBL Seminar Papers* (Atlanta: Scholars Press, 1988), pp. 609-35.

16. See Kloppenborg, *Formation of Q*, pp. 342-45.

a major secondary redaction(s) of the original document. The problem of the divergent pictures of Jesus is evident and unavoidable, since Q mostly is comprised of long speeches by Jesus. The 'image' of Jesus is, therefore, contained in the words of Jesus.

To start with, I accept the quite standard view that 'judgment to this generation' (see below) is Q's organizing principle. The redaction Q^2 is usually considered to be the level that dictates the appearance of Q as a final product. The supporters of the stratification think that the two redactions serve different purposes: the first has to do with the lifestyle and values of the compiling community, the second aims at attacking those who have not responded positively to this ethos of the Q group.[17] Seen this way, the first layer retains its original function and is legitimized by the second layer's use of the Old Testament theme of a 'prophet's fate'. This makes sense, but the larger question remains: Does the material really necessitate an hypothesis of *redaction*? The proposal of this article is that the answer is 'no'.

The passages dealing with the 'Son of man' are an important watershed in this respect. Some of them are viewed as reflecting the tendencies of Q's redaction, whereas some are considered to belong to the 'formative stratum'.[18] It will be argued here that no such dichotomizing of the 'Son of man' material is needed. The 'Son of man' language is coherent and consistent with Q's organizing principle. In the following I shall argue that even those passages that most often have been assigned to the formative layer of Q are firmly at home in the 'deuteronomistic' argumentation of Q as a whole. The 'Son of man' language appears to be a flexible and illuminating way of giving voice to the Q community's manifold experiences.

It is necessary to define briefly what is meant in Q by the sayings that announce judgment to contemporaries. For a long time it has been

17. See Mack, 'Kingdom That Didn't Come', pp. 624-26; J.S. Kloppenborg, 'Literary Convention, Self-Evidence and the Social History of the Q People', *Semeia* 55 (1992), pp. 77-101 (91-99); and Cotter, 'Prestige, Protection', pp. 124-38.

18. Kloppenborg (*Formation of Q*): Q 7.34; 11.30; 12.8-10, 40; 17.24, 26, 30 belong to Q's redaction, while Q 6.22 and 9.58 are part of the formative layer. See also Vaage, 'Son of Man', pp. 107-27: the sayings of the formative stratum are Q 9.58 and 7.34 ('less certainly'). R. Uro is more cautious and avoids direct stratigraphical locating ('Apocalyptic Symbolism and Social Identity in Q', in Uro (ed.), *Symbols and Strata*, pp. 67-118 (98-118)).

acknowledged that Q contains many affinities to the Old Testament 'deuteronomistic view of history', located originally in the Deuteronomistic history book and in the Chronicles, but later on utilized in a variety of Jewish writings up to the second century CE. Accordingly, the 'deuteronomistic' view goes as follows: Israel has continually been disobedient to Yahweh's covenant, but in his mercy Yahweh has exhorted the people through prophets. When Israel has not repented but persecuted the prophets, Yahweh has avenged this disobedience. This has taken place through the historical catastrophes of 722 and 587 BC, but will recur when necessary.[19] Q elaborates this idea by viewing John the Baptist, Jesus, and the community itself as God's last prophets, the persecution of whom God will avenge.[20] The pattern was first identified as characteristic of Q by O.H. Steck,[21] and first proposed by A.D. Jacobson as the 'unifying principle' around which the whole was organized.[22] Kloppenborg, by contrast, points out that these passages of 'deuteronomistic' influence are only a small portion of Q-material.[23] Nevertheless, their placement at the framing positions of many individual units, and the fact that Q's beginning and ending carry these tones make it most probable, even in Kloppenborg's view, that the 'deuteronomistic' element dictates the composition as a whole.[24]

Before proceeding to a treatment of passages that have to do with the

19. See R. Uro, *Sheep among the Wolves: A Study on the Mission Instructions of Q* (AASF, 47; Helsinki: Suomalainen tiedeakatemia, 1987), p. 176; also Jacobson, *First Gospel*, p. 73.

20. For relevant passages in Q, see A.D. Jacobson, 'The Literary Unity of Q', *JBL* 101 (1982), pp. 365-89 (384-85).

21. O.H. Steck, *Israel und das Gewaltsame Geschick der Propheten: Untersuchungen zur Überlieferung des deuteronomistischen Geschichtsbildes im Alten Testament, Spätjudentum und Urchristentum* (WMANT, 23; Neukirchen–Vluyn: Neukirchener Verlag, 1967).

22. A.D. Jacobson, 'Wisdom Christology in Q' (PhD dissertation, Claremont Graduate School, 1978); see also *idem*, 'Literary Unity', and lately *idem*, *First Gospel*. D. Lührmann (*Die Redaktion der Logienquelle* [WMANT, 33; Neukirchen–Vluyn: Neukirchener Verlag, 1969], pp. 87-89) and P. Hoffmann (*Studien zur Theologie der Logienquelle* [NTAbh, 8; Münster: Aschendorff, 1972], pp. 158-90), too, emphasized the relevance of 'deuteronomism' in Q, but not as forcefully as Jacobson.

23. Kloppenborg, *Formation of Q*, p. 93.

24. Kloppenborg, 'Sayings Gospel Q', pp. 55-56. Further, see Hoffman, *Studien zur Theologie*, pp. 180-81; Jacobson, *First Gospel*, pp. 72-76; Cotter, 'Prestige, Protection', p. 117.

Son of man, I shall sketch some general outlines of characterization in Q.

Characterization in Q

The narrator[25] of Q makes a minimal effort at a close description of characters, by connecting them to a time or a place, be it temporal (historical connections), spatial (home town, etc.) or social (familial relations, social status, etc.). In terms of geographical places, Q relates John the Baptist's activity to the region of the River Jordan (Mt. 3.5/Lk. 3.3) and the healing miracle of a centurion's child to Capernaum (Q 7.1). There is no mention of rulers or other significant temporal landmarks in the flow of contemporary history. True, there are some names present in Q, but—apart from John and Jesus—all this data is either about Israel's epic history (Abraham, Solomon, Jonah, Sodom and Gomorrah, Nineveh, etc.) or about some experiences of Jesus and his followers (Chorazin, Bethsaida and Jerusalem).[26]

As a consequence of Q's limited exposition[27] we notice that the nar-

25. The concepts 'narrator' and 'author', which normally are distinct concepts in narrative criticism, might actually be paralleled in the case of Q. Some literary theorists suggest that it is not illegitimate to mix the concepts 'author' and their 'narrator' in 'the case of a historical narrative ...'; cf. G. Genette, *Narrative Discourse: An Essay in Method* (Ithaca, NY: Cornell University Press, 5th edn, 1993), p. 213; also R. Scholes and R. Kellogg, *The Nature of Narrative* (New York: Oxford University Press, 1966), pp. 242-44. Accordingly, the author lends his or her authority to the 'narrator' and thus becomes more or less merged with the last mentioned. For the sake of convenience, however, I shall retain the traditional distinction between author and narrator in what follows. For the difference of the concepts, see Genette, *Narrative Discourse*, pp. 213-14; Scholes and Kellogg, *Nature of Narrative*, p. 240; D. Rhoads and D. Michie, *Mark as Story: An Introduction to the Narrative of a Gospel* (Philadelphia: Fortress Press, 1982), pp. 35-36; S.D. Moore, *Literary Criticism and the Gospels: The Theoretical Challenge* (New Haven: Yale University Press, 1989), pp. 25-40; E.S. Malbon, 'Narrative Criticism: How Does the Story Mean?', in J.C. Anderson and S.D. Moore (eds.), *Mark and Method: New Approaches in Biblical Studies* (Minneapolis: Fortress Press, 1992), pp. 23-49 (27-28). Particularly see the article of Merenlahti and Hakola in this volume.

26. For more on Q's narrative world and Israel's epic history, see Kloppenborg, 'City and Wasteland'.

27. On 'exposition', see M. Sternberg, *Expositional Modes and Temporal Ordering in Fiction* (Baltimore: The Johns Hopkins University Press, 1978), and

rator seems to presuppose the reader's familiarity with the various cryptic symbols and concepts. The narrator seems to trust the reader's ability to make the right associations. It is also obvious that the narrator does not take pains to introduce characters or topics to the reader, but to *convince* the readers of the utmost relevance and importance of these quite familiar things to their existence. This is apparent in the paraenetic and imperatival manner of expression that Q often exhibits.[28]

The overall impression about characterization in Q is that the 'portraits' are extremely sparse. As with the Gospels in general, outward appearance is not an issue. Also, Q shows no interest in describing Jesus' gestures or other procedures used by him in the acts of exorcism or healing, in contrast to an author like Mark, who sometimes provides such details, as in Mk 8.22-26.

1. The narrator of Q creates and maintains a joint connection between the fate of *the main character Jesus* and those who consider themselves his followers. Examined from this point of view, the procedure of offering only very sparse circumstantial details becomes readily understandable. A deliberate tactic of contemporizing the situation of Jesus is probably behind this. In the readers' perception, it amounts to the analogy between their own situation and the one illustrated by the text. The readers' life is transparently visible in the text, without stating it *expressis verbis*. It is not so much the characters themselves that make it possible for the readers to fuse themselves into the narrated events—it is rather the *events* and Jesus' monologues with which the readers can sense familiarity.[29] The weight is on the argumentation and the defense that are contained in the words of Jesus.

The use of *common symbols* is of great benefit for a narrator who wishes to refer to a wide range of subjects in a compressed manner. A symbol is often obscure to outsiders or non-contemporaries, yet it

R.A. Culpepper, *Anatomy of the Fourth Gospel: A Study in Literary Design* (Philadelphia: Fortress Press, 1987), pp. 18-20.

28. See Q 6.27-49; 7.23; 10.4-11; 12.3-7, 22-33, 40-46, 58-59; 13.23-24; 17.3-4, 23. These are explicitly imperative utterances of Jesus; but in addition to these, there is a lot of indirect but clearly comprehensible exhortation in Q.

29. See S. Rimmon-Kenan's (*Narrative Fiction: Contemporary Poetics* [New Accents; London: Methuen, 1983], pp. 35-36) discussion of 'psychological narratives' and 'apsychological narratives'. Since narrated action is very limited in Q, we may add the observation that whereas characters are clearly subordinated to events, the events, in turn, are subordinated to *themes*.

launches a network of associations for those who are familiar with it.[30] There is no doubt that Q's compilers appreciated this possibility: the use of symbols like 'Son of man' compensates for the paucity of elaborate exposition by pointing to some shared codes that are inherent in these symbols. The Jesus of Q appears to be an ever-present oracler with few personality traits or biographical identifiers.[31] This limited exposition/characterization leaves the door open for the readers to step inside the text and sense the similarity to their situation.[32] The boundaries between the text world and the real world become blurred. The minimal exposition and the use of symbols indicate that the narrator is not concerned with credible history writing, but with the process of *re-actualization* in the lives of the readers.

These are the *actions* ascribed to Jesus in Q: opposing Satan in the wilderness (Q 4.1-13), performing an exorcism (Q 11.14), healing (Q 7.2-10) and—most of all—teaching. There is a huge emphasis on the teaching activity, which is further underlined by the fact that the other three actions clearly direct attention to the teaching or to the paradigm that is associated with the actions. The exorcism is at best an introduction to the polemical section (Q 11.15-26, 29-35, 39-52), and in one pericope (Q 7.2-10) Jesus actually *does* nothing; it is the Roman officer's faith that cures his child, and he thus becomes a paradigm of true faith. In Q 4.1-13, Jesus is very passive as first the Spirit and then

30. On 'symbol,' see Friedman, *Form and Meaning*, pp. 292-302; J.-P. Vernant, *Myth and Society in Ancient Greece* (trans. J. Lloyd; New York: Zone Books, 1988), pp. 235-41; T. Todorov, *Symbolik och Tolkning* (trans. M. Rosengren; Moderna franska tänkare, 5; Stockholm: Symposion Bokförlag, 1989), pp. 19-23; B.J. Malina, *The New Testament World: Insights from Cultural Anthropology* (London: SCM Press, 1983), pp. 21-24; Culpepper, *Anatomy*, pp. 180-98; Powell, *What Is Narrative Criticism?*, pp. 27-32. See Uro on Q and symbols, 'Apocalyptic Symbolism', pp. 89-91, 116-18 (and H. Räisänen's critical discussion of the symbolistic approach, 'Exorcisms and the Kingdom: Is Q 11.20 a Saying of the Historical Jesus?', in Uro [ed.], *Symbols and Strata*, pp. 119-42 [136-41]).

31. 'A trait is a personal quality that persists over time' (Malbon, 'Narrative Criticism', p. 29); however, traits can also be 'developing ... or even conflicting'. See also the discussion of O. Lehtipuu in this volume.

32. K. Syreeni notes the same kind of effect in Luke's use of the 'typical' in characterization ('The Gospel in Paradigms: A Study in the Hermeneutical Space of Luke–Acts', in P. Luomanen [ed.], *Luke–Acts: Scandinavian Perspectives* [PFES, 54; Helsinki: The Finnish Exegetical Society; Göttingen: Vandenhoeck & Ruprecht, 1991], pp. 36-57 [45]). Of course, Luke's characters are much livelier than Q's.

Satan transport him from one place to another.

An interesting contradiction occurs in the characterization of Jesus. At first, great expectations are evoked by the anticipation in John the Baptist's words about 'the coming one' (ὁ ἐρχόμενος, Q 3.16). These expectations are initially fulfilled in Jesus' defeat of Satan and his temptations in Q 4.1-13, and then explicitly affirmed in Jesus' answer to John's messengers in Q 7.22-23: 'Blessed is he who takes no offense in me.' Further, Jesus' words in Q 6 affirm to the reader the seriousness related to the teaching: it is crucial to follow these instructions.[33] Q comes full circle in Q 13.35 with the picture of Jesus as one triumphantly returning, ὁ ἐρχόμενος.[34] But alongside these noble characterizations, surprising things are revealed of this 'Son of God' (Q 4): he is said to be a 'glutton and drunkard' (Q 7.34), is accused of being demon-possessed (Q 11.15), defines himself as a homeless itinerant (Q 9.58), and is evidently a trouble-maker (Q 12.51). These features of unconventionality are *tensive traits* in Q's character of Jesus. As will be shown, these details contribute to the theme of the rejection of God's messengers.

2. *John the Baptist* plays a very important role in the literary design of Q and is in fact the only character (apart from Jesus) introduced by his proper name. It is therefore necessary to observe the way(s) in which he is characterized. There is an obvious literary strategy at play in the utilization of John as the introducer of Q's main theme, the judgment proclamation.[35] As many have already noted, Q aligns John and Jesus on the same side of the front line of debate. John spells out the same judgments as Jesus, he is a 'fore-runner' for Jesus' mission, and

33. Cf. Q 6.46-49 ('Why do you [[call]] me Lord, Lord, and not do what I say?' and the parable of the 'Two Builders').

34. R. Uro has argued that 'the coming one' may function as a link to Q's contemporary messianic hopes, but is foremost a device of literary 'plot' in Q (R. Uro, 'John the Baptist and the Jesus Movement: What Does Q Tell Us?', in Piper [ed.], *Gospel behind the Gospels*, pp. 231-57 [240]). The narrative logic in Q's use of the title is aptly described by Uro.

35. Sternberg (*Expositional Modes*, p. 20) illustrates the importance of a document's beginning: 'Since every work does establish a scenic norm and since the scenic treatment accorded to a fictive time-section underscores its high aesthetic importance, the first scene in every work naturally assumes a special conspicuousness and significance'. Cf. the interesting remarks by Cotter on Q's beginning ('"Yes, I Tell You"', pp. 138-40).

people have spoken ill of him, too.[36] But it is unlikely that in the composition history of Q John would ever have enjoyed a position almost paralleling that of Jesus. Neither is there any need to identify some passages dealing with John as more original than others because they portray John as a more independent messenger of God than the other passages do.[37] It is difficult to make such distinctions, because the message attributed to John in ch. Q 3 corresponds closely with the overall proclamation and polemic of the document as a whole. Thus, we can only say that John's and Q's 'voice' are uniform.[38]

According to Josephus (*Ant.* 18.116-19), John seems to have been honored as something like the 'last great prophet'. R. Uro holds that the compilers of Q borrowed the authoritative status of someone who was, in the view of the society, a far greater name than Jesus.[39] It must have been a powerful strategy to employ a widely honored figure to fight the community's fight, a means of creating a special sense of dignity among otherwise marginalized sectarians.[40] This may have been the

---

36. Note some parallel ideas and motifs.

	John	*Jesus*
Teaching: Trees and human nature	Q 3.8-9	Q 6.43-44
Proclamation of judgment	Q 3.7-9, 16-17	Q 10.12-15; 12.51, etc.
Rejection of 'legal heirs'	Q 3.8	Q 13.28-29
First mentioned in the wilderness	Q 3.2-3(?)	Q 4.1-13
Both being scorned and rejected	Q 7.33	Q 7.34; 11.15(?)

37. Thus argues L.E. Vaage, 'More Than a Prophet, and Demon-Possessed: Q and the "Historical" John', in Kloppenborg (ed.), *Conflict and Invention*, pp. 181-202. In his view, the Q redaction subordinated John to function as a mere 'precursor', whereas sayings in the formative stratum (Q 7.24b-26, 28a, 33) depicted John as 'rather like a Cynic' (p. 194). Also, M. Sato's view is that one of the main reasons for Q's first redaction ('Redaktion A') was the need to draw a clear line between the status of John and Jesus; cf. Sato, *Q und Prophetie: Studien zur Gattungs- und Traditionsgeschichte der Quelle Q* (WUNT, 29; Tübingen: J.C.B. Mohr [Paul Siebeck], 1988), pp. 33-37.

38. Cf. Arnal, 'Redactional Fabrication', pp. 171-76; Uro, 'John the Baptist', p. 243.

39. See Uro's argument, in which he supposes that John as a character 'has been used to support the authority of Jesus as an even more powerful figure'. In a footnote (n. 27) he discusses John's authoritative status in the light of Josephus's reference and Mk 11.30; Uro, 'John the Baptist', p. 241.

40. On the concept of 'marginal/liminal situation' in sociological terms, see V. Turner, *The Ritual Process: Structure and Anti-Structure* (Hawthorne, NY: Aldine de Gruyter, 2nd edn, 1995), pp. 94-130 (111-12); Berger and Luckmann,

importance of John's characterization in Q. Furthermore, if we can assume that the narrator of Q is well aware of John's favorable position in the eyes of those *opposing* the narrator's message, we can see the irony in the narrator's strategy. John joins in the document's judgment theme, the target of which are those who *appreciate* John as the most recent great prophet!

Q presents conflicting accounts about John: he is viewed as 'more than a prophet' (Q 7.26), greatest among those born of women (7.28a), yet those who are 'in the kingdom of God' surpass him (7.28b). Also, he is a forerunner (7.27) and not even worthy to remove the sandals of Jesus (3.16); he is insecure about the identity of Jesus (7.18). Vaage thinks that the passages with a strong positive flavor originated in the formative stratum of Q (see n. 37 above), while he assigns the others to redaction Q^2. This kind of splitting of the material is, however, unnecessary and forced.[41] Evidently the narrator of Q had two interests in mind when developing John as a character: first, to elevate the status of Jesus, and second, to make sure that the strength of John as a character will not interfere with the primary aim. The strategy is to point out how magnificient a standing John enjoyed in God's plans—affirmed by his 'actual' reputation—and simultaneously to reject any too far-reaching claims.[42]

3. The only two instances in Q that demonstrate Jesus' healing power contain some *additional characters*. In the first passage (Q 7.1-10), Jesus' counterpart in dialogue is a Roman officer. He received a very limited characterization. The words he is allowed to utter and the astonished response of Jesus, however, quickly make it clear that he is a purely *paradigmatic* figure.[43] His no-proofs-seeking faith deserves the praise of Jesus: 'I say to you, not even in Israel have I found such faith.'

Social Construction, pp. 114-20. Also, with respect to the Bible, L.G. Perdue, 'The Social Character of Paraenesis and Paraenetic Literature', *Semeia* 50 (1990), pp. 5-33 (10-11).

41. Kloppenborg and Cotter, for example, believe that the material in Q 7.24-26; 16.16; 7.27-28, 31-35 derives from one and the same literary stratum, Q's redaction. Both, however, consider the unit a composite one (Kloppenborg, *Formation of Q*, pp. 115-21; Cotter, ' "Yes, I Tell You" ', pp. 140-48).

42. Vaage acknowledges the possibility of such an interpretation (in his discussion of Q 7.24b-26), but concludes that 'it would quickly be a counterproductive move, for the kind of person evoked in 7.24b-26 might easily "steal the show" ' (Vaage, 'More Than a Prophet', p. 191).

43. On paradigmatic characters, cf. Syreeni, 'Gospel in Paradigms'.

Many have pointed out that, in addition to providing a model for imitation, the pericope creates a contrast between a Gentile's faith and the unbelief of Israel, thus joining in the deuteronomistic thrust of the document.[44]

A similar kind of setting is apparent in the healing that leads to the 'Beelzebul controversy' of Q 11.14-23. This time an unidentified *group* serves as a negative paradigm: as the sick/possessed person is healed, some people rudely accuse Jesus, while others want further proofs (cf. Q 7.7 above). First, Jesus tackles the accusation of using evil medicine (11.17-23). Second, he refers to 'the sign of Jonah' (Q 11.29-32) and thus bluntly rejects the request for signs. Significantly, no further mention is made of the possible objections of these counterparts: they are condemned and classified as 'this evil generation'. The deuteronomistic theme is at play again.

We have taken a rather lengthy look at the ways in which Q presents its few characters. The relationship of the characterization to deuteronomistic theme becomes apparent in all cases. I noted how the narrator of Q uses characterization to *contemporize* the events that once happened to Jesus and John, so that the reading community would be able to see the similarity to its own situation. The analysis of the 'Son of man' passages will reinforce this impression. So far, the *disciples* have not been treated in this survey. Q contains surprisingly little information about the historical followers of Jesus, and no names. But this does not mean that we do not know from Q what they thought Jesus required of them, what they held themselves to be, and what was promised to them. Such an inquiry would demand a whole study of its own. I shall rather restrict myself to some aspects of the characterization of the disciples in the passages that relate to the 'Son of man' motif.

Jesus as 'Son of Man'

Q 6.22, Mockery and the Son of Man

> Blessed are you...when they revile you and they...and they...you...evil on account of the son of man.

The speech is addressed to the followers of Jesus. Despite the lack of proper characterization, the followers of Jesus are central to the

---

44. See Kloppenborg, *Formation of Q*, p. 119; Jacobson (*First Gospel*, pp. 110-11) emphasizes the resulting 'shame' of Israel.

message of Q, as is demonstrated by their essential role in the concluding verses of Q (22.28-30):[45]

...You [[ ]] who have [[followed me]] in the [[kingdom]] ‹. .› [[ ]] you
will sit on thrones judging the twelve tribes of Israel (IQP).

This promise of ruling power to the disciples assures the reader that
everything so far said is related to the well-being of Jesus' followers.
Thus, Jesus' first words to this group are of utmost importance. The
three eschatologically oriented macarisms define the disciples in a

45. Currently R. Uro has argued that Lk. 22.28-30 par. may not have been a part
of Q (see Uro, 'Apocalyptic Symbolism', p. 78 n. 32). His cautiousness is justifiable, but perhaps it exaggerates the point. The saying is indeed outside of any Q-
context in both Matthew and Luke; there are also a lot of differences in the expression of the variants. Nevertheless, when viewed in its assumed position concluding
Q, the saying certainly appears as a 'highlight' and a culmination point. It is therefore justifiable to think that it was more easily detachable for the purposes of the
evangelists. Since the saying was a highlight (resembling the concluding words of
Matthew and Luke; cf. Mt. 28.18-20 and Lk. 24.49), the evangelists perhaps wanted
to find a special place for it in their narration. Matthew has it in the midst of the
private instructions of Jesus to his disciples as they are about to arrive in Jerusalem
(Mt. 19.28). Following the saying is a comforting saying (promise of a hundredfold
reward for leaving familial ties), which may be a deliberate hint at the austere and
unconditional saying in Q 14.26 ([If anyone] does not hate his [[own]] father and
mother ...; IQP). Although there is some textual distance between Q 22.28-30 and
14.26, it may betray that while Matthew read and relocated the *final* Q-saying, he
remembered something in Q that he needed to 'soften', and so he did that in 19.29.
Thus, his procedure may betray the Q-origin of 19.28. Luke, on the other hand, may
have realized the potential of Q's conclusion to serve as a temporary farewell
promise, and for this reason he incorporated the saying in the last supper scene. As
for what Uro says about the foreign nature of such 'kingdom-language' in Q, his
view allows too little room for variation. In fact, elsewhere Uro argues convincingly
for the *flexibility* of symbolic language, and he summarizes the 'kingdom of God'
language in Q: 'The 'meaning' of the kingdom in Q cannot be restricted to one
referent only, but it is capable of evoking many associations and images. The kingdom can symbolize the realm of God's healing power; sometimes it is a symbol for
the group, sometimes it is more like the ideal order of the group. Often several associations play at the same time. Even described in terms of *different* 'meanings' the
symbol remains opaque and hard to define' ('Apocalyptic Symbolism', p. 89; italics
original). For discussion about the inclusion in Q of Lk. 22.28-30 par., see J.S.
Kloppenborg, *Q Parallels: Synopsis, Critical Notes and Concordance* (Foundations
and Facets: Reference Series; Sonoma, CA: Polebridge Press, 1988), pp. 202-203.

marginal position: they are poor, hungry and sorrowful.[46] However, in prophetic tones, Jesus promises that the eschatological reversal of status[47] will revolutionize their situation. Jesus' very first instructions in Q are thus parallel to his last sentences (Q 22.28-30). Already this sets the focus on what is said in between. Given the overall scope of Q on the issue of marginalization, it appears to be the fourth macarism that best identifies the situation of the addressees. According to it, the disciples are reproached and reviled by some people from outside their own circle. The cause is made explicit: they are followers of the 'Son of man'.[48]

The expositional value of the designation 'Son of man' in the Q-characterization of Jesus is interesting. The self-designation gradually creates a contradictory effect. According to some of the Q sayings about the Son of man, the figure should be identified directly with the description in Dan. 7.13-14 of 'one like a son of man', who is given heavenly power to rule. According to other sentences, the Son of man is somehow socially unsettled and offending (Q 7.34 and 9.58). Q 6.22 clearly belongs to the latter group of sayings. I previously noted these tensive traits in the characterization of Jesus. Now we can address them in more detail.

As G. Theissen has observed, many of the Son of man sayings draw a specific analogy between this figure's fate and that of the Son of man's followers: they follow the same lifestyle and are likewise rejected by others.[49] Theissen concludes: 'Evidently the images of the Son of man

---

46. For more discussion, see R.A. Piper, 'The Language of Violence and the Aphoristic Sayings in Q', in Kloppenborg (ed.), *Conflict and Invention*, pp. 53-72. Piper reconstructs the text (and order) in Q 6.27-36 more according to Matthew than Luke (pp. 55-60), and sketches a picture of a community reluctant—at any cost—to deal with the judicial system of their day (pp. 63-66).

47. On this concept, see Turner, *Ritual Process*, pp. 166-203. Perdue, 'Social Character', pp. 10-11 (Perdue follows Turner's ideas here).

48. Matthew (5.11) substitutes 'Son of man' with Jesus' first-person statement (ἕνεκεν ἐμοῦ, 'for my sake'), but this procedure is obviously redactional (cf. Lk. 12.8-9/Mt. 10.32-33). For argumentation, see D.R. Catchpole, *The Quest for Q* (Edinburgh: T. & T. Clark, 1993), pp. 93-94; for a different point of view, see V. Hampel, *Menschensohn und historischer Jesus: Ein Rätselwort als Schlüssel zum messianischen Selbstverständnis Jesu* (Neukirchen–Vluyn: Neukirchener Verlag, 1990), p. 212.

49. G. Theissen, *Sociology of Early Palestinian Christianity* (Philadelphia: Fortress Press, 5th edn, 1989), pp. 25-29. Theissen does not restrict his observations to

christology had a significant social function.'[50] This social function has to do with the very central Christian *paradox* of 'humble beginnings, glory thereafter'. What makes it into a paradox (instead of a natural progression), was the first Christians' firm belief that they already participated in the 'Kingdom of God', and manifested its power through preaching and healing.[51] Yet, not many of those outside their circles were likely to subscribe to their bold claims: instead, these claims were opposed and scorned. Such rejection was experienced as persecution (whether Q 6.22-23 refers to actual persecution is impossible to decide) and resulted in marginalization. However, gradually a rationalizing strategy of legitimation evolved:[52] the movement's founding figure had had an analogous fate, and yet, he is the 'Son of God' (Q 4) and an eschatological judge (12.8-9). It is difficult to decide whether the distribution of different types of Son of man sayings in Q is a result of careful planning, but we may note that the three sayings portraying the Son of man as a rejected figure of the past come *first* in the order of representation (Q 6.22; 7.34 and 9.57). The other passages that follow (12.8-9, 39-40 and 17.24, 26, 30)[53] emphasize his role as the bringer of judgment. In the same way as the founding figure was elevated in God's plans and not left with his shameful earthly destiny, thus his followers can expect that this will happen for them also.

Those who support the stratigraphical division of Q into different layers are clearly correct in defining Jesus' opening sermon in Q 6 as mostly 'sapiential' in nature. Nevertheless, there is confirmation in 6.22-23 that the first unit of the sermon coheres with the reasoning of the assumed secondary layer. It is therefore surprising that Kloppenborg (for example) does *not* ascribe these verses to layer Q^2 where they would be at home; rather, he ascribes to Q^2 only the second, minor clause in Q 6.23c.[54] The arguments are not very convincing, as he

Q material, but inspects all the relevant data on the 'Son of man' in the synoptic Gospels.

50. Theissen, *Sociology of Early Palestinian Christianity*, p. 27.

51. On the symbol 'Kingdom of God' in Q, see Uro, 'Apocalyptic Symbolism', pp. 75-91.

52. On 'legitimation', see Berger and Luckmann, *Social Construction*, pp. 87, 110-46; especially interesting and illuminating is the discussion on pp. 125-26.

53. The passages Q 11.30 and 12.10 are more complex; see below.

54. Kloppenborg, *Formation of Q*, pp. 172-73, 187-90. Similarly Sato, *Q und Prophetie*, pp. 258-59; and Jacobson, *First Gospel*, pp. 100-101, 127, though arguing for different layers of redaction; cf. also Tuckett, 'Son of Man', pp. 204-208.

maintains that these few words have an altogether different scope than the rest of 6.22-23. It would be more consistent of him to do away with these verses altogether.[55] But if one wishes to preserve the coherence of the assumed Q^1 sermon, one has to account for the link between vv. 6.20-21 and 6.27-35. The latter deals with loving one's enemies and refusing to defend one's legal rights. If vv. 6.22-23 were taken from between these two blocks, there certainly would be no elegant connection between them. The words about receiving contempt and being overlooked are needed in order to introduce the theme of radicalized love.[56]

What further enhances the close relationship of the whole unit of beatitudes to the unifying theme of 'judgment to this generation' is the fact that, besides being sapiential in form, these beatitudes reflect a strong inclination to an apocalyptic thought-world. The anticipated reversal of status is hardly an earthly incident that would result from the society's sense of justice; rather, it is eschatological in nature.[57] The characterization of Jesus as the Son of man, therefore, emphasizes the judgment motif as the valid background for the beatitudes (cf. Q 12.9; the Son of man as prosecutor in the heavenly court).[58]

More cautiously Uro, *Sheep among Wolves*, p. 194 n. 147. However, Catchpole (*Quest for Q*, p. 91) assigns Q 6.23b rather than v. 23c to a secondary layer.

55. This is what is actually done by Vaage, 'Son of Man', pp. 108-109. Cf. also Mack ('Kingdom That Didn't Come', p. 610 n. 4), who views Q 6.22-26 as Q^2 material (note that the 'woes' in Lk. 6.24-26 are usually held to be Luke's redaction).

56. Cf. similar criticism by M. Myllykoski, 'The Social History of Q and the Jewish War', in Uro (ed.), *Symbols and Strata*, pp. 143-99 (152). Also acknowledged by Kloppenborg, *Formation of Q*, p. 187. Catchpole (*Quest for Q*, pp. 94, 115) stresses the joint connection between Q 6.22-23 and 6.27-35, although he attaches material from the Lukan 'woes' (Lk. 6.24-26) in between them. L.E. Vaage's observations concerning the unity of the 'sermon' (Q 6.20-49) seem to support the conclusions reached above (Vaage, 'Composite Texts and Oral Mythology: The Case of the "Sermon" in Q [6.20-49]', in Kloppenborg [ed.], *Conflict and Invention*, pp. 75-97).

57. Kloppenborg, *Formation of Q*, pp. 188-89; Tuckett, 'Son of Man', pp. 206-207. As R.A. Piper has shown, Q reflects a clear mistrust in the distribution of justice in secular institutions; see n. 46 above.

58. Although it is not my main concern to address the question of Q's possible redactions, one has to note the following emerging observations. If the verses Q 6.22-23 (even without the supposedly redactional v. 23c) appear to share fully in the *redactional* thought-world of 'judgment to this generation', what else is there

Q 7.34, The Offending Son of Man

The son of man came eating and drinking and you say, Look, a glutton and a drunk, a friend of tax-collectors and sinners.

The verses Q 7.31-35 form the conclusion of Q's first main section (Q 3-7). The immediate context began with John's question about Jesus' identity (Q 7.18-23), in which one finds a good example of the technique of 'flashback': the question picks up John's earlier words in Q 3.16 (anticipation of 'the coming one'). After Jesus' affirmative answer, the narrator has Jesus give information on John and how he is related to God's plans (7.24-26; 16.16;[59] 7.27-28). The narrating in Q 3 started *in medias res* with John preaching in full action: the scene permitted no halt to closer identification of John.[60] Now we get that identification through the words of Jesus.

Under the heading 'Characterization in Q' I observed a literary strategy that makes Jesus and John allies on the same side of the polemic. There is a culmination of this thought in the context of the Son of man saying under consideration now, after this, there is no trace of John in the rest of the document. The difficult parable of the 'Children in a Market-place' (Q 7.31-32) symbolizes the frustrating experiences of John and Jesus. The stress of the parable is on the dissatisfied and ungrateful responses of the audience, not on matters such as how well (or indeed how poorly) the complaining children function as represen-

---

that should prevent us from viewing these verses as contemporary with the other redactional material? In fact, the whole approach could be reversed: is not Q 6.27-35 but an explication about how to react to those who are openly opposing the views of the Q community? Why should we think the *instructions* came first and the information about the *cause* only second? The explanatory clause of 6.23c is in balance with its context and shows no interruption in logic: on the contrary, it better articulates the conviction of the Q-tradents and also foreshadows the information given in Q 11.49-51 (rejection of God's messengers). On the technique of 'foreshadowing' (and 'flashbacks') see Rhoads and Michie, *Mark as Story*, pp. 42-43.

59. The decision of the IQP was that Luke's location for Q 16.16 is the more probable one (cf. M.C. Moreland and J.M. Robinson, 'The International Q Project: Work Sessions 23–27 May, 22–26 August, 17–18 November 1994', *JBL* 114.3 [1995], pp. 475-85 [485]). However, I have followed Matthew's order in placing it in the section Q 7.18-35. For discussion, see Kloppenborg, *Formation of Q*, pp. 112-14.

60. For '*in medias res*—beginnings in literature' see Sternberg, *Expositional Modes*, pp. 35-55.

tatives of Jesus and John.[61] The parable only emphasizes that nothing is adequate enough for those who have hardened themselves. The complaining children of the parable have utilized different approaches to win the sympathies of their fellows, but in vain.[62] The irony that is hidden in the parable is explained in Q 7.33-35.

There is more at play in the utilization of different motifs in Q 7.33-34 than meets the eye. There are connotations that function as 'flashbacks' and 'foreshadowings' in this unit. The connection of the verb form ἦλθεν ('came') to the pattern 'the coming one' (ὁ ἐρχόμενος) may be readily noticed,[63] but the associations created by the explications in 7.33-34 probably require a more 'alert' manner of reading. First, the accusation of John in v. 33 is strange: his abstinence from eating and drinking may be considered quite ordinary for such a prophetic figure as is depicted in Q 3.[64] If this 'not eating or drinking' by and large refers to John's alleged habit of fasting (cf. Mk 2.18), there should be no grounds to make the blatant accusation that he is demon possessed.[65] However, once we realize that the central aim of this unit (7.31-35) is to *align John and Jesus* on the same side, we can see through the odd nature of this accusation. The intended parallel depiction of these two men is clearly indicated by the verbal similarities and sentence structure in vv. 33-34. Further, in Q 11.15, Jesus is accused of performing his exorcisms by the power of Beelzebul: stated simply, *Jesus* too is possessed. Thus it appears that the narrator wishes to portray both men being accused of the same offence.

The evolving picture of John in 7.33 is that of an ascetic, and the verse probably alludes to John's reputation as a prophetic character. The Jesus depicted in v. 34 could hardly have been considered either an

---

61. Kloppenborg notes the difficulty of identifying the *tertium comparationis* in the parable (*Formation of Q*, pp. 110-11); see also the discussion by Jacobson, *First Gospel*, pp. 121-23.

62. Similarly B. Lindars, *Jesus Son of Man: A Fresh Examination of the Son of Man Sayings in the Gospels in the Light of Recent Research* (London: SPCK, 1983), pp. 32-33; Hampel, *Menschensohn und historischer Jesus*, p. 215.

63. Hampel connects the earlier designation ὁ ἐρχόμενος (Q 3.16; 7.18-19) with the title 'Son of man' here, and argues for the relatedness of these concepts in Q's contemporary messianic understanding (*Menschensohn und historischer Jesus*, pp. 222-26). The interpretation is too daring.

64. Emphasized by Cotter, '"Yes, I Tell You"', p. 145.

65. Differently Vaage, who thinks that John's Cynic resemblance was the source of mockery ('More Than a Prophet', p. 191).

ascetic or a prophet by his contemporaries. Yet the title 'Son of man' is perhaps a conscious way of reminding the reader that Jesus really shares the same position as John, and even more.[66] It is illegitimate to conclude that here the title cannot bear its 'normal' apocalyptic connotations.[67] On the contrary, it hints in this direction, probably because the accusations aimed at Jesus seem to point to a very different interpretation.

Wendy Cotter has summarized the rhetoric of Q 7.33-34 aptly:

> Jesus' sociability is unconventional for a holy man. John's fasting is perfectly conventional... The problem is solved by inventing an outrageous and unwarranted judgment about John's reasons for fasting. Then, taking the doubts about Jesus to their extreme and insulting conclusion, namely, that Jesus is a glutton and a drunk, can be similarly labeled outrageous and totally unwarranted. Jesus' face is saved by John.[68]

As elsewhere in Q, the polemic against the community from outside is concerned with *credibility and authority* (cf. the lament in 7.31-32).[69] The myth of a powerful 'Son of man' (as identified with Jesus) was useful in the counter-argumentation. Yet another myth, that of Divine Sophia in search of recipient humans, was evoked in 7.35 to assist this argumentation.[70] It is evident that not just John and Jesus, but the whole

66. The designation 'Son of man' is quite peculiar in this context and forces Jacobson to treat it as a surrogate for 'I' (*First Gospel*, p. 123). Thus already H.E. Tödt, *Der Menschensohn in der synoptischen Überlieferung* (Gütersloh: Gütersloher Verlagshaus Gerd Mohn, 1959), p. 109, with modifications. Lindars (*Jesus Son of Man*, pp. 32-34) is forced in arguing for a generic usage ('any man') of an Aramaic בר אנשא idiom.

67. Against Jacobson, *First Gospel*, p. 123. Tuckett suggests, too, that between the 'Son of man' sayings of Q 'there is an element of overlap' regarding the 'present and future' emphases in these sayings (Tuckett, 'Son of Man', p. 206 n. 1).

68. Cotter, ' "Yes, I Tell You" ', pp. 145-46.

69. Cf. Lindars, *Jesus Son of Man*, p. 33; R.A. Piper, *Wisdom in the Q-Tradition: The Aphoristic Teaching of Jesus* (SNTSMS, 61; Cambridge: Cambridge University Press, 1989), pp. 124-26.

70. I am content to note that some Old Testament passages entertain the idea of Divine Wisdom being rejected and returning to its heavenly dwellings, to which the 'deuteronomistic' theme in Q may allude. In fact, such a tone has often been detected in at least Q 11.49-51 and 13.34-35; see Kloppenborg, *Formation of Q*, p. 228; Uro, *Sheep among Wolves*, pp. 179-84; Jacobson, *First Gospel*, p. 212; P.J. Hartin, ' "Yet Wisdom Is Justified by Her Children" (Q 7.35): A Rhetorical and Compositional Analysis of Divine Sophia in Q', in Kloppenborg (ed.), *Conflict and Invention*, pp. 151-64; generally, cf. Piper, *Wisdom in the Q-Tradition*.

Q movement is meant by 'Wisdom's children'.[71] Thus here, as in 6.22-23 above, the polemic of Q is phrased in a way that connects the experiences of the compiling community with those of the text-world characters.

Q 9.58, The Homeless Son of Man

And Jesus said to him, 'Foxes have holes, and birds of the air have nests; but the son of man has nowhere to lay his head.'

Opinion is divided concerning whether 9.58 is integral to the deuteronomistic theme that organizes the document Q into a coherent whole. A.D. Jacobson has proposed that the saying develops the idea of the rejection of Wisdom in Q 7.35, which precedes it. He also concludes that the homelessness portrayed is involuntary and unnatural, thus presupposing rejection.[72] Consequently, according to Jacobson, 9.58 is a redactional addition.[73] An opposite view is taken by J.S. Kloppenborg: he thinks that 9.58 belongs to the formative layer (Q[1]) and that it 'says nothing of rejection', but rather reflects the radical ethics of the first Q movement. In this connection, Kloppenborg also points to the 'structural homologue between the Son of Man and his followers', first observed by Theissen (above, pp. 196-97).[74]

Jacobson seems to push his conclusions too far in arguing that the Son of man's unconventional mode of existence is involuntary: there is no explicit reference here to the kind of rejection that the deuteronomistic pattern usually exhibits. But Kloppenborg's decision to posit the saying in the formative stratum of Q is likewise too daring, because the 'structural homologue' is a constant feature of the deuteronomistic theme. It is, in fact, *an important means of legitimation* for the background community in seeking to explain their miscarriage in mission.

The following considerations should be taken into account. Clearly the focus of Q has now shifted to the disciples. In Q 9.57-60 (61-62?) and 10.2-16 the disciples get instructions on how to follow Jesus, how

---

71. Hartin, '"Yet Wisdom Is Justified"', p. 155.
72. Similarly Piper, *Wisdom in Q-tradition*, pp. 165-67. Catchpole and Uro do not emphasize the motif of rejection but refer to the connection between Q 7.34 and 9.58 (Catchpole, *Quest for Q*, p. 240; Uro, 'Apocalyptic Symbolism', pp. 108-109).
73. Jacobson, *First Gospel*, pp. 133-37.
74. Kloppenborg, *Formation of Q*, p. 192.

to proclaim his words, and how to deal with rejection (!).[75] In Q 10.21-24, they are blessed for being the followers of Jesus; and in 11.2-4, 9-13 they are encouraged to pray. The emphasis is on *being the followers*.[76] Thus it is not surprising that the next major section (Q 11.14-52) is marked with polemic against those who have rejected Jesus (11.15-23) and those he has sent (11.49-52, implicitly). After this, the rest of Q down to the final promise (Q 22.28-30) consists of exhortations, instructions and warnings to the disciples. The narrative line disappears, and the sayings of Jesus (from 12.2 onwards) should be treated as one extensive speech, in which his words are left echoing in the air.

Thus, Jacobson seems to be right in associating the saying with the deuteronomistic theme. But it is not about rejection that the saying speaks. Evidently the interests and rhetoric of the deuteronomistic editing and arranging of material will have to be taken more broadly. The only paraenetically impressive motifs are not those that stress the ill will and stubbornness that God's prophets have encountered through all times. The attitude of bitterness toward a common outside enemy is 'beneficient' for boundary making,[77] but hardly the most fruitful approach for creating the intimacy of insiders. Rather, anything that works to provide a common sacred tradition ('a communal myth') will

75. According to Q, the followers of the Son of man must always be cautious. They are to make no compromises (Q 12.33-34; 16.13), they should not hesitate (9.59-60, [61-62?]) or be half-hearted (11.23; 13.23-27; 14.27, 34-35; 17.33), and never become concerned with their status or position (12.42-46) or deny the Son of man (12.8-10). The 'fate of a prophet' is not an easy one. The disciples voluntarily (this is the emphasis of Q 14.27) accept the same kind of fate for themselves that their master has had. Note the saying in Q 6.40: 'A disciple is not above the teacher, [[but every one, when well trained,]] will be like his teacher.' The saying is quite odd in its context and is reconstructed by the IQP following Luke's wording (J.M. Asgeirsson and J.M. Robinson, 'The International Q Project: Work Sessions 12–14 July, 22 November 1991', *JBL* 111.3 [1992], pp. 500-508 [502]); Matthew's wording (Mt. 10.24-25) would seem more intelligible. Whatever the exact wording of the saying, it is possibly meant to stress the previous point: 'Do not expect to receive better treatment' (cf. Mt. 10.25, ἀρκετὸν τῷ μαθητῇ ἵνα γένηται ὡς ὁ διδάσκαλος αὐτοῦ...); cf. Piper, *Wisdom in Q-tradition*, pp. 132-33. Already Tödt (*Menschensohn*, p. 55) noted the resemblance between Q 9.58 and 6.40.

76. Cf. Tödt (*Menschensohn*, p. 114) on Q 9.58: 'Der Spruch will in erster Linie nicht nur vom Erdendasein des *Menschensohnes*, von seiner Heimatlosigkeit als solcher sprechen; er beabsichtigt vielmehr primär eine Aussage über den Character der Nachfolge' (italics original). Thus also Vaage, 'Son of Man', p. 114.

77. See Kloppenborg, *Formation of Q*, pp. 167-68.

contribute to a sense of 'togetherness'.[78] For the Q movement, this tradition was first and foremost the *image of Jesus calling followers* and
the *enthusiastic mission* that subsequently ensued.[79]

How these quite general observations relate to the rhetoric of Q 9.58
should be evident. Jesus' authority has been established through the
first section of Q (chs. 3–7), and now it is time to authorize his disciples. Thus, Jesus commissions them to carry on the same tasks that he
performed in the first section: in Q 10.9, the disciples are exhorted to
preach (cf. Jesus in Q 6; 7.22) and to heal (cf. Jesus in Q 7.1-10, 22).
The purpose of the present section, then, is to show that the disciples
are fulfilling the same mission that Jesus had.[80] Accordingly, the

---

78. On the meaning of mythic interpretation of past events, see B. Hargrove,
The Sociology of Religion: Classical and Contemporary Approaches (Arlington
Heights, IL: AHM, 2nd pr., 1979), pp. 40-41; Perdue, 'Social Character', p. 8.

79. Section Q 9.57-60, (61-62?) is in line with the 'Mission Charge' in 10.2-11:
both sections paint a vivid picture of a radical mode of existence. There are clear
indicators in these sections of an initial enthusiasm and of an anticipation of the
eschatological consummation: freedom from cares (Q 10.4), symbolic procedures
(Q 10.6, 9, 11), and offending radicalness and spontaneity (Q 9.57-60 [60-62?]).
Amidst the pain of admitting that the mission to Israel turned out not to be as successful as it was hoped to be, there was need to recall the community to its beginnings. And a part of these beginnings seems to have been the conviction—described
in a lively manner in many passages of Q—that since the End is at hand, there is no
time to pay attention to the 'normal' routines of life. Cf. the emphasis of Jacobson,
First Gospel, p. 144; and Uro, *Sheep among Wolves*, pp. 160-61.

80. Being marginal and despised may also emphasize the voluntary nature of
the community's ethos of burdened existence (see Turner, *Ritual Process*, pp. 111-
12; and J.M. Yinger, *Countercultures: The Promise and Peril of a World Turned
Upside Down* [New York: The Free Press; London: Collier Macmillan, 1982],
pp. 286-88). This is especially so, if the community's values include values such as
non-retaliation, abstinence from reciprocity, non-violence, going 'as «lambs»'
among wolves' (Q 10.3; IQP); for a description of this particular Q-ethos, see R.C.
Douglas, '"Love Your Enemies": Rhetoric, Tradents, and Ethos', in Kloppenborg
(ed.), *Conflict and Invention*, pp. 116-31; J.S. Kloppenborg, 'Literary Convention,
Self-Evidence and the Social History of the Q People', *Semeia* 55 (1992), pp. 77-
101 (88-91). The instructions for the mission are not simply 'hyperbolic', for the
mission is likely to have been a real event (against Mack, 'Kingdom That Didn't
Come', pp. 633-34). The instructions emphasize that all the specific orders adopted
by the community originally came from Jesus. This is evident from the concluding
assertion (Q 10.16) and the following macarism (Q 10.23-24). Also, it is significant
that, in the next major section, Q portrays Jesus facing opposition as he carries out

narrator wishes to emphasize (throughout 9.57-60 [61-62?]) that the followers of Jesus even share the same troublesome and demanding pattern of life as their leader, because it was Jesus' command to do so.[81] Therefore, any offense that the disciples of Jesus encounter is at the same time directed at Jesus also.[82] When seen in this way, the sayings in 9.57-60 (61-62?) are an important part of the rhetoric of the deuteronomistic theme.

Finally, we shall ask why Jesus uses the circumlocution 'Son of man' in place of the pronoun 'I' in the saying, 'the Son of man has nowhere to lay his head'.[83] Some have suggested that also this occurrence of the title 'Son of man' is really nothing more than a surrogate for direct self-reference; thus Jesus is plainly saying 'this here man'.[84] The 'Son of man' is a symbol, and when a symbol is repeated, one cannot exclude

basic missionary tasks: healing in Q 11.14 and preaching in Q 11.20 (cf. the similarity to the wording of 10.9).

81. Myllykoski draws different conclusions concerning Q 9.58: 'When Jesus the Son of Man was on earth, *no one* could follow him, because he was homeless like wisdom' ('Social History', pp. 180-81). However, Myllykoski joins Jacobson's emphasis on rejection as the saying's background.

82. See the similar emphasis of Tödt, *Menschensohn*, p. 114.

83. Already emphatically asked by Tödt, *Menschensohn*, p. 114. He argued that the title points toward Jesus' authoritative status, as it does elsewhere in Q-sayings that depict the Son of man's 'earthly works' (*gegenwärtigen Wirken*) (i.e. Q 6.22; 7.34; 9.58 and 12.10). Tödt was not thinking in terms of a symbol, and he has been criticized for viewing the 'Son of man' as a rather fixed *title*; see, e.g., Uro, *Sheep among Wolves*, pp. 150-51.

84. Thus D.R.A. Hare, *The Son of Man Tradition* (Minneapolis: Fortress Press, 1990), pp. 220, 271-73; Jacobson, *First Gospel*, p. 238. Lindars (*Jesus Son of Man*, pp. 30-31) distinguishes between what Jesus may have meant (if the saying is dominical, 'a man such as I') and the later christological interpretations (also of Q). Piper (*Wisdom in Q-tradition*, p. 175 n. 111 [p. 267]) seems to agree with Lindars. The interpretation has often been harnessed to support the theory of a common aramaic expression (בר אנשא) in the background, which apparently has been used with a variety of meanings, also to denote the current speaker; cf. J.M. Robinson, who emphasizes the 'generic' non-apocalyptic understanding of passages Q 6.22; 7.34; 9.58; 11.30 and 12.10 (Robinson, 'The Son of Man in the Sayings Gospel Q' in C. Elsas and R. Haffke *et al.* [eds.], *Tradition und Translation: Zum Problem der Interkulturellen Übersetzbarkeit religiöser Phänomene* [Festschrift Carsten Colpe; Berlin: W. de Gruyter, 1994], pp. 315-35 [320-25]). On the linguistic background, see C. Colpe, 'ὁ υἱὸς τοῦ ἀνθρώπου', *TDNT*, VIII, pp. 400-77 (401-405); and Hampel, *Menschensohn und historischer Jesus*, pp. 7-48 (also a tradition-historical survey).

the associations that are normally attached to it. In other words, it is not justified to state that '[h]ere again "the Son of Man" has no connotative force, only denotative effect'.[85] It is hard to imagine that a first-century Christian reader would not have presupposed the *apocalyptic* components of the 'Son of man' language in Q 9.58, too. Would any author, then, be unaware of the connotations at play as she or he chooses to refer to Jesus as the Son of man, rather than with the simple pronoun 'I'? The use of the title is deliberate: the narrator wishes to hint at the decisive role and high status of Jesus, so that the reader may be confronted with the apparent paradox characteristic of Q's depiction of Jesus. This paradox also parallels the situation of the distressed readers.

Q 11.30, The Sign of Jonah

> For as Jonah became a sign to the Ninevites, so [[also]] shall the son of man be to this generation.

As always, the broader context of this saying offers the key to its interpretation. Already in the previous discussion we remarked that Q 11.14-52 comprises a large polemical section, the climax of which is the series of 'woes' (vv. 39-52). The discourse unfolds with an accusation (v. 15) and, perhaps, a request for further proof by the crowd (v. 16).[86] Jesus' words in vv. 17b-23 point out how illogical is the accusation that he works under the powers of evil. The following parable (vv. 24-26, 'the Returning Demons') is somewhat awkward in the argumentation, but should nevertheless be treated as a counter-attack. It is intended to warn those who have witnessed/experienced Jesus' healings and who still doubt the force of the 'Kingdom' (v. 20). If one is not prepared to acknowledge God's power at work in Jesus, the consequences can be quite fatal.[87] The parable thus paves the way for the austere words in vv. 29-32.

85. Against Hare, *Son of Man Tradition*, p. 60 (in discussing Q 9.58). Cf. what Uro ('Apocalyptic Symbolism', p. 108) writes: 'As a symbol, the Son of man can play with several connotations at the same time. Even if it is clearly a self-designation of Jesus and seemingly just a surrogate for "I", it also evokes references to Jesus' own fate as well as to that of his followers.'

86. It is uncertain whether Lk. 11.16 was in Q, but in the light of v. 29 it may have been there; the IQP suggests a probability of 'C' on a descending scale from 'A' to 'D' (Asgeirsson and Robinson, 'IQP Work Sessions 1991', p. 503).

87. A lot of ambiguity is still left regarding the function of the parable. This is probably due to its origin as an independent saying; cf. Kloppenborg, *Formation of Q*, p. 126.

It is doubtful whether the unit (vv. 29-32) can be dissected into diverging pieces from a tradition-historical perspective.[88] The reasoning seems to flow smoothly. How is the 'sign of Jonah' to be understood? Basically three alternative explanations have been presented. (1) Some propose that the future ἔσται (v. 30) guides the interpretation: the 'sign' will become manifest in the future *parousia* of the Son of man.[89] (2) Some argue that there may be here an allusion to the *resurrection* of Jesus, which is otherwise not present in Q.[90] (3) Others note that the only likely correspondence between Jonah and Jesus is that they both proclaimed a message of repentance; thus, the sign would be the *proclamation* of Jesus.[91]

Caution is in order here, for an either-or explanation may not do justice to this puzzle. We are left with guesswork concerning whether the author alludes to the resurrection. Apart from the quite passing mention of 'cross' (σταυρός, Q 14.27), there are no references to Jesus' passion and resurrection in Q. However, in order for Jesus to return as the 'Son of man' he must somehow be alive.[92] One should not try to 'modernize'

---

88. For a different point of view, see Lührmann, *Die Redaktion der Logienquelle*, pp. 37-42; Hoffmann, *Studien zur Theologie*, p. 181; Jacobson, *First Gospel*, p. 166; Lindars, *Jesus Son of Man*, p. 42; Kloppenborg, *Formation of Q*, pp. 128-30; and Uro, *Sheep among Wolves*, pp. 168-72. According to these tradition-historical reconstructions, the sequence of compilation was: (1) Q 11.29, (2) addition of v. 30 as a commentary saying, and (3) expansion of the unit with vv. 31-32 (Lührmann and Uro consider the addition of vv. 30 and 31-32 as a simultaneous incident).

89. So Lührmann, *Die Redaktion der Logienquelle*, p. 40; Hoffmann, *Studien zur Theologie*, p. 181. Against this interpretation, Uro, *Sheep among Wolves*, p. 170 (cf., however, his 'Apocalyptic Symbolism', pp. 110-12).

90. Especially I.H. Marshall, *The Gospel of Luke: A Commentary on the Greek Text* (NIGTC; Exeter: Paternoster Press; Grand Rapids: Eerdmans, 2nd edn, 1979), p. 485; H. Schürmann, 'QLk 11,14-36 kompositionsgeschichtlich befragt', in F. Van Segbroeck *et al.* (eds.), *The Four Gospels 1992* (Festschrift Frans Neirynck; 3 vols.; BETL, 100; Leuven: Leuven University Press, 1992), I, pp. 563-86 (576-77). Against, see Kloppenborg, *Formation of Q*, p. 132.

91. Thus Jacobson, 'Literary Unity', p. 382 (also, *First Gospel*, pp. 166-69); Lindars, *Jesus Son of Man*, pp. 40-42 (though utilizing a troublesome generic understanding of the Son of man); Kloppenborg, *Formation of Q*, pp. 132-34; Uro, *Sheep among Wolves*, p. 170; Hampel, *Menschensohn und historischer Jesus*, pp. 94-96.

92. Cf. R.J. Miller, 'The Rejection of the Prophets in Q', *JBL* 107 (1988), pp. 225-40 (225 n. 3).

the first-century Q-people too much by stating that they may have been capable of understanding Jesus' *post mortem* existence in quite surprising ways. But what seems most certain is that any allusion to Jesus' resurrection is not the point of the saying. Also, were one to argue that the saying refers to Jesus' parousia, one would fail to see what the Son of man has in common with Jonah. Therefore, the best explanation is that Jesus' proclamation was the last warning to the people of Israel, as Jonah's was to the Ninevites.

But again we face the question of the specific relevance of the 'Son of man' designation. The choice of the 'Son of man' language in Q is not without consequences; the Son of man is the historical, rejected Jesus, but also the heavenly judge who will punish the impenitent.[93] The future verb form may not be incidental in this respect, after all.[94] It probably underscores associations with the future parousia of the Son of man. The passage illustrates the flexibility of symbolic language, namely, its ability to convey multiple connotations at the same time.

'This [evil] generation' represents all the opposition the Q community has faced. It is notable how Q raises *Gentile* counterparts to illustrate the 'shocking' condition of Israel.[95] There is an irony about the parallelism of 'this generation' and the Ninevites: Jonah, a reluctant prophet of God had preached, and all Nineveh immediately repented; then God's Son (Q 4) proclaimed, and he was put to death. The curious sayings of Q 11.33-35, (36?) then warn *anyone*—including the insiders—about the importance of responding. Kloppenborg summarizes the message of vv. 29-35, (36) thus: '[F]ailure to grasp the presence of the πλεῖον Ἰωνᾶ [more than Jonah] can only be interpreted as abject moral blindness, worthy of judgment and condemnation'.[96]

---

93. Hare emphasizes the nature of the designation 'Son of man' as pure self-reference (*Son of Man Tradition*, p. 61). For Hampel (*Menschensohn und historischer Jesus*, pp. 96-98) this saying is yet another proof of Jesus' (covered) messianic self-understanding. This view, however, is utterly doubtful.

94. Cf. the arguments of Uro, 'Apocalyptic Symbolism', pp. 110-11.

95. Since Lührmann's work (*Die Redaktion der Logienquelle*), most authors on Q have shared this view. The juxtaposition of Israel and Gentiles is visible in sayings such as Q 7.9; 10.12-15; 13.28-29. Also, Q 3.8 can be taken as polemic against overt national claims to God. Against this interpretation, however, see R.A. Horsley, 'Questions about Redactional Strata and the Social Relations Reflected in Q', in Lull (ed.), *SBL Seminar Papers*, pp. 186-203 (187-88).

96. Kloppenborg, *Formation of Q*, p. 138 (my translation of Greek).

Q 11.39-52 carries this polemic one step further. This section (the 'Woes') reveals the profound nature of the conflict between the Q-people and those standing in opposition to it. The section is filled with accusations, ridicule, exaggeration and jealousy. Q accuses the opponents of observing the will of God (vv. 39, 46, 52) in its minutest details (v. 42), but doing this out of a desire for social standing and recognition (vv. 43-44). 'Best seats in the synagogue' and 'salutations in the market places' are expressions of honor. Especially the seemingly innocent words in v. 43 may betray jealousy, since both groups—Q and its opponents—strive to establish their authoritative teaching for the society.[97]

Q 12.8-10, The Son of Man and the Criteria of Judgment

Every one who acknowledges me before men... also will acknowledge before ...;
but whoever denies me before men ... will ... deny before ...[98]

And whoever says a word against the son of man will be forgiven; but whoever [[blasphemes]] against the Holy Spirit will not be forgiven.

---

97. See the similar emphasis of Kloppenborg, 'Literary Convention', p. 98.

98. The three dots indicate that the IQP assumes there has been some text in Q here, but a reliable reconstruction was not possible. There are three such instances in vv. 8-9 (with a probability of 'A–B' on a descending scale from 'A' to 'D'): the first and the third consist of a choice between the title 'Son of man' (Luke) and a first-person pronoun (Matthew). Matthew displays some (christological?) interest in substituting the title 'Son of man' for a first-person expression. In Q we have Mt. 5.11//Q 6.22 as another example of this, but it is really the Markan parallels that can be used to argue for Matthean redaction. Cf. Mt. 16.21, in which Matthew uses a *periphrasis* to avoid the Markan (9.31) 'Son of man'. Note how Luke (9.22) follows Mark. On the other hand, Luke may have been strongly influenced by a tradition-historical variant of Q 12.9 which he found in Mk 8.38. Following its wording quite closely, Lk. 9.26 states: ὃς γὰρ ἂν ἐπαισχυνθῇ με καὶ τοὺς ἐμοὺς λόγους, τοῦτον ὁ υἱὸς τοῦ ἀνθρώπου ἐπαισχυνθήσεται ... ('For whoever is ashamed of me and these words of mine, of her/him shall the Son of man be ashamed ...'; my translation). In the order of the Lukan discourse, this saying comes first and may therefore have affected his formulation of Q 12.8-9. The conclusion that the title 'Son of man' did not stand in this passage of Q would also ease somewhat the clash between vv. 8-9 (Jesus/Son of man must be acknowledged) in contrast to v. 10 (you will not be punished for speaking in opposition to the Son of man); we shall consider this problem below. Nevertheless, I find it more likely that the Lukan 'Son of man' is the original Q expression.

An obvious shift in the rhetorical argumentation of Q occurs with Q 12.2 and onwards. No new narrative scenes are here, but only Jesus addressing his disciples. Jacobson identifies a smooth transition between 11.52 and 12.2-3: the former verse blames the Pharisees for 'lifting the key of knowledge' (τῆς γνώσεως),[99] to which the latter verses are linked through the theme of *revealing* what is hidden. The verb γινώσκειν (to know) may also imply a connection to 11.52.[100] It is plausible that 12.2-3 forms a bridge between the 'Woes' and the paraenesis that follows, but is more at home with the unit 12.4-12.[101] At any rate, the design of the whole is quite elegant.

The nature of Q 12.2-12 is paraenetic. There exists wide agreement that this unit presupposes some kind of persecution, and that vv. 11-12 point toward a situation in which the community members are questioned by the institution of the synagogue.[102] Bold confession about Jesus is needed in this situation, and hardships should not hinder one's readiness to preach. At first, there is a reminder of the community's mission to 'proclaim upon the housetops' (vv. 2-3), then come comforting words that emphasize God's care (vv. 4-7). But in these latter words there already exists a seed of the warning that follows in vv. 8-10: a very threatening tone is apparent in v. 5 ('Fear... the one who... «in» Gehenna'; IQP), resembling the end of the grotesque parable in Q 12.42-46 ('the Faithful Servant'). Therefore, there is no reason to view vv. 8-10 as anomalous, as if they belonged to later redaction. When Kloppenborg among others does so, he seems to subordinate literary observations to form-critical distinctions.[103] Kloppenborg states: 'Widely regarded [12.8-9] as a "sentence of Holy Law" with its origin in prophetic speech, it moves beyond the essentially sapiential idiom of 12.2-7, introducing the motif of apocalyptic reward and punishment.'[104]

99. The choice between Luke's 'keys of knowledge' and Matthew's 'kingdom' is a difficult one; the IQP voted for the Lukan expression with the probability of 'C' (descending scale from 'A' to 'D') (Asgeirsson and Robinson, 'IQP Work Sessions 1991', p. 505). However, cf. the critical remarks of Uro, 'Apocalyptic Symbolism', p. 84 n. 51.

100. Jacobson, *First Gospel*, pp. 184-86.

101. Against Jacobson, *First Gospel*, p. 186. He treats Q 12.4-12 as a distinct, separate unit (pp. 186-89).

102. Concerning the inclusion to Q of Lk. 12.11-12 par., see Kloppenborg, *Q-Synopsis*, pp. 126-27.

103. See the criticism on pp. 183-84 above.

104. Kloppenborg, *Formation of Q*, p. 211.

Following Lührmann, he argues that the focus shifts here from preaching to confessing, and he supports his argument by noting the christological interest in vv. 8-9.[105] Lührmann was the first to suggest that these verses are addressed to outsiders rather than to the community itself.[106]

However, nothing warrants the positing of a shift in audience. According to Kloppenborg, vv. 12.4 and 'especially 12.11-12' may have been the reason to introduce vv. 8-9 (and subsequently v. 10 in Q^3).[107] More likely, the motivation for vv. 8-10 lies in v. 5 with its explicit image of judgment. The difference made by many scholars between preaching (v. 3) and confessing (vv. 8-9) is unnecessary, since the two activities are so closely related. In fact, it appears that vv. 12.4-7 relate better to a situation of public confession than of preaching. As to the presumed christological interest, is the use of a title (or rather a symbol) all that counts? Is it not *Jesus'* words that ought to be preached, according to v. 3? Proclamation of someone's message means open confession of her or his authority. It is a thin line that separates preaching from confessing.

There are indications in Q of a period during which some community members were accused of not being devoted enough to following Jesus. Participation in this new community involved a high degree of identification with the community ethos and an attachment to its values, values that were not always identical with those of the macrosociety. No one lives without a family and/or social class background; therefore, it is likely that a community like Q, which is *challenging and subversive* in relation to society, will inevitably produce significant tension in the relationships of individual members. Explicit evidence of this are passages such as Q 12.51-53 and 14.26. Note how the severe exhortation to 'take one's cross' immediately follows the latter passage. Passages like Q 9.59-60 imply such a strong attitude against traditional, taken-for-granted values that it is no wonder if the community's members felt 'homeless'.[108]

---

105. Kloppenborg, *Formation of Q*, p. 211 (with reference to Lührmann, *Die Redaktion der Logienquelle*, p. 52).

106. Lührmann, *Die Redaktion der Logienquelle*, p. 52. Also, Hoffmann, *Studien zur Theologie*, p. 156; Kloppenborg, *Formation of Q*, pp. 211-16.

107. Kloppenborg, *Formation of Q*, p. 211.

108. A.D. Jacobson, 'Divided Families and Christian Origins', in Piper (ed.), *Gospel behind the Gospels*, pp. 361-80 (361-62). Q 9.58 can be interpreted

There is another aspect that more directly links the situation of persecution to Q 12.2-12. If indeed there were interrogations by the synagogue in which members of the Q community made public confessions, then those who had the courage to avow themselves may have been placed under serious pressure. An effective way of coaxing an individual to abandon one's undesirable ideology is to direct *material* sanctions against one, to make one an outsider. We can imagine what it might mean, for example, to a potter in a small agrarian town[109] if the people around him are instructed to avoid his services because of his heretical beliefs. Such a scenario is a plausible background for exhortations such as Q 12.22-31; such an exhortation is not simply a noble ideal of careless existence, wisdom for wisdom's sake. We may also recall Jesus' orders to pray for daily bread (Q 11.3) and the exhortations to beg from God who knows the needs of 'his children' (11.9-13). Even portions of the temptation narrative (Q 4.1-12) may be taken as a metaphorical paradigm: if you deny Jesus in order to be released from your distressed position, it is as grave as consenting to worship Satan.[110] Notice also how the beginning of Jesus' first sermon links poverty and hunger to rejection of the disciples (Q 6.20-23).

Considering these samples from different locations of the Q-document, it may be argued that Q 12.2-12 should be viewed against this background. The introduction of threatening tones along with wisdom paraenesis is a sign of the relative seriousness of the socioeconomic hardships.[111] Perhaps the interrogation before the synagogue was too

communally, according to which interpretation the community's experience of being rejected and isolated corresponds to the story-level Jesus who is homeless.

109. Cf. the illustration by G.E.M. de Ste. Croix, who maintains that under favorable conditions these 'other independent producers' lived 'not very far above the poverty-line' (*The Class Struggle in the Ancient Greek World: From the Archaic Age to the Arab Conquests* [London: Gerald Duckworth, 1981], pp. 271-72; more extensively see pp. 269-75; see the brief description of Palestine, pp. 427-33).

110. On a similar vein of thought, Myllykoski, 'Social History', pp. 165-66. Kloppenborg resists the paradigmatic interpretation as 'oversubtle' (*Formation of Q*, p. 251) and identifies in the temptation narrative an ancient testing story, appearing often at the beginning of ancient sayings collections (pp. 256-62). However, I fail to see why that kind of a story would rule out the paradigmatic dimension.

111. On socioeconomic factors, see also Theissen, *Sociology of Early Palestinian Christianity*, pp. 33-46; R.A. Horsley, *Sociology and the Jesus Movement* (New York: Continuum, 2nd edn, 1994), pp. 53-54, 88-90. Horsley's interpretation

much for some members of the Q-group. Therefore, the authorities of the group issued austere warnings. The usage of the symbol 'Son of man' in this context is a skillful move by the narrator, because until this point in the discourse the figure 'Son of man' has been (deliberately) associated with the lot of the followers. Connotations from these prior passages are unavoidably present here—'you experience nothing that the Son of man has not gone through'.[112] Verses 8-9 introduce the other side of the coin, the threat to the disobedient ones. It is customary in paraenesis that exhortations (even comforting ones) and warnings may alternate, as can be seen from 12.2 onwards.[113]

However we understand the integrity of the unit, Q 12.2-9, we are faced with difficulties in explaining the meaning of v. 10 in its context.[114] According to this saying, speaking against the Son of man is not fatal; however, blaspheming the Spirit causes judgment. This kind of distinction is problematic in itself, but it also creates tensions with regard to vv. 8-9, which demand full acknowledgment of the Son of man. Numerous proposals have been advanced regarding v. 10, but none of them seems to explain fully all the aspects.[115] Kloppenborg is certainly right in noting that the emphasis in the saying is on the latter part of the sentence (v. 10b, blasphemy of the Spirit) and that it refers to the outsiders' rejection 'of the spirit-inspired defense of the disciples in 12.11-12'.[116] If there was a reference to 'Spirit' in v. 12, this explanation is all the more probable. But it ignores the problems related to the

of Q as part of an extensive class struggle against Jerusalem hierocracy by a peasant Galilean movement is too one-sided a view and requires a very selective reading (cf. Horsley, 'Q and Jesus: Assumptions, Approaches, and Analyses', *Semeia* 55 [1992], pp. 175-209).

112. Hare (*Son of Man Tradition*, p. 62) opts for a plain self-reference here as elsewhere.

113. See the similar emphasis with respect to Q 12.2-9 in Piper, *Wisdom in Q-tradition*, pp. 59-61. Although Piper considers the vv. 2-3 and 8-9 as later additions to vv. 4-7, he stresses the integrity of the unit. It is also interesting how Piper links together functionally the two distinct sapiential traditions in Q, the 'deuteronomistic Sophia logia' and the aphoristic collections (the latter corresponds by and large to Kloppenborg's alleged Q¹). Piper argues that both traditions in Q reflect a situation of economic hardships and opposition from outsiders (*Wisdom in Q-tradition*, pp. 176-78).

114. Cf. Kloppenborg, *Formation of Q*, pp. 211-14.

115. Kloppenborg, *Formation of Q*, pp. 212-13.

116. Kloppenborg, *Formation of Q*, p. 213.

logic between vv. 8-9 and 10a. After having disposed as invalid several proposed solutions, Kloppenborg suggests that the compilers of Q were perhaps unsuccessful in locating v. 10a within its theology.[117]

Q 12.10 is (like 12.8-9) evidently a pre-Q tradition, as its parallel in Mk 3.28-29 shows (differences notwithstanding). Nevertheless, there is sound logic in the interpretation that distinguishes between two preaching eras in Q. W. Schenk argues that the saying also legitimates the ongoing mission to Israel.[118] Although there is no explicit chronological distinction in the saying, it is reasonable to think that the saying actually necessitates one. If '[[blasphemy]] against the Holy Spirit' is identical with opposition toward the community's preaching and confessing, then how is that different from 'saying a word against the Son of man'?

As a means to infer the logic of the saying, it may be best to assume that the symbol 'Son of man' depicts Jesus' significance to the community as a rejected figure of the past. One may ponder whether the veiled reference to judgment in v. 10b has something rather concrete (such as the destruction of Jerusalem; cf. Q 13.34) in mind.[119] Then we might also infer that v. 10a represents the community's view according to which the length of time between the killing of Jesus and the destruction of Jerusalem was a sign of God's mercy. Israel had been given one final chance, which was present in the mission of Jesus' disciples. They had the 'Spirit' to assist them, and any objection to their message was 'blasphemy against the Spirit'. They were probably able to conclude that the time of forgiveness had run out, as they saw the Roman troops wrecking their native soil.[120] In its literary context, however, the emphasis of the saying would not be in positing a threat to outsiders (which of course is present, too), but in underlining the importance of the disciples' mission and warning them not to deny their message.[121]

---

117. Kloppenborg, *Formation of Q*, p. 214.

118. W. Schenk, *Synopse zur Redequelle der Evangelisten: Q-Synopse und Rekonstruktion in deutscher Übersetzung mit kürzen Erläuterungen* (Düsseldorf: Patmos Verlag, 1978), p. 88.

119. This is not to overlook the clear reference to the ultimate judgment in Q 12.5.

120. Assuming, of course, that the Jewish War was a fact during the compilation of Q; see, e.g., Hoffmann, 'Redaction of Q', pp. 190-98; Myllykoski, 'Social History'.

121. Also, there is the possible explanation introduced by Jacobson and Uro, who suggest that the saying hints at a 'material difference' between the two actions

The observation of Kloppenborg, according to which Q treats the rejection of the disciples' message as equally offending as the opposition that Jesus faced, is valid even according to the interpretation suggested above.[122] Certainly the Q-community had to draw conclusions as to why the death of Jesus did not 'fill the cup of God's wrath', but needed also the failed mission of the followers. Whether Q's conviction was that this very point of departure equals the content of 12.10a (speaking against the Son of man) is impossible to prove for certain.[123] Nevertheless, we may suppose that contemplation upon bare historical experiences forced the Q community to an interpretation: the sins committed against the earthly Son of man *had to* wait for their avenging. Ultimately, 'the blood of all the prophets which has been shed from the foundation of the world' (Q 11.50; IQP), would be required of its contemporary Israel. Only then would the 'Son of man' reveal his true nature as a bringer of judgment, as can be seen in the remaining passages on the 'Son of man'.

(speaking against the Son of man and blaspheming the Spirit); cf. Jacobson, *First Gospel*, pp. 188-89; Uro, 'Apocalyptic Symbolism', pp. 105-107. In particular, Uro stresses the 'human' connotations of the symbol 'Son of man' in this saying, linking it to other Q-passages that entertain the idea of the humiliation of the Son of man. He also makes note of the correspondence within these 'Son of man' sayings between the fate of the 'Son of man' figure and that of his followers ('Apocalyptic Symbolism', pp. 107-109). This interpretation comes quite close to the one described above, as both accentuate the flexible symbolic dimensions of the 'Son of man' language. Jacobson, however, bases his argument on the observation that in Q 12.8-9 and 10 Jesus is not identified with the figure of the heavenly prosecutor. Therefore, he supposes that these sayings (particularly vv. 8-9) reflect a very early stage in the tradition process of the early church. The reason why 'saying a word against the Son of man' was not as harmful, according to Jacobson, is that the 'Son of man' figure was considered to be inferior to the 'Spirit', and only later was this figure associated with Jesus (*First Gospel*, pp. 188-89). Jacobson's hypothesis is not very convincing. It does away with the contradiction between Q 12.8-9 and 12.10 only at the stage of a very early hypothetical layer, but as soon as Jesus is seen to be identified with the 'Son of man', the problem emerges.

122. Kloppenborg, *Formation of Q*, p. 213.

123. Although arguing for the lateness of Q 12.10, Tuckett suggests the same conclusions: 'Many would see 12.10 as exercising some interpretative role on 12.8-9, perhaps qualifying and correcting it to assert that whilst rejection of the earthly Jesus by Jewish opponents in the past was not decisive, rejection of the disciple's preaching in the post-Easter situation is' (Tuckett, 'Son of Man', pp. 210-11).

Q 12.40, The Sudden Arrival of the Son of Man

> You also must be ready; for the son of man is coming at an hour you do
> not expect.

This exhortation is part of a concise parable, the Parable of the Thief (Q
12.39-40). The parable itself is attached to its preceding Q-saying
(12.33-34) with two catchwords (κλέπτης and διορύσσειν). There are
difficulties about the application (v. 40) of the parable. To begin with,
Q 12.39 is reasonable in itself: surely anyone would watch over one's
possessions, if one knew the whereabouts of the thief. Jülicher has
emphasized rightly that the parable offers a picture of a successful theft
due to the *unpreparedness* of the house's owner. But then the application (v. 40) continues as though the outcome could have been altogether
different and the theft hindered: 'You *also* must be ready ...'[124] Certainly we can see the point: because one cannot know the time of the
breaking in of a thief, the only protection from theft is to be alert *all the
time*. The other difficulty about the application is the emerging impression that the Son of man *wants* to take his own by surprise ('the Son of
man is coming at an hour you do not expect'; IQP). The threatening
tone of this saying far surpasses the sayings of Q 12.8-10 discussed
above.

Neither of these difficulties represents an anomaly in the document
Q, however. The parousia-parable immediately following, the parable
of the 'Faithful Servant' (12.42-46), elaborates the same theme of
unpredictability. The images used in this second parable are particularly
brutal and ominous. Also, the parable shows a clear structure that is
interrupted by a transparent address to the reader (v. 44: 'Truly I tell
you ...') and by a macarism (v. 43).[125] The emphasis of the whole unit
Q 17.23-24, 37, 26-27, 30, 34-35 is on the unpredictability of the return
of the Son of man. Likewise, the parable of the 'Trusted Money' (Q
19.12-26) likens the Lord to an extremely demanding and merciless
master of the house, whose return from a journey is not fully anticipated
by some of his servants.[126] The apocalyptic expectation of Q in general

124. A. Jülicher, *Die Gleichnisreden Jesu* (2 vols. in 1; Darmstadt: Wissen-
schaftliche Buchgesellschaft, 1976), p. 141.

125. On this unusual phenomenon, *see* R. Bauckham's apt description ('Synoptic Parousia Parables and the Apocalypse', *NTS* 23 [1977], pp. 162-76 [167]).

126. On the inclusion of the parable to Q, see Kloppenborg, *Q-Synopsis*,
pp. 196-99.

gives no room for special signs or calculations that normally characterize apocalyptic sections like Mark 13 par., Daniel 7–12, portions of *1 Enoch* and *4 Ezra*, and the Revelation.[127] Q has not given up end-expectation, but is clearly in a phase in which this expectation has to be reinforced.

As has often been observed, Q reacts to the phenomenon of the *delay of the parousia*.[128] The narrative motifs of the parables listed above are illuminating in this respect: both parables (Q 12.42-46; 19.12-26) focus on a master who is absent and on the obedience of his slaves. Q 12.42-46 introduces the motif of the master's delay as a parabolic element; besides being an 'innocent image' necessary for the servant's lack of control,[129] it is pejorative enough for any reader to see the similarity to their situation. In line with the 'Logia-apocalypse' in Q 17 and Q 11.29-30 ('Sign of Jonah'), the parable of the 'Faithful Servant' stresses the peculiar point of Q 12.40, namely that the Lord is about to return when he is *least* expected by his own (cf. 12.46). The narrator seems to open the explicitly paraenetic section in 12.2 with the confidence that all the previous argumentation has been effective, so that more austere tones can now be applied and that the judicial role of the Son of man can be 'revealed'. It is time now to present the demands of the 'Kingdom'. Only at the end of Q does the narrator grant rest to the readers.[130]

Q 17.24, 26, 30, The Apocalypse of the Son of Man

> For as the lightning comes [[from the east]] and [[shines as far as the west]], so will be the [[‹day› of the]] son of man.

> [[For as were]] the days of Noah, so will [[it]] also be [[in the days]] of the son of man.

> So will it also be [[on the day when the]] son of man [[is revealed]].

---

127. Cf. J.S. Kloppenborg, 'Symbolic Eschatology and the Apocalypticism of Q', *HTR* 80.3 (1987), pp. 287-306; Uro, 'Apocalyptic Symbolism'; Myllykoski, 'Social History', pp. 184-99.

128. Similarly Lührmann, *Die Redaktion der Logienquelle*, pp. 69-70; Kloppenborg, *Formation of Q*, pp. 149-50.

129. Emphasized by Hoffmann, *Studien zur Theologie*, pp. 34, 46-50.

130. This rough description does not imply, of course, that no comforting tones are present from Q 12.2 onwards, nor that there are no strict sayings to the community in the preceding sections. I only wish to emphasize the differing general thrusts in both halves of the document.

Q 17.23-37[131] follows quite abruptly the 'various parables and say-ings'[132] in Q 15.4-7; 16.13, 17-18; 17.1-4, 6. With regard to what pre-cedes it, the 'Logia apocalypse' could hardly have started without an introductory or transitory phrase; however, if that is so, nothing has remained of it.[133] By contrast, what follows the 'Logia apocalypse' in Q 19.12-26; 22.28-30 fits well with the contents of our present section.[134]

It has been customary to point out the oddity of the contrast in vv. 23-24 between the limited, locally oriented expectations of some people and the appearence of the Son of man as a cosmic phenomenon.[135] Often v. 23 has been isolated as an originally independent saying, quite unrelated to what follows.[136] Recently, M. Myllykoski has argued that v. 23 reflects a different phase in the life of the Q-community, namely a lively expectation of the End in which there was no refusal of signs (cf. Q 11.29-30, 'Sign of Jonah'). Conversely the following sayings reject any such expectation and are shaped during peaceful conditions.[137] The arguments of Myllykoski are plausible: according to his view, Q was finished during the rather peaceful years after the Jewish war, sometime around 75 CE. 'Deuteronomism' and apocalypticism flourished in the symbolic universe of the Q-community as the war machines of the Roman army smothered the resistance of their fellow Jews. But several years of expectation after the war transformed this apocalypticism into a cautious attitude of resignation: no signs will be given, and the End will be sudden.[138]

---

131. For the sequence of pericopes, consult the IQP databases (Moreland and Robinson, 'IQP Work Sessions 1994', pp. 483, 485).

132. Designation by Kloppenborg, *Formation of Q*, p. 92.

133. Myllykoski, 'Social History', pp. 189-90. Uro asks whether Q 13.34-35 was originally located immediately before v. 17.23 ('Apocalyptic Symbolism', pp. 114-15). Vaage suggests that the discourse begins with v. 23 and nothing else as a result of poor redaction (Q^2) ('Son of Man', pp. 120-21).

134. Lührmann, *Die Redaktion der Logienquelle*, p. 75; Kloppenborg, *Formation of Q*, pp. 164-65.

135. Hampel opposes the view according to which Q 17.23-24 refers to the Son of man's parousia; in Hampel's mind the Lightning-saying (Q 17.24) is about Jesus' 'zukünftigen Herrlichkeit' (*Menschensohn und historischer Jesus*, p. 62).

136. Kloppenborg, *Formation of Q*, pp. 159-60 (however, see pp. 160-61, 163-64); Jacobson, *First Gospel*, pp. 234-35; Myllykoski, 'Social History', pp. 191-92. Against this, cf. Catchpole, *Quest for Q*, pp. 254-55 n. 78.

137. Myllykoski, 'Social History', p. 192.

138. Myllykoski, 'Social History', p. 199. Also P. Hoffmann locates Q in the

This fresh view is also supported by a comparison of the triple-tradition material: Myllykoski points out that Mark shares many of the emphases of Q's apocalyptic material.[139] But it is difficult to see why the apocalyptic cautiousness (whether of Q or Mark) could only have originated as a reaction to *post-war* frustration with regard to a delayed parousia. There was a long period of community living before the war, during which this kind of frustration could already have emerged. Such was the case in the Pauline community in Thessalonica, as its members grew restless when witnessing the death of some of its believers (1 Thess. 4–5).[140] Myllykoski admits that the early Q community did expect the End and was perhaps more engaged in observing typical apocalyptic signs (cf. above). It is also likely that the 'Mission Instructions' in Q 10.2-11 contain some old information concerning the lively enthusiasm that was apocalyptic in nature.[141] Actually I do not object to the post-war dating of Q as a document, but I do object to the idea that the explicit dating of 'deuteronomism' as well as most of the apocalyptic fervor are dependent of that phase. Certainly, the war may have *intensified* hopes of divine intervention and boosted the deuteronomistic interpretation; but this is a different matter. An argument for the unpredictability of the parousia would have been effective at any stage.[142]

Most of the arguments related to the previous Son of man saying in Q 12.40 are relevant here; thus, there is no need to repeat them. We can see how the humiliation of the Son of man has totally vanished from these sayings in order to make room for the 'parousia-paraenesis' which, very much dictating the last section of Q, Q 17.23-37, is therefore a warning to community members to take heed not to end up with

context of the Jewish War, but in the midst of it rather than after (Hoffmann, 'Redaction of Q'); cf. also the summarizing views of Uro, *Sheep among Wolves*, p. 243.

139. Myllykoski, 'Social History', pp. 176-78.

140. Also Jacobson notes the parallelism between 1 Thess. 5.1-3 and Q 17.23-37; he points out (importantly) that both sections reject the possibility of special signs.

141. Cf. the discussion under the analysis of Q 9.58 above.

142. Actually, a whole study of its own would be necessary to verify the specific features and ways of expression in both the 'deuteronomistic' passages and in the 'parousia-paraenesis'. The article of Myllykoski is a welcome reminder that the close association of these two is problematic. Also, see A.D. Jacobson, 'Apocalyptic and the Synoptic Sayings Source Q', in Segbroeck *et al.* (eds.), *Four Gospels*, pp. 403-19 (417-18).

the horrifying lot of the outsiders. On the one hand, there looms the danger of being deceived by false eschatological hopes (warning of false alarms, Q 17.23). On the other hand, the community should not become careless and be misled by the quite ordinary course of the lives of others (Q 17.26-30)[143] and thus become like 'insipid salt' (Q 14.34-35). The allusion to the story of Noah is twofold: the flood was for the destruction of the godless as well as for the rescue of the pious. In this connection one may recall the reference in Q 10.12-15 to the fate of Sodom and Gomorrah. According to that particular analogy, 'one was taken and one was left' (cf. Q 17.34-35).[144] A far worse catastrophe is about to happen, and the followers of Jesus should be ready. Absence of particular signs may leave the community unprepared for the most drastic event ever to occur to the human race.

Conclusions

In the preceding discussion, literary observations of individual 'Son of man' passages were analyzed to reveal the literary planning of Q. When necessary, sociologically oriented questions were also addressed to the text. Certain recurring patterns were uncovered as a result. Perhaps the most notable of these is the way in which Jesus' characterization as the 'Son of man' functions as an (interpretive) link between the 'deuterono-mistic' material and what has most appropriately been termed 'wisdom-language'. As a consequence, the 'wisdom-language' need not be considered as separate (usually taken as prior) traditions, and the link with the deuteronomistic material need not be treated as secondary.

The first instance of this phenomenon is in the opening sermon of Jesus (Q 6). The macarisms (6.20-23) reveal the followers of Jesus to be in anguish for multiple reasons, but nevertheless blessed and deserving of future reward. The last macarism with its 'Son of man' vocabulary is the key to undertanding of the situations of the followers,[145] as

143. Cf. Kloppenborg ('Symbolic Eschatology', p. 302): 'One expects a catalogue of sins. But Q's interest lies not in their sinfulness nor even in the righteousness of Noah and Lot, but [...] in the *unapocalyptic* character of the events prior to the end' (emphasis original).

144. Kloppenborg ('City and Wasteland', pp. 151-53) shows convincingly that the Old Testament story of Lot and Sodom/Gomorra is also echoed in Q, and that its allusions are numerous. He connects the verbs συμπαραλαμβάνω and ἀφίημι in Q 17.34-35 with the language of Gen. 18.26 and 19.17 (p. 152).

145. As noted in the analysis of Q 6.22 above, G. Theissen's observations (in

well as the necessary link to the 'love of enemies' ethic. But an analogous thought is evident in the unit Q 12.2-34: the followers are under pressure to tolerate interrogations (and persecution?) for the sake of the Son of man, but God will provide whatever they need. The 'Son of man' sayings are the middle terms in both accounts, although the one in Q 6.22 offers consolation, whereas the other in 12.8-9 (10) is also threatening. Because of the slightly different aims of these units, one cannot speak of a common structure behind them. But in both cases it is possible to assign a specific function to the 'wisdom-language'. Its aim is to comfort and instruct the community about how to react to the pressures that the community is facing.[146] Both 'Son of man' sayings are placed prior to two of Q's most extensive wisdom speeches. Naturally, nothing forces one to conclude that these speeches could not have existed as some kind of collections before the compilation of our present 'version' of Q. On the other hand, *literarily* there is nothing in them to resist their classification as late constructs that originated purely for paraenetic and didactic reasons.

Sociology of Early Palestinian Christianity) about the social function of the 'Son of man' language are illuminating. But his views can only be applied to the study of Q with reservation: (1) his portrait of the 'wandering charismatics' is inapplicable to much of the material in Q and is too hypothetical, and (2) the material basis of his argument is rather uncontrolled (eventually all the Gospel material is included). See a similar criticism by Uro, *Sheep among Wolves*, pp. 126-31.

146. According to Mack ('Kingdom That Didn't Come', pp. 620-26), the situation behind these units was quite the contrary. The 'sapiential instruction genre' of Q^1 reflects a community that understood itself to be the fulfillment of God's reign (= the 'Kingdom') on earth, less interested in 'changing the world' than in expanding its influence through normal interaction between people. Mack proposes that some of the 'survival tactics' evident also in the formative stratum are comparable to the ways in which ancient Cynics prepared themselves to endure reproach. Kloppenborg's ('Literary Convention', pp. 81-91) explanation is more warranted, because it takes seriously the continuum between the ethos of the formative stratum and the secondary redaction. Already the first Q-community was 'radical' and engaged in missionary activities and had even started to 'form social boundaries' (p. 90; with reference to Q 6.22-23b). But even in Kloppenborg's view, only the redactional stratum is responsible for deuteronomistic polemic. Basically similar is the social reconstruction of W. Cotter, 'Prestige, Protection'. See, however, Piper's formulation of the community setting of Q's 'sapiential collections', which seems to point in the direction argued for in this article (Piper, *Wisdom in Q-tradition*, pp. 184-92).

The most important observation in regard of the 'Son of man' material is the thoroughly *paraenetic* use of it. The community is living at the 'threshold' of society,[147] liminal and despised; therefore the narrator of Q presents a Jesus of similar fate. His cross (Q 14.27) is a concise and grotesque symbol of the radical call to discipleship. It is more difficult to guess why it was the symbol 'Son of man' that the Q community felt would best articulate the humility of Jesus' earthly destiny—especially so since the last uses of the title in Q carry contrary connotations. The title is certainly more easily associated with the apocalyptic thought-world.

The document Q as a whole is a mixture of comforting assurances, ominous threats, and demanding exhortations that alternate between different units of the text. Therefore, it should not be surprising that the 'Son of man' language exhibits all these tendencies and ways of expression. In the literary planning of Q, the Son of man is at first a comforting figure whose fate foreshadows the rejection of his followers (Q 6.22; 7.34; 9.58 [12.10]). Then the expression of the sayings starts to shift toward the judgmental aspects that any Christian was likely to perceive in the title (Q 11.30; 12.8-9, [10]). In the end, this manner of expression takes over, and the last sayings warn the followers not to fall under God's wrath (Q 12.40; 17.24, 26, 30). At the same time, the implicit notion in the latter sayings about Jesus' *post mortem exaltation* also signals the proof that the faithful followers will share his future glory, just as they had shared his misfortunes (Q 22.28-30; though not a 'Son of man' saying). This flexibility and variation of expression is the result of symbolic language, which is a mystery to 'outsiders' but divine wisdom to those 'inside' (Q 10.21-24).

147. Cf. Turner's 'threshold people' (*Ritual Process*, p. 95).

A Character Resurrected:
Lazarus in the Fourth Gospel and Afterwards

Raimo Hakola

John's characters are traditionally discussed in connection with other topics that are held to be more significant for the Gospel as a whole. For example, characters are often subordinated to the theological message of the Gospel. The Gospel is about believing in Jesus as the Christ, the Son of God, and having life in his name (20.30-31). Consequently, the most essential thing concerning different characters is their response to Jesus. The positive and negative responses to Jesus serve as a foil for the reader to ponder over his or her own position in light of the message of the Gospel. Because the theological message dominates to such a great extent the way the characters are presented, Franz Overbeck's view of John's characters is understandable; according to Overbeck, the characters in the Gospel are but 'a mirror for the manifestation of an alien Being and are of no further significance'.[1]

Besides being regarded as a necessary mirror for the revelation of Jesus, John's characters are sometimes regarded as a window to the history from which the Gospel came into being. J. Louis Martyn has proposed that the Fourth Gospel may be read as a two-level drama that is a witness to Jesus' earthly life as well as a witness to the events experienced in the Johannine community.[2] When the Gospel is read in this way, the different characters are representatives of the groups that have had a special role in the history of the Johannine community.

The primary interest of the theological and socio-historical interpretations of John has not been the characters in the story. However, Johannine characters have attracted attention in connection with some

---

1. F. Overbeck, *Das Johannesevangelium: Studien für Kritik seiner Erforschung* (ed. Carl Albrecht Bernoulli; Tübingen: J.C.B. Mohr, 1911), p. 303.

2. Cf. J.L. Martyn, *History and Theology in the Fourth Gospel* (Nashville: Abingdon Press, 2nd edn, 1979).

other questions. It is the recent literary approaches that have aroused a new interest in characters and characterization in Johannine studies. Scholars have noticed the importance of characters for the reading process: the readers become involved in a story by identifying themselves with some characters and distancing themselves from others. However, in spite of the recent interest in characterization, the new literary analyses have not completely changed the traditional way of approaching John's characters. John's literary critics have had to admit that the characters in the story are not well presented, for stereotypical traits dominate the characterization. In the most complete literary analysis of the Fourth Gospel to date, R. Alan Culpepper notes that

> characters are individualized by their position in society and their interaction with Jesus. This means that they may easily become types. They are not so individualized that they have much of a 'personality.' ... The functions of the characters are primarily two: (1) to draw out various aspects of Jesus' character successively by providing a series of diverse individuals with whom Jesus can interact, and (2) to represent alternative responses to Jesus so that the reader can see their attendant misunderstandings and consequences.[3]

Although many characters in the Gospel appear in restricted roles, they have had a wide appeal for the readers. It is not only well-developed and complicated characters who live in the minds of the readers. Even marginal characters can become an object of vital interest, as different readers approach the story with their own questions and expectations. In the Fourth Gospel Lazarus is a good example of a figure whose role in the story is that of a marginal agent but who moves toward a genuine personality as the Gospel comes to be read and interpreted in new contexts.

In this essay, we follow the growth of the traditions about Lazarus. I ask what has made the development of Lazarus's character possible. We will notice that the creative imagination of different readers has had a great part in this development. However, we can also see different trends in the Johannine text, each of which has generated different

---

3. R.A. Culpepper, *Anatomy of the Fourth Gospel: A Study in Literary Design* (Philadelphia: Fortress Press, 1983), p. 145. John's characters are described in a similar way by R.F. Collins, 'From John to the Beloved Disciple: An Essay on Johannine Characters', *Int* 49 (1995), pp. 359-69. According to Collins, Peter alone appears as 'a complex individual' in John, while all other characters 'are cast in typed roles as representative figures' (pp. 365-66).

responses. It has thus been possible for different readers in different ages to connect the story to their own situation.

In the first part of the article, a close narrative analysis of the Lazarus episode in John is provided in order to show that the characterization of Lazarus is minimal, and his function is strictly connected to the plot and the major themes of the Gospel. Yet, there is a surplus of information about Lazarus, which has played a special role in the developing inter-action between the text and its many readers. In the second part, then, I look at how the depiction of Lazarus has grown and developed over time as John's story is read and interpreted by subsequent generations of readers. I review selected examples that illustrate how Lazarus as a character has fascinated many generations of John's readers—even though he makes but a shadowy appearance in John.

Lazarus in the Gospel of John

The Lazarus Scene in the Plot of the Gospel

The first major part of the Gospel (chs. 1–12) is often characterized as the Book of Signs.[4] Jesus' seven miraculous signs form a nucleus that concentrates on his self-revelation to the world. In the course of the story, Jesus' signs evoke different responses from various characters. These various responses to Jesus are essential to the plot development of the Gospel: John's plot is about whether Jesus' self-revelation is accepted or rejected.[5] The outline of this plot can already be seen in the prologue of the Gospel: Jesus, the Word of God and the light of the world, comes to the world and gives those who receive him power to become children of God whereas even some of his own reject him (1.9-13). Successive scenes raise the question of how different groups and individuals react to Jesus. In a sense, the plot of the whole Gospel is compressed into each individual episode.[6] Different scenes of the Gospel are not always connected successfully to each other with causal

4. See, e.g., C.H. Dodd, *The Interpretation of the Fourth Gospel* (Cambridge: Cambridge University Press, 1954), p. 289.

5. Cf. N. Petersen, 'Can One Speak of a Gospel Genre?', *Neot* 28 (1994), pp. 137-58 (156). According to Petersen, John's plot is oriented to disclosure and reception.

6. Cf. Culpepper, *Anatomy*, pp. 88-89. See also Dodd, *Interpretation*, p. 384. According to Dodd, each episode in the Book of the Signs 'contains in itself, implicitly, the whole of the gospel'.

links, and the story does not progress from one scene to another without inconsistencies. In spite of the problems surrounding the causal progressions of the story, the different scenes are held together by their common theme: each scene opens up the possibility of faith and warns of unbelief, as different characters are confronted with the manifestation of God on earth in Jesus.

Although the question of the significance of Jesus' signs in the Gospel has been disputed among Johannine scholars, it can be said that the sign stories in the first part of the writing are of crucial importance for the plot development.[7] As D. Moody Smith notes, 'the miracle stories are taken up or recounted in the first instance because they aptly put the question of Jesus' identity (and thus create the possibility of genuine faith)'.[8] On the one hand, the signs are demonstrations of Jesus' heavenly origin: they show that Jesus is really what the Gospel claims him to be, the Christ and the Son of God (20.30-31). In so doing, they evoke faith from those who come to believe. On the other hand, the signs bring out the unbelief of those who do not receive Jesus and emphasize the fatality of their decision: they have seen Jesus' signs in which God's glory was visible on earth and yet have turned their backs to him. As John's Jesus declares: 'If I had not done among them the works that no one else has done, they would not have sin; but now they have seen and they have hated both me and my Father' (15.24).

The twofold functions of the Johannine sign stories become evident in the material preceding the Lazarus story. The Jews challenge Jesus and demand that he should tell them plainly if he is the Christ (10.24). In his answer, Jesus refers to the works that he does in the name of his Father and which bear witness to him.[9] After Jesus has spoken to the Jews and maintained that he and the Father are one, the Jews pick up

7. Especially R. Bultmann has maintained that the evangelist had a critical attitude toward signs and toward faith based on them. See, for example, *Theologie des Neuen Testaments* (Tübingen: J.C.B. Mohr, 9th edn, 1984 [1948]), pp. 396-97, 409.

8. D.M. Smith, *Johannine Christianity: Essays on its Setting, Sources, and Theology* (Columbia: University of South Carolina Press, 1984), p. 177.

9. It is clear that the signs told in the Gospel are to be included in the works Jesus is referring to, although Jesus' works (τὰ ἔργα) have a wider scope of meaning than his signs (τὰ σημεῖα). See W. Nicol, *The Semeia in the Fourth Gospel: Tradition and Redaction* (NovTSup, 32; Leiden: E.J. Brill, 1972), pp. 116-19; C. Welck, *Erzählte Zeichen: Die Wundergeschichten des Johannesevangeliums literarisch untersucht: Mit einem Ausblick auf Joh 21* (WUNT, 69; Tübingen: J.C.B. Mohr, 1994), pp. 55-57.

stones to stone him. Jesus does not, however, remain voiceless in the presence of mortal danger: 'Many good works have I shown you from the Father; for which of these do you stone me?' he asks the Jews with irony in his voice (10.32). The Jews are compelled to correct Jesus' words: it is not a good work but blasphemy that has stirred up their anger. Jesus answers by referring to the law of the Jews, but in the end he returns to the theme of his works, which witness on his behalf: 'If I do not the works of my Father, do not believe me; but if I do them, even though you do not believe me, believe the works, so that you may know and understand that the Father is in me and I am in the Father' (10.37-38). The dialogue comes to a conclusion as Jesus escapes from the hands of the Jews and withdraws to the other side of Jordan. However, many continue to come to him, and to confess their faith evoked by the signs (10.41).

This incident sets the stage for another sign that testifies to Jesus and shows his unity with the Father. Jesus' ironic question about whether the Jews will stone him because of his good works (10.32) reminds the reader of the obstinacy of God's own people. Although the Jews have seen Jesus' good (καλός)[10] works, these works have evoked in them only murderous intent rather than faith.[11] It is not surprising, therefore, that the last and the most impressive of Jesus' good works—the raising of Lazarus—will lead to a plan to kill Jesus. The reader is well prepared to recognize in this sign another demonstration of Jesus' heavenly origin, but the reader is also prepared for the fact that this sign will intensify the negative response to Jesus.

The raising of Lazarus is connected to the signs told at the beginning of the Gospel. After hearing that Lazarus is ill, Jesus says that this illness 'is for God's glory, so that the son of God may be glorified through it' (11.4). Jesus further couples God's glory and his sign when he promises to Martha that if she would believe, she would see the glory of God (11.40). The connection between God's glory and Jesus' sign reminds the reader of what was said earlier in the Gospel about

10. For the translation of the adjective καλός' in 10.32 see C.K. Barrett, *The Gospel According to St John: An Introduction with Commentary and Notes on the Greek Text* (London: SPCK, 2nd edn, 1978), p. 383. According to Barrett, it is difficult to find a word equivalent to the Greek 'which suggests deeds of power and moral excellence, resulting in health and well-being'.

11. Cf. P.D. Duke, *Irony in the Fourth Gospel* (Atlanta: John Knox Press, 1985), pp. 46-47.

Jesus' signs (ἀρχή τῶν σημείων), when the narrator comments on the wine miracle in Cana by saying that Jesus manifested his glory in this sign (2.11). The first and the last of the signs, therefore, make it clear that the signs are demonstrations of Jesus' glory on earth.[12] They are an essential part of his self-revelation to the world. As the last of the signs is recounted, Jesus' public career comes to its end.

The raising of Lazarus is not only the conclusion of Jesus' public life but, as the greatest sign, its culmination as well. In the first part of the Gospel, only a selection of signs is reported; nevertheless, the signs are all impressive ones. Various details in the sign stories emphasize the miraculous aspect of the signs.[13] Jesus turns Jewish purificatory water into wine that proves to be of superior quality (2.10); he heals the son of the royal official from a distance by his word (4.46-54); he heals a man ill for 38 years (5.1-9); he multiplies 5 loaves and 2 fish so that 5000 men are fed and 12 baskets are filled from the fragments left over (6.1-14); and he gives sight to a man who has been blind from birth (ch. 9). It is no wonder that even some of the Pharisees are astonished as they witness such signs (9.16).

But Jesus' last sign surpasses his earlier signs in magnificence. After hearing that Lazarus is ill, Jesus waits for two days before he decides to go to Judea again (11.7). When he arrives near Bethany, he finds that Lazarus has already been in the tomb for four days (11.17). As the miracle is finally at hand, Jesus (and the reader) is reminded once more, this time by Martha, that Lazarus has been dead for four days and that his body already smells (11.39). These details assure readers that Lazarus really was dead, and they leave no doubt that Jesus' last sign is beyond all comparison.[14] Therefore, Jesus' revelation to the world finds

---

12. This is emphasized by E. Käsemann whose view of the signs in the Gospel is opposed to that of Bultmann. Cf. E. Käsemann, *The Testament of Jesus: A Study of the Gospel of John in the Light of Chapter 17* (trans. G. Krodel; Philadelphia: Fortress Press, 1968), p. 21; Cf. also Nicol, *Semeia*, p. 133. According to Nicol, Jesus' glory in flesh which is visible in his signs is 'genuine epiphany even to unbelievers'.

13. Cf. Käsemann, *The Testament of Jesus*, p. 22: '[Jesus'] glory cannot be without miracles and the greater and the more impressive they are the better'. Though not sharing Käsemann's view of the Christology of the Gospel, other scholars also note the emphasis on the miraculous aspect of the signs. Cf. M. Davies, *Rhetoric and Reference in the Fourth Gospel* (JSNTSup, 69; Sheffield: JSOT Press, 1992), pp. 222-23; Welck, *Erzählte Zeichen*, pp. 60-65.

14. The mention that Lazarus had been dead four days is probably to be seen in

its culmination in the raising of Lazarus. Jesus' signs reveal his close relationship to the Father, and the raising of Lazarus is the most impressive one of these signs.[15] It gives the most incontrovertible proof for Jesus' claim stated earlier in the course of the narrative: Jesus really does the works of his Father, which shows that the Father is in him and he is in the Father (10.37-38).

In view of Jesus' most impressive sign, the unbelief of the Jews is especially surprising. It is no wonder that the narrator calls forth the Scriptures of the Jews as a witness to explain their unbelief (12.37-42). In the introduction to the two citations from the prophet Isaiah, the narrator makes another reference to the greatness of Jesus' signs. The words τοσαῦτα δὲ αὐτοῦ σημεῖα πεποιηκότος ἔμπροσθεν αὐτῶν (12.37: 'Although he had performed so many great signs in their presence ...') may refer either to the great number of Jesus' signs ('so many') or to the impressive nature of these signs ('so great'). In this context, the latter meaning is probably to be preferred.[16] Not even the last and the greatest of Jesus' signs has convinced the Jews of Jesus' heavenly origin.

The story of the raising of Lazarus not only crowns Jesus' public career but also points forward in the narrative to the passion of Jesus. The story brings to a climax the hostile attitudes of Jesus' enemies. The reader is warned of the murderous plans of the Jews already in ch. 5:

light of the view expressed in rabbinic literature (*Eccl. R.* 12.6; *Lev. R.* 18.1). According to this view, the soul hovered near the body for three days; after that time death is irrevocable. See, e.g., Barrett, *John*, p. 401; C.H. Talbert, *Reading John: A Literary and Theological Commentary on the Fourth Gospel and the Johannine Epistles* (Reading the New Testament Series; London: SPCK, 1992), p. 172.

15. The Lazarus scene is also regarded as a culmination of 'The Book of Signs' by T.E. Pollard, 'The Raising of Lazarus (John xi)', in E.A. Livingstone (ed.), *Studia Evangelica. IV. Papers Presented to the Fourth International Congress on New Testament Studies Held at Oxford, 1969* (TU, 112; Berlin: Akademie Verlag, 1973), pp. 434-43 (436).

16. Cf. R. Schnackenburg *Das Johannesevangelium. II. Kommentar zu Kap. 5–12* (HTKNT, 4.2; Freiburg: Herder, 1971), p. 516; J. Becker, *Das Evangelium nach Johannes* (2 vols.; Ökumenischer Taschenbuchkommentar zum Neuen Testament, 4; Gütersloh: Gütersloher Verlagshaus Gerd Mohn/Wurzburg: Echter-Verlag, 3rd rev. edn, 1991), II, p. 475; R. Kühschelm, *Verstockung, Gericht und Heil: Exegetische und bibeltheologische Untersuchung zum sogenannten 'Dualismus' und 'Determinismus' in Joh 12,35-50* (BBB, 76; Frankfurt-on-Main: Anton Hain, 1990), pp. 171-72; Welck, *Erzählte Zeichen*, p. 76.

230 Characterization in the Gospels

the narrator reports in a narrative aside how the Jews all the more sought Jesus to kill him, not only because he broke the Sabbath but also because he made himself equal to God (5.18). From this point on, the plans of the Jews to get rid of Jesus are taken for granted in the narrative. The narrator tells readers that these plans explain Jesus' movements (7.1), and both Jesus (7.19; 8.37) and the crowd (7.25) know about these plans, even though Jesus' opponents want to deny them. Several times, the narrator tells readers that the Jews are at the point of fulfilling their aims (7.30; 8.59; 10.31; 10.39), but Jesus always escapes from their hands. The narrator also tells readers why the Jews are not successful in their efforts: the hour of Jesus has not yet come (7.30).

The raising of Lazarus gives another reason for Jesus' opponents to fulfill their plans: many people believe as a result of seeing Jesus' last sign, and the chief priests and the Pharisees become fearful about Jesus' success (11.45-48). The narrator hints that this time the efforts of the Jewish leaders will not be fruitless. Their plans will finally be fulfilled, but in a way hidden even to them. The narrator has the chief priest Caiaphas prophesy the death of Jesus, and the narrator also reveals the ironic meaning of Caiaphas's words (11.49-53). According to the political reasoning of Caiaphas, one man should die for the people so that the whole people should not perish (v. 50). For the narrator, Caiaphas's words disclose a profound truth, because Jesus indeed will die for the nation, and not for the nation only, but to gather into one the scattered children of God (vv. 51-52) The narrator thus connects the earthly plot of the Jews to the divine plot of the whole Gospel. In so doing, the narrator provides the Lazarus scene with its proper connecting function in the narrative, for the Lazarus scene serves as a narrative bridge leading from 'the book of signs' to 'the book of passion'. Together with ch. 12, where Mary anoints Jesus and Jesus comes to Jerusalem for the last time, the Lazarus story brings to a conclusion the story of Jesus' revelation to the world and, at the same time, points forward to Jesus' passion.[17] Thus, the raising of Lazarus serves an important function as the culmination of the first part of the Gospel and as the prelude to its second part. As such, the placement of the scene is by no means random but shows the deliberate design of the author.[18]

17. Cf. D.A. Lee, *The Symbolic Narratives of the Fourth Gospel: The Interplay of Form and Meaning* (JSNTSup 95; Sheffield: JSOT Press, 1994), p. 189; R.A. Culpepper, 'The Plot of John's Story of Jesus', *Int* 49 (1995), pp. 347-58 (355).
18. Cf. M.W.G. Stibbe, 'A Tomb with a View: John 11.1-44 in Narrative-

The Lazarus Scene and the Major Themes of the Gospel
The Lazarus scene is connected to the rest of the narrative especially by means of the theme of life, one of the major themes of the Gospel. Already in the prologue, life and light are connected to Jesus as God's eternal Word become flesh: in this Word was life, and the life was the light of humanity (1.4). It is noteworthy that the two last signs of Jesus deal with these two themes connected already in the prologue: in ch. 9 Jesus gives sight to a man born blind and shows that he is the light of the world (8.12; 9.5), and in ch. 11 he gives new life to Lazarus and shows that he is the resurrection and the life (11.25). In these last two signs there comes to expression the central christological idea of the Gospel that Jesus is the light and the life of the world.[19]

Earlier in the Gospel (5.17-29), Jesus himself gives theological reasons for the claim that he gives life to all who believe in him. Jesus defends his action on the Sabbath by saying that his Father is still working, and so is he (5.17). He clarifies his point by saying that the Son does whatever the Father does (5.19). The two activities that the Father has delegated to the Son are of special importance: like the Father, the Son acts as a judge and as a giver of life (5.21-22). Then Jesus' life-giving activity is described in even more detail: 'Very truly, I tell you, the hour is coming, and is now here, when the dead will hear the voice of the Son of God, and those who hear will live ... Do not be astonished at this; for the hour is coming when all who are in their graves will hear his voice and will come out ...' (5.25-29). These words form a background for the Lazarus story, for the raising of Lazarus serves as their demonstration.[20] After the stone has been taken away from Lazarus' tomb and Jesus has prayed to his Father, the narrator tells how Jesus cried with a loud voice to Lazarus (11.43). Lazarus hears Jesus' voice and comes out from the tomb. Thus he fulfills Jesus' earlier words about resurrection (5.25, 28).

Critical Perspective', *NTS* 40 (1994), pp. 38-54 (39).
   19. See Schnackenburg, *Johannesevangelium*, II, p. 396; Lee, *Symbolic Narratives*, p. 190.
   20. Dodd, *Interpretation*, p. 365; Brown, *The Gospel According to John, I–XII* (AB, 29; Garden City, NY: Doubleday, 1966), p. 437; Barrett, *John*, p. 388; J.H. Neyrey, *An Ideology of Revolt: John's Christology in Social-Science Perspective* (Philadelphia: Fortress Press, 1988), pp. 81-93; A. Reinhartz, *The Word in the World: The Cosmological Tale in the Fourth Gospel* (SBLMS, 45; Atlanta: Scholars Press, 1992), p. 95; Lee, *Symbolic Narratives*, p. 190.

In the material preceding the Lazarus story, Jesus affirms once more that he does the works of his Father (10.37). The giving of life is a work of God *par excellence*. So these words prepare the reader for the miracle of resurrection that shows the truthfulness of Jesus' claims. In the course of the story, the narrator emphasizes that Jesus' claims do not concern the distant future only. Martha misunderstands Jesus' words about resurrection and expresses her faith in terms of traditional belief, according to which everyone will rise in the resurrection at the last day (11.24). However, Jesus' words to Martha (11.25-26, 40), indeed the whole Lazarus story, emphasize that Jesus' claim to be the resurrection and the life is already realized. This is in accordance with Jesus' earlier words, according to which the hour is already present when the dead will hear the voice of the Son of God (5.25).

Lazarus's story is connected also to the story of Jesus' own resurrection: both these stories took place by a tomb closed by a heavy stone that is somehow taken away from the tomb (11.39, 41, 20.1); both stories present a women disciple of Jesus who is weeping (Mary of Bethany, Mary Magdalene); in both stories faith is an important theme (11.40; 20.8).[21] Regardless of these points of similarity, there are marked differences between these stories as well. Unlike the case of Lazarus, Jesus' resurrection is not described and takes place without a helping hand. Lazarus returns to ordinary life whereas Jesus goes to his Father (20.17).

The differences between these two resurrection stories are seen in a tiny detail common to both stories. Lazarus comes out from the tomb with his hands and feet bound with bandages and his face wrapped with a cloth (11.44). This detail could simply be an embellishment to the simple story, but the deeper symbolic level of meaning becomes evident as the story progresses. The word for the cloth that covered Lazarus's face (σουδάριον) recurs in the Gospel in the story of Jesus' resurrection (20.3-9). As Peter and the beloved disciple come to Jesus' tomb, the beloved disciple reaches the tomb first but does not go in: he stoops, looks in and sees the linen cloths lying there. As Peter enters the tomb he sees 'the linen wrappings lying there, and the cloth (σουδάριον), which had been on Jesus' head, not lying with the linen wrappings but rolled up in a place by itself' (20.6-7). The placement of

21. See Lee, *Symbolic Narratives*, pp. 214-16.

the cloth seems to be of special importance, because the beloved disciple does not enter the tomb until this point; and when he finally steps into the tomb he sees and believes. The properly arranged grave cloths are a special sign of Jesus' resurrection: they show that Jesus' body has not been taken away. Also, Jesus' grave clothes and especially the napkin placed separately remind the reader of the story of Lazarus's resurrection. Whereas Lazarus had to be freed from the bandages, Jesus has freed himself from them and left them behind as a special sign of his resurrection.[22]

The raising of Lazarus is thereby given its proper place in the Gospel: though being the greatest of Jesus' signs, it must not supersede the culmination of the whole Gospel, the resurrection of Jesus, which is also the first step in Jesus' departure to his Father. However important a role Lazarus and his story may have in the plot of the Gospel, this role is subordinated to the overall message of the Gospel.

The Characterization of Lazarus
Lazarus's name. The narrator presents Lazarus to the reader right at the beginning of the story about him. 'Now a certain man was ill, Lazarus of Bethany, the village of Mary and her sister Martha' (11.1). Lazarus's village is identified through two sisters who are not yet explicitly identified as Lazarus's sisters. What follows is a further characterization of one of the sisters: Mary is identified as the one who anointed the Lord and wiped his feet with her hair (11.2). This mention seems to appear too early in the narrative because the story of Jesus' anointing is not told until in ch 12. The misplacement of this narrative aside may be a sign of the redactional process of the text. As such, it seems to indicate that the narrator supposes that his readers have some prior information about Mary, if not of both sisters.[23] This verse also identifies

22. See R. Schnackenburg *Das Johannesevangelium.* III. *Kommentar zu Kap. 13–21* (HTKNT, 4.3; Freiburg: Herder, 2nd rev. edn, 1976), p. 367; J. Kügler, *Der Jünger der Jesus liebte: Literarische, theologische and historische Untersuchungen zu einer Schlüsselgestalt johanneischer Theologie und Geschichte. Mit einem Exkurs über die Brotrede in Joh 6.* (SBB 16; Stuttgart: Verlag Katholisches Bibelwerk, 1988), pp. 335-37.

23. Verse 2 is commonly held as a later addition to the text. Thus, e.g., B. Lindars, *The Gospel of John* (NCB; London: Oliphants, 1972), pp. 386-87. According to E. Haenchen, *Das Johannesevangelium: Ein Kommentar* (ed. U. Busse; Tübingen: J.C.B. Mohr [Paul Siebeck], 1980), p. 398, the narrator supposes the reader to know Mary beforehand. According to Culpepper (*Anatomy*, p. 60) the misplace-

Lazarus as Mary's and Martha's brother.

Although the narrator gives scanty information about Lazarus and introduces him through his sisters, the narrator reveals his name at the onset of the story. In the Fourth Gospel, it is by no means usual to name such a minor character as Lazarus. Many individuals whose meetings with Jesus are described in detail do not become known to the reader by name (e.g. the Samaritan woman and the man born blind). Yet each member of this family from Bethany receives a proper name as soon as they appear in the story. As such, they stand out in the Gospel as a special group. Out of all those who receive a miracle of Jesus, Lazarus is the only one given a name: the royal official and his son, the sick man at the pool of Bethzatha and the man born blind all remain nameless, even though they have more active roles in the narrative than Lazarus.

The naming of a character is of importance for the reader's response to the character. The character with a name is distinguished from other characters. The proper name makes the identification of the character easier for the reader, who collects various traits from the character's conversations, feelings and action, and unites them under the proper name of the character. The name opens up a new point of view for the reader to see the events of the story.[24] Nameless characters, on the other hand, tend to remain faceless.[25] Had Lazarus not been given a name, he would be but another example of Jesus' divine power. Lazarus's role in the narrative is restricted and closely connected to plot development, but he still stands out as a distinct person because of his name. His naming explains partially the appeal his figure has had among John's readers: although Lazarus makes but a brief appearance in the narrative, his name makes him memorable and invites the reader to fill the gaps of his life by creative imagination.[26] In John's narrative, the name

ment of the verse 'raises a questions regarding the possibility of editorial rearrangement of the text or of appeal to tradition known by the reader'. Stibbe ('A Tomb with a View', p. 52) suggests v. 2 to show that the narrator has in mind a reader who rereads the story several times.

24. The function of proper names in fiction is discussed by T. Docherty, *Reading (Absent) Character: Towards a Theory of Characterization in Fiction* (Oxford: Clarendon Press, 1983), pp. 43-86.

25. See M. Sternberg, *The Poetics of Biblical Narrative: Ideological Literature and the Drama of Reading* (Bloomington: Indiana University Press, 1985), p. 330.

26. The name Lazarus appears in the New Testament also in Lk. 16.19-31. For the analysis of this narrative, see O. Lehtipuu's chapter in this volume. In Luke's account the resurrection plays an important role, and some scholars have suggested,

'Lazarus' has no meaning in the Greek language, although his name has a special meaning in its Hebrew form.[27] It is quite natural that his name is mentioned together with his sisters' names; they are all characterized as Jesus' special friends, and the proper names of each member of the family bring a sense of intimacy to the story.

It is noteworthy that Jesus addresses only Lazarus by name in the course of the story. This takes place at the climax of the story when Jesus cries to Lazarus and tells him to come out from the tomb (11.43). There is an echo of Jesus' words about the good shepherd here: the good shepherd calls his own sheep by name and leads them out from the sheepfold (10.3). Later Jesus explains his words further and connects the hearing of his voice and the giving of eternal life: 'My sheep hear my voice. I know them, and they follow me. I give them eternal life ...' (10.27-28).[28]

Jesus' love for Lazarus. Through the message that the two sisters send to Jesus, the reader infers that Jesus loved Lazarus. In their reported message, the sisters do not directly ask anything from Jesus but simply inform him of Lazarus's illness: 'Lord, he whom you love is ill' (11.3). Though they do not appeal explicitly for Jesus to come and heal Lazarus, the sisters make their worry known to Jesus. From the very beginning of the story there are great emotions behind the scenes. The

therefore, that there is a connection between Luke's story and John's story of Lazarus's resurrection. For the discussion see U. Busse, 'Johannes und Lukas: Die Lazarusperikope: Frucht eines Kommunikationsprozesses', in A. Denaux (ed.), *John and the Synoptics* (BETL, 101; Leuven: Leuven University Press, 1992), pp. 281-306. According to Busse, John's story 'basiert sowohl auf synoptischen Vorgaben, deren Kenntnis bei allen am Kommunikationsprozeß Beteiligten vorausgesetzt wird, als auch auf dem dem Autor eigenen theologisch motivierten Intentionen' (p. 303). It is doubtful, however, that readers are supposed to read John's story with the Lukan parable in mind; whether or not the Lukan parable has played a part in the creation of John's story is a question that cannot be dealt with here.

27. The Hebrew form presupposed by the Greek is לעזר. This is a shortened form from אלעזר which etymologically means 'God helps'. See Barrett, *John*, p. 389. This time the narrator does not give the translation of the Hebrew name, and it is probable, therefore, that the etymological meaning of the name is not of great significance for him. In other contexts, the narrator gives a translation of those Hebrew (or actually Aramaic) words or names he is using: some of these words are very common ones (cf. 1.38; 1.41; 5.2; 9.7; 20.16).

28. For the connections between the raising of Lazarus and the parable of the good shepherd, see Reinhartz, *The Word in the World*, pp. 94-95.

sisters' message is an implicit call for help; they remind Jesus of his love for Lazarus in the hope that he will hurry to help their brother.

Jesus' love for Lazarus is an ambiguous theme in the story: as Jesus hears the message of the sisters, he does not respond as they might have hoped. Instead of hastening to Bethany, Jesus gives a theological reason for the illness (v. 4) and deliberately delays his departure from the place where he was (v. 6). This behavior does not show, however, that Jesus does not love Lazarus; this is made clear in the narrator's commentary in v. 5, where the narrator says that Jesus loved Martha and her sister and Lazarus. This narrative aside is awkwardly placed in the story, for it does not follow v. 4 smoothly, and the narrative does not continue in v. 6. without difficulty.[29] It is as if the narrator had in his mind a possible objection that Jesus' delay may arouse in the reader. At the cost of a smooth progression to the story, the narrator emphasizes that Jesus' action does not indicate he is indifferent to the concern of Lazarus's sisters.[30] The narrator seems to be aware of the tension between Jesus' action and Jesus' love for Lazarus.

Jesus' action shows his independence of human demands.[31] Just as he does in the other miracle stories in the Gospel, Jesus rejects at first the appeal to perform a miracle but then later exceeds the hopes put in him (cf. 2.4; 4.48).[32] It seems as if the love for Lazarus expressed in the

29. Various redaction-critical suggestions have been made to explain the awkward placement of v. 5 in the text. J.H. Bernard, *Gospel According to St. John* (2 vols.; ICC; Edinburgh: T. & T. Clark, 1928), II, p. 375, regards v. 5 as 'an explanatory gloss added by an editor'. R. Bultmann, *Das Evangelium des Johannes* (MeyerK, 2; Göttingen: Vandenhoeck & Ruprecht, 21st edn, 1986), p. 302, regards v. 4 as an addition made by the evangelist to the signs source in which v. 5 followed right after v. 3. Schnackenburg (*Johannesevangelium*, II, p. 399) ascribes both v. 4 and v. 5 to the evangelist who has edited his source. According to Brown (*John*, p. 423), v. 5. is 'a parenthetical insertion to assure the reader that Jesus' failure to go to Lazarus does not reflect indifference'.

30. Cf. Barrett, *John*: 'V. 5 corrects a possible misinterpretation of v. 6: Jesus' delay, and consequent death of Lazarus, were not due to lack of affection on his part'. Thus also Haenchen, *Johannesevangelium*, p. 399; J. Kremer, *Lazarus: Die Geschichte einer Auferstehung: Text, Wirkungsgeschichte und Botschaft von Joh 11,1-46* (Stuttgart: Verlag Katholisches Bibelwerk, 1985), p. 57.

31. Cf. Stibbe, 'A Tomb with a View', p. 44: 'Jesus' hesitation is quite evidently emblematic of his evasiveness, of his reluctance to operate with predictability and according to discernible, man-made time-tables.'

32. Those scenes (2.1-11; 4.46-54; 7.2-14; 11.1-44) where Jesus seems to act inconsistently are studied in detail by C.H. Giblin, 'Suggestion, Negative Response,

message of the sisters belongs to the earthly point of view from which
Jesus is distancing himself. The narrator takes good care, however, that
the reader does not draw too far-reaching conclusions from Jesus'
action and thereby misinterpret his motives. As a result, Jesus' love
appears in the story in a strange light, for the mention that Jesus loved
the Bethanian family is followed by v. 6, in which the narrator says that
Jesus stayed two days longer in the place where he was when he heard
about Lazarus's illness. The words ὡς οὖν ('so when') connect v. 6 to
v. 5, and this connection suggests that there is a logical continuation of
thought between these verses. Jesus' love (v. 5) is presented as a reason
for his action (v. 6). If the text is taken as it now stands, it appears that
Jesus shows his love by delaying his trip to Bethany.[33] Jesus and the
sisters understand love in different ways. The reader, who is supposed
to share Jesus' point of view and rise above the worldly level of understanding, may be bewildered as the story progresses: Martha's and
Mary's emotions in the face of death seem to be quite natural, whereas
Jesus' response toward these emotions is a puzzling one.

After waiting two days, Jesus decides to go to Judea. The narrative
concentrates on the exchange between Jesus and his disciples. The
reader learns through this exchange that Lazarus is already dead. This
information is conveyed in the form of a misinterpretation, a narrative
convention familiar from many scenes in the Gospel. Jesus speaks
about Lazarus's death with the metaphor of sleep, but his disciples take

and Positive Action in St. John's Portrayal of Jesus', *NTS* 26 (1979–80), pp. 197-
211. According to Giblin, one can discern a common narrative pattern in these stories in which Jesus proceeds to act positively after giving a negative response to a
suggestion. This pattern 'sets in relief Jesus' dissociation from the predominantly
human concerns of those who, by merely human standards, would also seem to be
rather close to him ... He never fails to attend to the situation presented to him, but
in doing so he acts radically on his own terms' (p. 210). Cf. also A. Reinhartz,
'Great Expectations: A Reader-Oriented Approach to Johannine Christology and
Eschatology', *Journal of Literature and Theology* 1 (1989), pp. 61-76. Reinhartz
suggests that the pattern manifested in the three signs-stories can also be applied to
the Gospel as a whole.

    33. See Bernard, *John*, p. 374. According to Bernard, v. 5, in its present posi-
tion, gives a reason why Jesus did not go immediately to Lazarus: 'Because he
loved them (Martha, Mary, and Lazarus), he wished to exhibit in their case the
greatness of his power and the reach of his compassion. If that were so, he was
content to leave the sisters in agony of grief for three days, in order that the glory of
God might be more signally vindicated in the end.'

his words literally, which in turn gives Jesus an opportunity to clarify his point (vv. 11-14). Jesus is presented as the master of the situation, for he knows exactly what he is doing and what is going to happen. Instead of feeling sorrow for Lazarus and his sisters, he rejoices that he was not with Lazarus, because Lazarus's death will offer an occasion for the disciples to believe (v. 15). Jesus regards Lazarus's death as an event that testifies to his message, but he does not seem to be affected by the feelings that death usually evokes in human beings.

There is, however, an allusion to Jesus' intimate relationship with Lazarus in the story. Speaking to the disciples Jesus calls Lazarus 'our friend' (11.11: φίλος ἡμῶν). This reminds the reader of what was said earlier about Jesus' love for Lazarus. The reader may not forget that Lazarus was Jesus' special friend. In the section of the Gospel following the story of Lazarus, Jesus' friendship is an important theme. In his farewell speech, Jesus calls his disciples his friends: 'You are my friends if you do what I command you. I do not call you servants any longer, because the servant does not know what the master is doing; but I have called you friends, because I have made known to you everything that I have heard from my Father' (15.14-15). Already before this promise to the disciples, Jesus has called Lazarus 'our friend'. The beginning of Jesus' friendship with Lazarus is not described in the Gospel, but it does not seem to be based on the revelation of divine secrets, which is the reason why Jesus calls his disciples his friends. Jesus' friendship with Lazarus is a mysterious and open theme in the story. At this point of the story, Jesus seems to be playing a game with the fate of his friend.

As the story progresses the reader is presented a different way to respond to death. The reader encounters the Jews who have come to console Mary and Martha because of their brother (v. 19). As in v. 3, the text tells only indirectly about the emotions of the two sisters; between the lines, however, the reader can get a picture of the mourning sisters. This picture becomes more vivid as the narrative focuses on the sisters' encounters with Jesus. Both of them in their turn come to Jesus and address him with almost the same words: 'Lord, if you had been here, my brother would not have died' (vv. 21, 32). Martha's words also include a confession of her faith: 'But even now I know that God will give you whatever you ask of him' (v. 22). This confession shows Martha's genuine faith in Jesus' ability to perform miracles. However, as the following dialogue shows, she still has to grow in her faith.

Unlike Martha, Mary does not express her faith in words, but her way of approaching Jesus is full of devotion: when she comes to Jesus, she falls at his feet (v. 32). Scholarly readers have thought that the two sisters represent different faith responses to Jesus; scholars are not, however, in agreement about which one of the sisters shows the more acceptable faith. Some favour Martha while discrediting Mary.[34] Others, however, think Mary personifies the true believer.[35]

There is no reason, however, to emphasize the contrast between the responses of the sisters. Both sisters have a role of their own in the story, and both of them are presented in a sympathetic light. They may have some shortcomings in their faith, but there are hints in the story, too, that they are progressing in their journey of faith and becoming models of true discipleship.[36] Regarding their relationship with Lazarus, their first words to Jesus are of importance. In light of what happened earlier in the story, the sisters' words are close to a reproach towards Jesus; although they have sent Jesus a word to come and help their brother, Jesus seems to have turned a deaf ear to their request for help. A question about whether Jesus really loves Lazarus is again raised.

34. Already according to Wellhausen, Mary is but 'a shadow of her sister'. See J. Wellhausen, *Das Evangelium Johannis* (Berlin: Georg Reimer, 1908), p. 51. According to Schnackenburg (*Johannesevangelium* II, p. 418), the narrator compares and contrasts the attitudes of the two sisters. Mary falls short in this comparison, because she gives 'an impression of being nothing but a complaining woman'. According to Pollard ('The Raising of Lazarus', p. 441), Jesus' love for the two sisters has elicited contrasting responses: 'Confident trust on the part of Martha, and hysterical weeping on the part of Mary.' Martha's faith and Mary's lack of faith are contrasted also by T.L. Brodie, *The Gospel According to John: A Literary and Theological Commentary* (New York: Oxford University Press, 1993), pp. 392-94.

35. Cf. E. Hirsch, *Das vierte Evangelium* (Tübingen: J.C.B. Mohr [Paul Siebeck], 1936), pp. 290-91. According to Hirsch, Martha and Mary are contrasted on purpose in the text. Mary pronounces the same words as Martha but 'in an attitude of adoration'. Furthermore, her silence shows the right Christian attitude towards pain and suffering: her grief has become a silent and expecting appeal. Mary's faith is contrasted to that of Martha also by F. Moloney, 'The Faith of Martha and Mary: A Narrative Approach to John 11,17-40', *Bib* 75 (1994), pp. 471-93. For Moloney, Mary is 'the character in the story reflecting genuine Johannine faith, while Martha has fallen short of such faith' (p. 483).

36. Cf. A. Reinhartz, 'From Narrative to History: The Resurrection of Mary and Martha', in A.-J. Levine (ed.), *'Women Like This': New Perspectives on Jewish Women in the Greco-Roman World* (SBLEJL, 1; Atlanta: Scholars Press, 1991), pp. 161-84 (172-81); Lee, *Symbolic Narratives*, p. 219.

This time the question is raised implicitly by the words of the two sisters and is connected to their point of view, whereas the reader has a different viewpoint from which to evaluate the events of the story. The reader is better informed of the situation than the sisters. The reader is aware of Jesus' words according to which 'the hour is coming, and is now here, when the dead will hear the voice of the Son of God, and those who hear will live' (5.25). The reader can anticipate, therefore, the happy ending of the story.

Jesus' way of dealing with Martha confirms the positive expectations of the reader. Jesus hints at the coming resurrection of Lazarus by saying that Lazarus will rise again (v. 23). Martha misinterprets Jesus' words and thinks that they refer to the coming resurrection at the last day (v. 24). Jesus' answer, however, promises more than this: 'I am the resurrection and the life. Those who believe in me, even though they die, will live; but everyone who lives and believes in me will never die' (vv. 25-26). Although Martha does not understand these words, the reader can recognize how deep a consolation there is in Jesus' words. Two levels of understanding as well as two different ways to face death are clearly evident in the dialogue between Jesus and Martha.

Things become more complicated, however, as the narrative focuses on Mary's meeting with Jesus. After falling at Jesus' feet Mary repeats the words her sister has already said to Jesus (v. 32: 'Lord, if you had been here, my brother would not have died'). After that the narrative takes a surprising twist. The narrator gives the reader a glimpse into Jesus' inner feelings: after seeing Mary and the Jews weeping, something happens in Jesus, who has thus far in this story not been affected by human feelings. Just what Jesus feels when he faces the weeping crowd is in dispute among the scholarly readers of the story. The narrator describes Jesus' emotions with two different verbs: ἐνεβριμήσατο τῷ πνεύματι καὶ ἐτάραξεν ἑαυτόν (v. 33). These words can be translated in two different ways: either 'he became angry and troubled' or 'he was deeply moved in his spirit and troubled'. What makes the translation difficult is the rare use of the verb ἐμβριμάομαι. This verb is used elsewhere to denote an angerlike feeling or action stirred up by a feeling of anger.[37] The verb 'refers to an aggressive style of behaviour

---

37. Surveys of the use of the verb ἐμβριμάομαι in classical, biblical and patristic literature are offered by C.I.K. Story, 'The Mental Attitude of Jesus at Bethany', *NTS* 37 (1991), pp. 51-66 (53-55); B. Lindars, 'Rebuking the Spirit: A New Analysis of the Lazarus Story of John 11', *NTS* 38 (1992), pp. 89-104 (92-96).

rather than to the emotion of anger as such; the emphasis is on outward expression rather than on inward feeling'.[38] In many cases, the meaning of the verb comes close to the meaning of the verb 'to rebuke'. In view of the meaning of the verb in other texts, many scholars consider that the word as it is used here in John refers to Jesus' anger.[39] The question remains, however, why Jesus would become angry when he saw Mary and the Jews weeping.

According to the most prevalent explanation given to the question, Jesus' anger was provoked by the tears of the mourners, because their tears indicated a lack of faith on their part. The mourning crowd overcome by grief cannot receive the salvation Jesus offers, and therefore they represent the unbelief of this world in the face of which Jesus becomes angry.[40] If interpreted in this way, Jesus' attitude towards Mary and the weeping crowd seems to be severe indeed, especially since the behaviour of the mourners seems to be a natural response. Some scholars, therefore, have tried to soften Jesus' attitude; according to them, Jesus' anger is not against Mary or the wailing crowd but against the power of death,[41] or against the final rejection of Jesus.[42] The problem of all these interpretations is that the reader must infer a profound theological rationale for Jesus' attitude from the very scant description in the text; furthermore, these interpretations do not fit the context without difficulty.

It is problematic to interpret the verb ἐμβριμάομαι to refer to Jesus' anger, because a few lines further Jesus cries too. Jesus' own

38. Lindars, 'Rebuking the Spirit', p. 96.

39. This interpretation is firmly attested in the German tradition, since already Luther understood the verse in this way. See G.R. Beasley-Murray, *John* (WBC, 36; Waco, TX: Word Books, 1987), pp. 192-93. Beasley-Murray offers a useful list of the commentators, both German- and English-speaking, supporting this translation: Bultmann, Büchsel, Strathmann, Schnackenburg, Schultz, Haenchen, Becker, Hoskyns, Barrett and Brown.

40. Cf. E.C. Hoskyns, *The Fourth Gospel* (ed. F.N. Davey; London: Faber & Faber, 2nd edn, 1947), pp. 403-405; Bultmann, *Johannes*, p. 310; Schnackenburg, *Johannesevangelium*, II, pp. 421-22; Pollard, 'The Raising of Lazarus', p. 441; Beasley-Murray, *John*, p. 193. According to Moloney ('The Faith of Martha and Mary', p. 486) Jesus is 'severely disappointed' because Lazarus's death and the grief evoked by it threaten the incipient faith of Mary.

41. Kremer, *Lazarus*, p. 73.

42. Lee, *Symbolic Narratives*, p. 212

tears have been regarded as tears of anger because of unbelief[43] or tears of sadness because of the darkness of the present world.[44] If Jesus' tears are interpreted in these ways, the statement that Jesus cried is awkwardly placed in the story.[45] The natural place for Jesus to cry would have been after v. 33, when the narrator reports Jesus' emotions elicited by the weeping crowd. Jesus' cry is not, however, reported until after v. 34; in this verse, Jesus asks where Lazarus has been laid, and the crowd invites Jesus to come and see. After this, there follows the asyndetic sentence that is not united to the preceding context with connectives. According to this reference, 'Jesus burst (cf. the aorist ἐδάκρυσεν) into tears' (NRSV: 'began to weep'). It seems, then, that Jesus' weeping is caused by the thought of Lazarus in the tomb[46] rather than by the weeping of the (allegedly unbelieving) mourners. The interpretation of the verb ἐμβριμάομαι as a reference to Jesus' anger is thus at odds with the mention of Jesus' own tears. Another meaning, therefore, needs to be considered for the verb.

In the English-speaking world, ἐμβριμάομαι has been understood to refer to Jesus' emotional state of mind; the rendering 'he was deeply moved (NRSV: 'greatly disturbed') in spirit' and other synonymous expressions have been offered as translations of the text.[47] The advan-

43. Hoskyns, *The Fourth Gospel*, p. 405. Hoskyns refers to Lk. 19.41 where Jesus weeps over Jerusalem.

44. Schnackenburg, *Johannesevangelium*, II, pp. 421-22. Schnackenburg refers to the texts that speak of the tears of Jesus or of his followers (Heb. 5.7; Acts 20.19; Rev. 7.17; 21.4). Schnackenburg is followed by Beasley-Murray, *John*, p. 194.

45. Already Wellhausen (*Evangelium Johannis*, p. 52) paid attention to the awkward placement of v. 35. Later many scholars proposed that there is a redactional seam between v. 34 and v. 35. For example, vv. 35-37 are regarded by Schnackenburg and Fortna as an insertion to the original story. See Schnackenburg, *Johannesevangelium*, II, p. 400; R.T. Fortna, *The Fourth Gospel and its Predecessor: From Narrative Source to Present Gospel* (Edinburgh: T. & T. Clark, 1988), pp. 106-107.

46. Thus Brown, *John*, p. 426.

47. Different translations for the text are presented by Beasley-Murray, *John*, p. 192. Various versions include the following translations for the words ἐνεβριμήσατο τῷ πνεύματι καὶ ἐτάραξεν ἑαυτόν: 'he groaned in the spirit and was troubled', 'he sighed heavily and was deeply moved', 'he was deeply moved in spirit and troubled', 'he spoke in great distress', and 'his heart was touched'. The two latest official Finnish versions (1938, 1992) have followed this translation tradition as well; previously, however, the text was translated so as to follow Luther's version. Beasley-Murray mentions the following scholars as supporters of

tage of this interpretation is its suitability to the present context: Jesus becomes emotionally affected when he thinks of his dead friend, and he shares in the grief of the mourners.[48] The problem with this interpretation is the lack of evidence for this kind of meaning for the verb ἐμβριμάομαι.[49] Furthermore, Jesus' emotions are now not in accordance with his earlier behaviour. Many scholars want to deny, therefore, that the cause of Jesus' tears is the grief over Lazarus; according to these scholars, Lazarus's death leads Jesus to ponder over his own approaching death in the face of which he is overcome by emotion.[50] This deeper theological explanation for Jesus' mental attitude is, however, too obscure to be persuasive.

However, a more obvious interpretation is at hand for the reader because of the immediate narrative context. Even though the text seems to leave the reason for Jesus' emotions indeterminate, nevertheless, the immediate context of vv. 33-35 suggests that Jesus takes part in the grief of the weeping crowd. This is the most natural explanation for Jesus' tears.[51] This interpretation, of course, raises a question about the consistency of Jesus' behaviour: why does he feel sorrow for Lazarus and his grieving sisters now, after disregarding their distress? Has Jesus changed his mind and begun to regret his earlier indifferent attitude?[52]

this kind of translation: Bernard, Temple, Strachan, Sanders, Morris, Marsh, Lindars, Bruce, Lagrange and F.M. Braun.

48. The significance of the textual context for determining the meaning of ἐμβριμάομαι is emphasized by J.N. Sanders, *A Commentary on the Gospel According to St. John* (ed. B.A. Mastin; BNTC; London: A. & C. Black, 1968), pp. 271-72; Lindars, *John*, pp. 398-99; Lindars, 'Rebuking the Spirit', p. 102; I. Dunderberg, 'Lasaruksen kuolleistaherättäminen: Kirjallisuuskriittinen analyysi jaksosta Joh 11, 1–46' (The Raising of Lazarus: A Source-Critical Analysis of Joh 11, 1-46) (Lic. Theol. thesis, University of Helsinki, 1990), p. 109.

49. Lindars ('Rebuking the Spirit', p. 96) sees clearly that the interpretation he is supporting ('Jesus was deeply moved in his spirit') does not accord with the use of the verb ἐμβριμάομαι in other contexts. He explains the choice of the verb in John by ascribing it to John's source. The verb refers to the underlying source that was an exorcism story in which Jesus 'rebuked the spirit' (p. 99). John adapted the exorcism to depict an actual case of raising a dead man (p. 101). He repeated the verb ἐμβριμάομαι, but gave it a new meaning that could be inferred from the narrative context.

50. Sanders, *John*, p. 272; Kremer, *Lazarus*, p. 73; Lee, *Symbolic Narratives*, p. 211.

51. Thus Lindars, 'Rebuking the Spirit', p. 92

52. See Story, 'The Mental Attitude', p. 64. According to Story, Jesus regrets

There are no answers to these questions in the text: Jesus' emotions are inconsistent and their deeper reasons simply remain unresolved.

For the reader who has wavered between Jesus' reserved attitude toward human distress and Martha's and Mary's natural grief in the face of death, the tears of Jesus come as a relief. Despite his earlier behaviour, Jesus finally shows his solidarity with the weeping mourners. Jesus' tears shed new light on his love for Lazarus, too. The thought that Jesus cried because of his love for Lazarus is placed into the mouth of the Jews. However, this point of view could be a sign that the reason for Jesus' tears is not grief for Lazarus.[53] Remembering the role the Jews played in previous episodes of the Gospel, the reader could interpret the remark of the Jews as another misinterpretation on their part. It belongs to the rules of irony in the Gospel, however, that those who misunderstand Jesus' words or behaviour often express the truth without realizing it themselves. In this connection, too, the two comments of the Jews hit the mark (vv. 36-37: 'See how he loved him!', 'Could not he who opened the eyes of the blind man have kept this man from dying?').[54] As the narrator has already stated, Jesus loved Lazarus and, as the following story shows, he acts to rescue his friend from death. As in the beginning of this story, Jesus' love for Lazarus is an ambiguous theme: Jesus indeed loved Lazarus, but not in the way the Jews could have imagined.

As soon as Jesus weeps out of grief for Lazarus whom he loved, the narrative logic of the whole Lazarus story begins to change. The two different ways to approach death, which are kept apart in the first part of the story, now intermingle with each other. The hidden emotions, from which the reader is supposed to distance themself, now take hold of the protagonist. As Jesus becomes touched by the human emotions that the death calls forth, the atmosphere of the narrative assumes unexpected features. What might have been a simple story, one that

---

his delay in arriving at Bethany when he sees the grief of the sisters and, therefore, he 'rebukes his spirit'. The verbs in question could be translated as follows, 'Why did I not come sooner and save my friends their grief and the grief of their friends as well?' Story's solution is hardly a convincing one, if it is meant as an explanation for the intended meaning of the text. His solution does, however, reflect the problems and questions that the indeterminate text arouses in the reader.

53. Thus Lee, *Symbolic Narratives*, p. 209.

54. See Barrett, *John*, p. 400.

exemplifies Jesus' power over death, achieves a new depth when Jesus weeps with the other mourners.[55]

The narrator refers to Jesus' emotions once more when telling about Jesus approaching the tomb of his friend: 'Then Jesus, again greatly disturbed (ἐμβριμώμενος ἐν ἑαυτῷ), came to the tomb' (v. 38). After that, there are no signs of Jesus' puzzling emotions. His emotional state is quickly over, and the narrative returns to its former logic. It is as if Jesus had pulled himself together after the brief outburst of emotion upon entering the tomb. He tells the bystanders to take away the stone from the tomb, and he gives his final lesson to Martha, who is still not able to anticipate what is about to happen (vv. 39-40). Jesus also prays to his Father,but the prayer is not a sign of Jesus' helplessness or hesitation. Rather, the words of the prayer are meant for the people standing nearby, so that they may believe that the Father has sent Jesus (vv. 41-42).

The culmination of the whole story, the actual raising of Lazarus, is described with only a few plain words: Jesus cries with the loud voice to Lazarus, the dead man comes out from the tomb bound with bandages, and Jesus tells the crowd to unbind him and let him go (vv. 43-44). This is a fitting conclusion to this story which is another triumph for the Gospel's hero. However, the narrative has suggested that there is more going on behind the scenes. It is as if the narrator has forgotten Martha's and Mary's distress for their brother and Jesus' love for Lazarus, because the narrator gives no hints as to the precise emotions Lazarus's resurrection has evoked in the characters, including Jesus. Instead of telling of the reunion of the two sisters and Lazarus, the narrator directs the attention of the readers to the response that Jesus' greatest sign evoked among the Jews. The reader is hardly ready, however, to forget the grieving sisters and their brother who were Jesus'

---

55. According to Stibbe ('A Tomb with a View', p. 41) the reader should respond to the story 'as a comic interlude prior to the dark and tragic intensity of the passion story'. For him, the motif of love in the story is 'part of the author's repertoire of comic ingredients, since love is frequently the most common motive for the protagonists of comedy'. Even if the story met some characteristics of a comic story, the reader would have difficulties reading it as such, because not even the protagonist manages to get through the events without being affected by the perplexing emotions that the death evokes.

special friends. For the reader who has identified with the emotions of the characters, the conclusion of the story is all too terse.[56]

Lazarus's new life. Lazarus does not disappear altogether in the Gospel after the story of his raising is completed. At the beginning of ch. 12, Jesus takes part in a supper in Bethany, where Lazarus is one of those at table with Jesus (12.2). Not unlike the previous scene in ch. 11, Lazarus is given but a minor role in this scene, which focuses on Mary anointing the feet of Jesus. Lazarus's presence with Jesus is mentioned because it evokes a variety of reactions among the Jews. A great crowd of Jews comes to Bethany, not only because of Jesus but also to see Lazarus (v. 9). This is enough for the chief priests, who make a decision to kill Lazarus, because many Jews have gone off and believed in Jesus on account of him (vv. 10-11). The chief priests are zealous enough to destroy not only Jesus but also Lazarus, who exists as living proof of Jesus' divine abilities.

The plan of the chief priests unites Lazarus' fate to that of Jesus. Like the one who restored him to life, Lazarus is persecuted—and without cause. However, there is a notable difference between the dangers that threaten Jesus and the dangers that threaten Lazarus. In the case of Jesus, the reader can anticipate his coming fate: Jesus will be killed by the Jews, although this is not the end of his story. Lazarus's destiny, however, is concealed from the reader: the narrative does not tell whether the Jews ever fulfilled their plans to get rid off Lazarus or, if

---

56. See H. Windisch, 'John's Narrative Style', in M.W.G. Stibbe (ed.), *The Gospel of John as Literature: An Anthology of Twentieth-Century Perspectives* (NTTS, 17; Leiden: E.J. Brill, 1993), pp. 25-64. (Originally appeared as 'Der Johanneische Erzählungsstil', in H. Schmidt (ed.), *Eucharisterion: Studien zur Religion und Literatur des Alten und Neuen Testaments* [2 vols.; Festschrift H. Gunkel; Göttingen: Vandenhoeck & Ruprecht, 1923], II, pp. 174-213.) Windisch extols the literary achievement of the writer of the Gospel in his article, but notes that on some occasions 'the joy of narrating has been smothered down by the compulsion to preach and bear witness' (p. 39). The end of the Lazarus story is one of these occasions: 'The scene is broken off prematurely; the creative touch goes lame, or rather the joy of narrating is extinguished after the fact of the miracle has been demonstrated, which has been sufficiently prepared for in what precedes it. This narrator wishes only to depict the 'legal sequel' in order to show how the mighty deed provided the last push towards the tragic outcome of the earthly story of Jesus' (p. 37).

they did not kill Lazarus, what happened to him. These questions are left for the reader to ponder.

The above analysis has shown how tightly Lazarus's story is connected to the plot and the major themes of the Gospel. The story brings Jesus' public career to its culmination and points forward to the story of his passion. Lazarus's character serves as a proof of Jesus' claims to be the giver of life whom the Father has sent into the world. The narrator does not tell much about Lazarus directly, but the reader is compelled to draw conclusions regarding his character from the words and actions of the other characters. Although the characterization is minimal, there still is a surplus of information about Lazarus that is not strictly connected to the function of the character in the deveplopment of the plot. The narrator reveals Lazarus's name to his readers, tells of his intimate relationship with Jesus, and suggests something of Lazarus's life after he was raised from death. Jesus' love for Lazarus, which is referred to several times in the course of the story, is an ambiguous and indeterminate element in the story.[57] It is precisely the indeterminate aspects of the story that make the diverse responses of various readers to Lazarus's character so interesting. Because of Lazarus's limited role in the story, it has been the task of various readers to unbind Lazarus and give him a life of his own.

The Many Lives of Lazarus

Despite Lazarus's restricted role in John's story, his character has fascinated various readers in different times. Christian theologians,

---

57. According to Stibbe, the narrator emphasizes that Jesus loved Lazarus, because the narrator wants to depict Lazarus as the beloved disciple, who appears in the other parts of the Gospel. See M.W.G. Stibbe, *John as Storyteller: Narrative Criticism and the Fourth Gospel* (SNTSMS, 73; Cambridge: Cambridge University Press, 1992), pp. 77-82; Stibbe, 'A Tomb with a View', p. 48. According to Stibbe, Lazarus is the only person who can be regarded as the beloved disciple, if John's story is read on its own terms. What is obvious for Stibbe is not so obvious to most Johannine scholars, however. It is precisely the internal evidence of John's narrative that makes Stibbe's solution problematic. For example, the chief priests planned to kill Lazarus (12.10-11), whereas the other disciple in 18.15, who is identified with the beloved disciple by Stibbe and many others, had access to the court of the chief priest because he was known to him. The historicity of Lazarus, as well as the historicity of John's story of his resurrection, is, of course, doubtful, which makes Stibbe's solution even more problematic.

preachers and laymen as well as various artists have reinterpreted John's story and used Lazarus's character in different ways for their own purposes. The most complete survey of the use of Lazarus's character is given by Jacob Kremer in his book *Lazarus: die Geschichte einer Auferstehung*. Kremer concentrates on the use of Lazarus's character in theological commentaries, homilies and liturgy, but he also gives examples of the reception of the story in Christian popular belief and art as well as among modern writers. Walter Puchner, in his study, concentrates on the views about Lazarus in popular belief.[58] Besides being used in the theology of the official church, Lazarus has lived in folklore, in legends and songs, and even in proverbs. In modern times, the figure of Lazarus has inspired a wide range of novelists, poets and playwrights. Leslie M. Thompson has surveyed the influence of the Lazarus motif in modern literature, and he introduces, for example, how Lazarus's character appears in the great novels of Fyodore Dostoevsky, Nikos Kazantzakis and Per Lagerkvist, as well as in the dramas of Eugene O'Neill and Robinson Jeffers.[59]

For our purposes, I do not wish to offer a complete survey of the Lazarus material. Rather, relying on the work done by other scholars, I simply wish to offer a few selected examples that illustrate the various responses the Lazarus story has evoked. The selected examples show how readers who have approached the story from different points of view have emphasized different aspects of the story. Various and even contrary renderings of the story share one point in common, however. The readers of the story have given new and unexpected meanings to

---

58. W. Puchner, *Studien zum Kulturkontext der liturgischen Szene: Lazarus und Judas als religiöse Volksfiguren in Bild und Brauch, Lied und Legende Südeuropas* (Österreichische Akademie der Wissenschaften, philosophisch-historische Klasse, Denkschriften, 216; Vienna: Verlag der Österreichischen Akademie der Wissenschaften, 1991).

59. L.M. Thompson, 'The Multiple Uses of the Lazarus Motif in Modern Literature', *Christian Scholars Review* 7 (1978), pp. 306-29. For the use of the Lazarus motif in Dostoevsky's *Crime and Punishment*, see P.-L. Dubied, 'Lazarus—Raskolnikow: Eine Begegnung mit vielschichtigen Verwicklungen', in M. Rose (ed.), *Johannes-Studien: Interdisziplinäre Zugänge zum Johannes-Evangelium: Freundesgabe für Jean Zumstein* (Zürich: Theologischer Verlag, 1991), pp. 159-73. For Lazarus in O'Neill's play *Lazarus Laughed*, see William H. Shurr, 'American Drama and the Bible: The Case of Eugene O'Neill's *Lazarus Laughed*', in G. Gunn (ed.), *The Bible and American Arts and Letters* (SBLBAC, 3; Philadelphia: Fortress Press; Chico, CA: Scholars Press, 1983), pp. 83-103.

the story. In this process, Lazarus's character has received new features as well.

Lazarus as a Theological Symbol

At an early stage, the story of Lazarus was taken as a proof for certain theological truths. Both Irenaeus (*Adv. haer.* 5.13.1) and Tertullian (*De resurrect.* 53.3-4) mention the raising of Lazarus as an example that testifies to the corporeal resurrection of the dead.[60] According to Irenaeus there is another kind of theological symbolism in the story as well. He pays attention to the detail about Lazarus coming out from the tomb, 'his hands and feet bound in bandages.' According to Irenaeus this detail is 'symbolical of a human being who has been entangled in sins' (σύμβολον τοῦ ἐμπεπλεγμένου ἐν ἁμαρτίαις ἀνθρώπου).[61] This explains, in Irenaeus's view, why Jesus gives the command to unbind Lazarus and let him go.

This interpretation, according to which Lazarus's raising from death is symbolic of the freeing of a human being from the 'bandages' of sin, became a prevalent interpretation among many subsequent Christian readers of the story. It was represented, for example, by Origen, Ambrosius and Augustine.[62] This tradition of interpretation does not give a very favorable portrait of Lazarus: he becomes a symbol of a sinful human being whom Jesus calls into repentance and new life. Lazarus's friendship with Jesus mentioned in the Gospel does not help him, but, on the contrary, makes his alleged lapse even worse. In the surviving fragments of his commentary on the Fourth Gospel,[63] Origen notes that the fate of Lazarus shows how human nature is mutable (τρεπτή ἐστιν ἡ ἀνθρωπίνη φύσις), since even Jesus' friend can become weak and die, when Jesus is not present (*Frg. 77 in Joh*).[64]

60. See Kremer, *Lazarus*, pp. 114-15.
61. Text in SC, 153.
62. See Kremer, *Lazarus*, pp. 119-34.
63. Origen's commentary on John contained 32 books, 9 of which have survived. One of the surviving books is the twenty-eighth book, where Origen comments on the end of the Lazarus story (from 11.39 onward). A few fragments dealing with the first part of the Lazarus story have survived in the collections of fragments compiled from Origen's writings by later theologians. The history of tradition of these fragments (catenae) and their relationship to Origen's commentary on John is complicated. See Erwin Preuschen's introduction to Origen's commentary in GCS, X, pp. lxi-lxxvi.
64. Text in GCS, X, p. 544.

When Origen refers to Lazarus's state with the verb ἀσθενέω (to be weak or sick), he is not speaking merely of Lazarus's physical weakness or sickness. In his commentary, Origen explains that Lazarus is not alone in his fate, but is a representative of a larger group of people. Origen compares Lazarus to 'the one who has fallen away from Christ and returned to the Gentiles' life after he has received knowledge of truth and been enlightened' (*Comm. in Joh.* 28.55).[65] Origen is not interested in Lazarus as such; rather, he tries to find affinities between the Lazarus story and the situation of his supposed audience.

The tradition of interpretation that regarded Lazarus as a representative of sinful human beings found its culmination in Augustine's rendering of the story. For Augustine, Lazarus is not only a sinful person, he is an archetype of those whose sin is of the worst kind. After giving a spiritual explanation for the two other New Testament stories in which Jesus raises a dead person (Mt. 9.18-25; and par. Lk. 7.11-16), Augustine clarifies his view of the deeper meaning of the Lazarus story (*In Joh. Ev. Tract.* 49.3).[66]

> The third dead person is Lazarus. There is a monstruous kind of death; it is called bad habit. For it is one thing to sin, it is another to make a habit of sinning. He who sins and is immediately corrected quickly returns to life; because he has not yet been ensnared by habit, he has not yet been buried. But he who sins habitually has been buried and it is well said of him, 'He stinks.' For he begins to have the worst reputation, like the foulest odor. Such are all who are accustomed to crimes, abandoned in character … And yet, no less was the power of Christ for raising him up.

Also, Augustine connects Jesus' tears to the great sins of Lazarus. Lazarus's sins make Jesus' miracle even greater, because not even Lazarus's great sins could prevent Jesus from performing this miracle: 'He [Jesus] groaned, he wept, he cried with a loud voice. With what a difficulty does he whom the bad habit presses down rise up! But nevertheless he rises up' (*In Joh. Ev. Tract.* 49.24).

The Lazarus story is used also by readers who want to show the

---

65. Text in SC, 385. The English translation in Origen, *Commentary on the Gospel According to John: Books 13–32* (trans. R.E. Heine; FC, 89; Washington, DC: The Catholic University of America Press, 1993), p. 302.

66. Text in CChr SL, 36. The English Translation in St Augustine, *Tractates on the Gospel of John 28–54* (trans. J.W. Rettig; FC 88; Washington, DC: The Catholic University of America Press, 1993), p. 241. For a detailed analysis of Augustine's interpretation see Kremer, *Lazarus*, pp. 128-33.

superiority of Christianity over Judaism and to emphasize the obstinacy of the Jewish people. This polemical use of the story is attested already in the second half of the second century. In his book *On Pascha*, Melito of Sardis lists the miracles of Jesus that should have convinced the Jews to believe in Jesus. He blames the Jews because not even 'the most unprecedented sign, a corpse roused from a tomb already four days old', had won their respect (*Peri Pascha* 78).[67] In the fourth century, Amphilochius, the bishop of Iconium, in his sermon based on this story said that nothing has exasperated the Jews like the raising of Lazarus (*In Lazar.* [orat. 3] 1).[68] The chief priests turned the miracle into a slander when they decided to kill Jesus after the raising of Lazarus. This is the only miracle that they could not explain away, however. The Jews knew Lazarus, because he was a notable (ἐπίσημος) man. Amphilochius uses the notion of Lazarus's reputation (not found in John's story) to show that even the Jews had to recognize Jesus' greatest miracle. For Amphilochius, Lazarus is a symbol not only of Jesus' divine power but also of the stubbornness of God's own people.

In all these interpretations the stress is laid on theological truths to which the story refers and which can be found if the various minor details in the story are 'interpreted' in a right way. If it is necessary, certain new character traits are added to Lazarus's character, traits that are not found in John's story.[69] Lazarus is described as a notable man, whose resurrection even the Jews could not explain away

67. The text and the translation is from Melito of Sardis, *On Pascha and Fragments* (texts and translations ed. S.G. Hall; Oxford Early Christian Texts; Oxford, Clarendon Press, 1979), pp. 42-43. Cf. Kremer, *Lazarus* 114.

68. Text in CChr SG, 3.

69. In his own interpretation of the story, Kremer agrees with the tradition of interpretation originating in Christian antiquity according to which Jn 11 is about freedom from the power of sin (*Lazarus*, p. 341). He even states that it is unimportant whether the Lazarus story testifies only to the forgiveness of sins Jesus gives or also to the temporary recalling of a dead person into life. In light of old Christian teaching, 'the incomplete raising from death' is not a greater miracle than the forgiveness of sins (p. 337). In John's story there are, however, no allusions to the forgiveness of sins, and Lazarus's death is not connected to his sins in any way. Furthermore, Kremer maintains that the factuality of this miracle is not a central message of Jn 11 (p. 333), although John's story emphasizes clearly the factuality of the miracle (see my analysis of the story). Kremer's interpretation, therefore, may be seen as an example of the ways the interpreters of the Gospel have tried to make the story more relevant for their contemporaries by reading new meanings into the text.

(Amphilochius), or he is regarded as a representative of sinful human beings (Origen, Augustine).[70]

The Elaboration of the Story

In the Fourth Gospel, the description of the actual raising of Lazarus is rather meager. It is no wonder, therefore, that in many interpretations the plain narration of the Gospel is made more dramatic. In the Fourth Gospel, Martha makes an allusion to the state of Lazarus's body in the tomb in the course of telling Jesus that her brother has been dead for four days and already smells. The Christian interpreters of the story have not refrained from thinking how this kind of a corpse could come alive. Ampilochius describes the moment in which life returned to the dead body of Lazarus (*In Lazar.* [orat. 3] 5):

> On one note he awaked from the sleep the one who was sleeping by himself by saying: 'Lazarus come out.' ... The Lord only shouted 'Lazarus come out,' and instantly the flesh (of the corpse) was filled up, the hair was planted again, the sutures of the bones were bound together, the veins were filled with clean blood.[71]

Lazarus's story was embellished especially by Christian poets, who tried to render the Gospel stories according to the model of classical Greek or Latin poetry. The starting point of these poets was the text of the Gospels, but they put more emphasis on the emotional features of the stories and also elaborated the plain narration of the gospels where they thought it was needed. In the case of the raising of Lazarus, additions of this kind can be found in the poets, especially when they retell the ending of the Lazarus story. C.V.A. Juvencus (fourth century) mentions that Jesus sent happy Lazarus home after he was freed from his bandages.[72] In *Carmen Paschale*, C. Sedulius (fifth century) says that, after his raising was celebrated in a decent way, Lazarus lived a new life as one who was untimely born.[73] In the background of these additions, one can notice the need to make the abrupt conclusion of the story more satisfactory. In addition, there was a growing interest in

70. Theological interpretations of this kind prevailed also in later times as succeeding generations of theologians explained the story in their commentaries and sermons. See Kremer, *Lazarus*, pp. 166-92.

71. Lazarus' raising is described in a similar way also in a commentary on Jn 11 that was preserved under the name of Hippolytus. See Kremer, *Lazarus*, p. 141.

72. Kremer, *Lazarus*, p. 147.

73. Kremer, *Lazarus*, p. 150.

Lazarus himself and in those stages of his life not reported in the Gospel.

As an example of the efforts to describe the raising of Lazarus according to a classical poetic standard I cite a poem of Aurelius Prudentius Clemens (died c. 410).[74] In his *Liber Apotheosis*, Prudentius defends Trinitarian doctrine against various heresies. In a section in which he attacks those who follow Christ half-heartedly and who do not confess that he is God, Prudentius describes in a vivid manner the miracles of Jesus that testify to his divinity. Prudentius's description of the raising of Lazarus is dramatic. He does not forget Lazarus's sisters, and he makes an allusion to their joyful reunion with their brother (*Lib. Apoth.* 753-62).[75]

> Before the entrance to the tomb, closed fast
> By monstruous stones set in the tunneled rock,
> The Lord stands still and calls his dead friend's name.
> Then lo, as stones roll back, the loathsome grave
> Gives up the living bones, a walking corpse.
> Loose now, you joyful sisters, fragrant bands!
> The only odor there exhaled is scented balm,
> And breezes do not waft corruption's stench.
> Eyes freed from oozing matter glow again
> With bygone luster; by degrees the cheeks
> Once putrefied take on a rosy hue.

After describing the miracle, Prudentius concludes that no one else but the creator can give life back to a dead corpse. In his combination of poetic dramatization and theological reasoning, Prudentius uses the story of Lazarus's raising as proof for the correct doctrine concerning Jesus' divinity.

In these renderings of the Lazarus story we notice a growing tendency to embellish the plain story that the Fourth Gospel tells of Lazarus. Readers of the story are curious to know more about Lazarus and his life. This natural curiosity about what a person's life would be like having been raised from the dead is satisfied as different legends about Lazarus develop. The figure of Lazarus is especially conducive to the development of legends: the Fourth Gospel presents Lazarus as a special individual who in one moment of his life has an important role

74. See Kremer, *Lazarus*, pp. 148-49.
75. The English translation in Prudentius, *Poems*, II (trans. M.C. Eagan; FC, 52; Washington: The Catholic University of America Press, 1965).

in the divine plan, but the Gospel is silent about the rest of Lazarus's life. In different legends, the gaps in the the life of Lazarus are filled. According to a popular medieval belief, for example, Lazarus did not laugh any longer after he saw the horrors of the underworld. Later, this belief found its way into the proverbs of Greek folklore. Someone could be described as 'not laughing, like Lazarus'.[76] Another medieval legend knows Lazarus as a judge who together with his sisters owned a castle, the village of Bethany, and even a large part of Jerusalem. After Jesus was taken into heaven, the family sold everything and placed the money at the feet of the apostles. According to the same legend, Jesus raised Lazarus out of love for Mary Magdalene, who was regarded as Lazarus's sister.[77] In the cultic legends of the eastern church, Lazarus was connected to Kition (later Larnaka) in Cyprus.[78] According to these traditions, Lazarus and his sisters escaped the Jews and came by boat to Cyprus. Lazarus was made the bishop of Kition by the apostles, and he lived 30 years after his resurrection. His relics were supposedly transported to Constantinople in 890.

The development of these legends is not based on the story of the Gospel itself, but on different associations or even misunderstandings.[79] The interest in Lazarus reflected in these legends is different from the interest many theologians have had towards the story. Whereas many theologians have sought the deeper symbolical lesson to which the story refers, the legends directed attention to Lazarus's person and life. The reasons why the story was told and retold were varied and did not always correspond to the reason why the story was originally created.[80]

---

76. Puchner, *Studien zum Kulturkontext*, p. 55.

77. See Kremer, *Lazarus*, pp. 193-94.

78. Puchner, *Studien zum Kulturkontext*, p. 35.

79. It was a common view in the Middle Ages, for example, that Lazarus later became a bishop of Marseilles. This view was probably based on the confusion of the biblical character with the bishop Lazarus who lived in the fifth century. See Kremer, *Lazarus*, p. 194.

80. Puchner (*Studien zum Kulturkontext*, pp. 58-59) notes how the use of the figure of Lazarus in popular belief has been different from the use of his character in the official theology of the church: 'Das in der christlichem Dogmatik streng regulierte und kontrollierte Verhältnis von Bezeichnendem und Bezeichnetem ist in der Volksreligisiotät gelockert: In der Verbindung der Zeichen mit ihrem Bedeutungen gehen oft die Konnotationen vor den Denotationen. Der Prozeß der Semiosis (der Bedeutungszuweisung) untersteht nicht einem durchstrukturierten Code (christliche Dogmatik und Exegese), sondern mehreren labilen Subcodes. Die

The growth of the Lazarus story illustrates how readers have not been satisfied to take the story as 'it was meant to be taken'. Just as writers use characters for their own purposes, so readers identify themselves with these characters and start to look at the events of the story from their own point of view. The less the writer reveals of a certain character the more there is room for the readers to read their own experiences into the text and connect these experiences with the character in question. In the case of Lazarus, it is evident that the fascination with his character among different generations of readers of the Gospel is due more to the readers' ability to use their creative imagination than to the Gospel's characterization of Lazarus.

The Modern Lazarus

The creative imagination of readers has guaranteed that the figure of Lazarus is no less attractive to modern readers of the story. From the nineteenth century onward, this biblical character and the story of his raising have inspired novelists, poets and playwrights. What is characteristic of the reconfiguring of the Lazarus story is the freedom with which various artists have interpreted the story. In the background of the free renderings of the story is, of course, the Enlightment and the attacks of 'the higher criticism' against the supernatural aspects of Christianity.[81] The Lazarus story was no longer regarded as an accurate report of Jesus' greatest miracle. Consequently, the artists who used the story were free to read the story even against the intentions of the author.

Modern artistic renderings of the Lazarus story represent a departure from earlier theological interpretations, for various artists did not even try to be faithful to the original story, but they used the figure of Lazarus to develop their own point. In these new versions of the story, Lazarus appears in a new light. However, new renderings have some points of contact with the earlier interpretations, and the modern Lazarus resembles in a way his biblical prototype. New aspects of the story and new traits in Lazarus's character come up when the story is read in new contexts. The theme that repeatedly appears in many modern versions of the story is the marginal and subordinated role that Lazarus has in the story of his own resurrection.

strenge Funktionsfestlegung wird durch assoziatives Denken gelockert, und die Funktionszusammenhänge können sich vervielfachen.'
    81. Cf. Thompson, 'The Multiple Uses', p. 309.

The Lazarus story deals with the enduring themes of life and death that makes the story especially fascinating. In writing about these themes, many modern writers have not hesitated to associate the experiences and problems of their own time with Lazarus. In this way, Lazarus has become a symbol of the situation of modern life, as Leslie M. Thompson points out:[82]

> Rather than using Lazarus merely as a symbol of resurrection, many modern writers have emphasized such diverse topics as his individualism, his human weaknesses and desecration of his new life, his intense alienation and loneliness, his prolonged, agonizing existence, and his indifference to death. Such tendencies, of course, reflect the insecurity of living in the modern, infinite world with its concomitant fragmentation, uncertainty, and lack of a cohesive mythic structure.

As Thompson's summary of the use of the Lazarus motif makes clear, the medieval interpretation of the fate of Lazarus continued its influence in modern renderings of the story. According to this interpretation, Lazarus's return to earthly life with all its miseries was an unhappy event. Oscar Wilde develops this view in his short story 'The Doer of Good'.[83] In the story Jesus walks through a city at night and meets different people. It turns out that they have all previously experienced some of Jesus' miracles, the results of which, however, have been evil. In the last encounter, Jesus meets a young man who is seated by the roadside and is weeping (p. 255):

> And he [Jesus] went towards him and touched the long locks of his hair and said to him, 'Why are you weeping?'
> And the young man looked up and recognised Him and made answer, 'But I was dead once and you raised me from the dead. What else should I do but weep?'

Wilde's short story had a profound influence on W.B. Yeats who had heard an earlier version of the story from Wilde himself.[84] Yeats later used the character of Lazarus in his play *Calvary*.[85] On the way to

82. Thompson, 'The Multiple Uses', p. 307.

83. *The Complete Shorter Fiction of Oscar Wilde* (ed. with an introduction by I. Murray; Oxford: Oxford University Press, 1979), pp. 253-54. Originally published in 1894. Cf. Thompson, 'The Multiple Uses', p. 311; Kremer, *Lazarus*, pp. 306-307.

84. See Thompson, 'The Multiple Uses', 311.

85. W.B. Yeats, *The Collected Plays* (London: Macmillan, 2nd edn, 1952), pp. 447-57. 'Calvary' originally appeared in 1920. Cf. Thompson, 'The Multiple

Calvary, Jesus meets Lazarus and Judas, who both make accusations against him. When Jesus reminds Lazarus of the gift of life he has given to him, Lazarus is not at all grateful to him:

> Christ: I gave you life.
> Lazarus: But death is what I ask. Alive I never could escape your love,
> And when I sickened towards my death I thought,
> 'I'll to the desert, or chuckle in a corner,
> Mere ghost, a solitary thing.' I died
> And saw no more until I saw you stand
> In the opening of the tomb; 'Come out!' you called;
> You dragged me to the light as boys drag out
> A rabbit when they have dug its hole away;
> ...
> I thought to die when my allotted years ran out again;
> And that, being gone, you could not hinder it;
> But now you will blind with light the solitude
> That death has made; you will disturb that corner
> Where I had thought I might lie safe for ever.

Lazarus's words echo the isolation of modern humanity: death is seen as a relief that gives a rest from the loneliness of life. Lazarus speaks for the right of every individual to determine their own fate, too. The salvation Christ offers, without asking whether his love is hoped for, threatens this individualism. Yeats's criticism is thus directed against a kind of a religion that sacrifices the needs and the will of a human being to satisfy the divine authority. Lazarus, who in the Fourth Gospel experiences God's saving act, thus becomes a victim in a divine play.[86]

Uses', pp. 311-12; Kremer, *Lazarus*, p. 307.

86. H. Daiber's rendering of Lazarus's story in his 'Argumente für Lazarus' resembles that of Yeats. Daiber's short story is referred to and cited by Kremer, *Lazarus*, pp. 307-308. Like Yeats's Lazarus, Daiber's Lazarus also accuses Jesus: 'Nein. Du kommst zu spät. Ich bin langsam gestorben, gliedweise, tagelang. Ich habe den Ekel vor mir in den Augen meiner Frau gesehen, die zusammengepreßten Lippen meiner Tochter. Und troztdem hätte ich gerne weitergelebt. Aber Du hast mich zu Ende krepieren zu lassen ... Nun sehe ich aber, warum Du mich auf so furchtbare weise verrecken ließest: damit die Erweckung um so effektwoller wäre. Es war eine Schaustellung für Dich, deren zweiter Akt nun kommt. Wer weiß, welchen Exitus der dritte bringen soll. Aber ich spiele nicht mehr mit ... Ich will kein Object mehr für Deine Demonstrationen sein.' According to Kremer, Daiber's interpretation 'enstammt ganz der marxistisch gefärbten Kritik an der christlichen Religion'. Daiber's interpretation may be an anachronistic one, but it successfully emphasizes certain aspects of the story that offend the eye of the modern reader. It

The criticism in Anna Kavan's short story 'I am Lazarus' is more subtle than the treatment in Yeats's play and is aimed in a different direction.[87] The name Lazarus appears in the title of the story, but there is no character in the story explicitly called Lazarus. The story begins when an English doctor comes to a French clinic. He had reluctantly promised to a rich lady named Mrs Bow that he would visit the clinic and see her son who had been taken there for treatment. The exact quality of the illness of Mrs Bow's son is never revealed to the reader who must draw conclusions from how the other characters and the narrator describe the son. As the doctor meets Mr Bow (the son) in a workroom of the patients, there seems to be nothing wrong with Mr Bow's appearance. Although he seems fit, the patient does not at first reply in any way to the greeting of the doctor. Only when the superintendent of the clinic asks about the article the patient is working with does Mr Bow smile and begin to tell about the belt he is making. The reader learns that Mr Bow likes making the belt and is pleased to have someone notice it. When speaking about his belt, Mr Bow looks 'satisfied, sure of being on safe ground' (p. 9). However, after the meeting, the English doctor is not at all comfortable with what he has seen.

The focus of the story now shifts to Mr Bow himself, and the reader learns something of his inner life. In the workroom, Mr Bow is totally concentrated on his work with the belt and does not take any notice of his surroundings. For him, other people in the workroom are only 'different coloured shapes whose mouths opened and closed and emitted sounds that meant nothing to him' (p. 10). The reader soon learns that there is another thing close to Mr Bow's heart in addition to making belts. As the lunchtime arrives, Mr Bow reluctantly leaves his belt with a man who belongs to the staff of the clinic, and he starts for the dining room across the grounds where the grass is not cut but grows tall. The grass has a special meaning for Mr Bow (p. 11). The narrator says that when he touches the grasses, 'they respond felinely; like thin sensitive cats they arch themselves to receive the caress of his finger-tips'. Mr Bow picks one of the grasses, which 'touches his skin lightly, prickingly, like the electrified fur of a cat in a thunderstorm'.

Mr Bow's happy moment is soon over as the gym director of the clinic arrives. She does not understand why the patient is picking up the

is far too easy to silence Daiber's criticism by labelling it as Marxist.

    87. A. Kavan, *I Am Lazarus: Stories* (London: Peter Owen, 1978), pp. 7-16. The collection of short stories was published originally in 1945.

grasses, and she is not willing to listen to what Mr Bow tries to tell her. She takes the grasses from his hand and throws them away and offers something better in place of them: 'Nobody picks grass. We could pick some flowers though, if you like ... There, aren't they pretty?' According to the narrator, the gym director was 'very good-natured' about what she did for Mr Bow. Her attitude reflects how the staff members at the clinic treat their patients: the patients are not allowed to enjoy life in their own way; the staff knows best what is good for them.

The tragic story comes to a conclusion after the lunch, when Mr Bow tries to enter the workroom where the belt is. The doors of the workroom are closed, however, because the patients are not supposed to work in the afternoon, a time that is devoted to recreation. A doctor in the clinic tells Mr Bow to join the other patients. Mr Bow goes away because he is afraid of the doctor who had previously 'put him into a hideous sleep with poisoned needle'. The doctor and his colleague watch Mr Bow as he goes away. The words of the doctor to his colleague show how Mr Bow's fate is compared to that of the Biblical character referred to in the title of the story (p. 16):

> 'He doesn't know how lucky he is, said the dark doctor. 'We've pulled him back literally from a living death. That's the sort of thing that encourages one in this work.'

The narrator's final words reveal that the doctor's view of his patient is perhaps not an accurate one, however:

> Mr. Bow walked carefully in the sunshine. He did not know how lucky he was and perhaps that was rather lucky as well.

In the story, Mr Bow's life is compared to that of Lazarus. Like Lazarus, Mr Bow has been raised from 'a living death'. As in many of the medieval and modern reinterpretations of the Lazarus story, the new life of Lazarus/Mr Bow is not considered to be a fortunate one. There is another point that Mr Bow and his biblical prototype share in common. The criticism of the story is directed especially toward the way the medical staff treats its patient: Mr Bow is an object, whose inner needs the experts supposedly know better than he does. The staff is not really interested in Mr Bow; they are only keen on showing the efficacy of their treatment. As referred to in the title of the story 'I am Lazarus', Lazarus serves as a symbol of how a person is used for the higher purposes. Kavan's story is thus related to W.B. Yeats's and H. Daiber's renderings of the Lazarus story discussed above. The way in which the

writer of the Fourth Gospel uses Lazarus to promote his larger message
with little interest in Lazarus for his own sake, is shown to be offensive
when read in this modern context. Such a critical attitude towards the
Biblical story is, of course, a modern attitude. And yet, as the story
continues to be read and interpreted in new contexts, the critical voices
cannot be silenced.

Italian dramatist Dario Fo, the Nobel Prize winner 1997, describes
the raising of Lazarus from a fresh point of view in his satirical play
Mistero Buffo, where he gives new renderings of medieval dramas
based on the Scriptures.[88] The resurrection of Lazarus is told from the
point of view of spectators who have gathered in a graveyard where
they witness the raising of Lazarus. The scene consists of the exchange
of the spectators, while the main characters of the biblical story, including Jesus and Lazarus, remain voiceless. The event is stripped of every
mysterious aspect of a miracle and made into a well-organized
spectacle:

> 'Isn't there someone here who knows this Jesus Christ, who could go
> and get him to hurry up, because we're all here, waiting? After all, you
> can't wait for miracles for ever, eh?! They should set a timetable and
> stick to it!'
> 'Chairs! Who wants chairs! Chairs for hire, ladies! Two pence per chair!
> Make sure that you've got a seat, ladies, because when the miracle hap-
> pens and the Holy Man brings Lazarus back to life, and he starts talking,
> and singing, and moving around, then you'll get a fright; you'll see his
> eyes glistening and gleaming, and you'll faint. You'll finish up falling
> backwards and banging your heads on a rock, and you'll end up dead!
> Dead! And this Holy Man only does one miracle per day! Chairs for
> hire! Only two pence!'

Fo's subversive way of reading biblical stories becomes evident in his
choice of the point of view from which the familiar events are seen: his
narrators or chief characters are not the heroes of scriptural stories but
mostly outside observers of the events. By telling the events from an
unusual point of view, Fo suggests that the way common people unde-
stand the miracle is different from the way the miracle is interpreted in
the official church. In his rendering of the story, Fo keeps up the tradition of the carnivalistic genre of literature, using Mikhail Bakhtin's

---

88. Dario Fo, *Plays: One*, *Mistero Buffo* (trans. E. Emery; London: Methuen,
1992), pp. 1-84. The resurrection of Lazarus occurs on pp. 66-70.

terminology.[89] In carnival, authority of all kinds of dogmatic institutions is called into question by laughter. According to Bakhtin, a carnivalistic sense of the world 'with its joy at change and its joyful
relativity, is opposed to that one-sided and gloomy official seriousness
which is dogmatic and hostile to evolution and change, which seeks to
absolutize a given condition of existence'. The carnival liberates an
individual from dogmatic seriousness, but it does not trivialize the
described phenomenon because 'there is not a grain of nihilism in it,
nor a grain of empty frivolity or vulgar ... individualism'.[90] In his version of the Lazarus story, Fo combines laughter with a warm and lively
presentation of those characters who do not usually attract much
attention:

> 'There's no way he can do it, never! Impossible for anyone to bring
> *that* back to life. He's all gone rotten! What a joke! Lousy bums! They
> told him that the man had been dead for three days! It must be a month at
> least! What a sight! Poor Jesus!'
> 'I say he can still do it, though! This man is a holy man, and he can do
> the miracle even when the body has been rotting for a month!'
> 'I say that he can't do it!'
> 'Do you want to bet?'
> 'OK, let's have a bet!'
> 'Right! Two pence! Three pence! Ten pence! What do you want to
> bet?'
> 'Shall I keep the money? Trust me! Here we all trust each other, don't
> we? Alright, I'll look after the money!'

One of the characteristics of carnival is the incorporation of things that
are usually distanced from one another. As Bahktin says, 'carnival
brings together, unifies, weds, and combines the sacred with the pro-
fane, the lofty with the low, the great with the insignificant, the wise
with the stupid'.[91] This happens also in Fo's rendering, where everyday
cares of the people intermingle with what should be a divine manifestation. As the culmination of the story is at hand and the dead man comes

89. For carnivalization in literature, see M. Bakhtin, *Problems of Dostoevsky's
Poetics* (ed. and trans. C. Emerson; introduction by W.C. Booth; Theory and History of Literature, 8; Manchester: Manchester University Press, 1984), pp. 106-109,
122-80.
  90. Bakhtin, *Problems of Dostoevsky's Poetics*, p. 160.
  91. Bakhtin, *Problems of Dostoevsky's Poetics*, p. 123.

from the tomb, someone notices that there has been a theft among the witnesses of the miracle.[92]

> 'Quiet! Look, he's risen up onto one knee!'
> 'Who? Jesus?'
> 'No! Lazarus! Heavens, look!'
> 'Nooo ...! It's impossible!'
> 'Let me see.'
> 'Oh, look! He's moving, he's moving, he's on his feet, come on! Oh, He's fallen! Now he's moving again, he's on his feet.'
> 'A miracle! Oh, a miracle. Oh Jesus, sweet creature that you are, and to think, that I didn't believe in you!'
> 'Well done, Jesus!'
> 'I've won the bet. Let's have the money. Hey, don't mess about ...'
> 'Well done, Jesus!'
> 'My purse! They've stolen my purse! Stop, thief!'
> 'Jesus, well done!'
> 'Stop, thief!'
> 'Well done, Jesus! Well done, Jesus ...!'
> 'Stop, thief!'

In the examples given here, the biblical story is read against the grain of the original story, but not in an arbitrary way. The whole story appears in a new light when characters who appear in marginal roles in John's story come to the fore and the events are seen through their eyes. Many writers have paid attention to the restricted role of Lazarus in John, by which Lazarus is but an example testifying to Jesus' heavenly abilities. This attitude is perhaps not totally surprising on the basis of my analysis of the story. We noticed that already in the story there is a certain ambivalence about the way Jesus deals with Lazarus. Jesus does not act as Lazarus's sisters had hoped he would; but later the narrator hastens to emphasize that Jesus really loved Lazarus. It is as if the narrator had anticipated the criticism that later generations of readers have aimed at Jesus' behaviour.

---

92. When introducing the resurrection of Lazarus in *Mistero Buffo*, Fo refers to a wall painting that has inspired him (*Plays: One*, pp. 64-65). As the final fresco was removed for restoration in a Pisa cemetery, the well-preserved cartoon of Lazarus's resurrection was revealed. In the picture appears the crowd struck with amazement, and one of the characters dips his fingers into the purse of a spectator standing near him and takes advantage of the miracle.

Conclusion

The Lazarus story and its later use exemplify the way in which indeterminate aspects of a biblical story have not been an obstacle to reading; on the contrary, they have generated various and fascinating responses from different readers. The modern interpreters, especially, have paid attention to those features of the story that were not in the strict control of the narrator of the original story. Different readers in different ages and with various ideologies and expectations have been able to read their own experiences into the text because there are already in the text trends that point in a variety of directions. It seems that literary critics of the Gospels should pay more attention to the gaps and inconsistencies in biblical stories, gaps and inconsistencies that have made various and unexpected responses to these stories possible. There is a danger in the current literary criticism of the Gospels that something of the richness of biblical stories may be lost when these stories are interpreted in the way that emphasizes only their unity and their coherence.[93] Certain interpretations are preferred over others, although there is in the text disparate aspects on which different interpretations can be based.

What has made possible the fresh approach to Lazarus as a character is the change in the point of view from which the events of the story are seen. John's story is told from the point of view of a narrator who is outside the storyworld and is not interested in the inner life of the characters of the story. However, as soon as the events of the story are told from the point of view of one of the characters, the whole story appears in a fresh light. New questions emerge: How has this character experienced the events? What kind of influence have these events had on the character? The change in the point of view is, of course, made against the grain with which the original story was supposed to be read. The writer of the Gospel uses Lazarus for his own purposes and does not intend for his readers to become emotionally involved in the fate of this character. The real readers of the story have not, however, been satisfied with this shadowy figure of the Gospel, and so they have filled this character with new and unpredictable meanings. They have made an exciting character out of a silent agent of the Gospel. The bound Lazarus has been freed and given many lives of his own.

---

93. For the discussion of the narrative unity of the Gospels, see the chapter by P. Merenlahti and R. Hakola in this volume.

NARRATIVE CRITICISM: PRACTICES AND PROSPECTS

David Rhoads

Introduction

Narrative analysis of New Testament writings had its beginnings in the
1970s with the seminal works of Norman Perrin, Thomas Boomershine,
Joanna Dewey, Werner Kelber, Norman Petersen, Robert Tannehill and
Mary Ann Tolbert. It came into its own in the early 1980s with efforts
to produce narrative analyses of each of the Gospels as a whole. Since
then it has become popularly known among New Testament scholars as
narrative criticism and has generated many fine studies of the narratives
of the New Testament.[1] It has been a privilege and a delight for me to
be a part of this project by Finnish scholars and their mentor Kari
Syreeni to lay their own claim to narrative criticism and to contribute to
its development. As is evident from these essays, narrative criticism
continues to change and grow.

The purpose of this essay is to consider the practices and prospects of
narrative criticism by reflecting first on critiques of narrative criticism,
followed by some ways narrative analysis of the New Testament is
being sharpened and broadened, then by showing how some traditional
disciplines and some newer methods in biblical studies are being incorporated into the practice of narrative criticism, and, finally, by dealing
with the relationship between narrative interpretation and the ethics of

---

1. M. Powell, *What Is Narrative Criticism?* (Minneapolis: Fortress Press,
1990). See also, e.g., S. Porter, 'Literary Approaches to the New Testament: From
Formalism to Deconstruction and Back', in S. Porter and D. Tombs (eds.),
Approaches to New Testament Study (JSNTSup, 120; Sheffield: Sheffield Academic
Press, 1995), pp. 77-128; and David M. Gunn, 'Narrative Criticism', in
S. McKenzie and S. Hayes (eds.), *To Each its Own Meaning: An Introduction to
Biblical Criticisms and their Application* (Louisville, KY: Westminster/John Knox
Press, 1993), pp. 171-95.

reading. Where appropiate, I will make comments relevant to issues of characterization.

Narrative criticism has come to be understood as (1) the analysis of the storyworld of a narrative and (2) the analysis of its implied rhetorical impact on readers. First, the analysis of the storyworld focuses on the world inside a narrative with its own times and places, its own characters, its past and future, its own sets of values, and its series of events moving forward in some meaningful way. This story-world is neither the historical world depicted by the story nor the historical world of the situation in which the story was first told.[2] Rather, it is the imaginary world created by the narrative in its telling. Second, the analysis of a narrative's rhetoric focuses on the implied impact of a narrative both from the *story itself* as well as from the *way* it is told—with its distinctive style and point of view, set of literary techniques, and order of recounting.

Narrative criticism has been one of many new methodologies to arise in biblical studies in the last several decades. Narrative criticism has recovered the text as a story to be experienced, an experience that had been all but lost during the last two centuries of biblical studies.[3] As such, narrative criticism has recovered the story as a whole, instead of the fragmented pieces of historical criticism. In this way, narrative criticism has opened up new questions and areas of analysis of the text. It has helped to establish literary rhetoric as a legitimate way to study New Testament narratives and to pave the way for the use of reader-response criticism.

Narrative criticism's major contribution to biblical scholarship in general has been the establishment of the surface narrative of the text as a legitimate object of study. Many writers of monographs, commentaries and articles now regularly deal with the narrative in its final form and of the storyworld of the New Testament narratives without sorting out tradition and redaction or engaging in historical reconstruction.

Narrative Criticism and its Critics

Narrative criticism arose in the context of the predominance of traditional historical-critical methods—source criticism, form criticism and

2. N. Petersen, *Literary Criticism for New Testament Critics* (Philadelphia: Fortress Press, 1976).

3. H. Frei, *The Eclipse of Biblical Narrative* (New Haven: Yale University Press, 1974).

redaction criticism. These methods generally explored the text for layers of tradition in order to construct the history of the early church from the time of Jesus to the time of the evangelists. As we have said, narrative criticism provided an alternative approach by shifting the focus from the world outside the Gospel to the world of the story itself. It involved other shifts as well: from the study of brief form-critical units to the study of a Gospel narrative as a whole; from reconstructing the layers of tradition and redaction to the analysis of the single surface layer of the final story; from the author as redactor to the author as creator of a story; and from how the author may have constructed the Gospel to how the readers may have experienced it.

In general, these shifts have meant the bracketing of earlier methods, because treating the reader's experience of the narrative in the integrity of its final form was methodologically incompatible with the layering of the text into redaction and tradition. Because the several methods could not easily be mixed into one method, there was need for narrative critics to embrace the new method as a discrete discipline.

Some critiques of narrative criticism, then, have come from those who use traditional methods. Other critiques have come from those who have moved beyond narrative criticism to postmodern literary methods. I would like to reflect briefly on four critiques of narrative criticism.[4]

Coherent Narratives?

Some scholars using traditional methods have argued that the Gospels are really such a patchwork of embedded traditions and authorial redactions that they cannot legitimately be treated as whole cloth. They argue that narrative criticism emphasizes too much the coherence of the narrative or assumes a unity that is not really there. Therefore, although redaction criticism is itself far from exact, some scholars will continue to use redaction criticism as the primary basis for recovering the purposes of the Gospel writers, in some cases combining it with composition analysis. This is an important enterprise that will allow for helpful comparisons of the results of the two methods.

---

4.   For an account of these shifts and a helpful critique of their problems, see S. Moore, *Literary Criticism and the Gospels: The Theoretical Challenge* (New Haven: Yale University Press, 1989), and *The Postmodern Bible: The Bible and Culture Collective* (New Haven: Yale University Press, 1995). See also the helpful insights of Raimo Hakola and Petri Merenlahti in the opening chapter of this volume.

Narrative critics have used the coherence of the text as a *working hypothesis, a heuristic device* to discern fully the coherent patterns of storytelling on the surface level of the final narrative. In the case of Mark, some narrative critics have been so impressed with the pervasive signs of the coherence of the narrative world as to argue that it will be difficult now for scholars to distinguish tradition from redaction. Narrative critics might say the same with regard to Matthew or Luke, except that, with the Markan source in hand, they can see how these authors have changed their traditions. Nevertheless, narrative criticism does not necessarily weigh differently what authors of the Gospels have kept of their traditions and what they have added. Matthew's free editorial hand, for example, could have omitted any part of Mark; as such, the author of Matthew may have kept parts of Mark precisely because they served his purposes every bit as much as the redactions. At a minimum, the evangelists have included or omitted material, modified it to a greater or lesser extent, and ordered it into a consecutive narrative. In the end, then, both tradition and redaction combine together to form the narratives of the Gospels as the subject matter for interpretation.

Narrative analysis can certainly be aided by information about an author's redaction of sources. In many cases, such observations will confirm and inform a narrative analysis, as can be seen from several of the essays in this collection. We would be foolish to ignore insights that come from an integrated approach with form and redaction criticism. And attention to redaction and sources can help to reconstruct the trajectories in the tradition, as Petri Merenlahti has shown in his chapter in this volume.

Nevertheless, the shift in narrative criticism from author to reader/ hearer makes the study of redaction somewhat limited in value, for narrative criticism seeks to recover the final story the author has created *for the reader*. A first-century audience hearing a Gospel would have experienced it as a whole and not as pieces of earlier tradition. Readers/ hearers of a Gospel were surely not listening to sort out tradition from redaction. Nor does the narrative reveal what its author rejected of its sources, Rather, hearers were absorbed in the story as it was being presented to them. And, in general, the Gospel writers succeeded in creating rather coherent reading/listening experiences for their audiences.

So, narrative criticism deals with how a reader experiences the story in its final form, even when there are places in which the story does not cohere so well. Thus, narrative critics may show where they find the narrative to be coherent and at the same time be open to its lack of coherence *as a narrative*. We see the problem most clearly, for example, in the Gospel of John, where there are awkward breaks in the narrative and where some characters are first mentioned as if they had already been introduced. Nevertheless, instead of returning to redaction criticism, narrative critics still take seriously the final form of the narrative as an audience might have experienced it—with all its faults and failures as a narrative. This caution about overrating the coherence and consistency of the Gospels is an important part of the contribution of Raimo Hakola and Petri Mehrenlahti in the first chapter of this volume. Their argument implies that we need to develop a narrative poetics for each Gospel so as adequately to take into account all the peculiarities of that narrative without forcing it into a straightjacket of coherence.

Detached from History?

Some critics argue that narrative criticism, by focusing on the story, has detached the narrative from its historical moorings. After all, the Gospels were about historical events, and the Gospels indirectly reflect historical events and circumstances at the time of their writing. As we have noted, before narrative criticism, the literary methods of source, form and redaction criticism were pursued primarily in the service of historical reconstruction. Narrative criticism has succeeded in showing the value of the narrative in its own right, without serving as a handmaid to historical reconstruction. Nevertheless, narrative criticism affirms that a Gospel narrative is a historical artifact, a first-century contextual document fully conditioned by its time and place. More than ever, interpretations of the Gospel narratives are drawing upon our knowledge of the history, society and cultures of the first-century Mediterranean world *as a means to help us understand the story better.*

As the fruits of narrative criticism become evident, it will be important to reassess traditional historical-criticial disciplines in light of the results of narrative criticism. Rethinking redaction criticism and source criticism will be appropriate. It may also be possible for narrative criticism to find some new ways to make inferences from the Gospel stories and their rhetoric about the authors, audiences and circumstances of the Gospels.

Narrative critics treat the Gospels as different 'fictionalized versions' of the events they are depicting. At some level, therefore, the accuracy or inacuracy of the events as recounted may not be so significant to an appreciation of the Gospels as first-century narratives. Nevertheless, it is an important part of the rhetoric of the Gospels that they do in fact make implied or explicit claims to be faithful depictions (the claims made by Luke and John) of actual people and events. As such, we can only fully understand the rhetorical impact of the Gospels if we see them as narratives presented as being about real events.

An Autonomous Narrative World?

Narrative criticism arose when New Criticism was prevalent among secular literary critics. New Criticism argued for the study of the text in its own right apart from authorial intention or reader responses. Texts were seen to have an independent autonomy, a kind of life of their own. However, even though we cannot recover the intentions of an author,[5] subsequent literary studies have made clear that there is no storyworld apart from social context, and there is no storyworld apart from the reading experience. This is equally true of ancient readers and modern readers. Apart from the reading experience, the text is only a series of marks on a page.

Hence, readers who are engaged in the act of reading give meanings to words, use their imagination, attribute emotions, fill in gaps, make connections, among many other tasks. For example, the spareness of language in characterization of the Gospels especially invites reader participation.[6] One of the results of such reader participation is that there is no single authoritative reading, only various readings. As such, narrative critics will deal with the role of a reader in analysis and interpretation—both the construction of ancient readings as well as the readings of modern readers, including critics. Thus, when narrative critics are constructing the reading experience of a hypothetical 'ideal reader' or the imaginative reading experiences of possible ancient audiences, it is, of course, the narrative critics themselves as readers who are constructing these imaginary reading experiences of the first century.

5. See the discussion in the first chapter of this book about limited and cautious inferences we may make about an author.
6. On the reader's role in the interpretation of character, see J. Darr, *On Character Building: The Reader and Rhetoric of Characterization in Luke–Acts* (Louisville, KY: Westminster/John Knox Press, 1992), and F. Burnett, 'Characterization and Reader Construction in the Gospels', *Semeia* 63 (1993), pp. 1-26.

Unified Narratives?

While the earlier critique about coherence comes from traditional, historical critics, a somewhat different concern about unity comes from literary postmodern critics. As we have said, narrative criticism tends to look for the unifying patterns of a text as the basis for interpretation. Each line is interpreted in the context of the whole. Where paradoxes and contradictions occur, the narrative critic seeks to relate them to each other in light of the whole. However, postmodern critics point out that by its very nature, at a fundamental level, narrative is not unified— not just ancient Gospels, but even carefully crafted modern fiction.[7] Narratives overflow with a surplus of meaning, and they are full of gaps, fissures, contradictions, multiple meanings and connotations, and a lack of connection between possible causes and consequences. Therefore, any effort to provide an airtight unified interpretation of a writing will do violence to the complexity and multivalence of the narrative. So, postmodern critics read and interpret 'against the grain' of standard interpretations in order to expose the gaps and contradictions in texts and interpretations.

Narrative critics will do well, therefore, to acknowledge the complex nature of narrative. Perhaps the goal of narrative criticism is not so much to discern the unity of a text as it is to assess its *impact*—to see in what ways a narrative coheres adequately to give a satisfying reading experience. With this more modest goal in mind, narrative critics will continue to look for patterns of coherence and at the same time be aware of what we notice and also learn from reading against the grain. They will continue to interpret portions of narrative in light of the whole, seeking to avoid imposing unity where it does not exist and with the recognition that efforts to find total unity in texts are clearly elusive.

---

7.   See S. Moore, *Poststructuralism and the New Testament: Derrida and Foucault at the Foot of the Cross* (Minneapolis: Fortress Press, 1994). See also F. Kermode, *The Genesis of Secrecy: On the Interpretation of Narrative* (Cambridge, MA: Harvard University Press, 1979); D. Seeley, *Deconstructing the New Testament* (Leiden: E.J. Brill, 1994); G. Phillips, 'The Ethics of Reading Deconstructively', in E. McKnight and E. Struthers Malbon (eds.), *The New Literary Criticism and the New Testament* (Valley Forge, PA: Trinity International Press, 1994), pp. 283-325; and A.K.M. Adams, *What Is Postmodern Biblical Interpretation?* (Guides to Biblical Scholarship; Minneapolis: Fortress Press, 1995). See also the bibliographical references above in n. 4.

Sharpening and Broadening Narrative Criticism

The parallel to narrative criticism in secular literary criticism is the dis-cipline of narratology—the theory and practice of narrative analysis. There are many works in narratology dealing with narrative as a whole, and there are works that represent particular developments in the under-standing of character, plot, setting, standards of judgment, point of view, and literary-rhetorical analysis.[8] These developments in narra-tology will continue to be of benefit to narrative critics of the Bible. Thus, narrative critics of the Bible may continue to sharpen their capacity to do narrative analysis. For example, narrative critics continue to grow in the discernment of patterns of storytelling, such as paral-lelism, forms of repetition[9] and irony.[10] Work is being done with the symbolic language of the Gospel of John.[11] Style could become a greater focus of attention. Point of view can be informed by a treatment of the narrator's tone in addressing the audience. The concept of stan-dards of judgment is yielding many insights into the moral world of a narrative. The study of setting is taking greater account of all the struc-tures of the narrative world, including the sociopolitical ethos and the cosmology.[12] The analysis of character can enable critics to clarify an author's view of the human condition.[13] There could be greater efforts

8.   See, e.g., S. Rimmon-Kenan, *Narrative Fiction: Contemporary Poetics* (New York: Methuen, 1983), M. Bal, *Narratology: Introduction to the Theory of Narrative* (Toronto: University of Toronto Press, 1985), and W. Martin, *Recent Theories of Narrative* (Ithaca, NY: Cornell University Press, 1986); as well as works by R. Alter, W. Booth, S. Chatman, J. Culler, G. Genette, W. Kort, S. Lanser, G. Prince, M. Sternberg and B. Uspenski, among many others, on particular issues such as rhetoric, style, irony, and so on. On character studies, see especially B. Hochman, *Character in Literature* (Ithaca, NY: Cornell University Press, 1985).

9.   See J. Anderson, *Matthew's Narrative Web: Over, and Over, and Over Again* (JSNTSup, 91; Sheffield: JSOT Press, 1994).

10.   See, e.g., P. Duke, *Irony in the Fourth Gospel* (Atlanta: John Knox Press, 1985); and J. Camery-Hoggatt, *Irony in Mark's Gospel: Text and Subtext* (Cam-bridge: Cambridge University Press, 1992).

11.   C. Koester, *Symbolism in the Fourth Gospel: Meaning, Mystery, Community* (Minneapolis: Fortress Press, 1995).

12.   See, e.g., A. Reinhartz, *The Word in the World: The Cosmological Tale of the Fourth Gospel* (Atlanta: Scholars Press, 1992).

13.   For recent development in character studies of biblical narratives, see E. Struthers Malbon and A. Berlin (eds.), *Characterization in Biblical Literature*

to understand the interrelation between plot, conflict, setting and tone as a way to see more clearly the 'world' offered by the narrative to the reader.[14]

In general, narrative critics have tended to aim their work at the whole narrative of a Gospel.[15] However, there are now also appearing detailed and careful treatments of particular episodes, as they can be understood in their context in the whole Gospel.[16] This is the significance of Outi Lehtipuu's careful and detailed character analysis, in this volume, of the parable of the rich man and Lazarus in Luke.

Narrative criticism will continue to give greater attention to the reader by combining its treatment of narrative with *reader-response criticism*.[17] Reader-response critics range from being text-centered (the text determines the reading experience) to being reader-centered (the reader determines the reading experience). Narrative critics lean toward the text-centered approach because they want to understand the narrative better as a means to assess what impact the narrative might have had on first-century readers. In this regard, various theories about ideal readers have become useful—the ideal reader being not a real reader but a construction of the possible implied responses of an ideal reader through the course of the narrative.[18]

(*Semeia* 63 [1993]) as well as the article by Outi Lehtipuu in this volume.

14. W. Kort, *Story, Text, and Scripture: Literary Interests in Biblical Narratives* (University Park: Pennsylvania State University Press, 1988)

15. For recent narrative-critical treatments of whole Gospels, see M. Stibbe, *John as Storyteller: Narrative Criticism and the Fourth Gospel* (SNTSMS, 73; Cambridge: Cambridge University Press, 1992), W. Carter, *Matthew: Storyteller, Interpreter, Evangelist* (Peabody, MA: Hendrickson, 1996), and S. Smith, *A Lion with Wings: A Narrative-Critical Approach to Mark's Gospel* (Biblical Seminar, 38; Sheffield: Sheffield Academic Press, 1996).

16. See, e.g., D. Rhoads, 'The Syrophoenician Woman in Mark: A Narrative-Critical Study', *JAAR* 62 (1992), pp. 342-75.

17. See the anthologies of S. Suleiman and I. Crossman (eds.), *The Reader in the Text: Essays on Audience and Interpretation* (Princeton, NJ: Princeton University Press, 1980), and J. Tompkins (ed.), *Reader-Response Criticism: From Formalism to Post-Structuralism* (Baltimore: The Johns Hopkins University Press, 1980). Note also E. Freund, *The Return of the Reader, Reader-Response Criticism* (New York: Methuen, 1987); as well as works by theorists W. Iser, S. Fish, W. Booth, and others.

18. Examples of such constructions include R. Fowler, *Let the Reader Understand: Reader-Response Criticism and the Gospel of Mark* (Minneapolis: Fortress Press, 1991); and J. Staley, *The Print's First Kiss: A Rhetorical Investigation of the*

Thus, text-centered reader-response criticism is interested in the *literary rhetoric* of a story. The rhetoric of a narrative refers to the overall impact of a story in its telling. Rhetoric is more than the impact of the events of the story. It is more than the stylistic features and literary devices by which the story is told.[19] Rhetoric is a combination of both in the diachronic experience of the narrative by the readers. Thus, rhetoric has to do not only with what the story *means* but also with what the story *does* in the course of its telling. A narrative like one of the Gospels affects the readers in the process of reading so that readers are led to become something different as a result—people who embrace certain beliefs or values, faithful followers of Jesus, disciples who teach what Jesus has taught, followers who will share their wealth, or people who believe and have eternal life.

The New Testament narratives offer a significant challenge to critics seeking to understand the dynamics and power of their rhetoric, for they were composed as part of an effort to create and shape communities, to make available divine resources for transformation, and to announce judgment and salvation. One of the tasks of narrative criticism, then, is to deal with these questions: What are the New Testament narratives doing? And, literarily, how do they do it?

Also, *reception criticism* can be of assistance here as a helpful way to discern how actual readers from ancient times to the present have reacted to a particular writing. Reception criticism can thus be seen as a branch of reader-response criticism, because it looks at the way in which readers down through the ages have received, understood, and appropriated a Gospel—often evident in the history of commentaries on a particular writing. For example, insights into the Gospel of Mark come by seeing how Matthew and Luke reacted in their reading of Mark—as implied by their revisions of Mark. In this volume, Raimo Hakola, in addition to providing a fine character study of Lazarus, offers interesting insights into some neglected aspects of the Gospel of John by identifying what some readers through the centuries, reading against the grain, have seen in John.

Implied Reader in the Fourth Gospel (Atlanta: Scholars Press, 1988). See also Fowler's Introduction to the subject, 'Reader-Response Criticism: Figuring Mark's Reader', in J. Anderson and S. Moore (eds.), *Mark and Method: New Approaches in Biblical Studies* (Minneapolis: Fortress Press, 1992), pp. 50-83.

19. W. Wuellner, 'Where Is Rhetorical Criticism Taking Us?', *CBQ* 49 (1987), pp. 448-63.

Further insights about the impact of a narrative on the reader may also come from the literary branch of study called *speech-act theory*. Speech act theory assesses a whole range of the performative functions of language in the interaction between speaker and receiver.[20] This approach began in the philosophical analysis of language and it has many important implications for the study of biblical narrative and dialogue.

Finally, narrative criticism is broadening its scope and proving to be useful in analyzing literary works that are not primarily narrative in nature but which have narrative dimensions. This is the contribution and promise of the interesting article on Q in this volume by Arto Järvinen, who teases out for character analysis the narrative elements of a text comprised primarily of sayings. In addition, it is possible to analyze the occasional letters of Paul by reconstructing the chronological story of the past events that are portrayed or mentioned in the letter and the potential future events projected by the letter, and then to see the letter as a moment in the story surrounding the letter—with its own plot, characters, settings, point of view, tone, standards of judgment, and rhetoric.[21] Also, writings such as the book of Revelation may be analyzed for the same formal features of narrative.[22]

Incorporating Some Traditional Disciplines

Narrative critics enhance their analysis of biblical narratives by *comparison with other ancient literature*. They begin by consulting treatments of narrative in ancient literary handbooks, such as Aristotle's *Poetics*, and then also study the features of narrative expressed in ancient writings that are parallel to the New Testament narratives.[23] Also, the presentation of characters in ancient biographies and novellas

20. J.L. Austin, *How to Do Things with Words* (Cambridge, MA: Harvard University Press, 1975); and S. Petrey, *Speech Acts and Literary Theory* (New York: Routledge, 1990). On biblical studies, see D. Neufeld, *Reconceiving Texts as Speech Acts: An Analysis of 1 John* (Leiden: E.J. Brill, 1994).

21. See the groundbreaking work of N. Petersen, *Rediscovering Paul: Philemon and the Sociology of Paul's Narrative World* (Philadelphia: Fortress Press, 1985).

22. See D. Barr, *Tales of the End: A Narrative Commentary on the Book of Revelation* (Santa Rosa, CA: Polebridge Press, 1998).

23. See parallel guidelines for classical rhetorical analysis in M. Mitchell, *Paul and the Rhetoric of Argumentation: An Exegetical Investigation of the Language and Composition of I Corinthians* (Tübingen: Mohr Siebeck, 1991)

can be an important means for understanding New Testament narratives.[24] Not only analogies with Greco-Roman literature but also recent narratological studies of the Hebrew Bible should be explored more extensively as ways of enhancing our understanding of the dynamics of New Testament narratives.[25]

In addition, *genre criticism* is increasingly important for narrative analysis. Seeing a Gospel as representing a particular genre—whether tragedy or biography or romance or apocalypse—helps to identify an implied audience, the social ethos, the issues being dealt with, and the expectations that an audience brings to a story.[26] Thus, genre studies help to imagine contexts for the reception of the Gospels in antiquity. Genre studies are complex, because narratives seldom fit into a single generic category. One may decide that a Gospel represents a mixed genre or a subversion of a familiar genre or even a new genre. Nevertheless, any comparisons and contrasts with other similar writings of the time can be helpful in clarifying the nature of a Gospel.

For example, a recent approach to genre analysis of the Gospel stories deals with *rhetorical criticism*, and employs classical, Greco-Roman rhetoric of argumentation.[27] Critics take individual stories from the Gospels and analyze them as the narrative equivalence of speeches—representing species of argumentation, showing an order of argumentation, and manifesting techniques of ethos, pathos and logos.[28] Such analysis may be a helpful way to inform an understanding of plot

24. See, e.g., M.A. Tolbert, *Sowing the Gospel: Mark's World in Literary and Historical Perspective* (Minneapolis: Fortress Press, 1989); and V.K. Robbins, *Jesus the Teacher: A Socio-Rhetorical Interpretation of Mark* (repr.; Minneapolis: Fortress Press, 1992).

25. A. Berlin, *Poetics and Interpretation of Biblical Narrative* (Sheffield: Almond Press, 1983), R. Alter, *The Art of Biblical Narrative* (New York: Basic Books, 1981); M. Sternberg, *The Poetics of Biblical Narrative* (Bloomington: Indiana University Press, 1985); and S. Bar-Efrat, *Narrative Art in the Bible* (trans. D. Shefer-Vanson and S. Bar-Efrat; JSOTSup, 70; Sheffield: Almond Press, 1989).

26. For an articulation of the importance of genre studies, see Tolbert, *Sowing*, pp. 48-84.

27. G. Kennedy, *New Testament Interpretation through Rhetorical Criticism* (Chapel Hill: University of North Carolina Press, 1984); and D. Stamps, 'Rhetorical Criticism of the New Testament: Ancient and Modern Evaluations of Argumentation', in Porter and Tombs (eds.), *Approaches*, pp. 129-69.

28. See B.L. Mack and V.K. Robbins, *Patterns of Persuasion and the New Testament* (Sonoma, CA: Polebridge Press, 1989).

and character, point of view, standards of judgment, and the narrative rhetoric of persuasion. The fruitfulness of this approach is just beginning to be apparent, and it is not yet clear if the approach can be sustained over the narrative of a whole Gospel.[29]

Incorporating Some New Disciplines

While narrative criticism has many parallels to narratology, narrative criticism is taking its own unique shape because of the particular nature of the literature under study. For example, the Gospels are examples of oral/aural literature that was designed to be heard and not read. Also, the Gospels originated from a culture very different in time and place from our modern world. As a means to take full account of such factors, narrative critics are incorporating insights and approaches from other fresh disciplines in New Testament studies.

For instance, *orality criticism* focuses on the aural reception of oral performances of literature in an oral culture. It is clear that the Gospels were written to be performed to audiences in a predominantly non-literate culture. Considerable work has been done on the qualities and features of oral literature and on the context and impact of the aural reception of it.[30] Most of the work has been done on the Gospel of Mark,[31] but all the narratives of the New Testament were written to be heard.[32]

---

29. For an integrative approach to Mark using several disciplines of New Testament study, see V.K. Robbins, *Exploring the Texture of Texts: A Guide to Socio-Rhetorical Interpretation* (Valley Forge, PA: Trinity Press International, 1996).

30. See the works of W. Ong, such as *The Presence of the Word: Some Prolegomena for Cultural and Religious History* (Minnesota: Minnesota University Press, 1967); and *Orality and Literacy: The Technologizing of the Word* (New York: Methuen, 1982).

31. See, e.g., various articles by J. Dewey, 'Mark as Interwoven Tapestry: Forecasts and Echoes for a Listening Audience', *CBQ* 53 (1991), pp. 221-36; 'Oral Methods of Structuring Narrative in Mark', *Int* 43 (1989), pp. 32-44; and 'The Gospel of Mark as Oral-Aural Event: Implications for Interpretation', in McKnight and Malbon (eds.), *New Literary Criticism*, pp. 145-63. Also see P.J.J. Botha, 'Mark's Story as Oral Literature: Rethinking the Transmission of Some Traditions about Jesus', *Hervormde Teologiese Studies* 47 (1991), pp. 304-31; and C. Bryan, *A Preface to Mark: Notes on the Gospel in its Literary and Cultural Settings* (New York: Oxford University Press, 1993), esp. pp. 67-171.

32. P. Achtemeier, 'Omne Verbum Sonat: The New Testament and the Oral

The connection with narrative criticism (and reader-response criticism) is immediately obvious. Critics are reframing narrative criticism by conceiving of the narrator as a performer, of a temporal rather than a spatial experience of a Gospel, of forecasts and echoes rather than foreshadowings and retrospections, of hearers (probably in a group as an audience) rather than readers, of type scenes rather than forms, and of diverse examples of repetition with variation.

Hearers of a Gospel can listen to the narrative for its sounds and rhythms.[33] Here careful attention is given to word order—foregrounding, backgrounding and elision, as well as to synonymous and antithetical parallelism and chiastic patterns. The development of 'sound charts' to identify repetitions and alliteration help to bring out the aural experience of the text.[34] The Gospel of Mark, for example, offers a hearing experience of verbal echoes both within and between episodes. The teaching of the Sermon on the Mount reveals parallel and chiastic patterns of sound and rhythm. The alliteration and lilt of the Gospel of John may be part of a rhetorical aesthetic designed to draw hearers into the experience of eternal life. Also, 'hearers' of narrative will have a different experience of characters in a Gospel than 'readers' do. Because the performer addresses the hearers directly with the speech of each character, hearers are led to identify, in some sense, with all the characters. In this way, the story also becomes an emotional experience (similar to viewing a film), rather than simply a source of information.

The interpreter may also relate to narrative in terms of *performance criticism* and may even practice being the narrator as performer.[35] Preferably, this is done in the Greek language, but the experience also bears much fruit by performing translations that attend to the oral/aural

Environment of Late Western Antiquity', *JBL* 109 (1990), pp. 3-27.

33. Listening to the Greek text was a key methodological procedure in T. Boomershine's groundbreaking narrative analysis, 'Mark the Storyteller: A Rhetorical-Critical Investigation of Mark's Passion and Resurrection Narrative' (PhD dissertation, Union Theological Seminary, New York, 1984).

34. B.B. Scott and M. Dean, 'A Sound Map of the Sermon on the Mount', in *Seminar Papers of the Society of Biblical Literature, 1993* (Atlanta: Scholars Press, 1993), pp. 672-725.

35. See M. Maclean, *Narrative as Performance: The Baudelairean Experiment* (London: Routledge, Chapman & Hall, 1988); and R. Moore, 'The Gospel and Narrative Performance: The Critical Assessment of Meaning as Correspondence in D.F. Straus and R. Bultmann' (PhD dissertation, Rice University, Houston, Texas, 1992).

features of the narrative.[36] Such an experience of performing recovers a new level in the analysis of narrative, because oral performers must make interpretive decisions not only about what a line *means* but also decisions about *how* a line is to be delivered. Every line has a *subtext*—the message that is being conveyed by *how* the line is said. Every subtext is determined from the lines themselves in the context of the episode and of the story as a whole, as if one were seeking stage directions in a play. Oral performance can be a test of interpretation, because it is difficult to find a way to deliver some lines with the meanings attributed to them in some interpretations.[37]

One can readily see the applicability to character analysis, for example. Performers will place themselves in the position of each of the characters and clarify the differing points of view in a narrative. Performers will notice the distinctive speech patterns of the different characters and will attempt to identify subtexts for the lines of the characters that are suggested by the text. Also, the interpreter as performer will bring out emotive dimensions of the text in new ways, because characters speak with amazement or fear or surprise or irony. Obviously, one does not attempt to construct an ancient performance, which we cannot hope to recover, but rather to take into account dimensions of an oral text that might otherwise be neglected when treated only as a written text.

Narrative critics can also benefit from the discipline of *social-science criticism*. The world of the story represents one example of a social construction of reality. It is crucial, therefore, to use all the tools we have to understand the nature of that social construction. Because the narrative worlds of the Gospels reflect ancient society in particular geographical locations, interpretation becomes a cross-cultural process. The question is: how can we begin to construct the shared cultural assumptions that enabled ancient readers to understand the story and to fill in the gaps of the texts? In order to address this question, narrative

36. See D. Rhoads, 'Performing the Gospel of Mark', in B. Krondorfer (ed.), *Body and Bible* (Philadelphia: Trinity International Press, 1992), pp. 102-19. Note also how a performance can be influenced by an audience. For information about video presentations of some biblical works by the author, write to SELECT c/o Trinity Lutheran Seminary, 2199 E. Main Street, Columbus, OH 43209, USA.

37. For example, it is virtually impossible to deliver the line of Jesus to the disciples in Mark praising the poor widow as if it were a negative criticism of her gift to a corrupt temple system, as some commentators have interpreted it.

critics turn not only to the knowledge we have about the first century from literary and material artefacts, but also to the use of cultural models that help to organize and interpret the ancient cultural information in the narrative—thus helping us to avoid imposing the conceptions of the world we bring from our experiences in the twentieth century.

Social-science criticism employs models from sociology and anthropology as heuristic devices to enhance our understanding of ancient biblical cultures.[38] The Mediterranean societies of antiquity had parallels to modern Mediterranean cultures. Therefore, models based on studies of contemporary Mediterranean cultures—models dealing with honor and shame, dyadic personality, purity and defilement, economy of limited goods, patron–client relations, kinship patterns, among others—are helpful in understanding ancient society. Because a Gospel narrative is a relatively coherent slice of life from cultures that these models reflect, it is possible to use these models to unpack the dynamics of the storyworld. The use of the models helps to articulate reading scenarios, representing the framework of assumptions and expectations that first-century readers might have brought to their experience of the story.[39]

The social-science approach has been employed fruitfully to illuminate the narratives of the Gospels.[40] Issues of honor and shame illuminate the conflicts in the plot.[41] An understanding of ancient economy informs the standards of judgment regarding wealth and poverty.[42] Studies of purity and defilement help to clarify the ethos of the setting.[43]

---

38. See B. Malina, *The New Testament World: Insights from Cultural Anthropology* (Louisville, KY: Westminster/John Knox Press, 2nd edn, 1993); J. Elliott, *What is Social-Scientific Criticism?* (Minneapolis: Fortress Press, 1993); and R. Rohrbaugh (ed.), *The Social Sciences and New Testament Interpretation* (Peabody, MA: Hendrickson, 1996)

39. B. Malina, 'Reading Theory Perspective', in J. Neyrey (ed.), *The Social World of Luke–Acts: Models for Interpretation* (Peabody, MA: Hendrickson, 1991), pp. 3-23.

40. See all the articles in Neyrey (ed.), *Luke–Acts*.

41. Labeling and deviance theories in the social-science approach also help to chart the mutual accusations that comprise many of the conflicts in the plot. See B. Malina and J. Neyrey, *Calling Jesus Names: The Social Value of Labels in Matthew* (Sonoma, CA: Polebridge Press, 1988).

42. See H. Moxnes, *The Economy of the Kingdom: Social Conflict and Economic Relations in Luke's Gospel* (Philadelphia: Fortress Press, 1989).

43. D. Rhoads, 'The Social Study of Mark: Crossing Boundaries', in Anderson

So also do cross-cultural treatments of sickness and healing.[44] Models about the importance of eating and food shape our understanding of meal settings. Models of social change distinguish the features of the Jesus movement depicted in the various Gospels.[45] Social-science commentaries on the Gospels have helped to integrate many of these models into a greater understanding of the narrative.[46]

Especially in relation to character, the social-science approach is helpful as a means to understanding the dyadic cultures of ancient Mediterranean societies, that is, cultures in which people depend on the group to which they belong for their identity. Features of dyadic cultures include the tendency to stereotype, the importance of kinship (both natural and fictive), a contrasting treatment of insiders and outsiders, the lack of introspection—all these providing important heuristic insights into the portrayal of characters in the Gospel narratives.

Narrative criticism and social-science criticism work well together.[47] Social-science criticism helps to clarify the common assumptions made by author and hearers in the act of communication. At the same time, the detailed attention to the text offered by narrative criticism helps to give specificity and qualification to the general nature of the models and applies social-science criticism to the narrative *as a narrative*.

One of the most helpful aspects of the social study of the Gospels is the identification of *social location* within the structure of ancient society and its cities.[48] Pre-industrial, agrarian societies were organized hierarchically with (1) a small ruling elite (2–3 per cent) along with (2) their scribal and mercantile retainers, below which were (3) the

---

and Moore (eds.), *Mark and Method*, pp. 135-61.

44. See, e.g., J. Pilch's article, 'Sickness and Healing in Luke–Acts', in Neyrey (ed.), *Luke–Acts*, pp. 181-209, and bibliography.

45. See D. Rhoads, 'The Social System of the Jesus Movement as Depicted in the Narrative of the Gospel of Mark', *ANRW* 26.2, pp. 1692-729; and 'Mission in the Gospel of Mark', *CurTM* 22 (1995), pp. 340-55.

46. B. Malina and R. Rohrbaugh, *Social Science Commentary on the Synoptic Gospels* (Minneapolis: Fortress Press, 1992); and *idem*, *Social Science Commentary on the Gospel of John* (Minneapolis: Fortress, 1998).

47. For an integration of narrative criticism and social-science criticism in character analysis, see D. Gowler, *Host, Guest, Enemy, and Friend: Portraits of Pharisees in Luke and Acts* (New York: Lang, 1991).

48. See, e.g., R. Rohrbaugh, 'The Pre-industrial City in Luke–Acts', and D. Oakman, 'The Countryside in Luke–Acts', both in Neyrey (ed.), *Luke–Acts*, pp. 125-49 and 151-79 respectively.

masses of peasants (about 95 per cent) living at a basically subsistence level, in addition to (4) a small percentage of 'expendable' people comprised of unclean and other marginalized groups.[49] This economic and political ordering of an honor–shame society becomes an important framework for interpreting the narrative world of a Gospel—the ethos of the settings, the nature of the conflicts that comprise the plot, and the social location of the various characters.

Attention to social location especially helps to amplify character analysis, because characters can be identified by their cultural origin, social status, economic level, kinship identification, gender, honor rating, state of purity or defilement, health, occupation, education, religious allegiances, urban/rural origin, and so on. The idea is not simply to identify the social locations of the characters, but to use what we know of the society as tools to interpret better the narrative and the characters and conflicts in it.

Ideological criticism goes hand in glove with the identification of social location,[50] because it asks questions of power. Ideological criticism assesses the power relations between and among the characters from different social locations as the plot develops. What are the values and beliefs of the different characters? What access to differing kinds of power does each character and character group have? Who oppresses and who is being oppressed? Whose interests are served by the beliefs and values and the exercise of power of the different characters? These questions have led to studies that recover the political dimensions of the Gospel narratives.[51] Feminist critical studies in particular have unpacked the power dynamics between females and males in the world of the story and asked whether the plot works to overcome or to reinforce patriarchy, and in what ways.[52] Talvikki Mattila's treatment of the

49. G. Lenski, *Human Societies* (New York: McGraw-Hill, 6th edn, 1991).

50. See T. Eagleton, *Ideology: An Introduction* (London: Verso Press, 1991); D. Jobling and T. Pippin (eds.), 'Ideological Criticism of Biblical Texts', *Semeia* 59 (1992); and 'Ideological Criticism', in The Bible and Culture Collective, *The Postmodern Bible*, pp. 272-308.

51. See, e.g., C. Myers, *Binding the Strong Man: A Political Reading of Mark's Story of Jesus* (Maryknoll, NY: Orbis Books, 1989); and R. Cassidy, *John's Gospel in New Perspective* (Maryknoll, NY: Orbis Books, 1992).

52. Recent studies of the ambiguous treatment of women in Luke–Acts are good examples: T.K. Seim, *The Double Message: Patterns of Gender in Luke–Acts* (Edinburgh: T. & T. Clark, 1994); and B. Reid, *Choosing the Better Part? Women in the Gospel of Luke* (Collegeville, MN: Liturgical Press, 1996). See also

marginalization of women in the patriarchal structures of Matthew's passion narrative, in this collection, is a noteworthy example of this approach.

Analysis of social location and power relations can also helpfully be applied to the authors and audiences of the New Testament narratives.[53] Rather than simply identifying geographical origin and date of a writing, scholars can seek to infer from each Gospel a range of factors that help to identify the social location of the narrator/author and the implied audience of a writing. Where does this writing fit into ancient society? Whose interests do the beliefs and values promoted by the narrative serve? What power or rhetorical force does the narrative use to have its way? What kind of society does the narrative serve to subvert or reinforce or shape or generate? All these questions increase our capacity to clarify the rhetoric of a Gospel in relation to its audience. Kari Syreeni's narrative analysis in this collection shows very helpfully how a character such as Peter in the Gospel of Matthew can function symbolically to embody and promote an ideology for the readers.

In addition, it may be a helpful heuristic device to imagine the responses of imaginary readers from many different social locations in the society of the audience—elites, a slave, peasants, a Roman soldier, a leper and a Pharisee. Placing oneself in such imaginary roles of reading will better show how the text might have worked rhetorically in its ancient context—that is, what values and beliefs the narrative reinforces and which ones it seeks to subvert and replace.

E. Wainwright, *Toward a Feminist Critical Reading of the Gospel According to Matthew* (Berlin: W. de Gruyter, 1991), the commentaries and articles in E. Schüssler Fiorenza (ed.) *Searching the Scriptures* (2 vols.; New York: Crossroad, 1993), J. Capel Anderson, 'Feminist Criticism: The Dancing Daughter', in Anderson and Moore (eds.), *Methods*, pp. 103-34; E. Cheney, *She Can Read: Feminist Strategies for Biblical Narrative* (Valley Forge, PA: Trinity International Press, 1996); and L. Schottroff, S. Schroer and M.-T. Wacker, *Feminist Interpretation: The Bible in Women's Perspective* (Minneapolis: Fortress Press, 1998).

53. See R. Rohrbaugh, 'The Social Location of the Markan Audience', *Int* 47 (1993), pp. 380-95; V.K. Robbins, 'The Social Location of the Implied Author in Luke–Acts', in Neyrey (ed.), *Luke–Acts*, pp. 305-32; and several of the articles in D. Balch (ed.) *Social History of the Matthean Community: Cross-Disciplinary Approaches* (Minneapolis: Fortress Press, 1992), especially the one by A. Wire, 'Gender Roles in a Scribal Community', pp. 87-121.

Responsible Interpretation

Narrative criticism is also beginning to benefit from reflection on the relatively new field of the *ethics of reading*—reflection on the moral responsibility involved in the process of reading and interpreting as contemporary readers.[54]

Contemporary readers may think of reading as a dialogue—a meaningful exchange between the story and the reader.[55] Each partner has power and influence on what happens in the dialogue. On the one hand, a story seeks to influence readers—to affect them for good or for ill, to change people, and to shape communities. On the other hand, a reader also has power in this dialogue with the story. Readers can take a story seriously and be affected by it or they can be indifferent or resistant and have strong objections to the story. A reader can also use the story in ways that may be helpful or harmful to others.

To begin with, narrative interpreters are responsible to allow the story of a Gospel to have its influence in this dialogue, by reading the story on its own terms and for its own time. In this dialogue with a story, the reader has the responsibility to treat the story with respect, to listen carefully over and over again—seeking to limit our tendency to impose alien ideas and images onto the story. It is important to assume that the story will be different from what we expect it to say or want it to say or fear it might say. Aware of our limited and relative perspective, we can make our assumptions and perspectives explicit from the start,[56] thereby

54. On the ethics of reading in literary studies, see J.H. Miller, *The Ethics of Reading: Kant, de Man, Eliot, Trollope, James, and Benjamin* (New York: Columbia University Press, 1987); and W. Booth, *The Company We Keep: The Ethics of Fiction* (Berkeley: University of California Press, 1988). In biblical studies, see E. Schüssler Fiorenza, 'The Ethics of Interpretation: De-Centering Biblical Theology', *JBL* 107 (1988), pp. 3-17; D.J. Smit, 'The Ethics of Interpretation— New Voices from the USA', *Scriptura* 33 (1990), pp. 16-28; J. Botha, 'The Ethics of New Testament Interpretation', *Neot* 26 (1992), pp. 169-74; and D. Patte, *Ethics of Biblical Interpretation: A Reevaluation* (Louisville, KY: Westminster/John Knox Press, 1995).

55. H.G. Gadamer, *Truth and Method* (trans. J. Weinsheimer and D. Marshall; New York: Crossroad, rev. edn, 1989).

56. The importance of these dynamics were brought to scholarly attention by feminist critics. See, e.g., E. Schüssler Fiorenza, *In Memory of Her: A Feminist Reconstruction of Christian Origins* (New York: Crossroad, 1983). See also Aichele *et al.*, *Postmodern Bible*, *passim* and R.S. Sugirtharajah (ed.), *The Postcolonial Bible*

helping us to avoid inappropriately reading them into the story.

Of course, every interpretation will be only one interpretation in a range of faithful interpretations.[57] Given the multivalent nature of stories and the limitations of reader perspectives, it is not possible (or even desirable) to provide one correct and objective understanding of a story. The goal is to be faithful to the narrative and to learn from other interpretations as well.

Once we have allowed a Gospel to address us on its own terms, the dialogue can begin to move to the modern reader's side of the equation: How does the story relate to contemporary life? On the one hand, we may resist many parts of a Gospel narrative—certain beliefs, depictions of demons, a compromising duality, an anti-Jewish thrust, patriarchy or a glorification of suffering. Where the intepreter differs with the story, the idea is not to reinterpret the story to make it look acceptable, but to let the story say what it says and then to object honestly to those aspects of the story we find disagreeable or abhorrent.

At the same time, because this is a genuine dialogue, we need to be open to the ways in which the story as a whole may be potentially transforming for us.[58] Real dialogue involves risk, the possibility of being changed by our encounter with the text. We modern readers can enter the storyworld in imagination and by immersion can allow the story to work its magic on us, as well as be careful not to use the story in ways that can harm others. Thus, whatever our interpretation, readers have an ethical responsibility for their interpretations—to promote the ways in which interpretations may serve the good and to counter those interpretations that will bring harm and oppress people.

Narrative critics are also learning the importance of reading and interpreting with others from different social locations. Just as social

(The Bible and Postcolonialism, 1; Sheffield: Sheffield Academic Press, 1998).

57. For recent studies that emphasize the multivalent dimensions of Scripture, see D. Patte, *Discipleship According to the Sermon on the Mount: Four Legitimate Readings, Four Plausible Views of Discipleship and their Relevant Values* (Valley Forge, PA: Trinity Press International, 1996); F. Segovia (ed.), *What Is John? Readers and Readings of the Fourth Gospel* (Atlanta: Scholars Press, 1996); and C. Cosgrove, *Elusive Israel: The Puzzle of Election in Romans* (Louisville, KY: Westminster/John Knox Press, 1997).

58. W. Kort argues that it is precisely this willingness to risk in reading that defines our attitude toward a writing as Scripture, in *Take, Read: Texts as Scripture. Scripture, Textuality, and Cultural Practice* (University Park: Pennsylvania State University Press, 1996).

location can be applied to a story, to an author, and to ancient readers, so it is also being applied to modern readers and interpreters. Every reader has a relative perspective due to national identify, social location within that society, and personal experiences, beliefs and values.[59] Each perspective has its own angle of vision that may enhance understanding but that may also inhibit understanding.[60] Again the ideological questions apply: Whose interests are being served by this or that interpretation? How can interpreters take responsibility for their interpretations? The recent discipline of *cultural exegesis* recognizes the importance of reading with people from many different cultures and social locations at a round table in which no positions are privileged or no positions are marginalized, with each participant bringing unique insights and understandings from their perspective. This appreciation for diversity and collegiality is just one more reason to celebrate the Finish scholars who have here so enthusiastically joined the conversations about the narrative interpretations of the Bible.

Conclusion

There are many exciting new directions taking place in narrative criticism that are enabling students of biblical narrative to become even better practitioners of narrative analysis and at the same time to have that practice enhanced by integrating insights and methods from other approaches to New Testament narratives. All the writings of the New Testament, as well as many writings outside the canon, provide opportunities to bring narrative analysis to bear upon a better understanding of a wide range of ancient literature.

59. For an understanding of the way our social location affects interpretation, see F. Segovia and M.A. Tolbert (eds.) , *Reading from This Place. I. Social Location and Biblical Interpretation in the United States*, and *Reading from This Place. II. Social Location and Biblical Interpretation in Global Perspective* (Minneapolis: Fortress Press, 1995); B. Blount, *Cultural Interpretation* (Minneapolis: Fortress Press, 1995), D. Smith-Christopher (ed.), *Text and Experience: Towards a Cultural Exegesis of the Bible* (Biblical Seminar, 35; Sheffield: Sheffield Academic Press, 1995), and M. Brett (ed.), *Ethnicity and the Bible* (Leiden: E.J. Brill, 1996). See also the two volumes of Schüssler Fiorenza (ed.), *Searching the Scriptures*; and C.H. Felder (ed.), *Stony the Road We Trod: African-American Biblical Interpretation* (Minneapolis: Fortress Press, 1991).

60. As one specific example, see H. Kinukawa, *Women and Jesus: A Japanese Feminist Perspective* (Maryknoll, NY: Orbis Books, 1994).

INDEXES

INDEX OF REFERENCES

OLD TESTAMENT

NEW TESTAMENT

OTHER ANCIENT REFERENCES

JOURNAL FOR THE STUDY OF THE NEW TESTAMENT
SUPPLEMENT SERIES